THE PRINCIPLES OF POPULATION AND PRODUCTION

The Development of Industrial Society Series

John Weyland

The Principles of
POPULATION
and PRODUCTION
as They Are Affected by the Progress of Society with a View to Moral and Political Consequences

IRISH UNIVERSITY PRESS
Shannon Ireland

First edition London 1816

This I U P reprint is a photolithographic facsimile of
the first edition and is unabridged, retaining the
original printer's imprint.

© *1971 Irish University Press Shannon Ireland*

All forms of micropublishing
© *Irish University Microforms Shannon Ireland*

ISBN 0 7165 1777 9

T M MacGlinchey Publisher

Irish University Press Shannon Ireland

PRINTED IN THE REPUBLIC OF IRELAND BY
ROBERT HOGG PRINTER TO IRISH UNIVERSITY PRESS

The Development of Industrial Society Series

This series comprises reprints of contemporary documents and commentaries on the social, political and economic upheavals in nineteenth-century England.

England, as the first industrial nation, was also the first country to experience the tremendous social and cultural impact consequent on the alienation of people in industrialized countries from their rural ancestry. The Industrial Revolution which had begun to intensify in the mid-eighteenth century, spread swiftly from England to Europe and America. Its effects have been far-reaching: the growth of cities with their urgent social and physical problems; greater social mobility; mass education; increasingly complex administration requirements in both local and central government; the growth of democracy and the development of new theories in economics; agricultural reform and the transformation of a way of life.

While it would be pretentious to claim for a series such as this an in-depth coverage of all these aspects of the new society, the works selected range in content from *The Hungry Forties* (1904), a collection of letters by ordinary working people describing their living conditions and the effects of mechanization on their day-to-day lives, to such analytical studies as Leone Levi's *History of British Commerce* (1880) and *Wages and Earnings of the Working Classes* (1885); M. T. Sadler's *The Law of Population* (1830); John Wade's radical documentation of government corruption, *The Extraordinary Black Book* (1831); C. Edward Lester's trenchant social investigation, *The Glory and Shame of England* (1866); and many other influential books and pamphlets.

The editor's intention has been to make available important contemporary accounts, studies and records, written or compiled by men and women of integrity and scholarship whose reactions to the growth of a new kind of society are valid touchstones for today's reader. Each title (and the particular edition used) has been chosen on a twofold basis (1) its intrinsic worth as a record or commentary, and (2) its contribution to the development of an industrial society. It is hoped that this collection will help to increase our understanding of a people and an epoch.

The Editor
Irish University Press

THE

PRINCIPLES

OF

POPULATION AND PRODUCTION.

C. Baldwin, Printer,
New Bridge-street, London.

THE

PRINCIPLES

OF

POPULATION AND PRODUCTION,

AS THEY ARE AFFECTED BY THE

PROGRESS OF SOCIETY;

WITH A VIEW TO

MORAL AND POLITICAL

CONSEQUENCES.

BY

JOHN WEYLAND, JUN. ESQ. F.R.S.

LONDON:

PRINTED FOR BALDWIN, CRADOCK, AND JOY,

47, PATERNOSTER-ROW;

J. HATCHARD, 190, PICCADILLY; JOSEPH PARKER, OXFORD;
DEIGHTON AND SONS, CAMBRIDGE; WILLIAM BLACKWOOD,
EDINBURGH; AND JOHN CUMMING, DUBLIN.

1816.

DEDICATION.

TO THE

CHANCELLOR,

MASTERS, AND SCHOLARS,

OF THE

UNIVERSITY OF OXFORD.

My Lords and Gentlemen,

THE following work is an attempt to establish the elements of society, during the whole of its progress, from the lowest to the highest stages of civilization, upon the basis of sound morals ; and to deduce from the hypothesis certain plain and practical principles of moral and political economy for the use of the British student.

On considering to whom I could with the greatest pleasure and propriety dedicate such a work, my

mind was not long left in doubt. Brought up from
my earliest days within sight of an University of
which I subsequently became an unworthy member, I have since had ample opportunities of appre-
ciating the influence of the instruction there imparted upon the moral and political welfare of our
country.

That the work which I now presume to offer to
your consideration does in any degree merit an equal
rank with the books which have been instrumental
in producing that influence, I have not the vanity to
suppose. Concerning the station to which it may
be entitled by the presumed soundness of its principles or the justness of its conclusions, I shall cheerfully submit to your decision. But I may venture
to observe that the SUBJECT is of the utmost importance, and one upon which no British Gentleman
or Legislator should be permitted to go forth into
the world without clear and decided views. The
happiness of the people, derived from their comfortable subsistence, and from their moral conduct upon
all those points which are connected with the principle of population, is the only solid foundation of
National prosperity. Without it all the pains bestowed in the higher departments of policy are only

so many fruitless efforts to adorn a superstructure which the first blast of adversity must level with the ground. With it the edifice of the state is founded upon a rock, against which the waves will beat in vain; for it will be firm enough not only to be preserved from overthrow, but even to escape those temporary shocks which might injure the more minute arrangements for the comfort of the inhabitants. The mind of a British Statesman especially must be ill-furnished, and his efforts comparatively unsuccessful, who is ignorant of the principles upon which this essential foundation is to be laid; for a very slight acquaintance with the subject will show that the advanced stage of society, to which our Country has been happily carried, renders the knowledge of them peculiarly necessary, towards its maintenance and further progress.

Should the following work be calculated, in your opinion, to improve and to extend that knowledge, I shall be more than repaid for the labour of the composition : and my utmost wishes will be surpassed, should you think it worthy of occupying an humble place in those studies by which the youth of Britain are trained to be the strength and ornament of their country, and to be the instruments of

imparting a portion of their own blessings to the distant regions of the world.

I have the honour to be,

MY LORDS AND GENTLEMEN,

With every sentiment of respect and esteem,

Your most obedient humble servant,

THE AUTHOR.

PREFACE.

THE substance of a large portion of the following work was written some years ago, and at no very distant period from the publication of the second edition of Mr. Malthus's Essay on the Principle of Population. The subject had been so long and so deeply considered by that able and candid writer, and involved questions so vitally important to the best interests of mankind, that it would have been the height of presumption, and positively *an immoral act*, hastily and without mature reflection to publish what purported to be a general refutation of his hypothesis. I therefore thought it prudent to confine my public communications for a time to those particular parts of the system which more immediately obtruded themselves upon my notice in the duties and employments with which I was most conversant. Upon these I conceived myself entitled to bring the author's hypothesis to the test of experience, and, where any part of it appeared to fail, to endeavour to show in what respects the argument was faulty in its principle or in its application. This I attempted in the year 1807 by " A Short Inquiry into the Policy, Humanity, and past

Effects of the Poor Laws ;" a publication which at
the time attracted perhaps more notice than it deserved, but of which I may venture to say that I have
not yet seen it fairly answered. Since that period
the tremendous risks to which the vital interests of
the country, moral and political, have been exposed, not only indisposed the public mind towards
any statistical argument not immediately affecting the existence of the commonwealth, but also
called upon every individual, by his pen, by his
personal exertions, by every mode of influence
which his talents or situation would enable him to
exert, to take a part in questions and employments
which at other times he might fairly, perhaps, have
declined as objects of mere temporary interest.

In times such as we have lately passed through, to
use the words of an old writer, " I am deceived if
God allow any man for private." In such times
the citizens of a state blessed with institutions worth
preserving " are not so much their own as others
are theirs ; they must take to themselves firm fore-
heads, courageous hearts, hands busy, but not partial, to resist the violent sway of evils."

These considerations put together constitute the
true reason why this work was not some time ago
placed in the hands of the bookseller, although a
considerable portion of it was written, and wanted
little but arrangement to prepare it for the press.

The delay, however, has not been entirely fruitless ; as I have been enabled by laying detached
fragments occasionally before the public, as oppor-

tunity offered, to collect the opinions of competent judges, to obviate some difficulties and objections to which my hypothesis appeared liable,
and to present it now to the reader with less numerous faults than it might otherwise have contained. It will probably be admitted that, in an
argument which I believe to be so entirely my own
as that which I have ventured to hold in following
out the principles of the ensuing treatise, these precautions are not illegitimate; but it is fair to warn
the reader of one necessary consequence; that some
passages will of course be found which have been
previously submitted to the public eye. They are,
however, not so numerous as to bear more than a
very small proportion to the whole of the work;—
they are my own composition, and were taken from
those parts of the original manuscript in which I
have now replaced them. Although a writer is
fairly entitled to do what he will with his own, and
leave the public to exercise their discretion as to
the value of his whole performance;—although a
builder may justly use the rafters ultimately intended for the roof of a house he is employed to
construct, as a scaffold for the erection of the walls;
yet it is certainly a point both of candour and discretion not to fit in the materials so used to the
place assigned them in the original plan of the edifice, without notice of the purposes they have previously served. Having now performed this obvious
duty, and encouraged by the hope that my materials will only turn out to be the better seasoned by

the use which has been made of them, **I** proceed
to the few prefatory remarks which appear necessary
to introduce the following treatise.

I have observed at the very outset that the principle of population, in its practical operations upon
the condition of mankind, may be said to constitute a new department of science. It is also a
very intricate one ; conversant with so wide a circle
of facts and arguments, and with so many of the
most difficult questions of moral and political
economy, that to treat it in a popular manner, so
as to convey a clear conception of the subject
to a general reader, is a matter of no small difficulty. Yet I have thought that only such a mode
of treating it could lead to extensive usefulness.
A dry philosophical discussion, inapplicable to the
purposes of statesmen, and devoid of the interest
excited by an immediate reference to the conduct
and duties of individuals, may amuse the studious
and the speculative, but can lead to no good practical result in the improvement of society. The
reader, therefore, must not expect to find in the
following pages the neat conciseness of a logical deduction ; but rather a dissertation, in which fulness
has been sometimes studied at the risk of occasional
repetition, that ideas new to the mind might not
fail of their impression from any want of variety in
the views under which they are presented.

The political illustrations and allusions, and the
moral deductions scattered throughout the work,
have also been selected from many others which

might have been equally applicable, principally because they are presumed to be such as will affect
in the most lively manner the hearts and the consciences of those to whom they are principally addressed; especially with a view to the improvement
of their own country, and of others over which they
can exercise influence.

Of the political uses to which I have endeavoured
to convert the argument, it may fairly be said that
they embrace the most interesting topics among
those which may be called fundamental in the constitution of civil society, viz. the subsistence and
comfort of the great body of the people, and the
means by which those blessings are to be preserved
as society advances from the earliest to the latest
stages of its progress. It cannot be denied that these
objects lie at the root of all public prosperity; for
upon them mainly depend the contentment of the
people, the security of governments, and consequently the offensive and defensive power of nations. The political part of the argument, therefore, does not so much refer to the temporary interests of particular states, as to the great and original principles upon which may be said to depend
the existence and developement of the best systems
of social polity; to the foundation, in short, of the
temporal happiness of individuals and communities.

The moral uses to which the argument has been
converted are, I trust, yet more interesting. To enlarge or fortify the dominion of morals over human
happiness and prosperity, is at all times perhaps the

highest office in which a writer can be engaged. For surely it requires but little reflection upon the history of the past, and little experience of the actual condition of society, to perceive the utter insufficiency of mere political, or philosophical, or economical systems, to afford any permanence to the amelioration which they all profess to bestow upon the condition of mankind. The ties by which they endeavour to bind man to man are altogether too weak for the purpose without some further cement, and the principles upon which they are established are too much open to controversy permanently to command the assent of the human mind. System after system has been adopted with eager hope, and rejected in its turn with utter despair, in favour of another which has ultimately followed the destiny of its predecessor. And mankind, instead of reaping the expected benefits, have found their condition deteriorated and their minds disappointed and irritated. If there ever were a time in which these truths were more palpable than at another, it appears to be the present. From all the magnificent systems which, independently of pure morals, promised so much benefit, but performed so little but mischief to society, it has come out demoralized, degraded, impoverished, unsettled, insecure: and the most profligate politicians have at length been compelled to acknowledge (without, however, practically enforcing the consequence) that the only hope for the future is to be sought in a general moral amelioration. Such will ever be the end of systems which have fine sentiment on the surface, but base selfishness at the core. I have therefore thought the opportunity not unfavourable for openly asserting and endeavouring to demonstrate the necessary connexion of moral conduct, public and private, with political wealth and prosperity; that the former is in fact the centre round which the latter must revolve. It is in vain to deny that this has been at least overlooked in political speculations, which have usually been projected in an orbit not a little eccentric to their legitimate cycle. I hope therefore that I shall not be accused of merely asserting and proving a truism in the following pages. A truth, forgotten, neglected, and no longer acted upon, may to all practical purposes be admitted as no longer acknowledged. To revive its obsolete vigour is as necessary a task and often more difficult than the first establishment of its power; for long disuse is *primâ facie* evidence of want of utility, and constitutes an additional prejudice to be overcome· If, therefore, I have been successful in showing that a fair attention to moral principle is of itself sufficient to free the elementary operations of society from fatal political impediments, and that all other contrivances for the purpose tend only in the end to perpetuate the evils they profess to relieve, I trust that the execution of the attempt will meet with the indulgence due on the score of originality, as well as on that of utility. The principle is certainly as new in the practice of modern politics as it is simple and uniform in its application to society. It has too this peculiar advantage, that whereas in controversies purely political the very elements of which they are composed preclude the possibility of establishing any certain standard of reference, by which the dispute can be settled so as to lead to a safe result in practice ; so, by tracing the propositions up to their legitimate standard in morals, we at once obtain the proper test by which their permanent value may be tried, and (unless we mean to deny the continued superintendence of Providence,) by which the system when reduced to certainty may be also fixed for ever as an unerring rule of conduct. Politicians, when thus confirmed in the truth of their principles will naturally display augmented courage in opposing temporary obstacles, knowing that, although the course of this world is more or less of a struggle against the principle of evil, yet success will always be proportionate to the constancy of perseverance.

I am well aware that the introduction of morals (especially if founded upon religion) into political discussions is apt to excite feelings of disgust in some classes of readers. They delight to contemplate the superstructure of society in its various modifications and arrangements, but decline the less amusing task of inspecting the foundations, which they consider to be the exclusive concern of the professional builder. But all workmen are more or less prone to neglect that part of their work which they know will not be surveyed, till at length occasional omissions degenerate into a faulty habit. The statesman, who is the workman in the case before us, will necessarily

follow the custom and way of thinking of the age
in which he lives. If the fundamental doctrines of
morality have been habitually overlooked in the
practical application of politics, he cannot well restore their influence till the fatal effects of the omission have recalled the public mind to a general sense
of their necessity.

The press is the great medium through which the
public mind is influenced in a free country; and he
who writes with that object has this advantage over
the statesman, that he may, and indeed is frequently
bound in conscience to, run counter to the spirit of
his age, if it oppose the enunciation of what he conceives to be a profitable truth; and he may sometimes hope to reap the delightful reward of giving a
new and improved impulse to the public opinion.

I firmly believe that Christian morality is the very
root and principle of the questions discussed in the
following chapters. I have therefore referred to it
equally, as I hope, without disguise and without affectation, and must trust to the candour and propriety with which the several references are made, as
my best apology to those who are disposed to deprecate the practical association of morals and politics in
such discussions.

I do not wish to disguise the fact, that throughout the whole treatise I have never lost sight of the
application of the argument to our own country in its
present advanced state of society, and in the progress
through which it has arrived at it. This is to be ascribed to two causes. In the first place it is impos-

sible for an Englishman, discoursing on the elements of social happiness and prosperity, to avoid a continual reference to the land where his affections are centred, from whose system of society he has derived his own happiness, the sources of which he desires to transmit uncontaminated to posterity. And in the second place it appeared to me that, throughout the wide circle of political history, I could find no other country where the foundations are so fairly laid upon an enlightened view of moral and political expediency; and where society has advanced so far with so little necessary retrenchment of the comfort and happiness of the people. Such a constitution of things, therefore, presents points of illustration and comparison on the advanced stages of society which would elsewhere be sought in vain. I am well persuaded that none of my countrymen will think the time mispent which is employed in tracing such a system up to its *original elements*,—in investigating the principles upon which it may be preserved in vigour, and transmitted, perhaps with some improvements, to remote ages.

The Reader is entreated to recollect, that this Treatise proceeds little further than to the *elements* of civil society in the several stages of its progress; or to the principles which enable the community to subsist in comfort and happiness as it advances in wealth and population. Such an exposition is a necessary preliminary to all discussions on the higher arrangements of polity; for the people must be at ease in their circumstances before they can become the instruments of forwarding the views of the statesman for the wealth and glory of their country, as a member of the commonwealth of nations.

I wish to add in conclusion, that I should be sorry if any expressions used in enforcing the arguments connected with morals and religion should be thought to undervalue the labours of the metaphysical school of philosophy. As matter for intellectual exercise and improvement, as exciting and fostering a spirit of inquiry and reflection upon the operations of the human mind, the lucubrations of that school must be admitted to be of great importance. But the ambition of its professors takes a higher flight, and aims at establishing practical rules of political and moral conduct upon general and incontrovertible principles; and here I must be permitted to think that they outstep the bounds of the legitimate influence of their science, and, by leading their pupils to rely upon a vague and deficient standard of opinion, are peculiarly in danger of misleading their minds upon many important subjects of moral and political practice.

The fact seems to be that as scarcely any two philosophers ever exactly agreed in the practical inferences justly deducible from a metaphysical inquiry, the science is in itself insufficient for the establishment of general principles in morals and politics; and, when propounded for such a purpose as a department of education, is liable to contract the youthful mind instead of enlarging it, and to confine it within the trammels of its own particular school. It educates the politician to bend the circumstances of general society to a conformity with those peculiar views which his own school has been pleased to sanction with the name of *general principles*, although those principles are in direct opposition to the tenets of other schools equally worthy of credit and regard; and the contest is between the *ipse dixit* of one set of philosophers and the *ipse dixit* of another, rather than between the natural infirmity and selfishness of mankind, and that enlarged view of moral and religious philanthropy which can be drawn only from one source and sanctioned only by one reference. But it is upon the result of this last-mentioned contest that many important elementary principles in politics depend.

Fully admitting, therefore, the usefulness of metaphysical inquiry as a means of intellectual exertion, and as an instrument for promoting what its advocates are pleased to term " the progress of mind," I do not think that a writer can be fairly said to undervalue it, although he may wish to qualify the insinuation of one of its ablest and most eloquent professors, that the " *diffusion of the philosophical spirit*," and its " application to the natural or *theoretical history* of society, to the history of the languages, the arts, the sciences, the *laws*, the *government*, the *manners*, and the *religion* of mankind, form the peculiar glory of the latter half of the eighteenth century." *

* See 1st Dissert. prefixed to Suppl. Encycl. Brit. by Dugald Stewart, Esq. F.R.S. &c.—P. 54.

Now the practical efficacy of the two last-mentioned objects (if not of the two which precede them,) upon the welfare of mankind does not upon the whole appear to have been promoted by the *philosophical spirit* of the latter half of the last century. It may therefore be doubted how far a just view has yet been taken of their " *natural* or *theoretical history*." Are we in fact authorized by history, experience, or revelation, exclusively to rest our hopes of moral and religious improvement, or in many cases even of political amelioration, upon the bare cultivation of our intellectual faculties ? And is not that system peculiarly liable to abuse in its application which confines those offices to the improvement of the understanding, the full discharge of which must at least be aided by a reformation of the heart, and by the abandonment of the selfish principles of our nature; operations which lie beyond the scope of mere intellectual exertion ?

It may be perfectly true that in arts and sciences, on which men reason with minds comparatively unprejudiced, and where the conclusions themselves are the result of strict induction from facts previously demonstrated, every new fact or established argument is a solid addition to our knowledge, and serves as a stepping-stone to further acquisitions. Bu every man at all in the habit of reflecting upon moral evidence, is aware that moral and political truths rest upon principles very different from those by which scientific truths are established. The assent of the mind is with difficulty obtained by

reasoning alone to conclusions resting upon premises which we cannot investigate to the bottom,
and which frequently run counter to the natural
and selfish dispositions of mankind. Neither can
propositions thus supported furnish ground for the
establishment of further truths; for, as it has been
well observed, " the first conclusion not being universally true, but true only in a certain proportion,
out of a given number of cases, we are in danger of
building our second process of reasoning on one of
those cases in which it may fail. In our third process we run two risks of assuming a false ground;
and in our fourth process we run three, and so on:
whence it is evident that it cannot be completely
safe to proceed more than one step; or, to place this
matter in a plainer light, the first conclusion is not
certainly but only *probably* true. The second will
be probable only on a supposition that the first
should in the event prove true; that is, it is only a
probability of a probability: and the third conclusion will be probable only on a supposition that both
the former should prove true; *i. e.* it is the probability of a probability of a probability. Thus in the
progress, the uncertainty of the conclusion is continually increasing."

Now that this is true of moral reasoning, (except
in so far as it depends upon revelation,) does not, I
think, admit of doubt. It appears equally true of
all inquiries determinable by mere moral evidence.
Hence the impossibility, on any authority less than
that of revelation, of establishing *general principles*

in those inquiries; and also the notorious fact, that
what have in their day been called such have frequently turned out in the end to be nothing else but
mischievous delusions.

That it also applies to all argument upon natural
religion, or that knowledge of God and his will
which can be acquired by the unassisted operation
of human reason, or by " *the progress of mind*,"
seems equally clear. Hence the fanciful and immoral
systems which from time to time have been invested with the name and character of religion.

To the same causes may perhaps be ascribed the
little service which the progress of metaphysical inquiry seems to have hitherto rendered to the cause of
Revelation, or that it can ever be expected to render
to that cause, so long as its professors persist in sub-
stituting a mass of doubtful conclusions for the certain dictates of revealed truth, instead of explaining
and enforcing those dictates where they are plainly
applicable to the subject under inquiry.

In opposition to these systems of investigation, an
attempt has certainly been made in the course of the
following pages to add to the proofs already existing,
that (at least in the *elements* of society, considered
either in its " natural or theoretical history," or in its
actual progress,) political truth can only be discovered
with certainty, and political improvement will, therefore, be most surely promoted, where a clear reference
can be made to morals; and that moral truth and
improvement depend in like manner upon a reference
to Revelation. Thus, within the limited extent to

which the following inquiry reaches, we may aid our
political researches by referring to an unerring
standard upon many questions, which must otherwise, by their very nature, be for ever suspended in
the fluctuating balance of doubt and controversy.
Upon the rest we must perhaps be ˙satisfied to remain in that state of uncertainty to which the con-
tingencies of human affairs, in the varieties incident
to their progress, have hitherto condemned the most
enlightened conclusions of mere human reasoning.

CONTENTS.

BOOK I.

VIEW OF THE PROGRESS OF SOCIETY, WITH ITS EFFECTS ON
THE PRINCIPLE OF POPULATION.

CHAPTER I.

CHAPTER II.

CHAPTER III.

CHAPTER IV.

CHAPTER IX.

BOOK II.

POLITICAL CONSEQUENCES DEDUCIBLE FROM THE PRINCIPLES MAINTAINED IN THIS TREATISE.

CHAPTER I.

Consequences to be deduced from the first principle, viz.
" that population has a natural tendency to keep within

CHAPTER II.

CHAPTER III.

CHAPTER IV.

CHAPTER V.

CHAPTER VI.

CHAPTER X.

CHAPTER XI.

BOOK III.

MORAL CONSEQUENCES DEDUCIBLE FROM THE PRINCIPLES
OF THIS TREATISE.

CHAPTER I.

Application of the third principle:—"that the tendency of
population will neither be materially altered nor diverted
from its natural course (as exhibited in the foregoing
chapters), in a country whose government, laws, and
customs, are founded *in the main* upon principles of
religion, morality, rational liberty, and security of person
and property; although these principles may obtain only

CHAPTER II.

CHAPTER IV.

CHAPTER V.

CHAPTER VI.

CHAPTER VII.

CHAPTER VIII.

CHAPTER IX.

CHAPTER X.

THE
PRINCIPLE OF POPULATION.

BOOK I.

VIEW OF THE PROGRESS OF SOCIETY, WITH ITS EFFECTS ON THE PRINCIPLE OF POPULATION.

CHAPTER I.

Introductory Remarks.

THE Principle of Population in its moral and political effects, or in its practical operation upon the condition and interests of mankind, may be said to constitute a new science. Till within these few years it has been treated either as a matter of curious historical research, unconnected with inferences for the regulation of the conduct of nations and individuals; or as a subject upon which no ground of dispute existed, inasmuch as every practice, having an apparent tendency to increase the numbers of mankind, was assumed, on that account only, to merit the encouragement of statesmen. It is not surprising that, with such views of the subject, many unsatisfactory conclusions should have been arrived at, and much political mischief produced; nor that such men as Mr.

Hume and Mr. Wallace should have held notions so indistinct concerning the connexion of the Principle of Population with the progress of society, as to assert; the former, that in small republics, where each man has his little house and field to himself, population may go on doubling every generation; and the latter, that great political advantages would ensue, were all the persons now employed as manufacturers to quit their present pursuits and to be equally industrious in raising grain and breeding cattle. The first of these positions seems tantamount to the declaration, that men in each succeeding generation can subsist upon the half of that which supported their fathers; and this down to the lowest point to which the infinite divisibility of matter can reduce their pittance: the last seems to assume, on the contrary, that the only healthy condition of society is that, wherein *every citizen* raises not only food enough for the support of himself and his family, but a surplus store sufficient for four or five other families. There must evidently have been a great want of science and of clearness in the conception of a subject, upon which men so ingenious could have come to conclusions so strange, and so discordant.

In proportion, therefore, to the deficiency that existed, is the merit of those who have in any degree supplied it: for no man, I apprehend, will be disposed to deny that the question involves considerations emphatically interesting to the welfare of his species, and is conversant with the most important departments of morals and politics. On these grounds, too much can scarcely be said in commendation of Mr. Malthus's Essay upon Population. It at once raised an important object, from the confusion of desultory thought and blindfold speculation, to the dignity and precision of philosophical inquiry; nay more, to the highest rank of philosophy, viz. the knowledge of the principles upon which the practical improvement of mankind, moral and political, is to be conducted. When we reflect that the confusion previously existing was reduced in the Essay to a regular and tangible system, scientifically arranged, fairly argued, and founded upon principles not merely speculative, but drawn from facts candidly stated though perhaps somewhat misapplied, it is impossible not to admit that valuable progress was made towards the establishment of truth. Those who differ the most from the conclusions must at least be thankful for the facilities afforded to the argument. They certainly ought to admit that their own minds would neither have been so well informed, nor their ideas so well arranged, nor their means of reply so amply furnished, without the lucid order and indefatigable industry displayed in the Essay. As one of those who differ the most from the Author's conclusions, I am not ashamed to confess my obligations to him, and my admiration that so much was effected upon a first attempt, rather than any regret at what I conceive to be the untenable nature of his principles, and their consequences. It is of inexpressible advantage to a fair controversialist to have the power of at once proceeding to the *merits of his case.* This Mr. Malthus has conferred upon all who oppose him; and had they universally availed themselves of it, it would have been as advantageous to their own credit as to the cause of truth. If I may presume to rank myself among his fair adversaries, it is not because I enter-

tain the slightest doubt that we are both honestly engaged in the same pursuit, viz. the improvement of
society ; but because it is impossible to discuss a question which he has so ably and logically argued, with
any material difference of opinion, without carrying
the opposition up to the principles from which the
conclusions appear to be so fairly deduced.   Nor indeed should I have had the vanity to constitute myself in any degree his adversary, if the question concerning the Principle of Population could have been
fundamentally treated, without continual and almost
exclusive reference to the only writer, of whom it
may be said with reference to this subject, that his
prism has collected the scattered rays of light from
the literary firmament, and refracted them in their regular series of lively colours upon the fair surface
of his pages.   In a word, I consider Mr. Malthus's
Essay upon Population to be the point from which
every subsequent discussion of the subject must necessarily diverge.   With these preliminary remarks I
proceed at once to the statement of my subject.

Statement of the Subject.

THE first command of God to man was that
he should increase and multiply, and replenish the
earth and *subdue* it, that is, labour upon it for his
subsistence.   Experience and common sense inform
us, that as man cannot live without eating, the species can only increase and multiply in proportion as
food can be raised from the earth by human industry:
and we learn from the whole tenor of the sacred

writings, as well as from the suggestions of natural conscience, that none of these objects are to be attempted by means inconsistent with virtue.

The fair result of these three propositions seems to be, that it is incumbent, as a moral duty, upon governments and individuals, to use every exertion which appears conducive to the multiplication of the human species, together with, and in proportion to, the extension of industry and civilization, which ensure subsistence and happiness. In other words, the object of a sound politician should be to place his country in that progressive state, which Dr. Adam Smith, in his Treatise on the Wages of Labour, has justly and clearly shown to be the cheerful and hearty state to all the different orders of the community.* (Wealth of Nations, b. i. c. 8.) And the final view of all rational politics being, as Dr. Paley observes, to produce the greatest quantity of happiness in a given tract of country, it follows that it is also our duty to use every exertion for the purpose of preventing a country from resting in the stationary condition, which Dr. Smith designates as " *hard* " and " *dull*," or from sinking into the declining state, which is described as " *miserable* " and " *melancholy.*"

---

* The passage is as follows: " It deserves to be remarked, perhaps, that it is in the *progressive state*, while the society is advancing to the further acquisition, rather than when it has acquired it's full complement of riches, that the condition of the labouring poor, of the great body of the people, seems to be the happiest and most comfortable. It is *hard* in the stationary, and *miserable* in the declining state. The progressive state is in reality the cheerful and the hearty state to all the different orders of the society. The stationary is dull—the declining melancholy."

Any system, which professes to found the happiness of a people upon measures having a tendency to produce either of these last-mentioned states, must be no less fallacious and unnatural than a scheme which should seek the same end by means inconsistent with sound political morality. In the following Treatise, therefore, I shall think myself at perfect liberty to argue that the Principle of Population has been adjusted with a view to the following truth, viz. that the condition best adapted to the nature of social man is that which most completely fulfils the end of his Creator in placing him in a social state; namely, a condition of progressive prosperity and of moral improvement.

Now if the moral and political progress of a people constitute the main ingredient in any estimate of their power and happiness, a particular inquiry into the mode in which the principle of population operates among them becomes essentially requisite to the correctness of such estimate. For whenever the due proportion between population and the food provided for its support is to any material extent deranged, a corresponding weakness will be infallibly introduced into some of the vital powers of the commonwealth, by an immediate deterioration in the moral and political state of the people. This consequence has seldom been positively denied: but politicians (of late years especially) have widely and warmly differed both with respect to the quantum of each which constitutes the due proportion between food and population, and to the means by which such proportion is to be maintained, when once established. Now it is evident that the solution of these questions must very much depend upon the relative progress which population and the production of food would *naturally* make in the state of society in which the country whose means we are investigating may happen to exist. If indeed, as hath been lately maintained,* " population hath in all cases a *natural* tendency to exceed the supply of food for it's support," the task of the politician is plain and obvious: he must, in all cases and in every state of society, exert his faculties in preventing the exuberance of the one, and supplying the deficiency of the other. But if, as I venture to contend in the following pages, the *natural* progress of population varies in its tendency with every variation in the state of society, and seldom, if ever, tends to a vicious exuberance, the duties of the politician must then be regulated according to the circumstances of each particular case; that is to say, he may encourage an increase of population under some conditions of society, although he may discourage it under others. It will, however, be a comfortable discovery, if it shall appear (as I think it will) that in most cases he will best fulfil his duty by leaving things in the hands of Providence; who will probably be admitted to be the most competent legislator in a case which concerns the whole world, and who, contemplating the natural man as a being compounded of mind and body, has been very far (as contended by Mr. Malthus) from regulating the laws relating to the increase of his species by the same calculations which govern the increase of the inanimate or brute creatures, the principle of whose multiplication has

---

* See Mr. Malthus on Population, *passim;* Edinburgh Review; Christian Observer, &c.

evidently been framed with a view to their consumption as food. But taking into view the higher
destiny of man, the rational as well as the sensual
part of his nature, Providence seems to have afforded
full security against every danger, in the spontaneous
operations of the human will, where they are not materially interfered with by bad government or evil customs, or vitiated by an extraordinary relaxation of
morals: that is to say, wherever an ordinary degree of
attention is paid to the express commands of the Creator. This I say would be a comfortable discovery, because it would exceedingly simplify the duties of the
politician. Instead of wandering through a maze of
intricate problems, uncertain as the capricious nature
of the beings it is his object to control, his march
would be directed to a few simple points, plainly
marked out by an unerring Guide: and what is
still better, certain though not complete success
would attend his career:—for although Providence
does in no instance hold out a prospect of *perfect*
success in the pursuit of moral objects, yet it is reasonable to infer that the happiness of mankind will
be proportioned to the earnestness of the pursuit,
and the degree of the attainment.

On whatever side of these conflicting opinions the
truth may ultimately be found to rest, one thing
seems very clear—that until we have ascertained the
truth we are working in the dark, and may probably
counteract our common object, the happiness and welfare of mankind, by the very means we adopt to promote it. Moreover, if we reflect upon the extreme
importance of the subject, that it involves nothing
less than the very foundations of the moral and political welfare of the whole community of nations as

well as of individuals, we must admit that a grave responsibility is incurred by wilful ignorance or apathy concerning it. It is the glory of this free country that our institutions rest upon the secure basis of candid inquiry and free discussion. It is the glory of such a system that, notwithstanding the ignorance, the prejudices, and the self-interest of mankind, and the mischiefs introduced among them by false but plausible reasoning, truth will ultimately prevail. I am very far, however, from suggesting this circumstance as even a palliation of wilful indulgence in false or superficial reasoning on important matters of policy. A profligate perversion of the mental powers in a pretended pursuit of truth is even more disgraceful than gross and wilful ignorance; and is by no means to be excused by the consideration that the deceit will ultimately be discovered, and further evil prevented, after it has served the purposes of the deceiver. It is not, therefore, without long and anxious consideration, that I have ventured to lay before the public the whole of the system embraced in the following pages. But being upon the whole conscientiously convinced, not only of the truth of my hypothesis, but of it's great importance to the moral and political welfare of my countrymen and of mankind, I now venture to submit it to their judgment. This conviction has been strengthened by a perusal of what has been advanced during the past five or six years in support of the opposite system. I believe my view of the subject to be in a great degree original; and under these circumstances I feel bound to state it in a manner as plain and as strong as that in which I view it: and my confidence in the success of the statement is weakened only by an unfeigned diffidence of my own ability to do it full justice. Having nothing in view but the discovery of truth, I deprecate no observations which my statement may call forth, except such as may superciliously condemn the argument without answering it. Let it be remembered that differences of opinion on such a subject do not involve a mere contest for victory on a question purely literary, but are conversant with the highest interests of man; that the subject is in itself difficult from the range over which the reasoning extends, and the depth from which much of it is drawn. To mix up with it therefore the petty interests of literary vanity instead of meeting it with honest argument, and, where necessary, with fair concession, would be not less absurd or unprincipled than if the congress of European powers had held its deliberations for the restoration of public justice and tranquillity in Europe amidst criticisms on the notes of Haydn, or in the intervals of a German waltz.

CHAPTER II.

*Statement of the Opinions lately promulgated on
the Principle of Population.*

A SHORT statement of the opinions lately received on the principle of population, with their obvious consequences, will best prepare the reader's
mind for the due reception and comprehension of the
principles about to be developed in this treatise. A
more eligible mode of effecting this object can scarcely
be adopted, than by a brief statement of the general
principles contained in the two first chapters of Mr.
Malthus's well known Essay on the Principle of
Population. He is deservedly considered as the
father of what may be called the new system; and
the *practical inferences* drawn from his theory by
others, rather than by himself, first drew my attention to the subject. He has indeed introduced
various modifications of his own original inferences
in his several editions, and explanations which amount
in some cases to little less than a direct retraction.
And no caution appears more necessary to the readers
of Mr. Malthus's Essay, than that of carefully dis-
tinguishing between the practical measures *ultimately*
recommended, and those obviously deducible from
the principles laid down. An insight will thus be
acquired, not only into the nature of the principles
themselves, but, I am happy to think, also into the
amiable disposition and enlightened humanity of their
author.

But to return to the principles themselves.

Population in very favourable circumstances (in the newly settled countries of America for example) has been found to double itself every twenty-five years : that rate, therefore is assumed to be (at the least) its *natural* rate of increase, which might go on *ad infinitum,* if interrupted by no *checks.* But it is evident that the increase of food, (land being an absolute quantity,) could by no methods be augmented to such an indefinite extent. It might possibly double itself for once in twenty-five years, while the best lands remained uncultivated; but so far from following up this ratio of increase in subsequent periods, it cannot even be supposed possible that its produce could be augmented even in the simple ratio of its original quantity.

" The necessary effects of these two different rates of increase" (says Mr. Malthus, and I beg the reader to bear the passage in mind), " when brought together, will be very striking. Let us call the population of this island eleven millions, and suppose the present produce equal to the easy support of such a number. In the first twenty-five years the population would be twenty-two millions, and the food being also doubled, the means of subsistence would be equal to this increase. In the next twenty-five years the population would be forty-four millions; and the means of subsistence only equal to the support of thirty-three millions. In the next period the population would be eighty-eight millions, and the means of subsistence just equal to the support of half that number. And at the conclusion of the first century the population would be 176 millions, and the means of subsistence only equal to the support of fifty-five millions, leaving a population of 121 millions totally unprovided for."

Extending this reasoning to the whole earth, it will be found that the population of the world would increase in a geometrical ratio as 1.2.4.8.16.32.64.128.256., and subsistence only in an arithmetical ratio, as 1.2.3.4.5.6.7.8.9. In two centuries the population would be to the possible means of subsistence as 256 to 9; in three centuries, as 4,096 to 13; and as of course there are ultimate limits to the produce of the earth, an end must come to any increase in the supply of food, while the principle of population still retains its full force.——Such is the account rendered by Mr. Malthus of the dispensation of Providence with respect to the *natural power* of increase in mankind and in their subsistence respectively; and I cannot but think that, if true, it affords a most singular and extraordinary exception to the admirable adaptation of means to ends which is so beautifully prominent in every other arrangement of the Creator.

But as it is evident that, in point of fact, mankind, unable to exist without food, do not increase in the abovementioned geometrical ratio, but precisely in that in which food is produced for their support; Mr. Malthus, in his second chapter, enumerates what he is pleased to call the *checks* to this exuberant power of production. They consist of " all those customs, and all those diseases, which seem to be generated by a scarcity of the means of subsistence; and all those causes, independent of this scarcity, whether of a moral or physical nature, which tend prematurely to weaken or destroy the human frame." These checks may be classed under two general heads, the preventive and the positive; the FORMER consisting of prudential abstinence from marriage, which when accompanied by irregular intercourse between the sexes, produces aggravated vice and misery; when accompanied by moral restraint produces comparative comfort. The LATTER, consisting of every cause, whether arising from vice or misery, which in any degree tends to shorten the duration or repress the productive power of human life; such as extreme poverty, wars, diseases, famine, pestilence, and the like. The obstacles to the increase of population, therefore, whether classed under the positive or preventive checks, are all resolvable into moral restraint, vice, or misery. And as the former (explained to mean an abstinence from marriage, unaccompanied by irregular gratification) is the only mode of escaping the encounter of the two latter in some form or other, it is evident that, upon this theory, the whole onus of counteracting, consistently with human happiness and virtue, the immense disproportion of the relative powers of increase above enumerated, rests entirely upon this single conservative principle. It follows of course, also, that the more it can be made to operate, the greater portion of virtue and happiness will be found in society. And as it is upon the lower ranks that the vice and misery alleged to arise from a redundant population particularly press, it evidently becomes the duty of governments so to model their political arrangements, and of individuals so to regulate their charities, as to lend encouragement to such protracted abstinence from marriage, from the moment that the produce of the land after it's first period of doubling sinks into the regular arithmetical progress; or, in plainer terms, from the moment that a country emerges from

the purely agricultural state of society into one compounded of agriculture and commerce.   Such is the
theory, and such are its consequences.

Granting the premises, it is indeed perfectly
obvious that this conclusion is undeniable.   Once
persuade a man against all experience that the oak
in his field hath a natural tendency to increase *ad
infinitum* in the same ratio as during the first fifty
years, and may in time overshadow his whole estate,
unless checked by the axe, and his prudent course of
conduct will not long remain doubtful.   But considering the extreme difficulty of such a general
system of abstinence at once from marriage and from
sensuality, where, according to the theory, it is most
requisite, i. e. among the lower orders of any country
(which indeed is fully admitted by Mr. Malthus); it
seems utterly impossible to reconcile his practical
conclusions either with the nature of man, or the
plain dictates of religion upon the subject of marriage.   But it is not by starting doubts and difficulties that the system, however apparently inconsistent with the goodness and justice of the Creator,
can be shaken.   I shall therefore proceed to state
the principles which appear to me to lead to opposite
conclusions, merely premising a few observations on
the mode in which Mr. Malthus has conducted his
argument, with the objections to which it is liable.

What he professes to have done, (see preface, p. vii),
in addition to the arguments found in the writings of
others, is, to state the subject more philosophically,
to illustrate more fully, by reference to history, the
various modes by which the level is preserved
between population and the means of subsistence,
and to draw new practical inferences of a general

nature for the political conduct of states and the
private conduct of individuals. Now with respect
to the works of others; Plato, Aristotle, Montes-.
quieu, Mr. Townshend, and other writers, who seem
to have believed in the natural tendency of population
towards a too rapid increase, either state the fact
incidentally, to illustrate some partial phenomena in
society, or draw their conclusions from a very confined view of it under an imperfect administration,
where slavery, ignorance, or tyranny, evidently
checked the industry of the people, and forcibly
diverted the progress of society from its *natural
course.* Even the state of society in the boasted
republics of ancient Greece cannot be exonerated
from some part of this imputation; and those of
Spain and France were too palpably open to it.
Observations, therefore, with respect to the vice and
misery arising from the difficulty of procuring subsistence, drawn from the view of those countries,
seem only to prove that they had not yet adopted
that system of polity for the government of the
mass of their inhabitants, which is consistent with
the views and ordinations of Providence. With
respect to the philosophical statement of the subject
it appears to be defective in one of its main branches
—the statement of the *natural* tendency of population to increase. The historical references appear to
have been made (as Mr. Malthus indeed in his preface
seems partly to admit) with a mind predisposed to
the theory with which it was impressed, and professedly in search of facts to corroborate it: and the
practical inferences (as far as they rest upon the
peculiar arguments arising out of the principle of
population) seem not to be borne out by the premises;

can in no case be *justifiably* acted upon; and are very evidently inapplicable to the advanced stages of society in a free and extensive Christian country, being calculated rather to check it's progress in wealth and happiness than to promote it.

If any success attend my efforts to establish the principles laid down at the commencement of the following chapter, it is probable that each of the preceding propositions will also be made out in the course of the argument. In the mean time I venture to suggest, as a further preparation of the reader's mind for the fair discussion of them, that the origin of what are conceived to be the mistakes and false reasonings, with respect to the principle of population, appears to be the assumption of a tendency to increase in the human species, the quickest that can be proved possible in any *particular* state of society, as that which is natural and theoretically possible in *all;* and the characterising of every cause which tends to prevent such quickest possible rate, as *checks* to the natural and spontaneous tendency of population to increase; but as checks evidently insufficient to stem the progress of an overwhelming torrent. This seems as eligible a mode of reasoning, as if one were to assume the height of the Irish giant as the natural standard of the stature of man, and to call every reason which may be suggested as likely to prevent the generality of men from reaching it, *checks* upon their growth. The natural and spontaneous tendency of the principle of population in distinct states of society varies its rate with every difference in their political condition; it is no more the same in the manufacturing, as it is in the agricultural, or in this as in the pastoral states of society, than the natural growth of an oak on a mountain top in Scotland is the same as it would be in the rich valleys of the New Forest. But the term *check* of course implies the prevention of that which would otherwise naturally take place; it is, therefore, very incorrectly applied to denote a relative difference, invariably fixed by the primary laws of nature, and the immutable decrees of Providence. From the deception caused by the wrong use of this term, we find writers supporting such positions as the following: " civilization does not weaken the principle of population;" (Monthly Review, June 1807, p. 137:) again, " assuming a peopled portion of the earth, there is a point at which it's produce would be a maximum; *there is no point*, however, at which the people upon it, however numerous, might not under advantageous circumstances go on increasing without number. Besides, while the soil is still capable of increasing its produce, yet if it be approaching somewhere near the limit of its capacity, the increase of its produce cannot possibly keep pace with the *natural*, or rather the *possible*, increase of the population upon it." (Christian Observer, July 1807, p. 452.)

These are, in truth, but natural corollaries from Mr. Malthus's premises, who asserts of population, " that a thousand millions are just as easily doubled EVERY *twenty-five years* as a thousand," and " population, could it be supplied with food, *would go on with unexhausted vigour;* and the increase of one period would furnish *the power of a greater increase* the next, and this without any limit." (Malthus, vol. i. p. 8.) And again, " it is not the question in England, whether by cultivating all our commons we could raise considerably more corn than at present, but whether we could raise sufficient for a population of twenty millions in the next twenty-five years, and forty millions in the next fifty years;"* as if it were possible, that the people of England, one third of whom are asserted by this very writer to live in towns, and consequently not generally to keep up their own numbers,† could by any possible means increase so fast as to double their total amount in twenty-five years; which is assumed as the quickest possible rate in the agricultural state of society, where the employment and situation of the people is most favourable to population. After these passages, however, we cannot be surprised at the opinions which they have engendered, or that another writer‡ should state, that " the greater part of those reasoners, who are in the habit of misunderstanding and misrepresenting Mr. Malthus, would have some chance of attaining clearer views on the subject of population, if they would attend to the very simple proposition from which his doctrines are deduced; namely, that the human race have a tendency to increase faster than *food can be provided for them.*" Mr. Malthus, in his Essay, does certainly intend to convey that idea. I cannot but think, however, that those reasoners who wish clearly to under-

* See Malthus, book iii. c. 11. p. 222. vol. ii.

† See Malthus, book ii. c. 7. The passage is as follows: " to fill up the void occasioned by this mortality in towns, and to answer all further demands for population, it is evident that a constant supply of recruits from the country is necessary; and this supply appears, in fact, to be always flowing in from the redundant births of the country." (Vol. i. p. 464.)

‡ Edinburgh Review, vol. xi. p. 102.

stand, and fairly to represent, the principle of population, would have a better chance of obtaining their end, if, instead of blindly acquiescing in these *assumed* data, they proceed to inquire into the degree in which the principle of population *naturally and really* operates in the several stages of society. They will find this to be very distinct from its assumed " possible" operation, and in most cases to be very far from having a necessary tendency " to push the number of people beyond the point at which food can be acquired for them." This is a broad and distinct difference *in principle*, which it is the object of this first book to make out to the satisfaction of my readers. It is hoped that the proof of the propositions assumed in the following chapter will lead to a full and fair establishment of the truth. The object of the following books will then be to show the consequences which may fairly be deduced from the propositions thus established.

CHAPTER III.

Fundamental Propositions of this Treatise.

IN opposition to the hypothesis detailed in the preceding chapter, the object of this Treatise is to maintain the truth and practical consistency of the following principles, viz. :

I. Population has a *natural* tendency to keep *within the powers* of the soil to afford it subsistence in every gradation through which society passes.

II. This tendency can *never* BE DESTROYED, and can only be altered or diverted from its natural course, so as to induce a mischievous pressure of population against the ACTUAL supply of food, by grossly impolitic laws, or pernicious customs,—either

1. Accelerating the progress of population considerably beyond its *natural* rate; or,

2. Depressing the productive energies of the soil considerably below its *natural* powers.

III. This tendency will neither be materially altered nor diverted from its natural course, so as to produce the evils mentioned in the last proposition, in a country whose government, laws, and customs, are founded in the main on principles of religion, morality, rational liberty, and security of person and property; although these principles may obtain only an imperfect influence. But

IV. This tendency will have its complete operation, so as constantly to maintain the people in comfort and plenty, in proportion as religion, morality, rational liberty, and security of person and property, approach the attainment of a perfect influence.

The various modifications, to which the alternate increase of food and population is liable, are all comprised within these general principles, which exclude the *necessity* of " vice, misery," or such a modification of " moral restraint " as includes *involuntary* abstinence from marriage, as *checks* indispensably arising out of the principle of population. Their consideration and consequences, moreover, will lead the attentive reader of the following pages to a fifth proposition of great importance in political œconomy, viz.:

V. During the alternate progress of population and subsistence in the earliest and most advanced stages of society, a *previous* increase of people is necessary to stimulate the community to a farther production of food; and consequently to the healthy advancement of a country in the career of strength and prosperity. It results from this proposition that the incipient pressure of population against the *actual* means of subsistence, or, more correctly speaking, the excess of population *just beyond the plentiful supply of the people's want*, instead of being the cause of most of the miseries of human life, is in fact (under the modifications just stated) the cause of all public happiness, industry, and prosperity.

These five propositions contain an outline of the argument maintained in the following Treatise; and in them is involved almost every question fundamentally important to the religious, moral, and political interests of mankind. The method by which I propose to establish their truth is to take a brief, but connected view of society in the several stages through which it has been found to pass, from the savage condition of man up to the highest state of civilization of which any authentic record is to be found; and even beyond that point, to the highest which he can be thought capable of reaching in the career of wealth and prosperity. These stages naturally separate themselves into four general divisions, viz.: 1. The savage and pastoral; 2. The agricultural; 3. The commercial and manufacturing; 4. The highly civilized and artificial states of society. Into the principles and practices of each of these conditions of society, and of the successive gradations which lead from one to the other, I have entered at some length in a separate chapter devoted to the particular stage then under discussion, and have endeavoured to show in detail the *effects* which those principles and practices naturally and spontaneously produce upon the progress of population. At the close of each investigation I have attempted to show that the *effects* produced in every stage of society can be no other than what are enunciated in four preceding propositions. If this attempt has been successful, I am certainly authorized to conclude that they are fundamental axioms of human society universally applicable to the purposes of the political œconomist, and to draw from them, for the benefit of mankind, such inferences as they may be fairly presumed to afford for the regulation and instruction of governments and individuals. For if the propositions be found true in every condition in which human society can subsist, they must doubtless be of universal operation; and being so, it is impossible, considering their obvious importance, moral and political, not to admit that they must lead to practical consequences deeply involving the best interests of mankind.

CHAPTER IV.

Of the natural Tendency of Population in the early Stages of Society.

BEFORE we proceed to a detailed investigation of the state of society among the barbarous, the hunting, or the pastoral tribes of mankind, who roam over millions of fertile but neglected acres, and whose idleness or ignorance condemns them to a scanty subsistence on the spontaneous produce of the earth, the following brief summary may perhaps be fairly introduced.

Throughout the earth, and in every separate division of it, there must have existed, before man could have multiplied so fast as to have occupied the land, a certain portion of animal and vegetable food in what is called a state of nature; offering itself to the first settlers without any labour or precaution of theirs, but simply that of seizing and devouring. This may be called the savage state; and as man in that state has few artifical wants, and therefore no temptation to labour except for food and, perhaps, a scanty portion of raiment, he would go on multiplying his species without regard to the existing quantity of food, till the continued increase of the former came to press upon the absolute quantity of the latter. The natural consequence would then be a degree of uneasiness among the inhabitants from a scanty supply of food; and two consequences must inevitably ensue: either contentions among the people for the food, in which the strongest would enjoy plenty and

the weaker starve; or an agreement among them to
enlarge the means of their subsistence by domesticating
some of the wild animals, thereby emerging from the
savage state, and making the first step in the progress of civilization. It is impossible for a society
to exist for many generations without making this
transition, unless repressed by their own vices, or the
selfish and cruel interference of others; for *naturally*
the pressure introduced by the increase of mankind,
though it might at first produce contests for the
existing supply of food, yet, considering the inconveniences attending them, would soon produce
another arrangement, unless it were artificially prevented. Some of the most acute among the savages,
observing the docile nature of many animals, and
that their docility is perhaps proportioned to their
domestic utility when tamed, would set about the
task of reducing them to a state in which, without
further diminishing the relative proportion of their
numbers to mankind, they might afford a continual
supply to their wants. Milk, and its various combinations, the changes of aliment to which it is con-
vertible, and the slaughter only of the superfluous
increase of the herds and flocks, with occasional
assistance derived from the wild animals still escaped
from extermination, would be the regimen of this
second stage of society in all widely-extended tracts
of country; and it may be called the pastoral state
of society. Upon this system it is evident that a
much larger number of persons can be supported on
the same extent of territory; the animals become
more numerous and healthy by being reduced under
the management of those who apportion to each
herd and flock its requisite extent of pasture, and

prevent the waste and accidents to which their erratic state is liable. The soil itself becomes capable of supporting a larger number; the less wasteful method of supplying man with food by the extraction of other nutriment from animals than mere flesh, creates a smaller demand upon the increased stock; and the progressive power of the country is improved in the double ratio of augmented force and removed obstruction. But as in land in a state of nature the capability of supporting herds and flocks is absolute, and determinable in no very long period of time, and as people increase at least as fast in a pastoral as in a savage state, the pressure of population will soon come to operate upon this increased supply; and the same necessity for contention, or rather perhaps for farther production, will occur. Observation quickened by necessity will have pointed out to some of the shepherds the vegetables most suited to their taste or climate; and the step from that observation to the cultivation of a small portion of the earth with rude instruments of agriculture, such as, first, a stake from a tree, next, one sharpened at the end with a flint, &c. is but a trifling advance in human intellect. But the increase it gives to the supply of food by introducing an enlarged supply of vegetable without materially reducing animal sustenance, greatly enlarges the power of the earth to support mankind; and a third stage in the progress of society ensues, that of the early and rude agricultural state—a change accompanied with this very important circumstance, that as it becomes the interest of the society that every man should be secure of the soil he cultivates, and that the whole society should ensure the whole collected produce by their protection, it necessarily becomes fixed to one spot; settled habitations are created, social ties formed, industry and other virtues excited, and the foundation laid of all those improvements in society which lead to more complete cultivation, to the division of labour, and to the development of those useful energies which lead to a farther progress in civilization. Now it is very evident that throughout the whole of this series of revolutions, population is kept very far within the powers of the soil to afford it subsistence; and that if in fact it presses against the actual supply of food, so as to bring a temporary inconvenience upon individuals, that effect is entirely to be ascribed to the laziness or ignorance of those individuals. It is no less evident, that this pressure is *necessary* to stimulate them to such exertion as would carry on the society to its next stage, and that any provision by which the pressure could be otherwise removed would be nothing less than a scheme for passing an eternal sentence of barbarism and ignorance against the unfortunate people, and for directly counteracting the ordinations of Providence for the replenishment and happiness of the world. To say, therefore, that in these conditions of society " population has a tendency to increase faster than food can be provided for its support" is evidently untrue, because the land is accessible and ready to make a tenfold return. It would be a much more tenable proposition to hold, that the wants of the people press against their own ignorance and apathy, and call aloud upon them in the name of Providence to remove the pressure. To ascribe the miseries of human life in these stages of society to the pressure of population would therefore be about as fair as to ascribe the sufferings of a criminal who forfeits his liberty or life to the offended laws of his country, to the operation of those laws, and not to the crimes he has committed. To assert that the assumed tendency of population to exuberance can only be repressed by vice, misery, or such a modification of moral restraint as includes an involuntary abstinence from marriage, is no less untrue; because the most ordinary exertion of industry on the soil would give to every man in want more than enough for the support of himself and his family; and this exertion, when it becomes general, will carry on the community to the next step in the progress of society. Therefore although under the amended system marriages would be multiplied, industry would also be awakened; although population would increase, the produce of the soil would much more increase; and a fair attention to the new duties introduced by new habits and pursuits would always maintain the community in a state of comfort and plenty.

Such, without any great stretch of presumption, may be predicated with some certainty to have been the intentions of Providence with respect to the earliest stages of society. It appears, indeed, that a people passing through them will not be permitted to enjoy any tolerable degree of comfort and happiness, except in the road which has been marked out as leading to their further progress. For if we consult the accounts rendered by different authors who have been eye-witnesses of men's actions in the early stages of society, when no attempts were making to lead them into the paths of civilization, it is to be feared that we shall too frequently find them of a nature grossly vicious, and calculated even to repress the population within the limits of that salutary pressure, against the actual means of subsistence which is necessary to the further development of their resources, and not only to keep it within those limits, but even to produce a gradual diminution in the scanty numbers of the people. Let us take as one example the case of the South Sea Islands;—an instance the more in point, as it has been relied upon by the advocates of the modern opinions respecting the principle of population as one of the strong holds of their argument.

It appears that in the island of Otaheite no regular cultivation has ever existed; the people have always been supported under the shade of their own forests by the almost spontaneous bounty of nature. Upon the first pressure of population against the existing supply of such food, the natives, instead of having recourse to agricultural exertion, preferred their original state of barbarism, and this against the repeated efforts of benevolence to induce them to adopt a better system. They removed the pressure of their population, necessarily arising out of such conduct, by the murder of their new-born infants, which became so regular a practice that nurses recommended themselves by their skill in the diabolical operation. But mark the effects of vice, and of the interference of human depravity with the order of nature, and the designs of Providence! The number of inhabitants, which in the year 1774, though perhaps much over stated at 200,000,* was certainly

* See Cook's Second Voyage, vol. i. p. 349. By tracing their history through the successive Voyages which have been published, a gradual diminution in the number of inhabitants is fully established.

very great, for whom nature had provided sustenance
with scarcely any exertion of their own to procure it,
gradually dwindled to such a degree, that at the beginning of this century it did not amount to more
than 5000; * and this in a climate delightful and
healthy in a very superior degree. No doubt, in
short, seems to remain, that the whole of the original
race of natives will soon be extinct. To complete
the argument, it is only necessary to state, that in
the Friendly and Sandwich Islands, where nature has
done less for the inhabitants in healthiness of climate,
and fertility of soil, the absence of this vice, and the
adoption of trade and cultivation, have kept them in
a gradual progress of improvement. The superiority
of the latter too (who have derived commercial advantages and civilized intercourse from their vicinity
to the north-west coast of America, and the convenience they afford to the piratical and smuggling navi-
gators of those seas) proves that the progress made
by the two has been exactly in proportion to their
industry and exertion. Nor has any inconvenience
been found to arise in these two last-mentioned groups
of islands from a redundant population; nor have any
extraordinary checks occurred to prevent it. Yet
upon them and Otaheite Mr. Malthus seems very
much to rely for the exemplification of his theory.
" Where," says he, " could they be disposed of in a
single century, when they would amount to above
three millions, supposing their numbers to double
every twenty-five years?" And in a note he professes to think, that they might perhaps increase in a
ratio still faster. But " *proh hominum fidem!* " the

* Turnbull's Voyage, vol. iii. p. 76.

island which has endeavoured to check its natural increase (for here the term *check* is applied correctly enough) instead of providing for it, has dwindled in 30 years from a numerous population to 5000 souls; while those who have permitted theirs to take its natural course, and have exercised their industry in the best method afforded by their circumstances and situation, have not only gradually increased in num--bers, but in prosperity and happiness. Nor have they been afflicted with any extraordinary quantity of vice or misery. Diseases are upon the whole less frequent among them than in more civilized states; and though havoc has certainly been made by war among their chiefs, yet their insular situation and limited means of transporting an army must have prevented that havoc from extending widely among the lower orders.

With respect to the island of Otaheite, there is something in the mode of checking population by infanticide, which rouses a feeling of horror in the mind, and deprives it of patience to calculate in detail the political consequence of such a *check*. It cannot be denied that so summary a method will certainly keep down the population: but its general result we have seen; and the foregoing statement gives every reason to conclude that effects of the same nature would arise from every other method taken to interfere with the laws of Providence for the due replenishment of the world. They all have a tendency to reduce a people to that point where the smallest exertion becomes irksome; the quantity of food, therefore, even where nature has performed nine-tenths of the task of producing it, will gradually decline, where any means, however horrid, can be found of dispensing with the trifling labour necessary to procure it.

Thus it is at Otaheite, where 5000 barbarians still prefer the destruction of their offspring to the moderate exertion necessary to provide them with food, in an island which previously supported more than twenty times that number, without vexing the earth with their instruments of tillage.

An investigation into the condition of the hunting tribes on the northern continent of America will give results not essentially different.

A very curious account of the state of some of these tribes is to be found in Hearne's Journey to the Copper-mine River, 4to, 1795. He appears to have been nearly the first European who visited them, and had therefore an opportunity of contemplating their moral and political condition in all its native deformity. The veracity of his account is, I believe, universally admitted. That of the main fact which he recorded, and of which he was the first discoverer, is fully established by the subsequent travels of Mackenzie, viz. the existence of a line of sea-coast to the north of North America, about the latitude of 73°. Nor is there any evidence, either internal or derived from subsequent experience, that throws reasonable doubt upon the faithfulness of the picture which he presents of savage manners. His journeys were performed on foot, in the years 1769-70-71-72, by a route leading from the western point of Hudson's Bay towards the north-west. A more striking proof of the general condition of the countries he traversed can scarcely be given than by recording the fact, that in a journey of some months he was precluded from any possibility of a change of apparel, even of linen, by the necessity under which he and his companions lay of reserving all their strength for the conveyance of necessary food. In p. 33. he writes, " It will be only necessary to say that we have fasted many times two whole days and nights ; twice upwards of three days, and once while at Shee-tan-nee *near seven days*, during which we tasted not a mouthful of any thing except a few cranberries, water, scraps of old leather, and burnt bones. On those pressing occasions I have frequently seen the Indians examine their wardrobe, which consisted chiefly of skin clothing, and consider what part could best be spared ; sometimes a piece of an old half-rotten deer-skin, and at others a pair of old shoes, were sacrificed to alleviate extreme hunger. The relation of such uncommon hardships may, perhaps, gain little credit in Europe ; while those who are conversant with the History of Hudson's Bay and are thoroughly acquainted with the distress which the natives of the country about it frequently endure, may consider them as no more than the common occurrences of an Indian life, in which they are frequently driven to the necessity of *eating one another*." (This, be it observed, in a country whose population is very thinly scattered in proportion to its productive powers.)

An Indian chief attributed the failure of Mr. Hearne's first journey to the circumstance of their not taking any women with them. " For," said he, " when all the men are heavy laden, they can neither hunt, nor travel to any considerable distance : and in case they meet with success in hunting who is to carry the produce ? Women, added he, are made for labour : one of them can carry or haul as much as two men can do. They also pitch our tents, make and mend our clothing, keep us warm at night : in fact, there is no such thing as travelling without

their assistance. Though they do every thing, they
are maintained at trifling expense, for as they always
cook, the very licking of their fingers, in scarce times,
is sufficient for their subsistence." (P. 55.) " Notwithstanding the northern Indians are at times so
voracious, they bear hunger with an incredible degree
of fortitude. I have more than once seen them at the
end of three or four days fasting, as merry and jocose
on the subject, as if they had voluntarily imposed it
on themselves; they would ask each other " if they
had now any inclination for an intrigue with a strange
woman." (P. 70.) " Finding great plenty of deer in
the neighbourhood of our little encampment, it was
agreed by all parties to remain a few days, in order
to dry and pound some meat to make it lighter for
carriage." (P. 73.) " A woman and her two children
joined us next morning, They were the first strangers .
we had met since we left the fort, though *we had
travelled several hundred miles.*" (P. 74.) " One of
their dishes is made of the raw liver of a deer cut in
small pieces, and mixed up with the contents of the
stomach' of the same animal, and the further diges-
tion has proceeded, the better it is suited to their
taste. They will eat venison, seals, and sea-horse
paws, though they have been a whole year sewed in
skin bags. Nay, I have even seen them eat whole
hands full of maggots produced in meat by fly-blows,
and it is their constant custom when their noses bleed
by any accident to lick the blood into their mouths
and swallow it. To such distresses are they frequently driven by hunger, that we are no longer
surprised at finding they can relish any thing, but
rather admire the wisdom and kindness of Providence
in forming the palates and powers of all creatures in

a manner most adapted to the food, climate, and circumstances of their situation." (P. 160-61.) " Several of the Indians being very ill, the conjurers, who are always the doctors, and pretend to perform great cures, began to try their skill for their recovery. They use no medicine. Sucking the part affected, blowing and singing to it, haughing, spitting, and uttering a heap of unintelligible jargon, compose the whole process of the cure. " Besides the above, they have recourse in the illness of a friend to a very extraordinary piece of superstition, pretending to swallow hatchets, ice chisels, broad bayonets, knives, and the like, out of a superstitious notion that undertaking such desperate feats will have some influence in appeasing death, and procure a respite for their patient." (P. 190-91.) Other superstitions are detailed of a nature too indelicate for recital in this place. My object also is to direct the reader's attention principally to those circumstances in the habits of these savage tribes which are more immediately connected with the hardships endured from a scanty supply of food, and with the causes to which the scantiness of that supply may be attributed. I wish to enable him to form a fair judgment whether the pressure of population against food in these regions be a dispensation of Providence from which they can only escape by a decrease in the number of the people ; or a salutary consequence of vice from which a little industry would relieve them. " We came to a tent of northern Indians, from whom Matonabee, an Indian chief, purchased another wife ; so that he had now no less than seven, most of whom would for size have made good grenadiers. He prided himself much upon the height and strength of his wives, and would frequently say few women could carry or haul heavier loads; and though they had in general a very masculine appearance, yet he preferred them to those of a more delicate form and moderate stature. In a country like this, where a partner in excessive hard labour is the chief motive for the union, there seems to be great propriety in such a choice." "The wives are all kept at the greatest distance, and the rank they hold in the opinion of the men cannot be better explained, than by observing the method of treating or serving them at meals. When the men kill any large beast, the women are sent to bring it to the tent: when it is brought there, every operation it undergoes, such as splitting, drying, curing, &c. is performed by the women. When any thing is to be prepared for eating, the women cook it; and when it is done, the wives and daughters of the greatest captains in the country are never served till all the males, even those who are in the capacity of servants, have eaten what they think proper; and in times of scarcity it is frequently their lot to be left without a single morsel. It is, however, natural to think they help themselves in secret; but this must be done with great prudence, as in such times it frequently subjects them to a very severe beating." (P. 90-1.) This chief, Matonabee, hanged himself about thirteen years after this period, an accident that was attended with the most melancholy consequences; no less than six of his wives and four of his children having been starved to death the following winter for want of his support.

"One of the Indians' wives, who for some time past had been in a consumption, became so weak as to be incapable of travelling, among these people the most deplorable state to which a human being can be brought. No expedients were taken for her recovery; so that without much ceremony she was left unassisted to perish above ground. This is the common, and indeed the constant, practice of the Indians. When a grown person is so ill, especially in the summer (when they cannot be hauled), as not to be able to walk, and too heavy to be carried, they say it is better to leave one who is past recovery, than for the whole family to sit down with them and starve to death; well knowing that they cannot be of any service to the afflicted. On these occasions, therefore, the friends and relations of the sick generally leave them some victuals and water, and perhaps a little firing. When those articles are provided, the persons to be left are acquainted with the road which the others intend to go, and then, after covering them up with deer-skins, &c. they take their leave and walk away crying. Sometimes persons thus left recover, and come up with their friends, or wander about till they meet with other Indians whom they accompany. The poor woman above-mentioned came up with us three several times, after having been left in the manner described. At length, poor creature! she dropped behind, and no one attempted to go back in search of her. A custom apparently so unnatural is not, perhaps, to be found among any other of the human race." (P. 202-3.)

" Old age is the greatest calamity that can befall a northern Indian; for when he is past labour he is neglected and treated with great disrespect even by his own children. They not only serve him last at meals, but generally give him the coarsest and worst of the victuals; and such of the skins, as they do not

choose to wear, are made up into clothes in the clum-
siest manner for their aged parents; who, as they had
treated their fathers and mothers with the same neglect, submit patiently to their lot, knowing it to be
the common misfortune attendant on old age. So
that they wait patiently for the melancholy hour,
when being no longer capable of walking they are to
be left alone to starve and perish for want. One half
at least of the aged persons of both sexes absolutely
die in this miserable condition." (P. 345.) " We
saw the tracts of some strangers. My companions,
the Indians, were at the trouble of searching for
them, and finding them to be poor inoffensive people,
plundered them not only of the few furs which they
had, but took also one of their young women from
them." (P. 273.)

I think that every crime of which human nature is
capable, except deliberate murder, has now been recorded of these poor half-starved savages. In exhibiting to view this yet remaining feature of the
depravity of their nature, I must recite a story, the
atrocity and cruelty of which can only be equalled by
the gross superstition of the perpetrators. I have,
nevertheless, been induced to record it in these pages,
with the feeble hope of exciting the attention of some
of the Benevolent Societies of Europe to so wide a
field for their philanthropic exertions. It seems that
in a glen on the banks of the Copper-mine River lay
a small encampment of harmless and peaceable Eskimaux, whom Mr. Hearne's companions, notwithstanding his remonstrances, resolved to murder and
to plunder. Having crept unperceived into ambush
within two hundred yards of their tents, the following
scene took place. The small number of their in-

tended victims rendered all idea of serious resistance impossible.

" While we lay in ambush the Indians performed the last ceremonies which were thought necessary. These chiefly consisted in painting their faces, some all black, some all red, and others with a mixture of the two : and to prevent their hair from blowing into their eyes, it was either tied before and behind, or on both sides, or else cut short all round. The next thing was to make themselves as light as possible for running, which they did by pulling off their stockings and either cutting off the sleeves of their jackets, or rolling them up close to their arm-pits; and though the muskitoes at that time were numerous, yet some of the Indians actually pulled off their jackets and entered the lists quite naked, except their breech-cloths and shoes. By the time they had made them-selves completely frightful it was near one in the morning; (in the summer solstice and within the arctic circle, therefore it was not dark;) when finding all the Eskimaux quiet in their tents, they rushed forth from their ambuscade and fell upon the poor unsus-pecting creatures, unperceived till close at the very eaves of their tents; when they soon began the bloody massacre, while I stood neuter in the rear. The scene was shocking beyond description. The poor unhappy victims were surprised in the midst of their sleep, and had neither time nor power to make any resistance. Men, women, and children, in all up-wards of twenty, ran out of the tents stark naked, and endeavoured to make their escape; but the In-dians having possession of all the land side, to no place could they fly for shelter. One alternative only remained, that of jumping into the river; but as none

attempted it, they all fell a sacrifice to Indian bar-
barity.   The shrieks and groans of the poor expiring
wretches were truly dreadful: and my horror was
much increased at seeing a young girl, seemingly
about eighteen years of age, killed so near me, that
when the first spear was stuck into her side she fell
down at my feet and twisted round my legs, so that
it was with difficulty I could disengage myself from
her dying grasps.   As two Indian men pursued this
unfortunate victim, I solicited very hard for her life;
but the murderers made no reply till they had stuck
both their spears through her body and transfixed her
to the ground.   They then looked me sternly in the
face, and began to ridicule me by asking if I wanted
an Eskimaux wife, and paid not the smallest regard
to the shrieks and agony of the poor wretch who was
twining round their spears like an eel!   Indeed after
receiving much abusive language from them on the
occasion, I desired they would dispatch their victim
out of her misery.   On this request being made, one
of the Indians hastily drew his spear from the place
where it was first lodged, and pierced it through her
breast near the heart.   The love of life, however,
even in this miserable state was so predominant, that,
though this might most justly be called a merciful
act to the poor creature, it seemed unwelcome; for
though much exhausted by pain and loss of blood,
she made several efforts to ward off the friendly
blow.   My situation, and the terror of my mind at
beholding this butchery, cannot easily be conceived,
much less described : even at this hour I cannot reflect on the transactions of that horrid day without
shedding tears.   The brutish manner in which these
savages used the bodies they had thus bereaved of

life, was 'so shocking that it would be indecent to describe it : " &c. (P. 152, &c.)

" Among the various superstitious customs of these people it is worth remarking, that after my companions had killed the Eskimaux at the Copper-mine River, they considered themselves in a state of uncleanness, which induced them to practise some very curious and unusual ceremonies. In the first place, all who were absolutely concerned in the murder were prohibited from cooking any kind of victuals, either for themselves or others. Two in the company who had not shed blood were employed as cooks till we joined the women. When the victuals were cooked, all the murderers took a kind of red earth or ochre, and painted all the space between the nose and the chin, and the greater part of the cheeks almost to the ears, before they would taste a bit; and would not drink out of any other dish, or smoke out of any other pipe but their own, and none of the others seemed willing to drink or smoke out of theirs." (P. 205.)

After this full survey of the savage state of society, I shall be satisfied with respect to the pastoral tribes with quoting a very few passages from Mr. Malthus's chapter " Of the *Checks* to Population among the modern Pastoral Nations."

" The Mahometan Tartars are said to live almost entirely by robbing and preying upon their neighbours as well in peace as in war." " The Usbecks, who possess as masters the kingdom of Chowarasm, leave to their tributary subjects, the Sarts and Turkmans, the finest pastures of their country, because their neighbours on that side are too poor or too vigilant to give them hopes of successful plunder. Rapine is their principal resource." The Turkmans are always at war with the Curds and Arabs, who often come and break the horns of their herds, and carry away their wives and daughters." " Neither the aptitude of the soil, nor the example which they (the Usbecks) have before them, can induce them to change their habits, and they would rather pillage, rob, and kill their neighbours, than apply themselves to improve the benefits which nature so liberally offers them." " And though they are often very illtreated in these incursions, and the whole of their plunder is not equivalent to what they might obtain with very little labour from their lands; yet they choose rather to expose themselves to the thousand fatigues and dangers necessarily attendant on such a life, than apply themselves seriously to agriculture." " The Mahometan Tartars in general hate trade, and make it their business to spoil all the merchants who fall into their hands. The only commerce that is countenanced is the commerce in slaves. These form a principal part of the booty which they carry off in their predatory incursions, and are considered as a chief source of their riches. Those which they have occasion for themselves, either for the attendance on their herds, or as wives and concubines, they keep, and the rest they sell." " They justify it as lawful to have many wives, because they say they bring us many children, which we can sell for ready money, or exchange for necessary conveniences. Yet when they have not wherewithal to maintain them, they hold it a piece of charity to murder infants new-born, as also they do such as are sick and past recovery, because they say they free them from a great deal of misery."—(Sir J. Chardin's Travels). " Under the feeble yet oppressive government of the Turks it is not uncommon for peasants to desert their villages and betake themselves to a pastoral state, in which they expect to be better able to escape from the plunder of their Turkish masters and Arab neighbours."

Thus then we perceive that in the rich islands of the Pacific, in the fertile plains of America, and the productive valleys of Asia, a population probably rather diminishing than increasing in numbers presses against a scanty supply of food derived from a soil whose productive powers are capable, with a very slight exertion of industry, to maintain a rapidly increasing population in comfort and plenty. It is plain too that in many instances the population declines, not from any general deficiency in the actual supply of food, but from the vicious, the cruel, the degraded habits of the people, derived from other causes. And in every instance the absence of cultivation, and of its necessary consequence the increase of subsistence, is to be ascribed altogether to moral causes. The land waits to be solicited, and is prepared to yield abundant returns. Providence is continually accumulating the intimations of its will, by adding misery to misery as the condition of a perseverance in idleness and vice, and as a stimulus to the efforts requisite to escape from them. But man, the creature of habit, prone to evil, and to an increasing deterioration of mind the longer he continues plunged in vicious practices, pertinaciously resists the suggestions of Providence, and frequently perseveres in his resistance till he has almost incapacitated himself as a subject for future amelioration.

In the foregoing picture then of the several gradations of savage and pastoral life, vice and misery
are indeed frightfully prominent; but it would be too
preposterous an abuse of terms to say that their office is to repress a mischievous tendency to exuberance in the population, when they are in fact the
positive means not only of preventing even a salutary
increase, but actually of inducing in many cases a
rapid diminution in the existing numbers.   As well
might the destruction of a city be called a salutary
precaution against its too great extension.   Neither
would it be more reasonable to argue that moral
restraint from sexual intercouse would remedy the
evils ; for in the first place such a virtue cannot be
singly implanted so as to flourish in a hotbed of
other vices ; nor if it were implanted under such conditions would the evils be remedied.   For regular
habits in this respect would soon rather increase than
diminish the number of the people, without having
any tendency to increase the quantity of food.   Industry therefore, and industry alone, with the moral
consequences thence arising, would be sufficient to
attain the object, by removing the impediments to
the farther production of food.   And I must again
be permitted to ask in what manner men drowned
in apathy and vice can be roused to *industrious exertion,* unless by the pressure of some misery which
may evidently be referred to the want of that exertion.

But the most unreasonable of all arguments upon
this state of society would be to maintain that the
pressure of population against subsistence (where
it is found to exist) is a *necessary* consequence of the
increase of the former, because it is perfectly obvious
that it is wholly to be ascribed to want of exertion

in the people who suffer under it.   Unless therefore
it can be proved that there is any *necessity* for their
perseverance in idleness, for their continuance in a
state of barbarism, brutality, ignorance, and vice,
it must be admitted that they possess immense resources in the productive powers of their soil, which
it only depends upon themselves to appropriate to
the purposes of their comfortable subsistence; and
that this end will be obtained precisely in proportion
to their general moral improvement.

Thus then we perceive, not only that the whole
mass of the population in these rude stages of society
has in all cases a *natural* tendency to keep within
the *powers of the soil* to afford it subsistence according to the first fundamental proposition in the last
chapter, but that any alteration of this tendency so
as to produce the pressure of individual want against
the actual supply of food comes under the second
head of the second proposition, viz., that it arises
from grossly impolitic customs depressing the productive energies of the soil considerably below its natural
powers; for not the slightest attempt has ever yet been
made to excite them into action.

With respect to the application of the third and
fourth propositions to these states of society, it must
of course be rather prospective than immediate.   If
religion and morality were introduced, that is, if any
progress were made towards a general and enlightened desire among individuals so to regulate their
actions as to produce happiness to others as well as
to themselves; if rational liberty and security of
property began to prevail, that is, if the public institutions of the country were in any degree calculated
for the general benefit, and with an equal view to

the happiness of the whole community; no reasonable man can doubt but that it would instantly
emerge from the states of society which we have
now been contemplating; and the improvement
would be complete, just in proportion as the means
producing it approached towards obtaining a perfect
influence: these propositions therefore call for no
farther notice on the present occasion except with a
view to one important practical inference. Doubtless a savage nation of its own accord, or rather
when urged on one side by the spontaneous energies
of a superior mind raised up for this purpose, and
pressed on the other by the wretchedness of the
savage state, might emerge in the course of time into
the light of civilization. This inference is fairly deducible from what has been handed down to us of
the native heroes of the East, and of ancient Greece
and the surrounding countries, whose deification is
at once a proof of the gratitude of their countrymen,
and of the miseries from which they were relieved.
The state of Mexico and Peru on the first discovery
of America may also be cited to fortify the same conclusion. But when we consider on the one hand the
difficulties arising from the free scope given to the
evil propensities of man while living in a state of
barbarism, and reflect on the other that the first step,
however small, made by a savage tribe towards the
attainment of the blessings enumerated in the third
and fourth propositions, will lead in the ordinary
course of things to their full development; how
gravely must it press upon the consciences of those
nations who have already run the career of civilization, and are actually living under the full blaze of
its meridian splendour, to look back upon the point

whence themselves first rose above the horizon of the moral world;—to recollect the means which have promoted their own advancement, and to impart them to such as now require their guidance and assistance. With this view, the encouragement of zealous but discreet missionaries, the moral uses of commercial intercourse, a provision for the religious interests of distant colonies, the abolition of all cruel, unjust, and oppressive methods of commercial enterprize, are at once erected into plain and positive duties. The Indian hunter must no longer be bribed by intoxicating spirits for the spoils of his chase, nor the African warrior for his more guilty spoils, even his fellow man; but they must be gently led to the knowledge of their duties and their happiness, and of the benevolent designs of Providence in their favour. And above all, these objects must be secured by a provision for keeping alive among the foreign agents of the more civilized country a sense of their moral and religious duties. It is thus, and thus only, that its intercourse with others can be either innocent, or ultimately useful to itself; or that it can be honoured by Divine Providence as the instrument of conveying His destined blessings to the uncivilized regions of the Earth.

This department of philanthrophy, however, is difficult in proportion to its importance; for the rare combination of zeal with discretion is essential to its successful pursuit. Enthusiasm, though useful and even commendable in some cases, must here be carefully tempered. The growth of zeal in the mind must be perceived only by the fruits of activity and perseverance, while the sincerity and simplicity of its views must be evidenced by the utmost wariness to avoid giving offence, and a cautious abstinence from any display of personal vanity or individual rivalship in the pursuit of philanthropic objects.

The neglect of skilfully combining temporal and commercial objects with the apostolic zeal of missionaries engaged in savage and barbarous countries, seems to have been the principal cause of failure in most of the cases where their benevolent designs have proved abortive. This appears evident from the accounts rendered of the missionary voyages to the South Sea Islands (see quarto Account of the Mission), of the mission in the Karroo Deserts (see Barrow's Cochinchina), and of all others, with a few judicious exceptions. The brightest of these is perhaps to be found in the account of two " Attempts made to civilize the North American Indians by the United Friends, 1. of Baltimore, and 2, of Philadelphia." (See two small Pamphlets under these titles.) The plan they proceeded upon was this:—that whereas most missionaries had (as an Otaheitan Chief expressed himself) bestowed on the objects of their care plenty of *parrow* (i. e. talk), but very few *hatchets* (i. e. objects of temporal convenience); these plain and benevolent missionaries, some of whom by the way were carpenters and blacksmiths, reversed this order of proceeding. They began by putting the spade, the hoe, the hammer, the saw, and the anvil, into the possession of the natives, and worked with them personally in constructing houses, cultivating fields, and making the coarser articles of furniture. When the savages with a customary jealousy, which reflects more disgrace on the *general* conduct of their civilized neighbours than on themselves, began to forget the benefits bestowed, to feel uneasy at the continued presence of their benefactors, and to doubt if so much kindness from a white man could be altogether free from some selfish design; the enlightened individuals, with a generosity and good sense truly admirable, made the Indian natives a present of every thing they had brought, and every thing they had done in the country, and instantly departed. The result was such as might have been expected. The houses soon got out of repair, the tools damaged or worn out, and the Indian attempts to remedy these evils were not the most successful. Deputations therefore were forthwith sent to Baltimore and Philadelphia, praying the return of the missionaries, who were seated for good in the confidence of the natives; and, unless the late war has interfered with their designs, have probably before this converted them to Christianity. At all events they have induced them to settle in regular villages, and have planted and watered the root, from which evangelical missionaries may in future gather an abundant increase.

I trust that this passage will not be construed into any reflection upon these last-mentioned missionaries: I admire their zeal and perseverance, and venerate the motives by which they are actuated; and have been indignant when writers of character have permitted the pride and prejudice of their hearts so far to overcome their better feelings, as to indulge in public sneers at what they are pleased to term " *lazy evangelical missionaries*." The ignorance betrayed by such reproaches is not less conspicuous than their malevolence. It is true that, among barbarous and savage tribes of the South Sea Islands, of North America, Africa, and so forth, the *manual* activity of the Baltimore and Philadelphian philanthropists is preferable; because *corporeal* improvement (if I may be allowed the term) is the first object in view. But when men's temporal wants are in some degree satisfied, and their minds begin to be accessible to reason and argument, (as among the heathens of Asia and other countries,) the *mental* activity and the spiritual zeal of evangelical missionaries are as appropriate and acceptable as the manual operation of their less educated brethren would then be misplaced. And I trust we have yet to learn that sacrifices of the higher qualities of the mind are less acceptable to God than those of the coarser operations of the hands. At all events the self-denial of the individual must be admitted to be great and praiseworthy in proportion to his possession of those attainments which give a charm to the intercourse of civilized society. Were Mr. Swartz and Mr. Martyn " *lazy* evangelical missionaries" because they did not drive nails and construct ploughs in the luxurious societies of India and Persia? Proh Pudor!

The reader may probably anticipate that some useful lessons may be deduced from the preceding arguments, when we inquire into those parts of the commonwealth of Britain, which include her colonial polity and her charitable institutions. I cannot, however, close this chapter without entering my protest against some mistaken doctrines that have found a comparatively easy entrance into the mind, through the custom prevalent among writers of denominating *uncivilized man*, man *in a state of nature* :—as if a responsible agent endowed with reasoning and moral faculties, and gifted with an immortal spirit, fulfilled the ends of his nature in proportion as his objects are confined to the mere animal gratifications and sensual pursuits of the brutes that perish; in proportion as all the great and nobler parts of his nature lie buried and obscured! Corrupt and fallen as it is, surely it is still the nature of man, for which all his moral and physical properties are best adapted, to pursue those objects which have a tendency to refine and enlarge the mind, to lift him from his fallen condition into one approaching to his original state, to lead him to the practice of the virtues and the charities of life, and to find his highest enjoyments in the praise of his Maker, and in promoting the happiness of his fellow-creatures. No one who has engaged in the pursuit of happiness, successively, in the career of sensual gratification and in that of Christian morality, will hesitate in admitting the superior happiness imparted by the latter. And what is superior happiness but a system of enjoyment the best adapted to our natural faculties, when renewed and confirmed by God's appointed means? Let us then no longer entertain the idea that the *brutal* state of man is his *natural* state, and that all those combinations of society, which call for the more refined and enlarged exertion of his mental faculties, are merely artificial inventions foreign to his original nature.

A *state of nature,* says Bishop Horne in his Discourse on the Origin of Civil Government, has *been supposed* by some writers of eminence, when men lived in a wild and disorderly manner, when they were mere savages, restrained by no laws human or divine, except the physical force and the unruly passions of their fellows.

The state of civil government has been opposed to this, as arising out of the inconveniences which men perceived to flow from the unbridled licentiousness of their natural state, and as becoming gradually more perfect from their experience of the benefits conferred by each successive improvement in the career of subordination.

The Bishop, however, doubts whether this theory afford a true account of the origin of civil society; and very justly infers that it is calculated to rob God of the glory which is due to his moral attributes, and to introduce a false and dangerous system of reasoning upon some of the most important relative duties and charities among mankind. For if the savage state be really that of nature, it seems to follow that, according to the opinion of some modern philosophers, it is also most consistent with the will of God and the happiness of man, and that so far from endeavouring to raise men above it, we are doing good service by reducing to their original and simple elements the *complicated* and *tyrannical* systems, which the inventions of man have falsely adorned with the epithet of salutary government. " But," says the eloquent and venerable Bishop, " the truth is, when we reflect a little farther upon the subject, we cannot but perceive our apprehensions greatly shocked at the supposition that the wise and good Creator, who formed mankind for society in this world, and designed to train them by a performance of its duties for a more noble and exalted fellowship with angels in the world to come, should place them, at the beginning, in the abovementioned wild and disorderly state of independence, to roam in fields and forests like the brutes that perish, and to search for law and government where they were not to be found; that he should give them no rulers by whom, nor rules how, they should be guided and directed, but leave them to choose for themselves, that is, to dispute and fight, and in the end to be governed by the strongest!" " But are these things so? Did God indeed, at the beginning, bring into being, at the same time, a number of human creatures, independent of each other, and turn them uninstructed into the woods, to settle a civil polity by compact among themselves? We know that he did not. He who appointed a regular subordination among the celestial hierarchies, who is the God of peace and order, provided for the establishment and continuation of these blessings among mankind by ordaining, first, in the case of Adam, and then in that of Noah, that the human race should spring from one common parent. Unless therefore some other origination of mankind be discovered, all equality and independence are at an end. *The state of nature* was a state of subordination; since from the beginning some were born subject to others; and the power of the father, by whatever name it be called, must have been supreme at the first, when there was none superior to it." ' To fathers within their families,' saith the judicious Hooker, ' nature hath given a supreme power; for which cause we see throughout the world, even from the foundation thereof, all men have ever been taken as lords and lawful kings in their own houses.' "

The Bishop then goes on to show how, from the Patriarchal, society spread into the lesser governments of States; till through the workings of corrupted nature disputes were engendered, which terminating in war, victory at last declared for one of the parties, and the other was obliged to submit. Thus the larger governments arose by conquest, and in their turn contended with, and overthrew, each other. In this state of things, and in the ignorance of what had happened in former ages, it is not surprising that heathen writers should have believed that civil government should at first have arisen by an agreement among independent savages. But in us who have the Scripture History before us, it would be something worse than unreasonable to overlook the information which that supplies to us, and have recourse to romantic schemes which owed their being to the want of it.

But if it be asked, how then comes it to pass that we do now actually find in different quarters of the world many tribes of these lawless and independent savages, who seem scarcely to have arrived at the infancy of society, but who will probably emerge from it in the progress of time? It may be answered, that after the first migration from the Patriarchal tribe into other climates, where few of the conveniences of life are to be procured, and cut off from communication with the rest of the world, men would almost necessarily degenerate. Strangers, for want of commerce, to arts and learning, they must continue in the deepest intellectual poverty, and would soon exchange the law of conscience imprinted on their hearts for superstitious customs and diabolical and idolatrous rites. And thus degenerating, as they must of necessity do every day more and more, they would come at last into that deplorable state of ignorance and barbarism, in which some nations are found at this day. But this is a state of *degeneracy*, not a state of *nature*. Could it then be the state in which the Lord of all things placed the noblest of sublunary beings, the heir of glory and immortality, when his own hands had formed and fashioned him, and he had breathed into him the breath of life? No surely! It is a state the most *unnatural,* in which rational creatures made in the image of their Creator can be conceived to exist! A state into which, through apostasy from revealed truth, and consequent loss of all knowledge, by the just judgment of God upon them, some nations were permitted to fall, and are suffered to continue, *in terrorem* to others.

Such is the amount of Bishop Horne's reasoning on this interesting subject, and I see but one way of escaping from it—a method indeed more apt to be tacitly adopted, than openly avowed, by the moral and political writers of Christendom. They seem to consider it as a matter of course that the Book, which is at once the most authentic history, and the most undoubted authority on all moral points, is studiously to be passed by in silence in all discussions upon either; that it is matter of good taste to draw principles of œconomy from the heathens, and elements of the philosophy of the human mind from their own unassisted reflections. But can any thing be more insincere, more unmanly, more inconsistent, than this mode of proceeding? They acknowledge the fundamental authority of the Sacred Oracles on these subjects, yet refuse to abide by their decisions, and build their systems upon a directly contrary hypothesis— like the reasoner who would prove one of the later propositions of Euclid by a reference to Aristotle's logic. They dare not deny the truth of Scripture, neither do they dare to risk offending the fastidious by a manly consistency in following it out into its consequences;—like the mechanic, who should refuse the assistance of the steam engine on account of the majestic beauty and variety of its construction, or of the noise it would introduce into his machinery.

But if those who pretend to enlighten a Christian community are not ashamed to fall into such contradictions, the community itself should at least convince them that it adheres to the truth of original principles, no less than if they had been duly admitted and argued upon;—and that it resists with as just contempt all consequences not fairly deducible from them, as it would repel an invading army that ravaged its plains and destroyed its cities, with the theory of humanity and the protection of property in the mouth of its commander. Let us in short, at least be consistent. If we pretend to be Christians let us act and argue upon Christian principles, and take them where they are only to be found. If we mean to reject the authority of Revelation, let us honestly say so, and hew out the best cisterns we can of our own materials. But half measures, especially in argument and deduction, are always contemptible. They will neither convince an opponent, nor fortify an adherent. For either of them, if he be endowed with the blessing of common sense, will soon discover that the arguer himself is little better than an hypocrite.

I have been the more anxious to place these observations at the close of this chapter, as the summary given at its commencement of the manner in which men, sunk in the miseries of the savage state, are driven, by the consequent inconveniences, to a gradual return towards the original condition in which the moral government of God had placed them,—may possibly be misunderstood; and be thought to imply that the savage state, because it is the lowest in the scale of society, is therefore that to which Providence originally adapted the nature of man.

CHAPTER V.

Of the Natural tendency of Population in the purely Agricultural State, and in the early Stages of the Commercial State of Society.

IN the beginning of the last chapter a sketch was given of the gradations, by which society passes from the savage and pastoral to the purely agricultural state, which is perhaps the most important period in its political course. The contrast between the new condition of the people, and that from which they have emerged, is as strong as opposition can make it. They are lifted from a state of penury and distress into one of comfort and plenty, and what is yet more important, they have made that step which almost necessarily ensures a future progress: for I believe that instances are very rare of a nation sinking from the purely agricultural state directly into that which is savage or pastoral. The argument of this Treatise, as applied to this condition of society, may be thus stated.

In newly settled and purely agricultural countries, where the progress of population is infinitely the fastest, *it can never* overtake the supply of food, as long as this state of society continues, for these plain reasons; that land will always produce, even in a very inferior state of cultivation, much more than sufficient food to support the cultivators, and the simple artisans attached to them; and that where good land can be had for nothing, the love of property and independence will find occupiers, although no immediate demand may exist for the produce beyond the place of its production, and the family which occupies the farm. The surplus produce, however, which such a country *is capable* of raising, will usually find purchasers among the commercial and manufacturing nations, whose wants create a demand for it. This demand will ensure its growth, and the returns, from its export to those countries, will afford to the growers many necessary or convenient manufactures, besides a capital which will enable them to settle their children upon fresh land. Where it is so easy to become a master there must always be a proportionate difficulty in procuring workmen, the demand for labour and the funds destined for its maintenance increasing still faster than the labourers themselves. This will raise wages to a considerable height; and as employment at high wages will always be to be had, " a numerous family of children, instead of being a burden, will be a source of opulence and prosperity to the parents." The *value* of children will operate as the greatest possible encouragement to marriage, and the liberal reward of labour will ensure a healthy subsistence to the offspring :— while the more immediate prospect of property and independence, the more simple manners of the people, and the more rare opportunities of reconciling occasional idleness with unlawful pleasure by a recurrence to licentious indulgences, will render the moral consequences of high wages less dangerous than in more advanced states of society. There will therefore be scarcely any natural or necessary impediments to the rapid progress of population. But subsistence will increase still more rapidly from the application made to the vigorous and unexhausted powers of the soil.

This state of society, and the rapid progress of population attending it, will continue, in the natural order of things, till all the best and most conveniently situated spots of land are occupied; and it would require the application of a large sum, on a remote prospect of return, to bring the remainder into cultivation. Till this point, a country may be said to be in the purely agricultural state of society, and the population is evidently far within the limits even of the actual supply of food; although individual instances of want or poverty may occur, caused by personal idleness or misfortune, or by impolitic laws and customs. But clearly, as long as this condition of society continues, the population cannot positively be said to press against the means of subsistence; since both food, and the means of acquiring it by ordinary exertion, are, or may be, within the power of every individual.

When a country however, has attained this point, the children of the farmers, unless their industry be violently depressed by ignorance or tyranny, will turn their views to trade and manufactures; which would then become the most profitable employment of capital. They would bring up their children also to the same occupations; and though capital made in trade might be occasionally realized in land, it would usually be by the purchase of that already cultivated, rather than by the cultivation of the barren and more ungrateful tracts. The surplus produce of the land, before exported to manufacturing countries, will now be consumed by the domestic workmen; and the goods before imported will be wrought at home; at first only in sufficient quantities for the domestic demand, but at length for the purpose of exporting them to other countries, who have not yet advanced beyond the agricultural state of society.

As soon as this manufacturing population is sufficiently numerous nearly to consume the surplus produce formerly exported, and it becomes difficult to procure grain for the various purposes of luxury or convenience, to which it is applied in all commercial countries, its price will rise; and this, let it be observed, before any actual pressure of distress for *a mere sufficiency of subsistence* occurs. This rise in the price will tempt the capitalist to lay out his money in bringing inferior waste land into cultivation, or in undertaking agricultural improvements by which the old lands may be made to produce somewhat more food with an equal quantity of labour. As this mode of procuring food, however, is evidently much slower *in operation*, and its increased quantity, in a given space of time or territory, less abundant than in the agricultural state of society, it is clear, that if the natural progress of population continued the same, it must shortly *overtake* the supply of food, and verify the positions just disputed. Let us see, therefore, whether the manner in which this manufacturing and commercial population immediately arranges itself, and the moral and physical effects produced by their employments, dispositions, and spontaneous distribution, do not naturally weaken the principle of population, as it originally subsisted, and reduce it as nearly to a par with the diminished power of production in the soil, as the views of Providence for a still farther amelioration will admit.

It is found that the convenience of the merchant

and manufacturer is much promoted by having their residences contiguous to each other, and by collecting round them the houses of those, who are employed in the various departments of their industry, and in supplying them with the necessaries and conveniences of life.   They will, therefore, fix upon a favourable spot, in the midst of an extensive neighbourhood; where first a knot of houses will be formed, next a village, and at length a town, by the accession of more manufacturers, and of many of those who before carried on trades in the country, but who are tempted by the superior convenience of markets and intercourse to migrate to the town.   From various other causes too, not necessary now to detail, towns will arise. (In manufacturing countries the rise of many has been witnessed even in recent times.)   Till at length the independent proprietors, the farmers and agricultural labourers, and the very simple artisans, will be the principal inhabitants remaining in the country. These will convey their stock or its produce to the market in the town, and return from thence with the manufactured goods they may want.   Two descriptions of inhabitants will thus be formed,—the townsman, and the countryman; and the habits, manners, and relative condition of each will naturally and spontaneously produce a very essential difference in their relative tendencies to contribute to the increase of population; while the progress of civilization, universally attendant upon commercial prosperity, will considerably diminish the absolute power of such increase throughout the whole community; and, as I hope to show in the course of this Treatise, without any necessary increase of vice and misery. Care, fore-

cast, anxieties of mind, emulation, severe attention
to business, various active avocations, and the general
incompatibility of the marriage state with this new
order of pursuits, form the first natural causes of a
diminished tendency in the population to increase,
incident to the prosperous conduct of trade and manufactures. For there seems to be no doubt, that in
proportion to the continued necessity of mental exertion or abstraction, many, who could well afford
to rear a family, are placed in situations and pursuits
where a voluntary abstinence from marriage, and the
incapacity and indisposition to rear large families,
become very general. Moreover, the comparatively
unfavourable state of the atmosphere even in towns *
of a moderate size, and the confinement and unhealthy occupations of the inhabitants, not only
weaken the robust state of health necessary to the
production of a numerous and healthy progeny, and
diminish the number of births; but likewise very
much shorten the period of human life in those situations, and increase the proportion of deaths. The

* See Malthus's Essay, book ii. c. 7. vol. i. p. 462. The
passage illustrates the position in the text so strongly, that I
cannot resist the desire to quote it at length. " There certainly
seems to be something in great towns, and even in moderate
towns, peculiarly unfavourable to the very early stages of life;
and the part of the community, on which the mortality principally falls, seems to indicate, that it arises more from the close-
ness and foulness of the air, which may be supposed to be unfavourable to the tender lungs of children, and the greater confinement which they almost necessarily experience, than from
the superior degree of luxury and debauchery usually, and
justly, attributed to towns. A married pair with the best con-
stitutions, who lead the most regular and quiet life, seldom find
that their children enjoy the same health in towns as in the
country."

average number of births to a marriage in towns has been calculated at between 3 and 4, while in the country it is said to amount to $4\frac{1}{2}$ or 5 *; and even in moderate towns, such as Newbury, containing a concentrated population of not more than about 4,200 souls, the annual deaths are to the population as 1 in 28 or 29; while in the purely agricultural villages, they often do not exceed the proportion of 1 in 50 or 60.† Here then are two natural and unavoidable causes, very strongly tending to weaken the *principle* of population.   Moreover, the artificial wants, which are converted into necessaries of life at every step in the progress of civilization, render the support of a wife and family more difficult, consistently with retaining other personal enjoyments, and cannot but farther diminish, in some degree, the proportion of marriages throughout the whole community.   So that the triple operation of a decrease in the number of marriages, diminished fertility in the human species, and an augmented proportion of deaths immediately begins, by the natural and unavoidable course of nature, to repress the progress of population, as soon as a part of the people are collected into towns.

This progress will indeed be retarded less during the earlier stages of the commercial and manufacturing states of society, than afterwards, when towns become larger, population more dense, and civilization more general.   Nor is it necessary that in these

---

* See Price's Reversion. Payments, vol. ii. p. 227. Perceval's Observations on Manchester, &c. vol. iii. of his Essays, edit. 1776, p. 60, 61 ; and Mr. Malthus's observations on this subject in his chapter on the fruitfulness of marriages.

† See Price's Rev. Paym. vol. ii. p. 40, and Malthus, book ii. c. 7.

earlier stages population should be so much retarded.
For as the power of the land is still capable of supporting a rapid increase of people from its surplus
produce before exported, some time must necessarily
elapse before population, though with a very trifling
abatement in its progress, would begin to press
against the actual supply of food. The labour of
one family employed in tilling the earth, even in
this early stage of agricultural improvement, may be
fairly accounted able to support itself and two others:
two-thirds of the whole population may therefore by
degrees become what Sir James Steuart (b. v. c. 5,)
calls *free hands*, i. e. engaged in manufactures and
commerce, in unproductive professions, or may be
living idly on the fruits of former industry, before a
demand arises for a further increase of food. But
long before a nation can have two-thirds of its people
thus occupied, a great proportion of it must reside in
large towns, and the introduction of luxury, and an
artificial state of society, must have produced various
imaginary wants among the country residents. Many
of the people will be also lifted above the rank
of the lower orders, and be affected by those artificial arrangements of society, which, though they
universally produce high mental cultivation, do very
much diminish the natural powers of increase in mankind.* Hence, from the diminished average of marriages and births, and the increase of premature
mortality, a large proportion of the population will
cease to reproduce its own numbers; and a consider-

* See, among other works, " Dr. Trotter's View of the
Nervous Temperament," for a detailed account of the effects
of civilization on the physical powers of a people.

able deficiency will remain to be filled up by the peasantry, or lower order of country residents,—the class most productive of people in every well-regulated community.

Thus it appears, that in proportion as the population advances towards an equality with the surplus produce, existing at the first emergence of a country from the purely agricultural state, in such, will its gradual progress naturally become slower, by the inevitable and unalterable laws of Providence; though the people be left as perfectly at liberty to follow the dictates of their own inclinations as is consistent with a free and well-regulated government. Let it be observed, also, that this effect will be produced by certain and unerring causes, which can by no human means be very materially altered. It is as impossible to render the residents in towns more fruitful, to make the air of towns more generally wholesome to infants, to induce any large proportion of those, who wish to abstain from marriage for their own convenience, to enter into that contract, as it would be to feed the increased population that would follow, supposing the possibility of their production to exist. The abatement in the progress of population is voluntary, natural, and unavoidable. It may be strictly termed its " *natural* tendency," however it may be modified or restrained by systems of policy or different forms of government. It is another question, which will be treated hereafter, how far it necessarily produces an increase of vice and misery, and how far that species of moral restraint, which consists in involuntary abstinence from marriage, be either necessary or useful to the welfare of the people. All that is here asserted is, that the abatement is *the necessary and natural consequence* of the progress of society; and that to exclaim against its effects is in fact to exclaim against all advancement of a country beyond the purely agricultural state.

That this advancement may be, and often is, retarded by gross tyranny and oppression, or a general relaxation of morals, is perfectly true. Nay, instances may perhaps be adduced where a nation, cursed with these evils, may even be carried by them with no slight rapidity in a retrograde direction, and instead of advancing out of the agricultural state, may sink into one compounded of the pastoral and agricultural; many of the peasants under the Turkish government are driven to desert their fields, and betake themselves to the pastoral state, to avoid the plunder and oppression of their masters, (Volney, as quoted by Malthus) : or, if the nation shall have emerged for a period into the commercial state, it may retain in its decline only the evils of that condition, viz. its towns and its vices, without its industry and its virtues.

The state of Spain during the past century is too lamentable an instance of the last-mentioned condition. Full of towns, the former seats of industry and activity, the hearts from which were propelled into the surrounding country the arterial currents of capital and enterprise, and which received in return the venous streams of agricultural produce, are now the mere receptacles of apathy and ignorance. The body through which the healthy action extended is lopped of almost all its members, and the utmost bounds of the reduced circulation are confined within the narrow valley immediately adjoining to the filthy and unwholesome town. The villages, which formerly gave a supply of labourers to the flourishing manufactures, or to increasing speculations in agriculture and commerce, are now over-populous from the stagnation introduced by ignorance and oppression, and their inevitable attendant, a want of demand for *free* labourers.

Mr. Townshend, in an account of one of the most fertile parts of Spain, (Townshend's Travels in Spain, vol. iii. pp. 104, et seq. edit. 1791,) states, that " throughout this elevated country there is little appearance of cultivation, although many considerable tracts of land over which we passed are good, and much of it might be watered." Yet speaking of this very neighbourhood he says, (p. 106), " On Saturday, April 28, we came to Cullar de Baza, a wretched village with many habitations excavated in the rock of gypsum. The little valley which supplies this village is about a quarter of a mile in breadth, enclosed by barren gypseous mountains; and although it is well watered and consequently fertile, yet the population bears too great a proportion to the extent of land susceptible of cultivation." " Looking down upon so rich, yet such a contracted spot, we instantly and evidently see, that the human race (however at first, and whilst their numbers are limited, they may rejoice in affluence,) will go on constantly increasing, till they balance their quantity of food : from that period, two appetites will combine to regulate their numbers. Beyond that period, should they continue to increase, having passed the natural limits of their population, they must suffer want. In these circumstances, beholding many of the poor naked and half starved, should they inadvertently ordain that no one in their community should want, that all should have food, and every man an habitation, is it not obvious that they would aim at impossibilities? and that by every effort to relieve distress, they would extend the bounds of human misery?" Here are, in few words, the general outlines of the Essay on Population, and its application, drawn from the observation of a little village in the mountains of a declining country. And thus it is that Mr. Townshend reasons generally from a few insulated facts.

But let us see how his argument agrees with his own subsequent observations on the same country. Comparing the density of population in the different countries of Europe with that of Spain, which he estimates at sixty-seven persons to a square mile; he says, (vol. ii. p. 211,) "Spain, if properly cultivated and well governed, might be the first in Europe, not excepting Holland, which to its wise and equitable laws is indebted for a population amounting to 272 on a square mile. All are agreed that Spain in more distant periods was much better peopled than at present, and many have attempted to assign the cause of its depopulation, &c. It may be useful to trace the various circumstances which have contributed to depress this once powerful nation, and to *desolate*, at least comparatively, one of the richest countries in Europe." He then proceeds to enumerate the causes which, in his opinion, have led to the depopulation, which are almost all resolvable into bad government. Here then we perceive the over-populousness of the mountain village, from which the general principle was drawn, to form merely one trifling feature of a commonwealth, in which the population is remarkably thin in proportion to the fertility of the soil. To convert the supposed evil therefore into a blessing, nothing more seems necessary than to draw off the surplus people of the village to those places and occupations in the towns and the country, where a demand for them probably first called them into existence. Thus an arrangement entirely consonant with the views of Providence would at once annihilate the general principle so pompously asserted, and would draw off the superabundant people of the villages to those occupations, in which they could not reproduce their own numbers, and where they would consequently want a continual supply from the same source, as that supply should arise as in the order of nature. And what prevents this arrangement? any law of nature, any principle inherent in the constitution of man? Clearly not. But let Mr. Townshend speak again for himself. Let him exhibit to us the means whereby a country, with natural powers capable of carrying its population in rapid progress to double or treble its present numbers, may actually be said to be overpopulous, unless they diminish in a ratio almost equal to their capacity for increase. (Vol. ii. p. 225.) " The people, thus every where plundered and oppressed, could not increase and multiply as they would have done under a free and equitable government." (Vol. ii. p. 88.) " The ploughman and the grazier, instead of being united in the same person, are here eternally at variance; and as the latter *is the best tenant*, the great proprietors give him the preference. Hence the country has been depopulated; and the lands which are in tillage, for want of cattle to manure and tread them, produce light crops of corn." (Vol. i. p. 230.) " Throughout the whole of Spain I cannot recollect to have seen a single country residence like those which every where abound in England." (P. 237.) " We passed by three monumental crosses all at the junction of four ways. In a country *where few people travel* a thief has little chance of passengers unless where two ways cross." (P. 294.) " They had once a canal made by Philip V. seven leagues in length, which brought to them the waters of the Jarama; but about twenty years ago the head proved faulty, and it has never been repaired. The loss (of produce) by this misfortune and neglect is almost inestimable." " They have no other implements of tillage except ploughs, being perfect strangers to the use of harrows. It must be evident to every one who has the least knowledge of the subject, that no plough can be worse adapted to the soil."

Thus much for the state of the country and of its agriculture and industry. Let us now inquire into that of the towns and their trade and manufactures. (Vol. ii. p. 8.) " Beggars, clothed with rags and covered with vermin, swarm in every street." (Vol. iii. p. 70.) " As for the manufactures, they are going to decay, and feel more than the common infirmities of age, receiving at best little encouragement from local situation, and being depressed and ruined by want of political wisdom in the government," &c. " Many laws were published, laying restraints on manufacturers, subjecting them to formalities and to vexatious fines, and fixing the price at which their manufactures should be sold. As a *compensation* the price of provisions was likewise fixed. But as the latter tended to hurt the market and to depress the farmer, so the operation of the former was to depress the quality of the goods, and to bring slow yet certain ruin on the manufacturer, under the absurd idea of favouring the consumer. The want of political wisdom has been here equally fatal to agriculture,

manufactures, and commerce." (P. 183.) " Previous
to the appointment of Don Francisco Pachecho to the
government of Alicant, the city swarmed all day
with beggars, and all night with prostitutes and
thieves. These were fed by the religious houses,"
&c." (P. 251.) " I was struck with the sight of
poverty, of wretchedness, and of rags, in every street."
(P. 17.) " With such encouragement for beggars no
wonder that they should abound in Malaga, where
the lazy can have no inducement to employ themselves in labour, and where the profligate, when they
shall have wasted their substance, may know for a
certainty that they shall never be in want of bread.
Hence it comes to pass that in the city few traces of
industry are seen, whilst filth and nastiness, immorality and vice, wretchedness and poverty, the inevitable consequences of undistinguishing benevolence,
prevail."—" Multitudes of beggars infesting every
street mark a bad police."—" For some time I could
not conceive the reason why, wherever I had supped,
I was constantly attended to my lodging by a servant
with a light. But observing, upon some occasion,
that such attendance would be needless, I was informed that the servant and the light were not merely
for comfort but for safety, because robberies and murders were frequent in the night. Indeed when I was
there, an officer returning unattended to his lodging
was assaulted in the street by thieves, and upon
making resistance was stabbed in the back by one,
while another robbed him. In the last sixteen months
they reckoned seventy murders, for which *not one*
criminal *had been brought to justice,* and in one
year, as I am credibly informed, 105 persons fell in
the same manner."

The enlightened and candid reader of these passages will find no difficulty in discovering the cause,
why in Spain, possessing less than half its complement of population, the people are yet half-starved.
Nor will he consider any reference to the principle
of population, as the cause of this distress, extremely
applicable to the case in question. He will, however, perceive in the great towns and crowded villages of Spain at once the magnificent wreck and the
proofs of its former grandeur and prosperity ; but in
the filth, and misery, and vice of those towns, and in
the *scanty* yet *redundant* population of the villages,
and the desolate state of the fertile lands, he will
discover the *causes* yet more clearly than the *proofs*
of its. present decline. Perhaps there cannot be a
more general or convincing proof of a declining commonwealth, than the co-existence of large towns and
a low state of agriculture ;—the former being, in
the natural order of things, absolutely the offspring
of a full cultivation, their very existence without it
is a proof that their vices and their crimes have destroyed their parent, at the period when, having
nursed them to maturity, it might fairly have expected the return of assistance now become necessary
to its old age; and the wretched condition of their
orphan state constitutes their just reward. A future
opportunity of illustrating this point more fully will
occur with reference to the modern state of China.—
In the mean time it may be observed that, in this
picture of the state of Spain, we again perceive the
necessary effects of a vicious interference with the
obvious designs of Providence for the advancement of
society. Instead of answering the selfish purposes
for which it was intended, or of rendering the natural

order of things compatible with immorality and oppression, by keeping affairs quiet while they are calling aloud for reformation;—we find that the very expedients, resorted to for these purposes, produce a
pressure thrice as heavy as that which they were intended to remove.   It seems also to follow, both as a
natural consequence, and as the result of historical
experience, that this pressure will increase in intensity till it can no longer be borne, but must either
crush the people, or rouse them with the energies of
despair to cast it from themselves on their oppressors.
This alternative may be most emphatically said to be
presented to the choice of the unfortunate people of
Spain at the present moment, (January 1816).

That the truth of the premises laid down in this
Chapter cannot fairly be disputed, is presumed with
some confidence.   The facts on which they rest seem
too obvious to require any further confirmation from
the aid of history.   That the newly settled lands in
America raise and export a surplus produce of food,
although their population is doubled in the shortest
possible period, will probably be admitted without reference to their statistical writers to prove it.   That
in those states which have been settled for a longer
period, the people having collected into towns export
less of their produce, and do not increase in so rapid a
ratio, will also be admitted.   Yet as they still export
some produce, their whole population cannot actually
press against the whole of their means of subsistence.
For it is evident that this effect cannot be produced
by any general law of nature, till we find a want
subsisting in the community for imported food, or
for a further produce from their own territory;—a
condition of society which belongs to the following

Chapter. The fact therefore that food is still *habitually exported* may suffice, instead of any historical illustration, to prove that the means, by which the progress of population is *naturally* regulated in the states of society treated of in this Chapter, are sufficient still to preserve it within the limits of the actual supply of food, which was first raised in the purely agricultural state.

We will proceed then to apply very briefly to this portion of the argument the fundamental principles stated at the outset of the treatise, (vide ch. iii.)— Population being, throughout the whole course treated in this chapter, preserved within the limits of the *actual* supply of food, it is evident that every conclusion tends clearly to establish the two first principles. For, first, population cannot exceed the powers of the soil to afford it subsistence, so long as a large surplus of food is actually derived from that soil ; nor, secondly, can the existence of such surplus consist with a mischievous pressure of population against the *actual* supply of food. With respect to the third and fourth principles, which are conversant principally with the conduct and condition of individuals, there can be no doubt but that the folly of a government, or the vices of the people, may introduce much want and misery notwithstanding the overflowing state of the national resources. The political constitution of the United States of America, leading to anarchy and idleness among some of the lower ranks, and the recent political conduct of their government, have actually introduced into that country a baneful interference with the comfort and happiness of many orders of society. I doubt not that some excellent individuals are to be found among them ; but to an English mind it does certainly appear, that their principles of " Religion " are superficial, their " Morality " exceedingly low, their " Liberty " verging to licentiousness, consequently not very " rational;" and that their persons and property, though secure against the government, are very liable to danger from the mob.

One of their own writers thus describes the progress of their politics since the period of their independence.—" No people had ever greater cause to be proud, none had before them a fairer promise to be happy. After many years of sanguinary trouble, to pass into a state of peace, security, and rest ;—to be relieved from unspeakable hardships and privations ;—to rise from dependance upon another and a far distant country, with all its subjections and restraints, into a state of self-government and exemption from foreign control ;—and to be left to the free choice of its own government, laws, and institutions ;—was a condition in which no enlightened people had ever before been found ; and was not only sufficient to fill them with immediate exultation and joy, and with the most happy forebodings of the future, but might naturally be expected to push their hopes and their pride a little beyond the bounds of moderation.   To men of unexercised minds, of little reflection, and of superficial knowledge, all around seemed lovely and felicitous ; and to the people, with very few exceptions, nothing seemed more impossible than that their harmony should be interrupted, that their happiness should be endangered for ages, or that any thing could arise to deprive them of the benefits and blessings they had obtained with the revolution.   Thus thought the many, and thus it was natural for the many to think.   They imagined that the supreme power being now at the disposal of a jealous people, from whom it could not be wheedled by fraud or flattery, nor wrested by force, would follow the natural course of the human heart, and find its way into the hands of the most deserving : and at the outset of the republic it was so. But time unfolded new views. to the multitude. Every day gave them a stronger sense of their own power, and greater inclination to evince it by abuse. It was soon perceived that that which was unappropriated to any might be aspired to by all; and the lower classes of ambitious men, and vulgar politicians, who felt themselves excluded by want of desert from all participation in power, resolved to make up their deficiency in merit by fraud and imposition; and to disturb and pollute the stream of public opinion, which, so long as it continued to roll in its natural purity, would run in favour of the most meritorious citizens." (Memoirs of T. Jefferson, New York, 1809, vol. i. p. 12, et seq.)

The licentious principles established by the French revolution, and previously disseminated no where with greater diligence than in the United States, lent great facilities to such a system of corruption. Nor was the early and absolute treachery of France sufficient to stem the torrent.

Another American writer (*Brief View of the Policy and Resources of the United States. Philadelphia*, 1810,) asserts, that the folly and passion in which the misfortunes of America have had their rise, are the *inseparable* concomitants of popular government, founded on the suffrages of the *multitude ;* who though *honest* are *ignorant ;* whose impressions are excited by *feeling*, not created by thought ; and least of all by the peculiar depth of reasoning, or elevation of view, which is indispensable to the attainment of political truth. In such governments we behold the passions which give rise to the keenest resentment, but not the wisdom or moderation requisite for the discovery or pursuit of the only means which can lead to redress. The genuine patriot deplores these evils, resulting from an excess of *that* democracy, which, under due modification, is the *best foundation* of government. (P. 26.)

It appears from these passages that although the laws of the United States are professedly founded on the principles of religion, morality, rational liberty, and security, they obtain only a very imperfect influence. It is still however sufficient to carry the country triumphantly through the purely agricultural state of society, which presents so many natural facilities. But as the difficulties incident to the commercial and manufacturing stages begin to arise, if a general improvement in the important respect just alluded to do not accompany them, it is easy to foresee the divisions and calamities which will befal the United States of America.

America has been said by one of her own advocates to be a new and rising country, whose progress, which is unprecedently rapid, may be retarded but cannot be stopped; therefore whatever bad consequences may result from her internal or external policy, they will be but momentary. She may suffer most severely in the first instance, but the consequences can be only transitory. I must beg leave to limit the truth of these positions, by confining the application of them to the present condition of society in America. Even now, in the midst of general prosperity, individual industry is interfered with, notwith-

standing all its natural advantages. Individual suffering is already the result; and the conflicting interests of commerce are daily aggravating the evil.
But it is evident that by the adoption of the
fourth principle, and in proportion as the obstacles to
the perfect influence of the blessings just enumerated
are removed, in such will individual suffering be
diminished, and a permanent progress in public prosperity be secured.—Nor can the actual or probable
evils be lessened, nay, they cannot be otherwise than
materially aggravated, by any other scheme of remedy.
It is surely superfluous to go about to prove, that in
proportion as men are quiet, industrious, and moral in
their private conduct; and charitable and considerate
towards others; and as their government acts upon
similiar principles; in the same degree will the happiness and comfort of individuals be increased, and
the progress of population promoted:—and, as in the
states of society here treated of the quantity of food
must *always* exceed its proportion to the wants of
the people, there can be no doubt that the increase
of their numbers will be sound and healthy, and
that they will not be driven into a state of vice and
misery through any want of food: therefore every
artificial impediment thrown in the way of the natural increase of population, or of any other spontaneous arrangement of the society, is not only unnecessary in point of policy, but also detrimental to
the general spread of public and private happiness.

We have no right to expect in this condition of
mankind to meet with any marks of high refinement;
it would therefore be absurd to complain of their absence. As the agricultural state is not favourable to
works of genius, so neither is it productive of exalted

moral feeling. The Romans, it has frequently been observed, showed scarcely any marks of poetical genius for many ages after the foundation of the city, and as little, it may be added, of the genuine principles of virtue. I know not how far the opinion of some philosophers may be thought fanciful, who assert that laxity of fibre, inconsistent with great muscular exertion, is necessary to that sensibility of feeling which leads to exquisite judgment and a correct taste. But this point seems at least well established, that the homely virtues are those of the agriculturist; and although he steps as much beside his moral advantage in aping the refinements, as he does beside his political interests in coveting the peculiar sources of prosperity of the more advanced stages of society, he is not the less bound to practise the duties of his own particular condition. He can scarcely be justified in tarring and feathering his neighbour, because they are incapable of reconciling their contending interests or opinions by a logical disputation on politics or morals.

CHAPTER VI.

Of the natural Tendency of Population in the more advanced Stages of Society.

IN the progress of society, beyond the stages treated in the preceding Chapter, population will at length overtake the supply of surplus food, so far as to press lightly against some of the luxuries to which it is converted, and will raise its price. And this is the first point, from the earliest states of society, in which the pretended universal aphorism, that population has a tendency to press against its *actual* supply of food, can be said even remotely to apply.

The elevation in the price of produce, from the increased competition, now encourages the capitalist to divest part of his funds from commerce and manufactures to the cultivation of inferior waste lands, or to agricultural improvements on those already cultivated. Let it carefully be observed, that this pre-existing demand for food from a population pressing against the *superfluities* of its supply, (if I may be allowed the expression), is the only possible mode by which a farther increase can now be elicited from the soil. For cultivators will not lay out their capital upon land of an inferior staple, until they find, by an enhanced price of its produce, that there is an increasing demand for it to compensate their additional expenses:—a fact which appears of itself sufficient to show the futility of the idea entertained by Mr. Malthus and others, that a manufacturing nation can ever permanently export large quantities of corn. This speculation indeed, implies the apparent absurdity of supposing that a commodity raised by one nation at a great expense, and sent abroad to a foreign market, can be sold there to a profit (expenses of carriage included), notwithstanding the competition of other nations, who can raise the same commodity at less than half the expense, and convey it to the same market with very inferior charges of freight. Neither is the fact stated more favourable to the position of the same economists, that an increase of people should always *follow*, and never *precede*, an increase in the produce of the soil:— which, when applied to a manufacturing society, appears to be nearly tantamount to saying, that an increase in the number of backs should always follow, and never precede, an increase in the manufacture of coats;—whereas surely a previous increase of wearers and consumers is absolutely necessary to the respective production of further food and raiment.

These questions will be more fully treated in a subsequent chapter, when we come to the consideration of the nature of Corn Laws. In the mean time it may be observed, that the produce of these new speculations in agriculture will set the people at ease till a further increase of population. But the improved methods, such as the consolidation of small farms into larger, ingenious implements, &c. will also enable a smaller number of cultivators to raise an equal quantity of produce, and will therefore set *free* a larger proportion of the people for manufactures and other occupations.* This new arrangement will

---

* These natural effects of the progress of society may serve to allay the anger of many *very honest* and plain spoken *political œconomists* against large farms, and other arrangements for obtaining such a surplus and disposable produce, as is absolutely requisite to the public good in the new distribution of the society.

also add to the number of people inhabiting towns:
while the accumulation of capital and of private fortunes, the increase of menial servants, and the various calls for men who are in situations and pursuits
of risk, danger, and the like, will add greatly to the
list of those who do not reproduce their own numbers even in the country.   So that it is only after a
longer interval than before, that the people again come
to press against the supply of food.   Thus an increased retardation takes place at every stage in the
progress of society.   The difficulty of procuring food
will evidently increase with each of these revolutions;
because the country will, after each, have approached
nearer to its acme of cultivation and production; and
the best remaining lands being occupied at each revolution, none but inferior and ungrateful soils will
at length be left.   But it is equally clear, from what
has been said, that the progress of population will
have become proportionably slower, and less capable
of overtaking the diminished power of the land to
supply it with food.

If it be necessary to make this proposition yet
more plain, by any addition to the preceding arguments, let it be considered that, after no long progress in this advanced state of society, one family employed in agriculture will be able at least to
support * itself and three others, in consequence of
the improved modes of culture, which the necessity
of a large surplus produce, and the application of
commercial skill and capital to agricultural pursuits
invariably introduce.   Three-fourths of the people
therefore will be left at large to follow manufactures,

* See Appendix to Dirom on the Corn Laws.

or non-productive employments, to be the menial servants of the higher orders, to navigate the ships, and
fight the battles of the country. Of these three-
fourths, at least two-thirds, or one-half of the whole
population, would cease to reproduce their own numbers of efficient people. This will be evident to any
one who considers that, in a state of society where so
large a proportion of the people are merchants, manufacturers, or idle persons, at least one-third of the
whole population must dwell in towns, some in very
large towns; and that the remainder of those, who
are calculated not to reproduce their own numbers,
principally consists of soldiers, sailors, men of good
families but small fortunes, servants, dependents, and
emigrants to colonies, or other places. These last are
usually taken out of the mass of the population in
the prime of life, but before they have contributed
children to replace their loss, which must therefore be
filled up by the children of others. And with respect to the towns, it is proved to demonstration,
that even of those of a moderate size, not one can
keep up its own *effective* population.* It appears
that, when our provincial towns were increasing much
less rapidly than at present, Dr. Short calculated that
nine-nineteenths of the *married* were strangers; and
of 1618 persons examined at the Westminster In-
firmary only 824 were found to have been born in
London. The continual influx of settlers, in the
prime of life, from the country, to repair the waste of
the towns, is indeed proved both by actual observation, and by the great excess of the births above the

* See Price on Rev. Paym. Perceval's Essays before quoted,
and Malth. b. ii. c. 7.

burials in the adjoining agricultural villages; although the population either of those villages, or of the towns to which the emigrations take place, by no means exhibits a corresponding increase. This excess of births above burials in some of the villages, where no numerical increase has taken place in the population, has been found to mount as high as 2 or 3 to 1; and as the excess of births above deaths is *naturally* the universal measure of the increase in the population, we may be sure that where that excess is great, in a situation where no increase has *actually* taken place, the surplus has been drawn off to other points.

If we suppose that, taking one town with another, a fifth of the inhabitants are not natives, but settlers from the country, the calculation will probably be found not exaggerated for towns with a stationary population, and to be much within the proportion that has been proved to exist in many towns that have rapidly increased their numbers. This may perhaps at first surprise many readers; but it will by no means appear exaggerated, if they attend to the following calculation. An excess of annual deaths above annual births of 7 in each 1000 of existing persons has been considered a low average in towns even of a moderate size. Upon this datum let us suppose a town to contain 1000 inhabitants, and it follows that seven emigrants per 1000 from the country must yearly settle in the town to keep up its population. We will suppose likewise, that the proportion of deaths to the population in this town is 1 to 28; i. e. that a number equal to the whole population dies in 28 years, or a twenty-eighth part (viz. $35\frac{4}{7}$ persons in 1000) on the average in every succeeding year. This is a rate of mortality less than that which is indicated by the best information with respect to the average mortality of European towns. It will appear reasonable, if we consider that the returns seem to prove that, (omitting all those sent into the country in the early periods of life, where a portion of them die without being included in the returns of the town), from a third to a half of the number born in towns usually die in the very earliest stages of life. The average expectation of life in a child just born in a town is never more than 19 years. In Vienna and Stockholm half the number born die under two years of age; in Manchester, containing 84,000 souls, under five; in Northampton, containing 7000 souls, under ten. Now in any space of 28 years, the number of acceders from the country settled in this town, at 7 in the 1000 per year, will be 196: and if they arrive there at the usual period of life (between 18 and 22 years of age), when they have all, one with another, an expectation of life equal to 30 years, i. e. an average prospect, which may be safely calculated upon, of reaching the ages of 48 to 52, the number will not be diminished in the course of the generation: on the contrary, 7 multiplied by 30 gives 210, which would be the number per 1000 of emigrants from the country always residing in the town after the lapse of the first 30 years. For though some may die within a few years of their arrival, others will live beyond the age of 48 or 52, so the average will be the same. But as a few may come to settle between the ages of 22 and 35, during which periods the expectation of life is in some degree lower, and continually decreasing, a subtraction must be made on this account from the number of 210 strangers. This, however, cannot be very large; and would scarcely do more than reduce the whole number of them to 200, the fifth of 1000, which is the proportion of settlers always existing, that I have been endeavouring to establish as a moderate calculation, and which appears from the foregoing statement to be indispensable in towns, when an excess of deaths above births equal to 7 in 1000 takes place among the inhabitants.

Such would be the case were the population of the town stationary; but if from an increase in the demand for labour, or other causes, it should be rapidly extending itself, of course a larger influx of settlers must take place. Supposing the number required to be no more than two individuals in a thousand annually, this would raise the proportion of strangers in the town from a fifth to above a fourth, and so on in proportion to the rapidity of the increasing demand for labour, or of the other causes of attraction to settlers. For all these reasons it cannot appear exaggerated to assert, that that third part of the population, which has been supposed to reside in towns in the state of society referred to, is not only incapable of keeping up its own number, but requires in each generation a number, at least equal to a fifth of its own, from the other two-thirds of the people, in order to prevent a diminution in its actual population. Still less can it be denied, that where a continually increasing demand exists for labourers in employments which are carried on in towns, a continually increasing proportion of recruits must also be afforded by the rest of the people. Let us see, therefore, to what extent the remaining two-thirds are capable of affording this necessary supply of recruits.

Of these two-thirds of the population not resident
in towns, we have already remarked three-eighths,
or a portion equal to one-fourth of the whole population, to be employed in agriculture. The portion
remaining to be accounted for, which does not live
in towns, and is yet not employed in agriculture,
amounts to five-eighths, or about two-fifths of the
whole population. These comprise the village shopkeepers and manufacturers, soldiers, sailors, and men
of fortune, with their descendants, families, and menial
servants; of whom (though some may be productive
enough of people), yet it may be difficult to say that
the whole keep up their numbers. A reference to
the state of England would probably show, that
about a fourth of this portion of the people consists
of men of rank and easy fortune, with their families,
and unemployed descendants, deriving income from
various funds, but many of them possessing not more
than enough fortune to afford their accustomed enjoyments in the single state. From these and other
causes, so many of them do not marry, or at least
not till late in life, and so many more, from the
various causes before-mentioned, do not rear families
of any size, that the aggregate amount of all their
descendants is not sufficient to replace their own
numbers; although they do not fall short of it in the
same degree with the inhabitants of towns. Of the
remainder of this portion, one-eighth may be said to
consist of the army, the mercantile and military navy,
emigrants to colonies, &c. with their families and
attendants; who are so far from keeping up their
own numbers at home, that they are a continual
drain to a very considerable amount, upon the most
robust and effective part of the people. The remain-

ing half and one-eighth of this portion of the people consists of the manufacturing labourers, and small proprietors, residing in the country, who (though the former,from occasional unhealthy occupation,fall short of the husbandmen in prolific power), are capable, upon the whole, not only of keeping up their whole numbers, but of affording a surplus, large in proportion to the means they have of sustaining their children by the remuneration of their labour. The same is the case with the agricultural fourth of the people.*
Thus we see that before a country has advanced very far in the commercial state, and long before it ap-

---

* In a country containing a population of nine millions, the following would be the distribution of the people according to the state of society supposed in the text.

1. One-third in towns (not reproducing their own numbers)..................................... 3,000,000

2. One-fourth in agriculture, (reproducing their own numbers and supplying the deficiences in the towns, &c.).................................... 2,250,000

3. A fourth of the remainder, men of rank and fortune with their families, unemployed descendants, and servants (not reproducing their own numbers) 937,500

4. Army, navy, mercantile, and military emigrants to foreign settlements with their families and attendants (almost entirely supplied from the classes reproducing their own numbers)................. 468,750

5. Country manufacturers, shopkeepers, small proprietors, &c. with their families (reproducing their own numbers, but affording no material supply to the deficiency of the other classes,............. 2,343,750

Total 9,000,000

The three classes not reproducing their own numbers leaving a deficiency of at least a fifth of their aggregate number, or 880,000 souls in a generation, to be made up by the two other classes, principally by that marked 2.

proaches to its *ne plus ultra* of cultivation, about
half of the population is incapable of reproducing its
own number of individuals, from moral and physical
causes of universal and spontaneous operation, unalterable, (to any material extent,) by human means.
It is evident, also, that with every step it takes in the
same progress,—or the nearer it advances towards a
fulness of people and the end of its resources in cultivation, the part of the community reproducing its
own numbers will still farther diminish its proportion
to the whole. The towns will increase, and all those
artificial wants and debilitating customs engendered
by wealth, civilization, and the progress of intellectual endowments, will act with accelerated force.

This exposition of the natural tendency of population in the more advanced stages of society seems to be
consistent with experience, and with the actual observation of those countries which are passing through
them. In all prosperous or (as Sir James Steuart calls
them) *growing* countries, towns have been universally found to increase both in number and size.
Witness London and Paris, Manchester and Lyons,
Liverpool and Petersburgh or Odessa, Glasgow and
Amsterdam. Their effects on population are so universally acknowledged, that they have been prover-
bially called " the graves of the human race." Neither
are the other causes of abatement which have been
recited less obvious to common observation in all
civilized communities. So that although the population of every growing country is actually on the
increase, yet such is the conservative principle inherent in the natural causes displayed in this chapter,
that it is not possible to point out one instance, where
it has surpassed the powers of the soil to produce a

further supply of food for its support; * (except indeed in those states, which consist exclusively of one great commercial city included in a narrow territory, and habitually supported on foreign produce, which is a case evidently without the scope of a general argument). Moreover, it is universally found that in proportion as a country is in a *growing* condition, or as its population is *in fact increasing*, in such will it ever be preserved within the limits of its *actual* supply of food; because the freedom and industry, necessary to place a country in a *growing* condition, will lead to the diversion of capital to the soil, before the demand for food presses against the bare necessities of the people: while in a declining country, whose population is actually decreasing, it will press the more severely against the supply of food, because in such a state of society industry is universally observed to decline still faster than population. In proof of these assertions let us look to the condition of England as compared with Spain; of the more civilized parts of Russia as compared with Turkey; of Scotland as compared with Sicily. I have purposely placed these countries in opposition to each other, because the natural advantages are entirely on the side of the less flourishing countries, and the mind is led at once to the moral and political phenomena which alone have made them to differ. Doubtless, the soil and climate of Spain, of Turkey, and of Sicily, are by nature more capable of fostering a rapid increase of population and production, than those of England, Russia, and Scotland. Yet in the

* If the reader should be tempted to suppose that China is in that state, I would beg him to suspend his judgment till he has perused the eighth chapter of this book.

three former a population diminishing in number presses severely against a scanty supply of food—while in the three latter a rapidly increasing population is amply supported on the produce of its own soil and labour. Such is the fair result of the natural and unrestrained progress of society.

In Great Britain the laws and constitution of the country have (comparatively speaking) very little interfered with the industry and spontaneous distribution of the inhabitants:—and in the more civilized parts of Russia, notwithstanding the despotic form of the government, so much attention has of late years been paid by the Sovereigns to the internal welfare of the country, that, for many of the practical purposes of political improvement, the effects have approached nearly to those of a free and liberal constitution. Of the three countries placed in opposition to them I have already said enough with respect to Spain. The causes of the misery and degradation of Turkey are sufficiently known to be of a moral nature. The following details, upon the authority of the latest travellers, may not however be altogether uninteresting to the reader. Mr. De Chateaubriand, in his Itinerary through Greece and Palestine, among many similar pictures, gives the following account of what occurred on his ride towards Sparta. " At noon we discovered a khan as poor as that in which we rested the night before, although it was decorated with the Ottoman flag. *In a space of twenty-two leagues they were the only houses we saw*. Hunger and fatigue obliged us to continue here longer than we wished. The master of the place, an old wretched looking Turk, was seated in a loft over the stables surrounded by goats, and in the midst of their dung. He received us without rising from his dunghill, or deigning to offer any refreshment to the Christian dogs. At length he called a poor naked Greek boy, whose body was all swelled with the stripes he had received, who brought us some sheep's milk in a dirty and disgusting vessel. I was obliged to descend from the loft to drink it at my ease, for the goats and their kids besieged me on every side, in hopes of partaking of the biscuit which I held in my hand. I had eaten bear's-flesh and the sacred dog with the savages,—I had shared in the meals of the Bedouin Arabs,—but never had I met with any thing so wretched as this Lacedemonian khan." (Tom. i. p. 70, 71.) On quitting Corinth he passed the Turkish guard at the Isthmus, and showing the order of the Pacha, the commandant invited him to smoke a pipe and drink coffee at the barrack. As they were seated together, the guard perceived a Greek countryman climbing the mountain at the side of the road, and ordered him to come down. Being at the time probably out of hearing, he did not obey, and the commandant seizing his carbine watched his opportunity and shot at the peasant, who then came down wounded and bleeding. The Turk, as our traveller expresses it, ordered him fifty strokes of the bastinado to cure his wounds. " If I had ever thought " (he adds, as a general reflection on his journey,) " that an absolute government was the best, a few months residence in Turkey would have cured me of that opinion."

The amount of Mr. Hobhouse's observations on the Turkish character and government show them to be a compound of indolence, cruelty, and oppression, depopulating or depressing the cultivation of whole districts of a country, which the Greek natives would soon replace in its ancient state of productiveness, were their industry fostered instead of oppressed by their conquerors. But some strong excitement is wanted to produce this change, and in the present state of religion and manners among the Turks, it is not easy to anticipate whence the impulse is to be given. In the mean time we may cite the authority of a still more recent traveller for the consequences of the present system. Dr. Holland, although he does not enter largely into the internal polity and condition of the Turkish empire, is significant enough when these subjects cross his path. Describing the very singular *aërial* monasteries at Meteora in Thessaly, he writes—" The monks received us with civility, and we remained with them more than an hour in their extraordinary habitation. The buildings are spread irregularly over the whole summit of the rock. They have no splendour either external or internal, and exhibit but the appearances of wretchedness and decay. Nevertheless the monks conducted us through every one of their dark and dilapidated rooms, and seemed to require a tribute of admiration, which indeed might conscientiously be given to the magnificent natural scenery around and beneath their monastery."—" Even their insulated and almost inaccessible situation has not secured these poor people from plunder and outrage. The property belonging to them is in the valleys below, and the inhabitants of a small village underneath the rocks supply food to these aërial inhabitants. The Albanian soldiers have frequently plundered this village, and either depending on the mandate of their superiors, or on other less licensed means, occasionally compel an entrance into the monasteries themselves, the miserable proprietors of which have little security against such acts of outrage. Before quitting the place we were conducted by the monks into their refectory, a dark room without a single article of furniture, where a repast was set before us consisting of a dish of rice cooked in oil." (Holland's Travels, p. 238.)

"Though the relative situation of the Turks and Greeks be that of masters and slaves, yet it will be found that all the other signs of degradation belong in greater degree to the condition of the Turks. The Greek town presents in general the aspect of useful and industrious life; and, unless when borne down by some of those circumstances of local oppression which are so *common* in Turkey, the population have an appearance of comfort." " In the towns chiefly inhabited by Turks, the most striking circumstance is the air of uniform indolence and unbroken monotony, which pervades every part of the scene. As you walk along the street few sounds of the human voice come upon the ear:—appearances of neglect and decay every where present themselves: houses falling for want of repair; the habitations of the lower classes wretched and comfortless; filth accumulating in the streets without removal; and a general want of those circumstances which give order and propriety to social life." (P. 268.) " I had myself the opportunity of observing, in part, the terror in which the Turks of Larissa are held by the Greek inhabitants of the place. The house of the Archbishop Polycarp resembled a prison, or a place of secret refuge. The gates conducting to it were always opened with a sort of suspicious anxiety; and an impression of alarm and distrust was ever visible among the inhabitants of this mansion. The Archbishop himself very rarely quits its precincts from the apprehension of insult. On the second day of our abode in his house, while sitting with him in his apartment, a Turk of surly and forbidding aspect, and evidently of the lower class, entered the room, seated himself unceremoniously on the sofa, filled his pipe, and took coffee from the attendants. The Archbishop was obviously embarrassed, but made no comment. After a short interval, he took a coin from his purse and put it silently into the hand of the Turk, who immediately disappeared." (P. 270.) " The (Greek) habitation, which our Tartar selected as one of the best in the village, consisted of a single apartment with naked mud walls, and a flooring of naked earth; one end of the room occupied by horses, the other inhabited by two large families, with no other furniture than a few wooden and earthen vessels, and the straw mats and woollen coats which they used for their nightly covering. There was an aspect of meagre wretchedness and of absolute privation about them, which I have seldom seen equalled. Our arrival, and the ferocious manner in which our Turkish attendants broke into the house, produced at first much alarm. The eldest daughter of one of the families, who in another sphere of life might have been a beauty, was hurried away into a neighbouring hovel. In the faces and manner of those who remained, there was silently expressed an habitual expectation of ill-usage, which it was painful to contemplate." (P. 384.)

Concerning Sicily, the last country named in the comparison, we have a cloud of authors, who have left us nothing to desire as to the knowledge of her internal situation. From Mr. Leckie downwards, through the writings of Mr. Galt, the Abbate Balsamo, Mr. Blaquiere, Mr. Thomson, and a variety of others, one uniform language is held. Houses unroofed, bridges broken down, large towns abandoned, immeasurable tracts of waste land without an inhabitant, are the usual objects which present themselves. " But to describe the sufferings of those, who are driven to mendicity without any resource whatever in their parishes, or the most distant prospect of obtaining employment, is far beyond the power of expression : and while the causes already mentioned must have contributed greatly to increase the number of the poor, *agriculture has been gradually declining* all over the Island. At no period of its history is Sicily recollected to have been so completely dependent upon strangers for support. It is said that, in the present year, near a million of dollars has been paid for imported corn." This is the testimony of one traveller. Another writes, " It will hardly be conceived, that although in this fertile soil it is only necessary to put the grain into the ground to ensure plentiful crops ;—yet, still in most of the villages there are seldom or never to be found the necessaries of life ;—meal *never*,—*often* not bread. Frequently I have not perceived any appearance of the country being inhabited or cultivated ; and even where it is, the population and the habitations are so thinly scattered as sufficiently to prove the oppressed state of the inhabitants." " There is nothing that conveys so pointed a stigma upon the present order of things in Sicily, as a comparison of the ancient and modern population."

Such are the accounts rendered by travellers of

credit of the " Sicula arva," the granary of Rome,
and one of the most fertile spots of the ancient world.
Mr. Leckie, who long resided in the Island as a
proprietor, has with sufficient clearness traced the
evil to its cause, in the tyranny and oppression, not
only of the government, but of every petty feudal
Lord of a village. Great Britain herself has had a
pretty sensible proof of the moral and political degradation of the people, inasmuch as when she had
generously given to the country a free constitution,
she was obliged to lend eighteen thousand disciplined
troops to secure to the inhabitants its *full* use and
enjoyment.

Such is the contrast afforded by the contemplation
of different countries, which have all, in the course
of their progress, far advanced beyond the agricultural into the commercial and civilized states
of society. In those where the people, under a
reasonably free government and a fair attention to
morals, have been suffered, in their habits, employment, and distribution, to follow the spontaneous
impulses given to their minds by the natural events
and circumstances of their progress ;—there they are
found subsisting, even in very inferior climates and
ungrateful soils, and notwithstanding their rapidly
increasing numbers, in plenty, comfort, and happiness : and I think it may be said, that a greater injury
could not be inflicted upon those societies, than to
check that tendency to increase in their population,
which is to urge them to a still further progress in the
career of civilization. On the contrary, where the
people, under a tyrannical government and a dis-
solute state of morals, have had their habits preverted,

their minds debased, and their employments and distribution violently interfered with, there, notwithstanding any superiority of climate and fertility of soil, the people, notwithstanding their rapidly decreasing numbers, have dwindled down to the extreme verge of want and misery: and I think it may be said, that a more atrocious injustice could scarcely be practised against such societies, than to search for means of obviating that grinding pressure of their population against the means of subsistence, by the inconveniences of which they could alone probably be roused to seek the efficient remedy. In the stages of society, therefore, treated of in this chapter, it does, I trust, appear manifest that, under whatever condition of government it may be, nothing but danger and deterioration can ensue from any attempt to tamper with the natural effects of the principle of population, but that it should be left to its appointed and ordinary operation.

I do not mean to imply, by the facts and arguments of this chapter, that the adjustment of the due proportions between food and population by the free operation of the laws of nature, as well as the adjustment of every other social interest, is not a more complicated affair in the advanced stages of society than in the earlier and more simple states. Every arrangement must of course increase in complexity the more particulars it includes. And when we consider the responsible condition of man, and the constant struggle against the principle of evil which his lot and his duties involve, it is reasonable to suppose that, in proportion to the advantages of knowledge and the facilities of intercourse which attend the progress of civilization, a corresponding difficulty should be imposed in the due preservation of the system. If the increased temptations of the civilized state were not met by the augmented necessity for exertion and moral precaution, which this difficulty brings with it, but were fostered by the same facilities of indolent gratification which may safely exist in the more simple conditions of society, there would not only be great danger of a total relaxation of morals, but a fair impeachment might be made of that *perfect moral equality*, which the wisdom and goodness of God have established among the several states of society, as well as among the individuals of each community. The present condition of Ireland may perhaps be cited in support of this reasoning. By its close connexion with Great Britain it has been exposed to the increased temptations of high civilization which is prevalent among some ranks of its society, while the mass of the people is in a situation very far behind that of the sister island, indeed very much below what ought reasonably to be expected from the intelligence of the higher ranks, and the vicinity of Ireland to the most civilized country in Europe. Into the remote causes of this state of things it is not my present wish to enter. But the proximate cause is evidently to be found in the want of that increased exertion and moral precaution on the part of the leading members of the community, which are necessary to oppose the temptations, arising out of the partial progress of prosperity, and the facilities of intercourse attendant upon the general improvement of the British empire. From this cause the people of that interesting country have been suffered to vegetate in the same indulgence of indolent gratification, in which they were found by a respectable traveller in the reign of Queen Elizabeth, who " freely professed, that Ireland in general would yield abundance of all things, if the people could possibly bee industrious therein ;—and if this publike good were not hindered by the inhabitants' barbarousnes, making them apt to seditions, and so unwilling to inrich their Prince and Countrey; and by their slothfulnesse, which is so singular as they hold it basenesse to labour." (Moryson's Itinerary, Book iii. p. 160.)

To the neglect of amending this unfortunate disposition by wholesome laws, the encouragement of industry, and the developement of the natural resources of the country, are to be joined other circumstances peculiar to Ireland, and particularly connected with the subject matter of this Treatise. From the mildness of the climate, the natural fertility of the soil, and the facility with which a turf cabin and a potatoe ground were to be acquired, through the neglect or mistaken kindness of the proprietors, a superabundant population has sprung up in many of the least improved parts of Ireland, totally uncalled for by the demand for labour, therefore totally unemployed, and, as a matter of course, altogether neglected as to their morals, habits, and pursuits, by their superiors. This moral deterioration has in its turn aggravated the evils which the injudicious neglect of the proprietors, and the mildness of the climate, originally introduced. By degrading the people, and preventing them from acquiring a taste for the comforts and decencies of life, premature marriages have been encouraged ; the offspring of which have been preserved in existence by the plenty of vegetable food, and the general benevolence of the people, until they now constitute a mass of population which would severely press against the means of subsistence, if those means were distributed as they necessarily must and ought to be among a decent, moral, and well ordered community; and which does in fact produce the extreme of wretchedness among individuals, especially in the principal towns. The very extent of the population, therefore, offers something like a *physical* impediment to the improvement of the society. But I am not entirely without hope that the check which has lately been given to the exportation of corn from Ireland, by reducing its price and encouraging its consumption among the lowest ranks of the people, may tempt them to desert their potatoes for bread, which would advance them more rapidly towards better habits than may at first sight be imagined. For by introducing into the character of a necessary of life a more expensive article of food,—as corn again rose in price, it would on the one hand become necessary for the peasant to increase his industry to procure it;—and on the other, premature marriages would be checked, by rendering the prospect of providing for a family more precarious : the quantity of surplus labour in the market would therefore be reduced. Thus by stimulating the industry of the people, and rendering it more valuable to their employers, the remuneration of labour would rise, to the obvious advantage of both; superabundant population would be checked, and the decencies and moralities of life proportionably encouraged, which would permanently prevent its future excess.

But whether this speculation be true or false, I apprehend that no reasonable and well informed man will deny, that the general state of Ireland is such as

it has been just represented, (though improvement is
rapidly spreading); and that it affords a striking
illustration of the truth of the first part of the alternative in my second proposition, (see chapter iii.) in
which the pressure of population against the *actual*
means of subsistence is ascribed to grossly impolitic
or pernicious laws, or customs, accelerating the progress of population considerably beyond its natural
rate. The most intelligent and patriotic among her
own natives are certainly of this opinion, and are
bending all their efforts towards the introduction of a
superior cast of habits and modes of thinking. One
of them, the Reverend Horatio Townshend, author
of a Statistical Survey of the County of Cork, executed in a manner by no means inferior to the best
of our Scottish and English reports to the Board of
Agriculture, specifically states the grand disiderata
(among others) to be " to make the tradesmen drink
less and behave better;—to make an idle gentry
better farmers and worse sportsmen;—to exchange
bad ploughs for good ones;—to remove dirt holes from
the doors of the lower orders, and put panes in their
windows;—to enlighten their minds, to enlarge their
scanty stock of ideas, to diminish their bigotry, and
to remove their prejudices." In short, he urges with
irresistible force, that the remedy must be sought in
the encouragement of industry and education among
all ranks, in a strict and regular administration of
justice, in stimulating the activity, advancing the
skill, and increasing the comforts of the slovenly
rustics, in promoting employment for an increasing
population by the advancement of agriculture, by
new manufactories, or the improvement of those
which exist. This is the way pointed out—and I

shall hope to find an opportunity, before the close of this Treatise, to say something of the means by which it may be successfully pursued.

It is now, I trust, upon the whole abundantly manifest that, in the more advanced stages of society treated of in this chapter, although the powers of production yet remaining in the soil are continually decreasing, yet the natural tendency of population to press against the supply of food is also decreasing in a still greater ratio; at least, in all countries where due attention is paid to religion, morals, and rational liberty. Whereas in countries where these duties and privileges are neglected or forgotten, the principle of population is diverted from its natural tendency, and numbers do actually press against the *existing* supply of food, on the one hand from the artificial acceleration in the procreation of the people, arising out of premature marriages among couples ill provided with the necessaries and comforts of life, and on the other from the depression of the productive energies of the soil below its natural powers, arising from vicious government and the discouragement of industry.

We have then several of the fundamental propositions of this treatise here distinctly asserted, and proved, with reference to the more advanced stages of society.

1. Population has a natural tendency to keep within the powers of the soil to afford it subsistence; because we see that where those powers are most called forth by industry and good government, and consequently approach most nearly to exhaustion, there the population presses *least* against them; while, on the other hand, where the powers of the

soil are permitted to lie most dormant by idleness, vice, and evil government, and consequently when the land has yet the largest resources left to unfold, there population presses *most* against them. The converse of which propositions must be true, if my first fundamental principle be false.

2. But, although in every country we find that the tendency of the population to keep within the *powers of the soil* to produce further food, (as proved by the first and admitted in the second proposition,) is fully established; yet as vice and bad government may check the progress of population in some degree, but will usually check industry and cultivation more, the pressure of the first against the *actual* supply of food in ill-governed and immoral communities generally arises from the unnatural depression of the powers of the soil, according to the second part of the alternative stated in my second proposition. But as this deterioration in society, when once established, demoralizes the people, and deprives them of their taste for the decencies and conveniences of life, it may, as in some parts of Ireland, in Sicily, Spain, &c. introduce the custom of premature marriages among the lower orders; which will have a tendency to accelerate the progress of population beyond the means of subsistence, which apathy and relaxed industry can now supply. This again produces, as we have seen, a pressure against the *actual supply* of food by the means stated in the first part of the alternative of the second proposition. (See chap. iii.)

3. But as we have moreover seen that, in moral and well-governed states, " whose laws and customs are founded in the main on religion, morality, rational liberty, and security of person and property,

although they may be far from approaching to what is altogether desirable in these respects, the people are well supplied with food from inferior land, although they are rapidly increasing in numbers; while in ill-governed states they are ill supplied with food from superior land, although not increasing in numbers at all; we may conclude, according to my third fundamental proposition, that, in the first mentioned countries, the tendency of population to keep *within the powers of the soil* will never be materially altered, or diverted from its natural course.

4. Few persons will probably deny the truth of my fourth proposition as a necessary consequence of those which have preceded it. It is, however, more a matter of argument and comparison than of positive proof from *facts:* and as it is conversant rather with the *most advanced* stages of society, treated of in the following chapter, than with those we have just been discussing, the consideration of it may as well be postponed to a subsequent page.

CHAPTER VII.

Of the natural Tendency of Population in the most advanced *Stages of Society.*

NOTWITHSTANDING the arguments detailed in the preceding chapters, it is still evident, that if a community, conducting itself even upon the most reasonable principles, is indefinitely to continue increasing in population, in however retarded a ratio, it must at length come to the end of its resources in food; the land being an absolute quantity, and only capable, when most fully cultivated, of making a definite return. Remote and improbable as this contingency may be, and without any sanction from history or experience, still there is nothing absurd or impossible upon the face of it; and its eventual arrival would certainly impeach the truth of the first and principal fundamental proposition of this treatise, " that population has a *natural* tendency to keep *within* the powers of the soil to afford it subsistence *in every gradation* through which society passes." In order therefore to establish the universal truth of this proposition, I have a farther task yet to perform, which is the object of this chapter: and it is thus that with some confidence I venture upon the proof; premising, however, that as no nation was ever found with its soil cultivated to the utmost, the reasoning in this chapter is introduced more for the sake of answering an hypothetical but plausible argument, which appears to me to arraign the wisdom and goodness of Providence, than with any such view to the practical conduct of mankind, as influenced the arguments of the preceding chapters.

In the further pursuit of the career, detailed in the last chapter, it seems very certain that there must be a point at which the whole population will *naturally* be incapable of a farther increase : and it appears that this will happen when the sterility of that part of the people, which does not reproduce its own numbers, becomes so great, (or rather when the sterile portion of the people becomes so numerous,) that the reproducing part will not be able, by any natural fertility of its own, to supply the deficiency :—when each couple among these last, for example, must produce seven or eight children on an average for the purpose. This I shall venture to call its POINT OF NON-REPRODUCTION. The period of its arrival will evidently differ in proportion to the climate, the healthiness of the people, the comfort and cleanliness of the habitations in general, and of the towns in particular; and it may be retarded or accelerated by a change in such of these conditions as are of a nature to be affected by human means. Still the point must at length be reached, as the size of the towns is enlarged, and the habits of a highly advanced stage of society are more widely extended through the several ranks of the people. But in order to make my argument complete, I must also show that this point will be attained before the country reaches its *ne plus ultra* of cultivation; otherwise the power of producing food would fail before the people ceased to increase their numbers, and a pressure would actually ensue without the means of meeting it. Now this proof, I trust, will be a matter of no great difficulty; for whatever specific objections may be made to the following data and calculations, I apprehend that no man will deny their general result to be satisfactory in establishing the fact which they are produced to prove. It is more than I will venture to predicate as an universal aphorism, at what particular stage in the progress of society a people will altogether cease to reproduce their own numbers. Arguing practically, however, and with a view to the civilized nations of Europe, it may perhaps be said that whenever much more than one-third of the population shall be constantly resident in towns of considerable size, and the *artificial necessaries of life* (if they may be so called) are as operative in producing celibacy among the remainder as so advanced a state of society usually makes them, then the people will have arrrived at ITS POINT OF NON-RE-PRODUCTION.

To prove this the following propositions must be established :—1st, Unless the marriages which take place in any district produce and rear children enough to supply the place of the parents themselves, as well as of all those individuals who die there in infancy or celibacy, or who habitually emigrate and die in other parts of the district, the population of that district cannot be kept up: and 2dly, Supposing that in an extensive country, thickly studded with towns, many districts are found where the population falls short by not fulfilling these conditions; unless the deficiencies in them are fully supplied by an excess of individuals from the other districts. living to the same age at which the deficient district loses its people, the whole population of the country must decline.

Now the deficient districts in the civilized nations

of the world are principally the towns. Arguing therefore upon them, we may assert, that wherever only half the numbers born live to a marriageable age, and not more than two-thirds of those who live to that age actually marry; then each couple must produce six children, of whom four must be reared to manhood, in order to keep up the population. They must, for example, rear two children to replace themselves; one to replace the individual who died in celibacy at or after the marriageable age; and they must also produce three other children to replace those, who, by the inscrutable ordinations of providence, seem to be doomed to a premature death in all large towns; a proportion which no human exertions can materially alter, so long as the state of society producing such towns shall continue to exist. (The reader is referred to a subsequent chapter for the establishment of this last fact of premature deaths, as well as for the proof that the happiness of the community is not thereby on the whole deteriorated.) In the mean time it may be observed, that this rate of mortality in infancy and celibacy agrees with that which takes place in most of the great towns of Europe. Judging, indeed, from the very extensive operation of the *preventive checks* detailed by Mr. Malthus, as taking place in England and the middle parts of Europe, where he says that not more than half of the prolific power of nature is called into action;—as well as from the many accurate returns and calculations of the proportion which dies in childhood in the European towns;—it is probable that the result above given falls rather short of the real mortality in celibacy and childhood in those situations: we may therefore assume that, at least, six births to a marriage are necessary to keep up the population of towns. Now Dr. Price states the general average of births to a marriage, in most European states, to be about *four* in towns, and *six* in the country: and although Mr. Malthus gives reasons which prove that Dr. Price, and indeed most other writers on political economy who preceded himself, have relied upon erroneous data in their calculations on this subject, yet his own opinion is not in effect very different; for he has little doubt that, on an average throughout Europe, each marriage, including town and country residents, yields considerably above four births, and he should think more than five. But as it is a fact fully admitted, that the number of births to a marriage in towns is less than in the country, in order to produce this average of more than five (say $5\frac{1}{3}$) in a state of society where one-third of the inhabitants reside in towns, these last must produce fewer than five, probably four; and the country residents more than that number, probably six children to a marriage.

We have already found that one third only of the numbers born in towns actually marry; it follows that the annual births are to the annual marriages as six to one, or two persons out of six that are born actually enter into the marriage contract. The proportion of births to a marriage in the course of its duration has also been found to be four in towns; but as half the numbers born die in childhood, two children, or one half of the produce of each marriage, must be taken out of the effective population; so that each married pair will only rear just enough to replace their own numbers: the total deficiency therefore in each generation must be equal to the number of those who live and die unmarried beyond the age of puberty, which we have before seen to be one third of the adults, or a *sixth* of the whole population born within the limits of the town. Unless, therefore, this number of recruits from the country flows into the town in each generation, the total numbers must decline, and very rapidly; for a deduction being made from each pair replacing its parents, in proportion to those among them who live and die in a state of celibacy, the number of marriages will decrease one third in each succeeding generation. The number of children will of course decrease in the same proportion; so that in eight or nine generations from the first in the series, the people would be absolutely extinct, supposing no supply to come from the country. These calculations do not materially differ from those made by M. Buffon, upon data taken from the town of Paris and its neighbourhood. He indeed, with levity enough, applies the data, taken from this confined view, to the whole human race. Mr. Malthus very properly points out this error, and shows that the argument by no means applies to the country residents. He admits, however, that the decrease, as it was found actually to exist in towns, is such as would very soon unpeople those particular districts, without the accession of recruits reared in the country.

It may perhaps be said, that if these recruits do not arrive, the demand for hands would induce a larger portion of the adults to marry. But this very supposition involves much delay and interruption to the public prosperity in so advanced a stage of society, and would carry it in a retrogade direction. Besides, in no town or country can all the adults marry: and we have seen that without this condition, the population of the town

must decline, and that with it, it can but just continue stationary.

We must now, therefore, proceed to inquire to what
extent the country districts, containing two thirds of
the whole population, are capable of supplying this
deficiency of one sixth in the population of the towns
in each generation. We have seen that the average
proportion of births to marriages, in these situations,
is six, and the proportion of early deaths to the
births is much less than in towns. The average may
be fairly stated at about one third before puberty ;
two thirds of the born therefore live to a marriageable age. The proportion of these who actually
marry in the country would at first sight appear to
be much greater than in towns, and in the natural
order of things it certainly would be so. But we find,
from the great porportion of births to deaths in
country villages, where a comparatively slow increase
of population has taken place, that many persons
emigrate (usually in the prime of life, and before marriage) to the army, navy, colonies, and towns ; and
though some of them do afterwards marry somewhere, their offspring is not numerous, and is generally assimilated with the population of the towns.
The whole supply therefore which the country residents could afford, in order to make up the deficiency
in the towns, which, as we have said, contain one third
of the population, may be thus estimated : I have ventured, as in the preceding chapter, to use an hypothetical number with a view to make the statement
more clear.

Suppose the whole population of a state to be
9,000,000, one third of which, or 3,000,000, reside
in towns, suffering a deficiency in each generation of
one sixth, or 500,000, which must be supplied from

the country. In the country the number existing is 6,000,000, four of whom are always at an adult age, or rising towards it. Of these 4,000,000, 500,000 are required in a generation (*or in thirty three years and a half*) to supply the deficiencies in the towns; and the same number is required to make up for the deficiencies left in the families belonging to persons in the army, navy, colonies, foreign trade, &c., who do not reproduce their own numbers: 3,000,000 of adults would therefore still remain in the country in a condition to rear families; and from their procreative powers a supply of 6,000,000 is to be raised, and constantly kept up to the ages at which they would respectively die or emigrate: *viz.* 1,000,000 would be wanted to supply the waste of the towns, army, navy, colonies, foreign trade, &c.; 2,000,000 for early deaths; and 3,000,000 to replace the parents. Now supposing that three fourths of these 3,000,000 of adults in the country, or 2,250,000, should actually marry, which is a high proportion, considering their various conditions in life, their progeny would amount to 6,750,000; and the whole increase of the population, upon this hypothesis, would be 750,000 upon 9,000,000, or a twelfth, in one generation of thirty-three years and a half, a rate of progress which would not double the population in three centuries. Such a rate of increase is surely sufficiently slow to alleviate any alarm concerning the vice and misery incident to a redundant population, and to preclude any necessity for extraordinary abstinence from marriage to keep down the exuberance.

I have purposely given these calculations in a manner more favourable to my opponents than the actual averages would warrant, that the subsequent argument may appear the more indisputable. If, for example, only two thirds instead of three fourths of the adults remaining in the country actually married, which the advanced state of society in a very civilized country may render probable, and the waste of the towns is supposed equal to one fifth instead of one sixth of the population born within their limits, then it is evident that the progeny of the country residents would barely replace themselves and the waste in other places, and there could on the whole population be no increase at all. But taking all the advantages of the hypothesis in the last paragraph, it is easy to perceive, that a short step towards the state of society, in which one half of the inhabitants reside in towns, would *naturally* bring the population to *its point of non-reproduction*. Nor is the whole case yet stated. The period of life being shorter in towns than in the country, a generation would sooner pass away in the former; that is, the whole number there existing will be dead, and require to be renewed sooner than those in the country. It will immediately occur, therefore, to those who consider this circumstance, that a larger proportion of emigrants from the latter, in proportion to the whole number existing in a generation, will be required, beyond what is calculated upon in the above hypothesis; because it is there supposed that the period of a generation is equal in both situations. Against this, however, may be set off the progeny arising from second and third marriages.

In a case where half the population resides in towns, supposing the whole number of the people to be 9,000,000, the demand of the towns for adults would be 750,000 in a generation, which, besides the 500,000 for waste, in naval, military, commercial, and other purposes above specified, must be supplied from the country residents in the prime of life. To afford this increased supply however, there would now be only a diminished number of 4,500,000, 1,500,000 of whom would never reach puberty, and 1,250,000 must emigrate in an adult state, but before they have materially added to the population; so that 1,750,000 only would then remain in the country to carry on the effective population: and supposing, by the most favourable hypothesis, that three fourths of these actually married, and that each couple had six children, their whole progeny would only amount to 3,937,500, instead of 4,500,000; that is, there would be a deficit of 562,000 in the whole population, at which rate of decrease it would be entirely extinguished in seventeen or eighteen generations. If it should be said that the increased demand for labour consequent upon its short supply would induce more than three fourths of the adults to marry, I do not deny that it probably would do so ; but then we must consider first, that this effect could not be produced without disordering the arrangements of the community, and throwing back the country in question to a less advanced stage of society ; and next, supposing even five sixths instead of three fourths to marry, their progeny would only amount to 4,425,000, and there would still be a deficiency. That no attempt may be omitted to illustrate this important and somewhat intricate part of the subject, let us state another case.

If the towns became so large, and the other causes of abatement acquired such force, that two thirds of the people should cease to reproduce their own numbers, while the deficiency of a fifth in each generation remained in this barren part of the people to be made up by the productive third, (a condition that may very possibly exist in a cool climate, and in a free and highly civilized country, where the wants of life are numerous,) there seems no doubt that the population could not be kept up, but must evidently decline: for let us consider; in order to keep population stationary, it is necessary that every married couple should rear two children, supposing every man and woman to marry once; the productive third of the people must therefore rear that number in the first instance to replace themselves. They must moreover rear on an average four fifths of another child from each marriage, to replace the deficiency of a fifth from the other two thirds of the people. This would induce a necessity that each marriage, supposing *all* to enter once into that contract, should rear two and four-fifths, or nearly three children, to keep up the whole population. But as it is not found that many more than half of the numbers born attain to a marriageable age,* it follows that, supposing all who do attain that age to marry once, each couple must rear $5\frac{3}{4}$ children, and consequently produce at least seven, on an average, to keep up the population. But if we consider further, that of those who live to a marriageable age many do not marry, and that some, even in apparently the most favourable circumstances, produce no children; by estimating this barren portion of the reproductive part of the community at an eighth, we shall find that the prolific part must pro-

* See Sir James Stewart's Pol. Œc. octavo ed. 1805, b. i. c. 12, p. 92, 93; and c. 21, p. 207. See also a Short Inquiry into the Policy, &c. of the Poor Laws. c. 2, sec. 35.

duce near eight children, upon an average, to make
it possible to keep up the whole number of the
people.

Now, supposing for a moment, that a manufacturing nation can prosper, while paying wages *to all its
labourers* high enough to enable the married peasantry to support eight children, to the respective
ages at which they would be cut off by the rate of
mortality existing in the country, it would be to the
last degree preposterous to believe the physical
powers of the procreating part of the community to be
capable of universally *producing* that number.   The
population must therefore decline; an increase of the
reproductive classes by further cultivation could not
prevent this effect, because cultivation cannot be increased in this state of society, except by the stimulus furnished by a previous increase of people.   Supposing a still greater rise in wages possible without
ruin to the national industry, the difficulty would not
be surmounted; for, as we have seen, the physical
powers of the people, in the actual state of their
distribution, and of society, render a further increase
impossible, without subtracting persons from occupations necessary to the public welfare, and naturally
arising from, and inherent in, the actual state of the
society.   Nor could the ordinary operation of the demand for labour so far alter the distribution of the
people, as to increase the proportion of the reproductive part of it.   The only method then left of promoting a further increase seems to be by contriving,
if possible, artificial means of enlarging, at the general
expense, that portion of the community which supplies the deficiency of the remainder, i. e. the peasantry.   The rich must give up a portion of their

superfluity for this purpose; and, as Sir James Steuart well observes upon another occasion, "the state must be at the expense of the children."

Now should any one be inclined to object, that the proportions of births, deaths, and marriages, on which the calculations in this chapter are founded, are more unfavourable to the progress of population than are usually found to occur, and to quote instances in agricultural countries, where the proportions are more favourable;—I would reply that the application of facts, drawn from the agricultural state, to the more advanced stages of society can only lead to error ; and that in these last, the proportions I have given are more favourable than is consistent with fact and experience, nor can ever be argued upon as less favourable than I have stated them, except by admitting the probability of some fanciful and theoretic improvement in the health and longevity of the people.

I have endeavoured to refer to the returns and calculations to be found in the works of several writers on political economy, and to check and correct them by the superior accuracy and ingenuity of Mr. Malthus. It is presumed that few who have studied the subject will impute extravagance to the conclusions I have drawn ; but those who chuse to alter the data may make the same sort of calculations upon data of their own, and may advance or retard *the point of non-reproduction* according to the differences in the proportion of births, deaths, and marriages, as they may be found to exist in fact, or as any calculator may please to suppose them.

Considering the intricacy and difficulty of all calculations in political arithmetic, I am not presumptuous enough to affirm that errors may not possibly be detected in the preceding paragraphs of this chapter; but I feel confident that every reasonable man will at least concede these points, which are all that I contend for: namely, That as society advances towards its highest stages, population with difficulty keeps up its own numbers; and that there is a point in the progress, where it cannot reproduce them by any natural efforts of its own, so long as the society continues in the same condition, and the same proportions of the people still remain in the same relative situations, in which they have spontaneously arranged themselves, and continue under the influence of the same habits and practices, in which they have been gradually confirmed by their progress in civilization.

Having now taken a view of the progress of society through all the gradations which I proposed to investigate, and brought it to a point higher than any of which history furnishes an instance, and beyond which it may fairly be presumed that it cannot proceed; I may perhaps be allowed to observe, that if the foregoing deduction of the progress of society be at all correct, Population, so far from having an inconvenient tendency uniformly to press against the means of subsistence, becomes by degrees very slow in overtaking those means. By the inevitable accumulation of a larger than the average proportion of the means of subsistence into the hands of rich individuals as society advances, and from other causes stated in the progress of my argument, the pressure of want may indeed operate upon a part of the people to that salutary extent, which insures their industry in order to supply their necessities; and the miseries, ascribed to the pressure of population, are more justly due to the backwardness of men to exercise that industry, or to grossly impolitic laws interfering with such exercise. But that the whole population is constantly pressing to a hurtful extent against the whole supply of food, or that the human race have a natural " tendency to increase faster than food can be provided for them," are perfectly untenable propositions. On the contrary, it is evident that there is a point beyond which the population cannot possibly advance further without artificial assistance. That the healthiness or insalubrity, the mildness or severity of the climate, that the excellence or depravity of the government, the freedom or slavery of the people, may, in different countries, accelerate or retard this point of non-reproduction cannot be denied ; but no salubrity of climate, nor any municipal regulations, consistent with a regular progress in industry and prosperity, could ever defer it (in a country of extended territory at least) till the period at which no more food could be raised, and no more people could of consequence be permanently supported.

Laws promoting the easy transfer and appropriation of waste land, or bounties upon the export of corn, may indeed delay it for a time ; because they will induce a preference of agricultural to commercial pursuits, and consequently establish a larger portion of people in country residences: yet still the point must come at last, when the further cultivation of the soil becomes ungrateful, and the capitalist will direct his principal attention to commerce, and the pursuits carried on in cities; and when nothing but a pressure of the population of these places against the supply of food will induce a further cultivation of the soil. Should it be objected that, by direct encouragements to the further cultivation of the wastes still remain-

ing an addition might yet be made to the reproductive part of the people, it may be answered, that it is
absolutely impossible to bring about such further cultivation in the state of society last supposed by any direct encouragement; for all the good lands being
already cultivated to perfection, and none but the
most ungrateful soils left unoccupied, nothing but a
very augmented demand from a domestic population
increasing fast in numbers, and shut out from a foreign supply, could possibly divert any more capital
to the soil. A mere encouragement to export would
evidently be insufficient; because corn, raised on very
inferior land by expensive processes, can never compete in the foreign market with the produce of the
purely agicultural countries. But the domestic population, in the case supposed, is either stationary or on
the decline, and therefore can afford no encouragement to the laborious cultivation of barren soils.

It is very true, also, that bad government and the
consequent vices; that a general relaxation of morals,
especially among the lower orders; that foreign violence or influence, rendering the political system of
a country subservient, not to its own interests, but
to those of its master-state; may often prevent the
further exertion of industry. The recent condition of the
continent of Europe affords but too deplorable an instance in point. It is true, also, that impolitic restraints upon agriculture may prevent the improvement and further cultivation of the soil at any given
point in the progress of society. The consequence of
such vicious interference, before the people have arrived at their point of non-reproduction, must evidently be the pressure of the population against the
supply of food, and the vice and misery so eloquently

pourtrayed by Mr. Malthus as the consequence of such pressure. This, however, is certainly no necessary effect of a law of nature, but of human oppression and folly. The removal of the oppression and folly would assuredly restore the comfort and happiness of the people ; whereas, were the pressure previously removed, it would take away that impulse which urges the individuals of a community to the improvement of their condition, and to resist whatever opposes it; and, contrary to the obvious designs of Providence, it would, humanly speaking, pass sentence of eternal slavery and ignorance against the unfortunate people. Tyrants only can wish to make the economy of human affairs consist with a state of ignorance, slavery, and oppression.

Without some such interference, then, with the natural rates of increase in produce and population, it is no " vulgar misconception to suppose that the evils of a redundant population can never be necessarily felt by a country, till it is actually peopled up to the full capacity of its resources." We may even go farther, and assert that, should this point of plenitude be ever attained, the evils of a redundant population would not even then be necessarily felt ; because the non-reproducing part of the people must bear too large a proportion to the whole, to permit any total increase in their numbers : and let it be observed, in aid of this argument, that a free scope for industry, a general system of morality, security of person and property, and a free constitution and practice of government, (which are all necessary to carry a country many steps in its progress in the commercial and manufacturing state of society, and consequently towards a full state of cultivation,) do also very much assist the causes before enumerated, in enlarging the non-reproductive portion of the people.

Thus we perceive, that every step which a country takes towards the end of its resources is accompanied by a correspondent abatement in the tendency of its population to increase; that although in *abstract theory* so many people, if they were all to marry as early as possible, and all to procreate and rear as many children as they might do, were they in different circumstances and distributed in a different manner, would very soon outrun the decreasing powers of the soil to afford food;—yet that necessary and anticipating alterations arise in the state of society, as those powers of the soil diminish, which render so many persons unwilling to marry, and so many more who do marry incapable of reproducing their own numbers, and of replacing the deficiency in the remainder, that the population is *in real fact* always prevented from having a natural tendency to exceed the feasible supply of food. So *fearful* indeed does Providence seem to have been of running the matter to *too great a nicety*, (if I may be allowed so to express myself), between the due return of the soil for the labour bestowed, and the power and patience of man to bestow it where the return becomes difficult or problematical, that it has fixed the point of non-reproduction of people in most cases far short of the extreme capability of the soil to return fresh produce; indeed, just so far short of it, in all free countries, as the artificial nature of the society has rendered further cultivation difficult, by the impediments thrown in the way of a speedy appropriation of new land to fresh proprietors.

It is equally clear, that had not the Divine Provi-

dence adapted the progressive power of the principle
of population to what it must have foreseen of the
effects of the progress of society, it would have made
a very inefficient provision for its professed purpose as
to the earth; viz. that it should be peopled, replenish-
ed, and *subdued*, or cultivated by the industry of
man. Omniscience, so far from having made its machinery too strong for the work it has to perform, as
the propositions I have ventured to controvert go to assert, has very nicely adapted its means to its ends, provided the workmen will comply with the regulations
given them for performing their task; that is to say, provided they will regulate their conduct by the laws of
religion and morality. If the workmen indeed choose
to alter or disarrange the machinery, with an auda-
cious confidence in their own superior wisdom, it is
more than probable that the work will be liable to
interruption and irregularity. But when their own
wilful blunders have impaired the beauty of the
structure, it is surely a very gross addition to the auda-
city of the workmen to ascribe the blame to the ma-
chinist, and to the principles upon which his work is
constructed, and not to their own misconception and
misapplication of his plan.

If the view I have now taken of the natural tendencies of population be founded on fact and right reason,
the theory laid down by Mr. Malthus as an inference from the assumed tendency of population to a
too rapid increase, in the more advanced stages of
society, is founded upon data perfectly supposititious;
viz. that a possibility exists, that the physical powers
of a people could double their numbers in 25 years in
a commercial and manufacturing state of society, because that effect has been produced in one purely

agricultural. It is evident that their tendency to such a rate of increase is as absolutely gone, as the tendency of a bean to shoot up further into the air after it has arrived at its full growth. The argument appears not even to be theoretically true—

" Frustra simulacra fugacia captas
Quod petis est nusquam."

It is a mere shadow—a theory built upon another theory, which, when brought to the test, is directly at variance with experience of the fact, and as unsafe to act upon, as would be that of a general, who should assume the force of a musket shot to be double its actual range, and then should calculate upon the death of all his enemies, as soon as he had drawn up his own men for battle within this line of assumed efficiency.

Nor is this last assertion confined to any one or two stages in the progress of society, but extends, as I trust this treatise has shown, throughout the whole career, from the lowest state of savage life of which any record can be found, up to a higher condition of civilization and culture than any community of men has ever reached since the world was made. I know not therefore that in point of argument any thing remains incomplete which I proposed to establish in this first book of this treatise. A few illustrations, however, and a brief recapitulation of the contents of the book, may tend to fix the hypothesis more strongly in the reader's mind, and enable him with more facility to judge of its moral and political consequences, as stated in the following books of this treatise.

CHAPTER VIII.

Farther Illustrations of the Subjects treated in the two preceding Chapters.

IT would undoubtedly have been my wish to lay before the reader, in this place, such an illustration of the preceding view of society in its highest stages, as might be afforded by the series of facts, and by the observations on human life and conduct, which have gradually led my own mind to the conclusions stated at the close of the last chapter. Some of them, however, are, as I have candidly acknowledged, more a matter of hypothesis than of experience; and upon investigating the others in detail, so many are found to refer to the COMMON-WEALTH OF BRITAIN, which fully deserves to be treated at length in a separate work, that I cannot anticipate the discussion in this place. I may be permitted however, to remark, that there is no record, in ancient or modern history, of a country in so advanced a state of society as Great Britain. I do not mean to assert, that higher degrees of refinement and luxury have not existed among what has been thought the favoured portion of the community in other countries;—in the Roman empire, for example, where the fish of the Epicure were fattened on the body of his *slave*. If this may be called civilization, states more civilized than Britain certainly have existed; and, doubtless, the view of society, taken in the preceding chapters, would be far from being borne out by any reference to the practical operations of a system, involving such a complication of enormities. But I do mean to assert, and with a feeling of honest joy and profound gratitude, that there is no record of any country, where *real civilization*, that is, where the moral and political equality of every individual, of all ranks and stations, has been *practically* secured to any thing like the same extent as in Britain; where the laws of the land and the spirit of the constitution have so amply guaranteed to every man the freedom to exercise his industry, and to seek his happiness in the way best suited to his interests and inclinations, and the assurance that the fruits of his exertions shall be preserved to him; and where the laws, and the actions of individuals are, upon the whole, and notwithstanding some lamentable exceptions, so much guided by the spirit of enlightened morality. It is therefore to a country, which has been thriving for many years under such a system, that the illustration of an hypothesis, drawn from the spontaneous operations and distribution of a community of moral agents, may most properly be referred. It is indeed from a detailed view of the *workings* of *such a society* that the truth or falsehood of *such an hypothesis* can alone be well determined.

I have no doubt that the result would be found to be, that although scarcely more than a third of the population resides in large towns, yet were not the restraining power, imposed upon the increase of the people by the progress of wealth and civilization, in some degree weakened by the system connected with the legal, public, and individual charities; the population, except in times of extraordinary demand for labour and consequent high wages, would scarcely be sustained at its actual number, much less would it increase so as to press against the diminishing powers of the soil to afford it a plentiful subsistence. Nay, is it not a *fact*, that, notwithstanding the rapid increase which by artificial assistance the population has attained, we find that food is comparatively so much more plentiful, (Jan. 1816,) and has increased so much more rapidly, even though produced from a soil whose most fertile spots have been long since occupied, that the actual difficulty is not now how to feed the people, but how profitably to dispose of the superfluity of the food raised for their support. Can a more convincing proof be imagined of the gratuitous nature of the fears entertained concerning the unobstructed increase of population, and the tendency which it *naturally* has in such a society to exceed the limits of the food provided for its support? Even actively excited, and accelerated beyond its natural rate, it has still kept considerably within those limits. The spring has been bent, much beyond the point which calculators assigned as its utmost limit, and so far from breaking, has only the better executed its purpose.

It must, however, be admitted that if an authentic account can be any where found of an extensive country cultivated up to its full capacity of production, in which the population shall nevertheless be found to press perniciously against the means of subsistence, my hypothesis cannot be sustained. The only nation which has ever been asserted to be in this condition is China. An inquiry therefore into the truth or falsehood of this assertion is very necessary. Now, I think, it will appear that much exaggeration has always prevailed with respect to the extreme populousness of China, and the alleged *necessity* for the practice of *infanticide* as a check to its redundant numbers.

In order to form a fair judgment upon this subject it is necessary, first, to inquire into the *extent of the fact* as far as materials for ascertaining it can be had; and, having thus reduced the evil to its real amount, to investigate its cause, and to form a judgment of its *necessity*. The accounts given by the missionaries and Jesuits concerning China must be received with great caution; the interests of their order having rendered necessary to them a continued residence in a country under a despotic government, peculiarly jealous of foreigners, it was incumbent upon them to report nothing which might eventually give it offence. Their desire also of magnifying their own importance, by enhancing the numbers, knowledge, and virtues of the people they had undertaken to convert, might naturally lead to exaggeration. When we read, therefore, of the crowded numbers, the perfection in arts, sciences, and agriculture, the full state of cultivation, the ingenious methods of improving land, and the various features of an high state of civilization, recorded of the Chinese by those authors, we cannot consent to receive the account as perfectly unprejudiced: particularly where it directly contradicts all the known principles of political economy, and is equally at variance with other accounts from persons who could have no possible inducement, either to form, or to state to the world, erroneous conclusions on the subject.

The embassy of Lord Macartney to China has produced such accounts, and has falsified, in a great measure, all the fine theories built upon the romances

of the Jesuits and missionaries, has reduced the
information to be obtained by a candid inquirer into
the condition of China to the level of common sense,
and has enabled us to argue upon its state of society
upon data applicable to the known principles of political economy. We are no longer to be told (without the power of detecting the imposture) of a
highly civilized, enlightened, and well governed
people exerting their utmost industry upon a soil
cultivated nearly to the utmost, yet unable to provide
subsistence for their still increasing numbers, and
reduced to the murder of their children from the
mere physical impossibility of supporting them! But
we are presented with the account of a country, from
the vices of its government, lying one third waste,
with industry depressed, property insecure, the
harvest (except in the immediate neighbourhood of
the towns) liable to be swept away by bands of
plunderers; and a people reduced to the lowest state
of distress, *not from any physical impossibility of
further improving their country*, or of raising further
produce, but from the want of capital to undertake
improvement, and the uncertainty of reaping any
of the profit. At the same time, China, from the
general uniformity and mildness of its climate,
from the fertility of its soil, and the prolific nature
of its staple article of food, rice, is even in its present
state capable of supporting a very large *absolute
population*, called into existence by direct encouragement to marriage, and the absence of all those moral
and political causes, which, among an enlightened
and well governed people, naturally and spontaneously produce an abatement in the progress of population. The public policy of China, therefore, is

precisely calculated for the double purpose of at once encouraging the increase of people, and diminishing the quantity of subsistence; thereby completely reversing the natural order instituted by a beneficent Providence, and acting the part of a farmer who should increase his stock in proportion as he diminished the size of the farm on which he raised their food.

Having premised thus much, let us now proceed to inquire into the number of deaths by infanticide in China. It appears from Mr. Barrow's information, collected during Lord Macartney's Embassy, (Barrow's China, 4to. p. 169, and seq.) that about 9000 exposed infants are picked up by the police in the streets of Pekin, a city containing 3,000,000 of inhabitants, and carried out of the town to be buried. Of these about 5000, or five-ninths, are supposed to be still-born, and exposed to save the expense of burial, which is so great in China, that instances have been known of corpses being kept a year above ground to save money for a suitable interment (Barrow's China, ibid.); the remainder, or 4000, may be laid to the charge of inhuman or distressed parents. It is farther calculated, from the best authorities, that the number of these deaths at Pekin are equal to one half of what take place in other parts of the empire; so that in a population of 230,000,000, about 8000 children are *known* to be annually exposed to destruction. Now the annual number of births in China, considering the climate and encouragement to marriage, cannot be calculated at less than 8,000,000 or 1 in 30. Therefore about one child in 1000 is murdered, or exposed by its parents, immediately upon its birth. The number exposed in times of famine, perhaps, in some degree exceeds the average of common years, but probably not to any great extent. The famines in China arise from the uncertain nature of their staple crop, rice; and, as it is known to be of a temporary nature, terminable at the next harvest, that is, within six months at farthest, there does not appear to be any great additional temptation to the exposure of an infant who consumes no rice, but subsists upon its mother's milk. The famines, by destroying many youths and adults, must certainly diminish the number of births, but cannot much increase the number of children exposed; neither is there any reason to suppose that many are privately murdered. Where the government indirectly sanctions the exposure of children, and provides publicly for their interment, it is impossible to suppose that any parent would prefer the horrid office of destruction to the milder expedient of exposure, where some hope, however faint, may still exist, that the infant's life may be saved by the humanity of the opulent. That this feeling does enter into their minds is evident from the practice of the numerous part of the Chinese population, which dwells upon the rivers. Whenever they expose an infant, they universally tie a gourd round part of its body to keep it above water, in hopes that, in its course down the river, some one may take compassion upon it and rescue it from death. These hopes are certainly very ill-founded. The fact, however, of the practice is a proof that they exist; for otherwise what parent would not rather tie a stone round its child's neck and hasten its end, than preserve it to die in the lingering torture of cold and hunger?

We see then the amount of the deaths by infanticide in China, a resource which has been asserted to be a principal and necessary check to their over-flowing population. It may throw light upon this subject to form a comparative estimate of the effect which the same proportion of exposed infants would produce in our own country. The annual births in England and Wales, may be fairly estimated at some-thing more than 300,000, and supposing every 1000th child to be exposed, the total number would amount to 300 for the whole kingdom. Let those who consider the annual admissions at the Foundling Hospital, together with the unhappy infants deserted by their parents, and admitted into the workhouses of all places where there is a considerable population; that few assizes pass where mothers are not indicted for the crime to which they are impelled through fear of shame, and that it must sometimes be per-petrated without discovery; let those who consider these things say how far the civilized and enlightened England, comes behind the brutalized China, in the crime of exposing infants. So many, indeed, are not ultimately lost to their country, because the humanity of the laws or of individuals preserves their lives; but if they were ultimately destroyed, it would be obviously absurd to count upon an annual destruction of 300 children as one of the principal drains upon the population of the country. The extended territory and the great absolute population of China are apt to cause much confusion in the mind of an English reader, unless he be familiar with the study of political arithmetic. When he hears of thousands and millions of persons employed in particular pur-suits, or enrolled, &c. the proportion which such a number bears to the whole population of his own country, or of any other with whose history he is familiar, and upon the contemplation of which his general ideas have been formed, makes the number appear enormous;—and he is constantly obliged to do violence to his habitual feelings that he may render the account consistent. It will probably surprise many persons to be told that the average population of England to a square mile is greater than in China, notwithstanding the great absolute population of the latter; yet such is the fact, England containing 188 inhabitants to a square mile, China not quite 180. Such is the effect of comparisons.

Infanticide, moreover, is found to be chiefly confined to the cities, and the numerous dwellers upon the water; this appears both by actual observation, and by inference from the state of society in China, where the agriculturist, being oppressed and plundered, and his markets under the control of a corrupt government, raises no surplus produce, except for the payment in kind of his tax of the tenth of the crop (see Barrow, p. 400,) to the general proprietor, the Emperor. Thus the inhabitants of cities and of the boats are very often left by the agriculturist without an adequate supply of food, the price of which rises among them to an enormous height, reducing the townsman to absolute want, and the waterman to a precarious subsistence upon fish alone (see Barrow's China p. 558). It is natural, therefore, for persons in such a situation to despair of their ability to support a family, and being encouraged by their public institutions to marriage, and not deterred from contracting it by any of the moral or political causes incident to a civilized state of society, that they should be sometimes tempted to expose their infants. The fact, however, of the crimes being confined to the great cities, and to those who dwell on the water (in both of which situations the people are crowded together in a very inconvenient manner, (p. 349,) and the want of cleanliness, and of preventive precautions, must be peculiarly unfavourable to early life, (see Price's Rev. Payments, and Malthus, &c.) and renders the amount of the drain upon the population, numerically speaking, much less. For as in towns and in the situations just described it is universally found that not more than half the born live to the age of two years, it follows that one half of the exposed children must be deducted, to form a fair computation of the positive drain upon the population; since had they been spared at that time they would never have reached the age of two years, and all the care and expense bestowed upon them would have been, politically speaking, a pure loss to the state.

In thus reducing the extent of the practice of infanticide in China within its proper bounds, for the purpose of correcting exaggerations and false statements, I am far from asserting that the people of that country are not often reduced to the lowest stage of want and misery; the public permission of such a practice, to any extent at all, is the strongest proof that the government are convinced of its apparent necessity, according to the actual state of affairs in the country, and to the existing condition and resources of the people. But I do most strenuously contend that that condition does not follow from any real necessity, arising out of a physical impossibility of finding recources of food equal to the plentiful supply of the existing population, or of any number to which it could reach under a free and good constitution; but entirely to the vices of the government, the consequent debasement of the people, and the unnatural state of society thereby produced.

We find that, even in the most frequented and commercial parts of the country, (see Barrow p. 70, 91, 564, et seq.), immense tracts of the richest land lie wholly waste and unimproved, that on the whole of that which is under tillage the most miserable modes of cultivation are adopted : ploughs are drawn by old women and asses in some parts of the country, and three fourths of the land are entirely managed with the spade and hoe. Few cows are kept; milk is not an article in common use. No beasts of burden but a few miserable horses, mules, and asses fed on straw and chaff in winter, and on the wastes and swamps in summer. There is no enclosed meadow land. It is scarcely necessary to say, that under such management there can be little surplus produce; and that every cultivator, (566. et seq.) like the Irish peasant, confines himself to the quantity necessary for his own consumption, with the addition of the tenth paid in kind as a tax to the government, the common proprietor of the soil. Tea, and silk, and cotton, articles of universal consumption, are cultivated in the same manner, and the part sold to foreigners is chiefly the produce of the taxes to government. There is no such member of society as a cultivator with skill, capital, and implements adequate to undertake the management of a large farm with few hands, and to produce a surplus produce to answer the demands of the towns; although it is perfectly evident that did such a character exist, there is no want of soil to bring into cultivation, nor any want of demand for its produce. Nothing, therefore, would be more easy, did the nature of the government and the state of the society permit, than to raise a plentiful supply of food for the existing people; and the very same improvements in society, which would produce this effect, viz. civilization, freedom, security of property, and the accumulation of capital, would also, as we have fully seen, naturally produce that abatement in the future tendency of population to increase, which the vice, the misery, the unnatural ignorance and barbarism of the people and the government have hitherto prevented.

Towns containing a large absolute population, and creating a demand for food, co-existing with rich but uncultivated soil, capable of bearing a surplus produce to answer that demand, yet still remaining untouched though no undue interference from the importation of corn prevent its cultivation, are certainly anomalies in political economy: but so is the whole condition of China. It is throughout a complete inversion of the order of nature, and of the designs of Providence; and it is melancholy to think of the ages, during which so large a portion of the people of the earth has groaned under it. The causes, however, are obvious, and have been fully stated. A good police to protect property; a good government to secure its free enjoyment; personal freedom and independence, as far as they are compatible with the public safety; an enlightened and unprejudiced people, to contrive or adopt improvements in the arts of life; and an established religion, to instil into the minds of youth moral sanctions for their conduct in after-life, in cases where legal sanctions are inadequate; are all so many ingredients in the condition of man in a civilized and advanced state of society. They are absolutely necessary to his progress in prosperity; and if in any period of that progress they are neglected or destroyed, his condition is proportionably deteriorated, an unnatural state of society intervenes, and he begins to feel those evils which never fail to follow any deviation from the laws of God for the government of man. If these things be so, we have only to express our surprise that the state of China is not more deplorable than it is. For these conditions of happiness and prosperity are, in every particular instance, absolutely reversed. Instead of a good police to protect property, the land is overrun with robbers, except in the immediate vicinage of the great towns and considerable villages; (Barrow, p. 570); and this to such an extent that the intermediate space of ground lies waste with scarce an habitation, and almost wholly useless. The bands of robbers are sometimes so numerous as to threaten even their populous cities with plunder.—Instead of a good government to secure personal freedom, and the free enjoyment of property when realized, the whole population from the prime minister to the peasant, each in his turn, is liable to be bambooed severely, at the caprice of any superior officer, some of whom he can scarcely stir abroad without meeting; and is, moreover, (P. 381), under the necessity of returning thanks for the fatherly correction. Judgments in cases of property are to the last degree venal (P. 377), and without appeal; and a man is afraid to be considered as wealthy, (P. 177), well knowing that some of the rapacious officers of the state would find legal reasons to extort his riches from him. Thus all spirit of enterprize is checked, and all temptation to the accumulation of capital by industry, and to its employment in beneficial purposes, completely destroyed : for where indigence and misery are the only security against plunder and oppression, it is equally impolitic and impossible for a man to use any exertions to raise himself into affluence and comfort.

No symptom is wanting of a declining country. The great pagodas are now in ruins (Barrow, 333, et seq). The great wall, with its towers, 1500 miles in extent, has been long in the same condition. The great canal was in a state of decay before the Tartar conquest : the emperors of that dynasty, of whom there have been four generations, have repaired and restored it, and it now conveys shipping during an uninterrupted course of 600 miles, *without a lock, or any interruption, except a few simple flood-gates* ; but its plan and execution are infinitely superior to anything the present state of the arts in China is capable of designing or executing.

The tyranny of the government has completely broken the spirit of the people, and confined their pursuits to the mere attainment of a scanty subsistence : so long as the multitude can procure their bowl of rice, the public peace is secure, but no longer.

Such is the account of an accurate and intelligent observer ; and in this state of things, it is not surprising that, instead of an enlightened and unprejudiced people, ready to contrive or adopt improvements in the arts of life, the Chinese should be a prejudiced and barbarous race, despising all foreign improvements, and exercising no talent of their own beyond the mere suggestion of means for providing their first necessities, and satisfying their most pressing wants. (Barrow, 177). It is natural that they should sink into such a state of brutality, as to occupy themselves in gaming to the extent of staking their wives and children, and in training animals to tear one another in pieces for their amusement. They not only train cocks and quails for this laudable purpose, but have extended their inquiries after fighting animals into the insect tribe, and have been fortunate enough to discover a species of gryllus, or locust, that will attack each other with such ferocity, as seldom to quit their hold without bringing away a limb of their antagonist. (Barrow, p. 159.) In the summer months, hardly a boy is seen without his cage containing these little animals, whose combats prepare the mind of their little master for the more serious amusements of his riper years. Notwithstanding this promising beginning, however, it does not appear, that they have yet attained to the practice of hiring and educating human creatures skilfully to slit or flatten each other's noses, to strike out each other's eyes, to break each other's arms and ribs, or take away each other's lives by dextrous hits on the throat, or behind the ears, for the amusement and edification of thousands of spectators, as is said to be the case with a small and degraded portion of the people in some Christian countries : the disciples of Confucius, and the worshippers of Fo and Poo-sa have not yet reached these enormities !

Instead of a national church, to instil moral precepts into the minds of youth, we find no established religion, no national clergy, no public worship, nor any religious rites, but a few solitary ceremonies of gross superstition, extorted by some impending temporal calamity, in which the worshipper is actuated by the dread of evil in this life, rather than by the fear of punishment in another. (Barrow, 486, &c.) " A Chinese can scarcely be said to pray; he is grateful when the event proves favourable to his wishes, petulant and peevish with his gods when adverse."

In such a state of society, where moral and political justice, in all its relations and arrangements, is so completely perverted, it is not surprising that consequences unnatural to the ordinary condition of man should have arisen: but it surely is to the last degree surprising, that any one should bring such a people as an example of mankind in the highest condition of society, populated and cultivated to the utmost of their physical means. The plain fact, with respect to China, seems to be this—that it has for some centuries been declining, both in population and produce, a circumstance reasonably to be expected from a recurrence to what is known of its history. Before towns of the immense magnitude which those in China are said to reach could possibly have existed in the regular course of society, as it has been traced in the preceding chapters, there must have been a considerable degree of freedom and civilization, and the general surface of the country must have been pretty fully cultivated. But that cultivation has now been in a great measure destroyed by foreign violence, intestine disorder, and domestic tyranny. The towns having thus been left without their adequate and legitimate resource of food, their inhabitants have become like garrisons placed upon a reduced allowance. The small portion of food, however, necessary to sustain bare existence in that country, the fertility of the soil surrounding the towns producing two crops annually, and the mildness of the climate, still admit of a large absolute population, though it has doubtless much declined, both in quantity and quality, from its former state, and will still further decline if the same vices continue. * But unless these vices are the *unalterable lot* of the Chinese, we are justified in concluding that, so far from the parents being under any *moral necessity* of killing their offspring, and the people of emigrating, because there is an absolute impossibility of procuring further produce from the land, they have recourse to those expedients merely because the industry of that part of the natives which ought to feed the remainder is unjustifiably interfered with; and because the want of civilization, and the brutal depression of the people, prevent some part of that abatement in the progress of population which is natural to so advanced a state of society. But the restoration of good government and agricultural industry would soon restore civilization and plenty, the one producing ample food for the existing people, the other preventing a future progress in population too rapid for the remaining powers of the soil; whereas the system of legalizing infanticide for the purpose of keeping down the population to the exigence created by bad government, if it were effectual to its purpose,

* The number of persons on a square mile in China is not, as I have observed, equal to that which is found in England : yet the quantity of grain which the land is capable of producing from its double harvest, and nearly double returns in the quantity of each harvest, (for rice returns about thirty for one), would indicate a power of supporting a proportion of people four times greater than England. Let us add to this, that the ordinary fare of an inhabitant of Britain would, upon the average, support three Chinese upon *their* ordinary fare, and we may form something like an estimate of the population that *might exist* in China without pressing against the means of subsistence.

would condemn the people to a perpetual state of moral debasement, to a progressive diminution of their numbers, and to all that complication of vice and misery which attends upon a retrogressive career in the scale of society. For although the industry of the remainder may be excited for a time by the rod and the bamboo, yet when the mental and corporeal energies are unnerved by such expedients, industry and morality will soon take their flight to happier regions.

Here then we find that the natural tendency of the population to keep within the powers of the soil to afford it subsistence, as stated in the first fundamental proposition of this treatise, is disarranged, so as to produce *actual* pressure against the *existing* supply of food, by the "depression of the productive energies of the soil considerably below its natural powers," according to the second fundamental proposition of this treatise. But as such depression is produced by a government, laws, and customs, *directly opposed* to " the principles of sound religion and morality, to rational liberty and security of person and property, the counteracting causes ascribed to the imperfect influence of these principles, in the third fundamental proposition, have no effect whatsoever. Their perfect influence, according to the fourth fundamental proposition, is of course entirely out of the question. We need do little more than thankfully contemplate the state of our own country, in connexion with the preceding view of the state of society in China, to perceive the effects which the introduction of religion, morality, liberty, and security, would operate in the latter : and as I think it may be asserted without incurring the imputation of national partiality, that there is no country in the world where sound religion and morality, rational liberty and security of person and property, approach so nearly to the attainment of a perfect influence as in Great Britain; the comparison of its actual condition with that of other states will best substantiate the proof of my fourth fundamental proposition, as applied to the highest stage of society, of which history or experience will afford an example. It is evident that the population, although increasing on a soil where the best spots have all been long occupied, does by no means injuriously press against the supply of food raised from that soil : and it is still more evident that this happy condition is to be ascribed equally to our substantial political advantages, which encourage industry and cultivation on the one hand, as to our sound moral institutions, which tend on the other to introduce habits and dispositions preventing all vicious exuberance in the *natural* progress of population.

Far be it, however, from me to contend, that we have arrived at any thing like perfection in morals or politics !—on the contrary, should I be permitted to execute the work which I contemplate on the " Commonwealth of Britain," there is too much reason to fear that a few of our laws and institutions will be found as defective in *political morality*, as some orders of the community undoubtedly are in *private virtue ;* and I should truly rejoice to find some abler hand engaged in a philosophical treatise, for the purpose of tracing the connection between these two subjects, which involves the legitimate influence of morals in affairs of legislation and civil government. What I am now contending for is, that as in no great country upon record has so much public liberty been found, co-existent with so large a portion of private morality, the progress which England has made, without any serious inconvenience from the pressure of population against subsistence, is a striking evidence of the truth of the fourth fundamental proposition of the third chapter of this book, which is entirely of a relative nature. If, indeed, I may be allowed to make any observation on the *positive* degree of liberty and morality, which are requisite to enable a state to proceed in its career of improvement, without serious impediments arising out of the principle of population, I should be disposed to fix the point still lower than that at which those blessings are sustained in this country, and to cite the fact as an additional ground of thankfulness to Providence.

The permanent pressure of population against subsistence is an evil of so fatal a nature, so entirely subversive of all virtue and happiness, so degrading in its consequences to the minds and bodies of the people, so productive of apathy in the governors, and despair in the governed, that nothing short of a total revolution in society, with all its attendant horrors, is sufficient to renovate the system. Without this desperate remedy, therefore, which even the most considerate of the existing community may well deprecate as almost worse than the disease itself, a country labouring under the misfortune stated may well be considered as placed under the ban of perpetual exclusion from all the highest privileges of social man, from the attainment of virtue, from the exercise of charity, from the enjoyment of civil and religious liberty. The moral and political condition of a country is never entirely desperate, so long as this extreme sentence is yet suspended over its head. We ought therefore to be thankful that Providence has not allotted a pestilence so fatal to society, as the punishment of any trifling deviations from public or private duty, but has reserved it for those signal instances of departure from his laws, which have in all ages called down the whole weight of his wrath against devoted nations! Minor transgressions are punished with lighter inflictions, which, so far from being fatal to society, may be said to act as its conservative principle; for they recall to the minds of a community, who, in the career of prosperity, have forgotten the Author of their blessings, the omissions of which they have been guilty: and this, while a sufficient degree of vigour yet remains in the body moral and political, to render the hint available; and the impulse which is thereby imparted renews the drooping energies of its efficient members. The revival is gradually imparted to the multitude, and the whole system comes forth as a giant refreshed, prepared again to run its course in the career of power and beneficence. The history of the Church of England for the last century, compared with its present progress in improvement, may be cited among many other instances in support of this last observation.

The present condition of the people of Ireland is also a case in point, although it must be confessed to be by no means so fertile of hope, nor, (if the expression may be allowed,) so complete in expectation as that just cited. Neglect of duty towards them has, it is true, worked its legitimate consequence; and an exuberant and vicious population presents very formidable obstacles to the operations of the statesman and philanthropist: but, as it was stated in the last chapter, there are peculiar circumstances in the situation of that country which abstract it a little from the ordinary course of argument deducible from the principles of political economy. It is to be presumed, from the ameliorated system of the last few years, that the enlightened individuals connected with Ireland are at length seriously awakened, by its misfortunes and its miseries, to a just appreciation of the causes from which they have flowed, and of the only practicable remedy. If they will honestly apply that remedy, doubtless the inherent capabilities of their country will answer with elastic bound to the attempt; and the sense of the evils they have escaped will add double force to the spring. But it is impossible for a writer, engaged in a discussion like the present, to avoid gently intimating that statesmen, who have been for a long time engaged, and *honestly* engaged, in vainly seeking a *political* remedy for the disorder, have at length been brought, by total want of success, to the unanimous conclusion, that *moral* means can alone operate the cure; and, to their honour, they have set about in earnest to provide those means. This is a tribute to their efficacy in affairs of civil government, which it would be criminal to pass unnoticed, especially when it has so direct a bearing upon the truth of the proposition I have just endeavoured to establish. Truly, were it not that this ray of light penetrates through the darkness which hovers over that devoted land, to cheer the mind, and direct the exertions of the philanthropist, he might well be tempted to close his eyes in despair; or, at least, to turn them from the dreary prospect to others more bright with hope, although less interesting in respect of their proximity.

I shall close this subject with the advice of a good

old writer to those who acknowledge the force of a moral influence upon public happiness:—" How commonly do men complain, yet add to the heap? Redress stands not in words. Let every man pull but one brand out of this fire, (*viz. himself,*) and the flame will go out alone. While every man censures, and no man amends, what is it, alas! but busy trifling? In such a cause God will not allow any man for private. Here must be all actors, no witnesses. His discrete admonitions, seasonable reproofs, and prayers never unseasonable, besides the power of honest example, are expected as his due tribute to the common-wealth. What, if we cannot turn the stream? yet we must swim against it. Even without conquest, it is glorious to have resisted. In this they alone are enemies, who do nothing."

The respect which I entertain for the candour and ingenuity of Mr. Malthus, and my earnest desire for the discovery of the truth on the important subjects of this treatise, make me unwilling to close this book, without endeavouring precisely to point out the difference between the results of the views we have respectively taken of the effects of the progress of society upon the principle of population. I think it will appear that, short of the point at which a people naturally ceases to reproduce its own numbers, the difference between us does not attach so much *to the matter of fact*, with respect to the increase or decrease of population, as to its natural tendency and rate of progress, and to the means by which that progress is regulated. However we may differ in *degree*, both agree in admitting, that population does *in fact* somewhat diminish its rate of increase, with every step in the advancement of a country in wealth and civilization, and towards a full state of cultivation. It may be said indeed that Mr. Malthus has noticed, under the denomination of *checks*, many of those causes which I have pointed out, as naturally and unavoidably abating the tendency of the people to multiply, as society advances. It is true that he has ; but it is also true, that contemplating the want of the means of subsistence as the only real or necessary impediment to the increase of population, and the other checks merely as artificial impediments to what might otherwise have existed, he has continued to argue upon the geometrical and arithmetical ratio, in the relative powers of increase of food and population in the advanced as well as in the early stages of society, as though population still retained all its original power of doubling in very short periods.* I trust that my endeavours to expose the fallacy and inconsistency of this mode of reasoning, and of the moral consequences necessarily deducible therefrom, have not been altogether unsuccessful. But the principles of Mr. Malthus, with their application as rules of conduct, could never have made so deep an impression on the minds of so many

* In addition to the passages quoted in the second chapter of this book, the following argument concerning China will not be here misplaced. " The *procreative power* would, *with as much facility*, double in 25 years the population of China, as that of *any of* the States of America;" (this of a society where there is a town containing 3,000,000 of citizens!) but we know that it cannot do this, from the palpable inability of the soil to support such an additional number. What then becomes of *this mighty power* in China? And what are the kinds of restraint and the forms of premature death, which keep the population down to the level of the means of subsistence?"—(Malthus's Essay, book i. c. xii.).

enlightened men, had they not some foundation in truth. They appear to me to be partially true, inasmuch as they assert the tendency of population gradually to overtake *the existing supply of food* in the earlier stages of society, which I have freely allowed; but instead of wishing to prevent or weaken that tendency, which in my opinion would only serve to check the public prosperity, I venerate it as a signal instance of the kindness of Providence, and a plain annunciation of its will, that society should progressively advance to a more perfect state of civilization. But they appear to be no less decidedly false, inasmuch as they go to assert, that the natural tendency of population to increase (as society advances) is, physically speaking, so rapid, that it cannot be kept within the powers of the soil to afford it a further supply of food, without the operation of extraordinary checks, producing either a curtailment of the happiness and enjoyments of the whole people, otherwise allowable, or an inevitable accession of vice and misery. Whereas the system which I have endeavoured to establish goes to assert, that the abatement in the natural progress of population, constantly and spontaneously occurring as society advances, will, of itself, be sufficient to prevent any mischievous pressure against the supply of food; and that such abatement is to be ascribed to causes arising out of the natural disposition of the people, under a reasonably moral government, and varies with every step in the progress of society. I shall further contend, in a subsequent part of this treatise, that these causes are so far from rendering necessary any curtailment of the people's enjoyments, allowable upon the general principles of religion and morality, or of producing extensive and irremediable vice and misery, that they do, in fact, by a beautiful system of compensations, only effect a change in the nature of those enjoyments among one portion of the people; while they leave to those, whose situation is least altered by the progress of civilization, the same portion of temporal enjoyment which previously contributed to the happiness of their existence. This appears to me to be a very decided opposition in *principle*, and the succeeding books of this treatise will show the *practical consequences* of the two systems to be, in many respects, no less at variance.

Results too of a directly opposite nature, with respect to the permanence of the prosperity of particular states, are necessarily derived from the two systems. According to Mr. Malthus's hypothesis of the arithmetical and geometrical progress of food and population; when a country has once approached toward its *ne plus ultra* of cultivation, such confusion must soon be introduced by the deficiency of food, and the utter impossibility of procuring it for a still increasing number of mouths, as must necessarily propel the community very rapidly in a retrograde direction down the scale of society. But, according to the hypothesis which I have ventured to suppose, there are no assignable limits to the endurance of any system of society founded upon the conditions of my third and fourth propositions. Take it at any point, from its first starting in the career to the extremest verge of high cultivation and civilization, still the natural causes, spontaneously arising out of the system, will be found to preserve a constant equilibrium between food and population;

an equilibrium which must necessarily endure, so
long as the causes producing it are permitted to
operate. These are, it is true, political causes derived from moral conclusions. But philosophy has
yet to learn that they are therefore less capable of
fulfilling the objects of a conservative principle.
The piece of machinery called the regulator of a steam
engine will permanently preserve the work from
danger, if it be constantly inspected and kept in
order by a superintendant well instructed in the principles of the machine. In like manner the frame of
society will be permanently preserved in vigour, if
moral integrity, which is the regulator of the political engine, be duly watched and preserved by a
superintendant acquainted with its principles : this
surperintendant is an enlightened legislature, tempered by the public opinion of a moral and instructed people. If they will do their parts, we may
say of Providence, as the poet said of nature,

" Continuò has leges, æternaque fœdera certis
" Imposuit natura locis."

CHAPTER IX.

Brief Recapitulation of the Contents of the preceding Book.

IT would not have been difficult to have enlarged the preceding sketch into a voluminous treatise, by the insertion of a greater variety of detailed illustrations, drawn from history, and from the accounts published by travellers of the different nations of the world. But many reasons have induced me to abstain from this course. Indolence, I trust, is not one of them; but principally a feeling, that few things are less convincing than such illustrations, especially when produced with the view of fortifying some specific system of philosophy. I make no doubt that authorities may be drawn from any given country, which has much occupied the attention of travellers and historians, to fortify almost any given hypothesis in political economy. The views of different men, contemplating the same scenes, and the same series of actions, are so diverse, that they will furnish materials almost equally solid, upon which to construct systems and conclusions diametrically opposite to each other; and the controversy, instead of being thereby cleared of difficulties, becomes doubly complicated by the addition of doubts and differences concerning the authenticity of the facts related, or the deductions drawn by the relaters. This is very obvious to the attentive reader of Mr. Malthus's animated descriptions of society, in the several nations to whose history he has referred for the proofs of his hypothesis;

and I cannot but think that his original positions are rather weakened than fortified by those amusing details.   I have therefore endeavoured to confine my historical and statistical illustrations to the turning points or *pivots* of the argument, (if I may use the expression,) and to a reference to facts, upon the authenticity of which no question will probably be raised.   I have thought the genuine account of one or two communities, actually passing through each of the stages of society to which I wished to refer, sufficient for my purpose, and less likely to withdraw the reader's attention from the main argument, than a desultory excursion through the paths of history, or the tracks of voyagers and travellers.   If the references contained in the preceding chapters are not sufficient to convince the reader of the truth of the positions, which I am now about to recapitulate, I do not think, that an accumulation of facts, selected to assist the force of the impression, would be likely to meet with better success;—though it would certainly afford additional matter for the amusement of a controversialist.   It is enough to show, that certain grand outlines distinguish certain conditions of society from each other, and that the progress of mankind, from one stage to the next, is to be traced to certain uniform causes, and is followed by certain general consequences.   I trust that this has been satisfactorily performed, and that facts enough have been produced to satisfy a candid and reasonable mind of the following truths.

And first, with respect to the earliest and most simple states of society, I think it has been sufficiently demonstrated, both by argument and from experience, (see chap. vi.) that population neither does nor can, by any possibility, increase beyond the powers of the soil to afford it farther subsistence, but that it does, in fact, keep at an immense distance within those powers. But as they are scarcely at all called forth, the numbers of the people will in time undoubtedly increase beyond the actual means provided for their sustenance. It is nevertheless evident that this natural tendency of population to exceed the spontaneous supply of food from the uncultivated land is absolutely essential to stimulate the people to industry, and to the further production of food, by the inevitable force of necessity. If this call upon their industry be answered, the law of nature, just enunciated, so far from making any addition to the hardships of any rank of the people, confers comfort and happiness upon individuals and the community. The pressure, therefore, instead of being the *cause* of the miseries peculiarly incident to these states of society, is, in fact, their *remedy;* being the leading motive to all industry, and the primary cause of all advancement in public happiness and prosperity.

With respect to the purely agricultural, and the early stages of the commercial states of society, (see chapter v.) it is, I trust, distinctly shown, that so long as a people is wholly employed in agriculture, and the simple trades connected with it, population, so far from exceeding the powers of the soil to return further produce, can never even approach to any thing like actual pressure against the existing supply of food; because one family, employed in cultivating good land, can always support itself and several others : but when, from the progress of this system, the best spots of land are already occupied, and men begin to turn their attention to manufactures and commerce, a population employed in these latter pursuits will gradually spring up and increase, till it has overtaken the surplus produce of food raised by the cultivators in the purely agricultural state of society. But I have shown that this progress of population will be considerably retarded by the spontaneous change in the habits, and by the diminution in the prolific powers, of the people, introduced in consequence of the change that ensues in their pursuits, employments, and places of residence: they will therefore very slowly overtake the actual supply of food, and their reasonable wants will by no means exceed the powers still inherent in the less fertile and yet unoccupied spots of land, which will now be cultivated for their subsistence. But still it appeared obvious, that unless the number of people did at length increase, so as to press against the actual supply of food derived from the surplus produce of the agriculturalists, no further cultivation would take place; because no man would be foolish enough to raise produce at an increased expense, without a previous and growing demand for it; consequently the state could make no further solid progress in wealth and prosperity. We find therefore that population does actually advance, though with abated rapidity, as the power of supplying it with food becomes more scanty and precarious. The means are nicely adapted to the end; and, by an admirable contrivance of Providential mechanism, the strength of the spring is spontaneously reduced, in proportion to the gradual diminution of the force it is destined to restrain. This is conceived to be made very evident in the sixth chapter of this book, upon the natural tendency of population in the more

advanced stages of society; where I have endeavoured to show, in some detail, the various causes
which, in all tolerably well regulated communities,
spontaneously operate in adjusting the increase of
population to the diminishing powers of the soil for
the further supply of food. These causes appear to
be of such powerful and certain efficacy, as to produce consequences which may, at first sight, appear
contradictory; although they are in truth nothing
more than the natural result of the Providential care,
which has made the comfort and happiness of man
dependent upon the fair discharge of his moral and
political duties; for I think it is established, by
the evidence of fact, in the sixth chapter, that the
nearer the industry of the people has brought their
country to a full state of cultivation, and consequently towards the end of its resources for a further
supply of food, the less will the population be observed to press against the actual means of subsistence. While on the other hand, the more the idleness and apathy of the people have induced them to
neglect the cultivation of their soil, and consequently
the more power it still retains to afford a further
supply of food, the deeper will be the distress produced by the pressure of population against the actual
means of subsistence. The solution of these apparent
contradictions is to be found, 1st, in the different use
which each party makes of the resources yet at its
disposal, whereby the one starves in the midst of the
means of plenty, while the other lives at ease with
very confined means;—and 2dly, in the different
habits adopted by the two parties, whereby the one
runs thoughtlessly like a spendthrift into engagements
which he cannot answer—while the other acts upon

feelings and principles, which, without any direct reference to the future, will from their natural effects always preserve him in a state of moderate competence. The one, in short, acts on the principle of increased industry and diminishing expenses, the other upon that of diminished industry and increasing expenses. Although the latter therefore may at some given moment be the richest in available means, he will always be the poorest in fact, because he will not turn his means to profit.

If a country, however, is to continue indefinitely increasing in population, in however retarded a ratio, it must at length come to the end of its resources of food, land being an absolute quantity and capable of making only a definite return of produce. In order, therefore, to make the argument of my Treatise complete, I have in the seventh chapter of this book endeavoured to show, that long before a country, conducting itself upon such a reasonable system as to carry it far towards the fullest possible state of cultivation, has arrived at any thing near to that condition, it will also have found itself in another predicament with respect to the increase of its people, which will have altogether ceased to re-produce their own numbers, or as I have ventured to state it, that the population will have arrived at ITS POINT OF NON-RE-PRODUCTION. I think I have shown that this effect would be produced by physical and moral causes spontaneously arising out of the habits and distribution of the people, which cannot be materially altered so long as the society continues in the same advanced stage. And although this part of the argument is introduced, more with the view of answering a plausible argument which appeared to arraign the wisdom and goodness of Providence, than with any view of practical policy, yet it seemed upon the whole necessary, in order to complete the circle of proof, that throughout the whole progress of society, from the lowest stage of savage life to a higher degree of civilization and culture than any people have ever reached, the first and principal proposition of this treatise, "that population has a natural tendency to keep *within the powers of the soil* to afford it subsistence in every gradation through which society passes," is strictly within the limits of truth.

Such appears to be the *natural* progress of society, when not materially diverted from its regular course ; but let it be carefully observed that, in each of the stages, it is a fundamental principle of my treatise, to submit the truth of the propositions, the freedom of of society from the vices and evils of a redundant population, and the consequent progress of mankind in political improvement, to some degree of dependence upon *moral amelioration.*   It will be observed that I have not merely had in view Mr. Malthus's principle of *moral restraint,* which includes only abstinence from early marriages, and from irregular sexual intercourse, but that general prevalence of moral principle, *in whatever degree,* which pervades the whole of the political body ; which, more or less, induces public men to act with public spirit and an honest regard to the *real* welfare of the people, and private men to seek their own advantage with an enlightened regard to the interest of others; and which, above all, produces a system of government and legislation, leaving men free to act in this praise-worthy manner, but repressing with more or less severity all *accessible* actions of a contrary nature.

Now I should be very sorry justly to incur the imputation of having made a parade of introducing
moral arguments where moral sanctions are misplaced, and where the question ought to be determined purely upon political grounds. Such a mistake
always indicates bad taste, and nine times out of ten
bad principle also; for it savours of hypocrisy, and,
like every other exaggeration, weakens the argument
it is produced to fortify. But I sincerely trust that
every candid reader will admit that the case I have
been arguing does really involve moral considerations
of the highest nature; that it is conversant with the
spontaneous actions of men towards each other, and
with the influence of laws and government upon those
actions; with the regulation, in short, of the human
will, disposition, and affections, as they operate upon
the progress of society, which is strictly within the
department, at least, of *political* morality. And if this
be so, I should be still more sorry justly to incur the
imputation of having made a parade of *omitting*
moral reasoning, where moral sanctions lie at the
bottom of the argument. For whether this be bad
taste or no, it is certainly the worst species of hypocrisy, being nothing less than the triumph of a cowardly fear of the worldly-minded over a manly regard
to reason and justice: it is in fact submitting to the
loss of more than half the argument, in the vain hope
of gaining proselytes incapable of half their duty, because deprived of half their means of knowledge, and
of more than half of their motives of action; which is
something like recruiting a regiment with men deficient of an arm and a leg: such soldiers and such
proselytes are little worth the cost of procuring.
Nay, it is worse than all this—it is depriving the

politician of his surest ground of action, of his only certain guide through the intricacies of his path. For let us look to history, and tax our own experience ; let us recollect the political axioms which have been held to be oracles in one age, and branded in the next as very mischievous things ; and we must admit that politics involve always a choice of difficulties, frequently a choice of evils, and are never reducible to determinate principles, unless when they can be traced up to a moral cause. But when this can be clearly done, let us again look to history, and tax our own experience, and declare whether any political action, or any improvement undertaken on moral grounds, was ever the subject of repentance or regret to the society which adopted it? Here then is the touch-stone by which every political speculation, that can be brought to it, may be examined and concluded on. When the symptoms of the pure ore are manifest, the politician may, nay *must*, if he is honest, declare the argument current: and we may conclude that the legislator is never *certainly* safe except when he proceeds on moral grounds.

To sum up the whole in a few words—where a moderately good government in its enlarged sense is found to prevail, there population will spontaneously restrain itself, while the production of food will be extended, and the community will make a healthy progress ; but where the vices of a bad government, and individual immorality and selfishness, are found to be predominant, there the production of food will be restrained, while population will make efforts to extend itself, which will be checked by misery and famine till a better system be adopted. I do not mean by this conclusion to lay every particular instance of private vice and public evil directly to the charge of the governments under which they may be found, any more than to fall into the opposite error of ascribing to the spirit of the government all private virtue and public prosperity : the utmost power of goverments can only lay the foundations of each, and lend a hand in rearing the superstructure; the spontaneous operations of the people will do the rest.   But my conclusion evidently does extend to this, that the *general nature* of those operations will depend upon the sort of foundation laid by the government, whether in just and moral, or in unjust and immoral laws; and it is certainly thus far responsible to God and to the country.   If public happiness and prosperity can rest upon political profligacy, the unprincipled use of power, the selfish traffic of individual interests, and the effeminate disregard of stern morals in affairs of state, then have the governments of past times clear consciences, and history much belies the general condition of the people who lived under them : but if, as I hope for some future opportunity of proving in a separate treatise, and as I think the brightening prospects of the world may lead a sanguine mind to anticipate, the converse of these propositions may be admitted as political axioms; if moral principle, and pure philanthropy may at length be considered as proper ingredients in the composition of a statesman, and legitimate influences in affairs of policy ; then may the people look forward to better days, in the removal of the impediments which have hitherto checked the designs of Providence in their favour.   For individual profligacy and selfishness, though shining with talent, will be discountenanced as useless : but individual morality, dilating itself as it always does into general philanthropy, and animated by zeal for the improvement of society, will be associated with the power of the state: their united force will be more than sufficient to fulfil the conditions under which (according to the principles of this treatise) mankind will spontaneously advance in the career of civilization and happiness.

BOOK II.

CHAPTER I.

*Consequences to be deduced from the first Prin-
ciple: viz. "That Population has a natural Tendency to keep within the Powers of the Soil to
afford it Subsistence, in every Gradation through
which Society passes."*

THE first obvious application of this principle, as
established in the preceding book, to the practical
purposes of political economy, may be thus stated.
An enlightened government, and an industrious
people, who will discharge their duties with an ordinary degree of practical wisdom and virtue, so far
from endeavouring to add force to the spontaneous
abatement in the progress of population, accom-
panying the civil and moral phenomena displayed in
the foregoing view of society, may safely venture upon
the removal of every *check* to population, which *really*
comes under that title by being of a nature to be removed by human power: they will, under ordinary
circumstances, leave the people to the natural rate
of increase inherent in the state of society which may
then be subsisting. In pursuing this course of conduct, they will not interfere with that necessity for
industry and exertion, which Omniscience seems to

have contemplated in calculating the force of the principle of population, and on which the happiness and virtue of all societies depend. But they will certainly feel it incumbent upon them to use every exertion for giving free scope to human industry, and indeed will consider that circumstance as a most important object of all rational politics. A full population, increasing as fast as the state of society in which it happens to be will permit, necessarily renders the people industrious; because in such a condition universal industry is absolutely essential to the sustentation and happiness of the people, and to the security of the government. In *ancient* China, which was eminently populous, idleness was a penal offence, and we are told by Strabo, lib. xv. that it was capital to lame an *artificer* in the hand, or to blind him of an eye, though not so with respect to other persons. These laws must have originated in the necessity of an universal industry in that country. As in such a situation it necessarily becomes expedient to the safety of the government, that every man should have it in his power to work without being deprived of the fruits of his labours, a free form and practice of government naturally ensue. The regular administration of justice, and the absolute necessity there is for encouraging industry by rendering property secure, are all so many bars to despotism. In truth, the attention which a full population, increasing as I have just stated, renders it necessary that a government should pay to the removal of all impediments to the people's industry, (particularly when employed upon the land,) and consequently to the welfare of the lower orders, is above all price. It was formerly the custom in India, at the beginning of a new year, for the kings and philosophers of the country to meet together and consult about the people's welfare; and those who had made any pertinent remarks, either relative to the fruits of the earth, or to animals, were exempted from tribute. What a magnificent board of agriculture and internal improvement! To bring one more instance of the effect of a full population on the people's industry and happiness, let us refer to the account given by a Syracusan classical writer of Egypt, the most industrious of the old states, and the mother of the arts and industry of Europe. He calls it "* Civitas opulenta, dives, fœcunda, in quâ nemo vivat otiosus. Alii vitrum conflant, ab aliis charta conficitur, alii lyniphiones sunt; omnes certè cujus-cunque artis et videntur et habentur. Podagrosi quod agant habent; habent cæci † quod faciant; ne chira-grici quidem apud eos otiosi vivunt."

But besides these obvious political duties, there are other considerations arising out of the principle we are now discussing, when coupled with the progress of society towards its higher stages, which demand the best attention of statesmen. Their duty consists not only in a careful removal of all impediments to the free progress of industry, and to the spontaneous distribution of the people, but also in adopting such measures, not inconsistent with these objects, as the interests of their country, involved in its geographical position, or its political relations, or its relative condition

---

* Vopisci Saturninus.

† See an account of the school for the indigent blind in St. George's Fields, instituted 1799, printed by the Philanthropic Society. The ingenious methods there detailed, of giving profit-able employment to the blind, exhibit a delightful combination of ingenuity and benevolence.

as to other countries, may seem to require. A nation may find itself, for example, under such circumstances with respect to the community of nations of which it forms a part, that the very prolongation of its existence may depend upon a career of prosperity more rapid than its bare natural resources would enable it to pursue. In such a case, without doubt, some hazard of ultimate failure may be incurred for the preservation of immediate welfare, and measures even attended with risk may be justifiably resorted to. But it is superfluous to state, that the least possible risk should be incurred, that all *forcing* measures should be used with the utmost caution, and that the plant should be restored to its natural climate, as soon as it can bear exposure to the surrounding atmosphere. If, for example, upon a deliberate view of the wants, resources, and political relations of a country, a full supply of disposeable hands be thought necessary for the security of the state, or for its advancement in the progress of prosperity; it should seem, if there be any truth in the principle treated in this chapter, that, relying on the natural tendency of population to keep within the powers of the soil to afford it subsistence, artificial encouragement may occasionally be afforded to its increase without any material danger.

To descend a little further into particulars; let us suppose a country of a cool climate, with a free constitution, and in an advanced state of society, seated in the middle of the ocean, and small in respect to territory compared with the rival nations who are contesting with it the palm of superiority, and whose interests it has been found impossible, from all past experience, permanently to reconcile with its own:

now such a country would naturally wish to augment its resources as much as possible, in order to place itself more upon a level with its rivals.

Again, should the supposed country not be actually surrounded by more powerful rivals, but should perceive, from its relative geographical position, that by increasing its internal resources it might raise itself from a bare independence to a superiority over its neighbours, and place itself out of the reach of any eventual combination against it; it would clearly be justified in seeking this object, provided it can be rendered consistent with the virtue and happiness of its people. This is more particularly evident, when we consider that the progressive state is the most healthy in which a country can be placed; and experience is far from informing us that any extraordinary redundancy of this species of healthiness will ever expose the patient to the danger of dying of a plethora, provided every part of the system receives its due portion of nourishment.

Once more—should the statesmen of the supposed country think with Sir James Steuart, that "it is not in the most fruitful countries of the world, nor in those which are best calculated for nourishing great multitudes, that we find most inhabitants : it is in climates less favoured by nature, and where the soil produces to those only who labour, and in proportion to the industry of every one, where we may expect to find great multitudes ; and even these multitudes will be found greater or less in proportion as the turn of the inhabitants is directed to ingenuity and industry—" Should they further agree with the same writer, in thinking that "the principal object of political economy is to provide every thing necessary for supplying the wants of the society, and to *employ* the inhabitants (supposing them to be freemen) in such a manner as *naturally* to create reciprocal relations and dependencies between them, so as to lead them by their several interests to supply one another with their reciprocal wants :"—and finally, should they consent to this further proposition of Sir J. Steuart's as applicable to the advanced stage of society in which their country is supposed to be : viz. that where agriculture is exercised as a trade, with a view to a surplus produce for sale, " the multiplication of people is the efficient cause of the increase in agriculture.* " If, I say, the statesmen of the supposed country should agree in these three propositions, they would doubtless be justified in giving encouragement to " *multiplication*" in order to encourage industry, production, and " reciprocal relations ;" and therefore a healthy increase of those " multitudes" which " we may expect to find in those countries where the soil produces to those only who labour." But the species of encouragement necessary to be given in such cases must depend upon a minute investigation of the state of society in which the country happens to be. If from a third to a half of its population reside in towns, and many of its best lands are brought under cultivation, and it is consequently advancing towards its point of non-reproduction of people; and if new fields of commercial enterprise are nevertheless continually opening to its view, it would, I think, be its interest to accelerate the rate of increase among its people by direct encouragements to population; for by that method only could it obtain either a supply of industrious labourers to meet the eventual exigencies of its political situation, to take advantage of its opening resources,

* See a subsequent chapter on this subject.

or to encourage a further production of food by a new demand for it. But then it must provide, that the demand for food among the newly raised population shall be a real and effective demand ; that is, that they shall be in a condition, by a corresponding increase of industry, to make a valid offer of remuneration for the supply of their wants. This is absolutely necessary to secure a healthy advancement in population, and without it I am perfectly ready to admit, that the expedient proposed would only lead to aggravated vice and misery.

Another precaution also seems very necessary : viz. not to accelerate the rate of increase faster than that at which the demand thereby created for food can be conveniently supplied, in time to prevent a *pernicious* pressure against the actual means of subsistence : for although we have seen that population will not *naturally* press in that manner, if left to its own course in a moderately good government, yet it is easy to conceive that artificial encouragements may be so constituted as to produce such an evil consequence. Now it should seem that there can scarcely be a better mode of escaping this inconvenience, than by providing that the same artificial means, by which the rate of population is accelerated, should be so contrived as to afford at the same time a corresponding direct encouragement to cultivation, without diminishing that which is due to commerce and manufactures. By this triple effect all the conditions necessary to a healthy progress in prosperity are fulfilled, and it becomes complete, permanent, and secure. But to afford at once this triple encouragement to sources of wealth, which are generally thought to thrive at each other's expense, may perhaps appear rather difficult. Let us consider, however, if some such provision as that which follows would not attain the object.

In the first place to rear the additional number of people at the least expense, it would be necessary to increase that of persons resident in situations best calculated for bringing up large families, somewhat beyond the natural demand of those places for labour. If it were not for fear of exciting a smile, where a serious impression is intended, I would word the proposition thus. If a country is in want of more hands than the *natural* rate of its population will supply, it must keep an additional set of healthy breeders for the community; and that all unnecessary expense may be spared, it must place them in situations most favourable to child-bearing, and to the health of children, and most favourable also to the preservation of their morals, that is to say, in the country villages. Here a smaller number of parents will produce an equal increase of stock; more of it will be reared to perfection; and the individuals when reared will be finer and more efficient animals. Just as the governor of Fort St. George, when he wished to procure a larger supply of fine horses for the cavalry of that settlement than the natural means of the country afforded, increased the number of breeders from the best stocks, and selected a favourable and sequestered spot in a country of rich pasture for the establishment of the stud. We must not indeed carry this comparison so far as to forget that man is a moral agent, and that he is never worth his country's having, unless he be both good in bodily health and also in moral quality; and that strength in virtue is as necessary to the preservation of a state as strength in numbers.

The object, then, being to raise an artificial increase of healthy and moral country residents, it follows that some expense must be incurred for its attainment, that donations in money, both to the parents and the moral instructors, form a necessary condition of the plan. But this would be a heavy burthen upon the industry of the country, if it were done by an universal rise in wages, and would materially interfere with agriculture, commerce, and manufactures, of which a corresponding encouragement constituted the other conditions necessary to render the progress in wealth healthy and permanent.

This objection would be obviated, and the additional numbers raised with a trifling expense, and kept up without any expense at all, if means could be found, either direct or indirect, to alter that equality in the remuneration of labour, which in all countries is calculated in proportion to the work performed and to the existing demand for labour, rather than to the wants of the labourer arising from the size of his family. By subtracting from the surplus earnings of the bachelor and childless labourer, all that is over and above what is necessary to enable them to live in comfort, and to make a saving by frugality for their declining years; and by applying the sums so subtracted to the support of such of the children of large families, as their parents cannot maintain upon the average rate of wages, it seems clear that the breeding stock would be supported without any expense to the public. But all *direct* attempts to assess wages in proportion to the wants of the labourer, and not to the work performed, have, from their extreme absurdity, been always found

impracticable, and Sir James Steuart and other writers
on political economy have much lamented this impossibility. Indirect means must therefore be resorted to for the purpose. The original stock must
indeed be raised by encouragements to marriage,
and by donations in money from the rich to the
parents of many children, who will thus be raised,
into effective men. This will be a real, but the
only real, outgoing to the state and the public. For
as soon as this first generation is reared, the succeeding ones will be maintained in the same manner, at
an expense merely nominal; for the redundant supply
of hands will have a tendency to lower the wages of
labour, below what they would naturally have been
without this redundancy. In a country with an increasing demand for labour wages may not perhaps
actually sink; that will depend upon the ratio of increase between such demand for labour and its additional supply : but they will certainly be at a rate
lower than they would otherwise have reached;
because, without this extraordinary supply of hands,
they would very much have risen, or the opportunity
for a further progress in publick wealth must have
been abandoned. This tendency towards a diminution of wages, to whatever extent it may go, will
equally affect the bachelor, the childless, and the
married man with a family; but the state may make
up the difference to the latter; and by a donation
in money make the whole remuneration of *his*
labour equal, not only to what it would have been
had no alteration taken place in the natural rate of
wages, (which is no where high enough permanently
to support a large family,) but also equal to his just
wants, whatever the size of his family may be.

Now if we consider what was stated in a previous chapter with respect to the small proportion of the whole labouring population which, in the advanced state of society here supposed, is in a condition (physically speaking) to rear many children, it is evident that the state will be a considerable gainer on this transaction; that is, it will save more on the depressed earnings of the bachelor or parent of few children, than it will expend in support of the excess of children in large families; and ultimately the result will be, that the saving in the *general* average, to which a rapid progress in prosperity, (if it could have been maintained under high wages,) would naturally have raised the *wages of all*, is greater than the *particular* expense of supporting the *large families only*.

It may be said, perhaps, that this process is liable ultimately to reduce the rate of wages too low for the average wants of the people, and to lead to a larger supply of hands than the wants of the state require. But let it be observed that, where liberty gives to industry a free scope for exertion, a slight tendency towards the depression of wages, or even the mere prevention of a rise in wages, when caused by a plentiful supply of hands, will give a considerable impulse to every kind of exertion, and, consequently, to a demand for labour in those departments where the labourers do not keep up their own numbers. Agriculture is also doubly encouraged by the increased demand for food from the augmented population, and from the additional facilities arising from a redundancy of labour. And thus the three conditions of a sound progress in public prosperity are fulfilled. And, upon the whole operation, it may perhaps be asserted

that, strictly speaking, wages are not so much *actually lowered* as industry and wealth promoted.
For unless the extra stock of labourers had been
previously raised to seize upon the opening sources
of wealth as they presented themselves, they must
probably have been abandoned, before the slow
operation of increased demand could have raised an
additional population to the condition of effective
workmen.   The rise in wages in that case therefore
would have been merely momentary, and they would
have sunk again only to plunge the labouring poor
in the deepest distress, and to annihilate the children
they had called into existence.   So that, whether on
the scorce of humanity or economy, the system appears unobjectionable.   And, again, let it be recollected that the previously existing stock of
labourers do, by their own demand, offer encouragement to every department of production, thus counteracting to a considerable extent the tendency towards lowering the price of labour which their
existence would otherwise have produced.   It should
appear, then, that the system here detailed doth
not, as it has been asserted, reduce the labouring
poor to the most scanty pittance of wages upon
which their bare existence can be maintained; but
that its real effect is to maintain an uniform rate of
wages, tending, indeed, rather towards a depression
than to an advance.   This circumstance, however, is
more than compensated, first, by the great impulse
given to internal industry, whereby the community,
and the condition of the labourer as an important
part of it, are kept in the healthy and progressive
state; and, secondly, by the uniformity introduced
into the particular remuneration of the different

classes of labourers, whereby the fluctuations so detrimental to their own health and happiness, and to the due support of their children, are excluded, and all disproportion between their wants and their means effectually prevented. The saving, nevertheless, made by the public by this system, may enable it, without injury to the public prosperity, to extend the donations in money beyond the mere supply of the wants of parents of large families. In the advanced states of society, where the saving is evidently the greatest, from the small proportion of the people who have large families, legal relief may even be extended to all cases of individual distress, and yet the public be a considerable gainer on the whole transaction.

Thus both the moral and political good consequences of the system appear evident ;—the first in removing temptations to vice, and in the general relief of individual misery ;—the second, in rendering these important objects co-existent with a rapid improvement in the public wealth. In short, as I have elsewhere written, the principle of encouragement to industry is found in the supply of effective labour constantly preserved in the market, ready to meet (and at a moderate price) the various and increasing demands of a powerful and progressive country. But a great and general rise in the wages of labour would, as I have already observed, (in a short period, and before a new set of efficient labourers could spring up to supply the demand in the market), annihilate the very industry which first gave the impulse. Preventing the necessity of this great and general rise is therefore an obvious benefit, for it could only end in misery to the population which

the prospect of an increased demand for employment had called into existence. The general consequence, therefore, is to produce, really and truly,
the same rapid progress of commercial and manufacturing prosperity under a regular but moderate
rate of wages, as could only be contemplated in
theory as possible under the previous operation of
very high wages. Thus it appears, as the practical
result of the whole system, that the fluctuations
in price, so pernicious to industrious employers and
consumers, and the fluctuations in wages and employment, so pregnant with vice and misery to the
poor, which the ordinary oscillations of society and
of the employment of capital bring with them,
are completely avoided; and the supply, the demand,
and the employment of labour, together with the
well-being of the employer and the employed, and
the progress of public wealth and private comfort,
run in an uniform and equable current.

Experience however is much more convincing
than reasoning, how just soever it may appear; and
to prove that the arguments here advanced are
(*politically speaking*) not the mere wild effusions
of a theoretic mind, I would appeal to the fact, that
in a country where this system, (established indeed
for other purposes, and *once* more requisite for the
purposes of charity than of policy,) has been in
operation for two centuries, the population is not redundant. Industry and wealth have been constantly
advancing more rapidly than elsewhere, and the
wages of labour have nominally risen, but in reality have uniformly continued sufficient to enable
the common labourer in ordinary times to support
himself, his wife, and two children without assistance;

a rate which, I believe, is no where exceeded in a manufacturing country, and which may be conceived to be equally advantageous to the employer and the employed, where the difference can be made up to the parents of large families. For it enables the batchelor, or married man without a family, to lay by a portion of his earnings for old age, if he be frugal, and does not, by a superfluity of money, tempt him to extravagance or excess. It affords also to the man, who does not choose to rely upon the public for any part of the maintenance of his family, the means of saving, in early youth, enough to be independent of all foreign support in a late marriage; at the same time that the assistance held out to those who decline that abstinence, and prefer the comforts of matrimony, with the chance of dependance upon the laws for a part of their maintenance, enables the lower as well as the higher ranks to enjoy without public injury the free option of marriage, upon a fair consideration of their moral state. That these effects have been produced, without any moral deterioration of the character of the people, arising out of the principle of the laws, a long observation of their effects, made with an unbiassed mind, enables me to affirm, and will, I trust, appear from the work referred to in the following page. I beg, however, to observe that this is predicated of the LAWS themselves, not of the abuses or inconveniences which the lapse of time, the alterations in society, and a long course of neglect or mismanagement, may have introduced into their *execution*. That these, however, have not been very general or injurious, and have been much counteracted by the conservative regulation, which places the expenditure of the fund in the hands of those very persons from whose pockets it is taken, (with a power of appeal afforded to both parties against abuse,) I think will plainly appear, upon reference to the extent of the humane results actually arising from the operation of the laws. Into the detail of these I am not entitled to enter in this place, but beg to refer the reader to a former work of mine on that subject.*

The augmentation therefore of the people's happiness, which such a system brings in the relief of individual misery and the accession of individual comfort, without injury to public wealth, is another political advantage, for which the public might well be satisfied to pay a high price, although, in fact, it is gratuitously conferred. The extent of this advantage is nothing less than the difference of feeling in the whole population, arising from the consciousness on the one hand, that they may starve and rot for any care which the state will take concerning them, or, on the other, that no circumstance can preclude them from that reasonable share of assistance, to which all human creatures in distress are entitled, so far as it is possible to afford it.

Upon the whole, then, of this argument, it may perhaps appear, that laws of this description are not quite so arrogant or inhuman as they have been sometimes declared; and that the Abbé Montesquieu did not greatly err, either in policy or humanity, when he wrote the following passages. " In trading countries where many men have no other subsistence but from the arts, the state is frequently obliged to supply the necessity of the *aged,* the *sick,* and the

* See a Short Inquiry into the Policy, Humanity, and past Effects of the Poor Laws.

orphan." " Those alms which are given to a naked man in the streets do not fulfil the obligations of the state, which owes to every citizen a certain subsistence, a proper nourishment, convenient cloth- ing, and a kind of life not incompatible with health." " The riches of a state suppose great industry. Amidst the numerous branches of trade it is impossible but some must suffer, and consequently the mechanics must be in a momentary necessity. Whenever this happens, the state is obliged to lend them a ready assistance, whether it be to prevent their sufferings or to avoid a rebellion."—(Esprit des Loix, b. xxiii. chap. 29.)

If these sentiments are confessedly humane, the principle stated in the title of this chapter seems to prove that they are also politic, and, in a free country at least, perfectly practical, and by no means obnoxious, as hath been asserted, to the arrogance of implying that the produce of the earth can be multi- plied *ad infinitum*, upon the *dictum* of the legisla- ture. Nor can I conceive any plausible objection to their validity, until a country is arrived nearly to the utmost verge of its power of cultivation. It may indeed then be said, that to maintain a breeding stock, when the power of raising food is nearly ex- hausted, is calling them into existence only that they may die of penury. But this objection will, I think, disappear, when we recollect that before the land is cultivated to the utmost, the whole popu- lation of the country would *naturally* have arrived *at its point of non-reproduction*. Deficiencies, there- fore, which may eventually arise in the actual numbers, must be made up, in the first place, by the population *artificially* raised; deficiencies, let it be observed, likely to increase with every subsequent advance in the progress of society, and which would therefore gradually absorb all the surplus stock of people; for these again would be continually decreasing, from the difficulty of procuring residences, and from that minute attention of proprietors even to the smallest portion of land, which a very full state of cultivation would induce. I have indeed attempted to answer this objection more with a view to illustrate, in every possible manner, the principle under discussion, than from a conviction that it can ever practically apply. An extensive country absolutely cultivated to the utmost, having never been known to exist in times past, it would be scarcely expedient to regulate our policy by any such expectation in future. An objection, therefore, resting upon the assumption of such a probability, can never weaken the practical policy of any system otherwise admissible.

Many other particular applications of the principle, which forms the title of this chapter, might be made to the varying circumstances of the different conditions of society; but it will be recollected, that it is the fundamental principle of the whole treatise, and therefore connected with the three other propositions (see chap. iii.) whose application is the subject of the following chapters. In those chapters, therefore, which concern the second propositions, many *political* references will of course be made to this original principle. In those which concern the third and fourth propositions it will equally be applied for the purposes of *moral* illustration. I will therefore at present venture only briefly to suggest as general propositions, 1st, that whenever it shall appear, either from what may follow in the subsequent chapters of this treatise, or from any other deduction, that an increase of people is necessary to the further progress of a nation in wealth and prosperity; a statesman may not only give direct encouragements to population without danger, but will frequently be bound to afford them upon principles of sound policy : and 2dly, that whenever any moral or political object is thought to be desirable and justifiable, save in its probable tendency to increase population ; that tendency by no means forms a justifiable ground of exception against the pursuit of the object, but may frequently be even an additional recommendation.

I shall now conclude this chapter with the following extracts from Sir James Steuart's work on Political Economy. He appears to have obtained a clear insight into the difficulties in the way of a permanent progress in prosperity, which the deductions in this chapter propose to obviate : but his observation does not seem to have extended to a clear view of the remedy.

" In order to have a flourishing state, which Sir William Temple beautifully compared to a pyramid, we must form a large and solid basis of the lowest classes of mankind. As the classes mount in wealth, the pyramid draws narrower, until it terminate in a point, as in monarchy, or in a small square as in the aristocratical and mixed governments. The lowest class therefore must be kept up, and, as we have said, by its own multiplication. But where every one lives by his own industry, a competition comes in ; and he who works cheapest gains the preference. How can a married man, who has children to maintain, dispute this preference with one who is single? The unmarried therefore force the others to starve, and the basis of the pyramid is contracted. From this results the *principal cause of decay in modern states.*"* " Could a method be fallen upon to prevent competition among industrious people of the same professsion, the moment they come to be reduced within the limits of the *physical-necessary* (that is, the fair supply of the necessaries of life) it would prove the best security against decline in a modern state, and the most solid basis of lasting prosperity. But, as we have observed in the first book, the thing is *impossible* while marriage subsists on the present footing. From this one circumstance the condition of the industrious of the same profession is rendered totally different. Some are loaded with a family, others are not. The only expedient therefore for a statesman is to keep the general principles constantly in his eye, to destroy this competition as much as he can, at least in branches for exportation; to avoid in his administration every measure which may tend to promote it, *by constituting a particular advantage in favour of some individuals of the same class above others;* and if the management of publick affairs necessarily implies such inconveniences, he must find out a method of *indemnifying* those who suffer by the competition."†

Few writers in political economy have taken a more comprehensive view of the operations of society in its advanced stages than Sir James Steuart. He has here pointed, in very express terms, to an evil which he thought irremediable, and therefore *one of the principal causes of decay in modern states.* I

---

* Sir J. Steuart, Pol. Ec. b. i. c. xii.   † Ibid. b. ii. c. xxi.

leave it to the candid reader of this chapter to consider how far the remedy detailed in the preceding pages may obviate the difficulty, and whether a method has not at length been fallen upon for fulfilling those conditions, which Sir James Steuart thinks would "prove the best security against decline in a modern state, and the most solid basis of a lasting prosperity."

I cannot refuse my readers the pleasure they will derive from considering one other passage from the great work of this amiable and enlightened philosopher. It exhibits his opinion of the principle which ought to regulate all systems of compensation among the lower orders of mankind.

" We are next to inquire, how it happens that many industrious people are rivalled in an industry which brings no more than a bare *physical necessary*, (that is, the bare necessaries of life.) This must proceed from some disadvantage either in their personal or political situation. In their personal situation when they are *loaded with a numerous family*, interrupted by sickness or other accidental avocations:— In their political situation, when they happen to be under a particular subordination from which others are free, or to be loaded with taxes which others do not pay. I shall only add, that in computing the value of the *physical necessary* of the lowest denomination, a just allowance must be made for all interruptions of labour. No person can be supposed to work every free day; and the labour of the year must defray the expense. This is evident. Farther, neither humanity nor policy, that is, the interest of the state, can recommend a rigorous economy in this essential quantity." *

* Sir J. Steuart, Pol. Ec. b. ii. c. xxi.

CHAPTER II.

Application of the Second Principle: viz. that the Tendency of Population to keep within the Powers of the Soil to afford Subsistence CAN NEVER BE DESTROYED, *and can only be altered or diverted from its natural Course, so as to induce a mischievous Pressure of Population against the* actual Supply of Food, *by grossly impolitic Laws and Customs; either,* 1st, *accelerating the Progress of Population beyond its natural Rate; or* 2dly, *depressing Agriculture below its natural Standard.*

IN the preceding book of this treatise, it appeared evident, that at no period during the whole progress of society did population increase so fast as to exceed the means of subsistence, which the soil, under reasonable encouragement, was capable of affording; and that any unnatural interference with the progress either of population, or of agriculture, would be so far from producing any good effect, that, unless influenced by moral circumstances as in the case stated in the last chapter, it would only disarrange the order of society, prevent the further developement of its resources,. and remain a dead weight upon the national prosperity, until the inconvenience arising from the load should rouse the community to cast it off, and set itself free to resume the natural course. The interference with the natural progress of population by the poor laws of England, and by the negligent facility of the proprietors of Ireland, are respectively conclusive on this point : in the former case, being founded on moral expediency, it has led to a healthy advancement both in population and produce : in the latter case, being directly in opposition to every principle of moral good, it has promoted the increase of a vicious and useless population, and by leading to political dis- orders, has retarded rather than advanced the pro- gress of cultivation ; so that in both cases it has left the powers of the soil perfectly capable, under a rea- sonable system, of answering all the demands that may be made upon it. Now if, notwithstanding an interference with the natural order of things con- ducted on two such opposite principles, the tendency of population to keep within the powers of the soil is not DESTROYED, but continues as complete as when the natural order of things was preserved, I think we may fairly conclude that that tendency NEVER CAN BE DESTROYED. But further, since no record exists of any country cultivated up to the full extent of its productive powers, or within a great distance from that point, we may safely venture to affirm, that none ever did exist in that condition. It will indeed ap- pear almost impossible that such a condition should practically exist, if we reflect that the advance to- wards the highest stages of society, which by their artificial habits introduce a progressive abatement in the progress of population, have also a strong ten- dency to convert a considerable portion of the land to the production of the luxuries, rather than of the necessaries of life. In proportion as a community advances from the purely agricultural state, the higher ranks of society multiply, more of the produce of the land is consumed for purposes distinct from the

mere physical support of the people ; more land especially is converted into pasture, with a view both to
profit and to pleasure, and it is well known that its
power of supporting people is thereby considerably
diminished. The proposition may be worded thus :
A constant advance in civilization being necessary to
a corresponding progress in cultivation after the
purely agricultural state of society is passed, and the
same cause also progressively diverting more and
more of the products of the increased cultivation
from the bare support of the people, in consequence
of the introduction of artificial habits ; it follows that
at no point during the continuance of such a system
can the land be cultivated to its utmost point of production, or be incapable, by any alteration of system,
of affording food for a further increase of people. In
this point of view therefore it may be also said, that
the tendency of population to keep within the
powers of the soil *to afford it subsistence* CAN
NEVER BE DESTROYED. But this is exceedingly
far from proving, that an unlimited encouragement
to population may not, during some steps in the
progress, cause it to press *perniciously* against the
actual supply of food, and even against that which
can be conveniently supplied, consistently with preserving the artificial arrangements of society in its
advanced stages ; in other words, consistently with
good order and regular government in those states of
society. It should seem that something like a competition must be introduced between the luxuries of
the higher orders and the necessities of the lower, the
object of which is to induce the agriculturist to raise
a supply for the respective demands of each party. It
is not difficult to foresee on which side of the alterna-

tive the competition will be successful (in a free country at least,) in producing the supply; but to point out the precise mode in which the victory will be obtained for the supply of the people's wants is not altogether so easy a task. In what manner to secure a further supply of food from the soil, for the wants of a commercial and manufacturing population, has been at all times a problem very far removed from mathematical demonstration. There is indeed scarcely any question in political economy, concerning which wider differences of opinion have prevailed: but as the application of the principle treated in this chapter essentially depends upon its solution, it will be absolutely necessary to investigate it in this place. The readiest mode of conducting such an investigation seems to be by an inquiry into the order of precedence between population and the production of food. I have freely given my own opinion upon this subject, and have not hesitated to argue upon it in the preceding chapters, as proved by the plain and obvious conclusion, that no man, after agriculture ceases to be the most profitable employment of capital, will expend his money in raising an inferior produce at an increased expense, unless he is impelled thereto by an extraordinary demand for that produce from a previously increasing population. But it is becoming, that on a point so controverted by political economists, especially when so many of great name hold an opposite opinion, that an inquiry into the truth should be regularly pursued by examining the arguments on each side.

CHAPTER III.

An Inquiry into the natural Order of Precedence between Population and the Production of Food.

TO establish this order of precedence on either side by an invariable rule, applicable to all states of society, would be an attempt quite as desperate, and almost as wise, as to determine the famous question with respect to the comparative eligibility of a black or a bay horse for the commencement of a journey. If the respective condition of the animals, and not their colour, is the true criterion by which to determine the question as to any two particular horses, the condition of the people, and the state of society in which they may happen to be, will afford data no less conclusive, on which to settle the order of precedence between population and production, as to any particular community. The object is to ascertain the precise means by which population can be permanently encouraged, and food provided for it; or in more technical phraseology, whether agriculture be the efficient cause of the increase of population, or population of the increase of agriculture. On this subject different opinions have been entertained by the writers on political economy, each very much according with the view of the question taken by its author in connexion with the particular system of society with which he has been chiefly conversant. Such a result is natural, and gives just ground for concluding that a comparison of their various opinions, conducted upon more enlarged principles, may lead to a reasonable compromise.

I shall not enter at length into the question as it relates to the earlier stages of society; indeed it scarcely admits of doubt or dispute. Before the hunter, or the shepherd, or the savage tribe of the desert, will betake themselves to the labours of husbandry, they must of course be urged to the exertion by the pressure of want. This pressure can only arise from a population increasing beyond the scanty means of subsistence; population is clearly therefore in this case the efficient cause of agriculture. But to advance to periods more interesting to ourselves :— It is perfectly clear that the ends of all cultivation are to provide subsistence for the cultivator and his family, and to raise produce in exchange for other articles the products of industry. In this all agree : and therefore it may fairly be considered as an established position—that it is the pressure of the want either of food absolutely, or of those necessaries for which food can be exchanged, that is the efficient cause of cultivation in agricultural as well as in commercial countries. It is therefore clear, says one party, that population, either foreign or domestic, is the efficient cause of agriculture; because without a set of manufacturers distinct from the cultivators, those objects could not exist, the desire of which prompts the agriculturist to extend or improve his speculations. But, says the other side, it is equally clear that without a *previous supply of food*, foreign or domestic, this manufacturing population never could have existed, nor have been reared into a capacity for producing the objects of the agriculturist's wishes. Agriculture, moreover, being capable of raising a surplus produce beyond the bare support of the cultivators, does also actually afford this previous supply of food, which is so necessary. It is not to be disputed therefore that agriculture is the efficient cause of population.

Dr. Paley has very ably explained and elucidated the first of these opinions, in the eleventh chapter of the sixth book of his " *Moral Philosophy*," where he asserts, that it is the business of one part of mankind to set the other part at work; that is, to provide articles which, by tempting the desires, may stimulate the industry and call forth the activity of those, upon whose exertions the production of food depends. Now this is clearly assigning the order of precedence to population; and that such was Dr. Paley's object, appears further from the following passage. " I believe it is true, that agriculture never arrives at any considerable, much less its highest, degree of perfection, where it is not connected with trade; that is, where the demand for the produce is not increased by the consumption of trading cities. Let it be remembered, then, that agriculture is the immediate source of human provision; that trade conduces to the production of provision only as it promotes agriculture; that the whole system of commerce, vast and various as it is, hath no other public importance than its subserviency to this end." (Ed. 1774. vol. ii. p. 375.) Now as the consumption of trading cities and commercial communities arises from the wants of their great population, it is evident that upon this hypothesis the existence of the population can alone with propriety be termed the efficient cause of the increase of agriculture; and wherever the state of society supposed in the induction is found to exist, the reasoning appears quite incontrovertible.

Dr. Adam Smith has not entered largely into this question, though, in refuting the capital error of the French economists, he of course admits that the labour and industry of the inhabitants of towns considerably augments the cultivation of rude produce in the country; which is an indirect admission that the increase of people is the efficient cause of such augmentation. It is true that in another part of his great work he says, that the cultivation and improvement of the country, which affords subsistence, must necessarily be prior to the increase of the town; for it is the surplus produce of the country only, or what is over and above the maintenance of the cultivators, that constitutes the subsistence of the town, which can therefore only increase with the increase of this surplus produce. These propositions are certainly true, and they convince us very logically that before men can be *supported* food must exist, at least in sufficient quantity to furnish a bare subsistence. But when we consider that in a state of society involving the existence of large towns, the people is never maintained upon so short an allowance, and that it is not absolutely a demand for food only, but for a variety of other products of the soil, that encourages further cultivation, we must admit that the propositions above mentioned, true as they may be, are far from establishing any general principle respecting the order of precedence which naturally takes place in calling food and population into existence. In a subsequent passage, (b. iv. c. ix. vol. iii. p. 41.) he admits the justice of this reasoning, and illustrates it very happily in the following words: " Whatever tends in any country to diminish the number of artificers and manufacturers tends to diminish the home market, the most important of all markets for the rude produce of the land, and thereby to discourage agriculture. Those systems therefore which, by preferring agriculture to all other employments, in order to promote it impose restraints upon manufactures and foreign trade, act contrary to the very end which they propose, and indirectly discourage that very species of industry which they mean to promote. They are so far perhaps more inconsistent than the mercantile system. That system, by encouraging manufactures and foreign trade more than agriculture, turns a portion of capital from a more advantageous to support a less advantageous species of industry; but still it really encourages that which it means to promote. The agricultural systems, on the contrary, really, and in the end, discourage their own favourite species of industry." There cannot be a clearer admission, that in some cases at least population, arising from commerce and manufactures, is the efficient cause of agriculture.

Sir James Steuart, who is referred to by Mr. Malthus *as having mistaken this subject,* states his opinion to be, (b. i. c. 18.) that the industry of the *free hands,* that is, of the people not employed in agriculture, may make a quicker progress in multiplying mouths, than that of the farmers in supplying subsistence; which must cause either a further supply from the domestic soil, or importation of food from abroad. In illustrating this point, he takes occasion to propose the following question: Is multiplication the efficient cause of agriculture, or agriculture that of multiplication? and he answers that multiplication

AND THE PRODUCTION OF FOOD.   195

is the efficient of agriculture, because, as this last always raises a surplus produce, which proves a fund for multiplying inhabitants, there must be a demand for it from those who have an equivalent, (viz. other labour and its products,) to give in return. It is this equivalent which is the spring of the whole machine ; for without it the farmer will not produce any surplus. Now because it is the effectual demand which makes the husbandman labour for the sake of the equivalent, and because this demand increases by the multiplication of those who have an equivalent to give, therefore, says Sir James Steuart, multiplication is the cause and agriculture the effect. So that industry will produce numbers, and those numbers, industriously employed, will in their turn promote an advance in agriculture.

Notwithstanding the objections of Mr. Malthus, I confess that this reasoning, when applied to certain states of society, appears to me quite incontrovertible : but it is surely rather extraordinary to find Sir James Steuart, in a subsequent passage on the necessary connexion between manufacturing industry and agriculture, remarking that " the precedence between them is a matter of mere curiosity and speculation ;" whereas, as Mr. Malthus well observes, it tends to practical conclusions by far the most important that can be drawn from studying the effects of the principle of population : for if, as he asserts, it is necessary to the happiness of the community that, population should always be strictly repressed within the limits of a comfortable supply from *the existing food;* then undoubtedly, unless it be feasible to increase this supply without first creating a demand for it from an augmenting population, neither this nor agriculture can ever proceed a step further in advance. Whereas, if the multiplication of mouths, to the extent of dividing the existing supply of food among a somewhat larger number, by producing a greater demand for it and advancing its price, induces the husbandman to cultivate; then the further progress of the country in population and agriculture becomes easy: and since industry, enterprise, and progressive prosperity are the surest foundations of a people's happiness, or as Dr. Paley has it, constitute the healthy state of their political existence, it follows, that in some states of society, the *encouragement to population*, according to the arguments of this treatise, or according to Mr. Malthus, *the permission to extend itself* up to a gentle pressure against the actual supply of food, is as certain a method of strengthening those foundations, as the repression of the population within the limits of the existing supply from the soil, as distributed in the advanced states of society, is of undermining them.

Let us now turn to the arguments used by Mr. Malthus, to prove that a previous increase of food should always exist, before the people are allowed to multiply *up to it*. He begins by comparing the policy of those who hold opposite sentiments, even in the modified sense of the writers lately quoted, to the antient and exploded errors concerning specie, the abundance of which was held by the old political economists to be the *cause* instead of the *effect* of wealth, as population is now held in some cases to be the cause and not the effect of production. " So," says Mr. Malthus, " the annual produce of the land and labour became in both instances a secondary consideration, and its increase, it was conceived, would naturally follow that of specie in the one case, and of population in the other. Yet surely," he continues, "the prejudices with respect to population are the most absurd of the two ; for, however impossible in fact, one may *conceive means* by which a quantity of specie beyond the demand might be retained in a country ; yet when the population has once been raised to such a height, that the produce is meted out to each individual in the smallest portions that can support life, no stretch of ingenuity can ever conceive the possibility of going further."

This last limb of the comparison will evidently lose its strength if we refer once more to the facts established in the preceding pages :—1st, that population, as it advances towards a pressure against the surplus food of the agricultural state, so arranges itself as never to press against " *the smallest portions which can be meted out to each individual,*" but only against the comforts and luxuries of life : and 2dly, that every step in this advance introduces a corresponding abatement in the progress of population. It is therefore by no means necessary to exert any ingenuity in discovering a process by which the people may be fed, after a country is fully cultivated, and every portion of the food is meted out to the inhabitants so as barely to support the existence of each ; the predicament upon which this limb of the comparison rests for support cannot exist, and the limb itself must fail. With respect to the comparison, it may also be further remarked, that specie, as is well known, being merely a circulating medium, the mistake of the old economists lay in supposing that it constituted real riches, instead of being only the instrument by which riches are transferred from one person to another. The absurdity of their opinions therefore rests entirely upon the discovery since made, that the value of specie depends wholly upon its instrumentality. But how can this be made to apply to population? All are agreed that a healthy and increasing people do in fact constitute the *real riches* of a state; that their increase therefore is the absolute and essential object in all rational politics, whether it be caused by encouraging manufacturing industry, or by a further production of food. The ultimate *value* of population does not consist in being the mere *instrument* by which to raise an increased supply of the products of land and labour, but the value of these last depends chiefly upon the existence of a population in a state to consume them, and to pay for the labour bestowed. Population is therefore the ultimate object in one case, while specie is merely a temporary instrument in the other; and thus the other limb of the comparison appears to drop off, and the whole entirely fails.

If indeed population had been compared to *capital* instead of specie, a pretty close resemblance might have been shown in some of their intermediate operations. Capital is well known to be that which sets further industry in motion, and raises further annual products of land and labour. Its accumulation is one great object of all industry, and cannot but lead to further exertion by the demand it creates for employment. Increase it even by means foreign to domestic production, and you will soon perceive that a real increase of domestic industry and produce will follow. This has been fully proved by the effects of the capital brought of late years into England from the colonies and from the East. Although it was by no means the legitimate offspring of the land and labour of the country set in motion by former capital, but the profits of adventures, (often without capital,) made out of the land and labour of the opposite side of the globe, the demand created by it is no sooner brought into operation at home, than industry is immediately set to work to produce a corresponding supply. So an increase of population, proceeding at the rate in which it can be produced in any free and civilized country in the state of society in which it may happen to be, can always make an effectual demand upon the industry of others, by offering a portion of their own in return. By whatever means the increase was produced, however unconnected with any previous production of food, it will immediately, by its demand for food, set industry at work to procure it.

Mr. Malthus also observes, that all the countries, whose inhabitants were sunk in ignorance or oppressed by tyranny, were very populous in proportion to their means of subsistence, because ignorance and despotism do not destroy the sexual passion, though they effectually destroy industry, and consequently cultivation; and that they do moreover reduce a people to such a hopeless state of indigence as almost to destroy all spirit of exertion among them. All this may be very true; yet surely it is no proof that the pressure of population is not the efficient cause of further cultivation, although it may prove that the effect may be delayed by ignorance and oppression. Remove these, and the demand for food would be instantly supplied, and all the operations of society would proceed with their accustomed facility. Although population does in fact continue to press against the means of subsistence, yet the ultimate

cause is in the ignorance and tyranny complained
of, and can no more be said to be derived from the
population, than the relaxed spring of a clock gone
down can be said to be the ultimate cause of its not
performing its functions. The owner has nothing
more to do but to wind up the clock and the functions will be instantly resumed. His laziness then,
and not the condition in which that vice has placed
the spring, is certainly the ultimate cause of the
clock's default.

In the following paragraph Mr. Malthus admits,
sub modo, that an increase of population is absolutely
necessary to a further increase of annual produce.
But then it is said, that this is not the *natural*
order of progress; because " we know that multiplication has in numberless instances taken place,
which has produced no effect upon agriculture, and
has merely been followed by an increase of diseases."
" But perhaps," he continues, " there is no instance
where a permanent increase of agriculture has not
effected a permanent increase of population somewhere
or other." In the preceding paragraph, we have
certainly a notable instance in which multiplication
fails of its due effect in producing an increase of
agriculture, and is therefore followed by an increase of diseases; and I fully admit that an increased
cultivation can alone render an increase of people
permanent after the agricultural state of society is
passed. But these propositions constitute no proof
whatever, that the augmented population is not
naturally the efficient cause of the increase of cultivation. If the people, when born and reared, are forcibly prevented from exerting their industry to provide for themselves, and precluded from profiting

by the industry of others, their increase cannot of course be permanent. And wherefore? Because the *natural* effect of the demand they create is obviated by tyrannical interference. But if they are permitted and encouraged to exert themselves, the increase both of population and produce then becomes permanent; but the latter is evidently engendered by the former.

We have next an attempt to prove, that complaints for want of food cannot be justly founded even in a country where much good land remains uncultivated: because, it is said, the effect of uncultivated land operates merely as the possession of a smaller territory, and does not by any means alter the proportion between the food and the people. Now really this is something like saying that a starving people, with money in their pockets, would have no ground of complaint were a large granary full of imported corn locked up, and the key forcibly detained till the contents were spoiled, because it would operate *merely as the possession of a smaller quantity;* and that, never having been in the domestic market, it does not by any *means alter the proportion* between population and production. This sort of reasoning may be very just on the supposition that any tyrant, endowed with sufficient power, had entered into a fixed resolution that the waste land should *always remain* uncultivated; and such a check to the due course of society, and to the progress of his people's happiness, would be a very characteristic exercise of despotic authority. But if no unjust impediment be thrown in the way of agricultural improvement, it would be as impossible to prevent individual interest from " *altering the proportion between the food and the people,*" by augmenting the produce of the soil to answer an increased demand, as to enable any ingenuity to prove that such augmented produce would not stop the very reasonable complaints of the people for want of food.

It is next observed, that " no country has ever reached, nor probably ever will reach, its highest acme of cultivation ;" whence, I suppose, is meant to be inferred, that the continued pressure of population cannot for ever be met and obviated by a continued increase of cultivation. But it has been shown, in a former chapter, that the further pressure of population will be *prevented*, before any point at all approaching to this " highest acme of cultivation" could be arrived at, at least in all those countries with which Europeans are best acquainted ; because the people will have reached *their point of non-reproduction*, before the land has attained to its *ne plus ultra* of cultivation. If this be so, it is neither " the want of industry, nor the ill direction of that industry," which is the limit to a further increase in produce and population, nor yet " the absolute refusal of nature to produce any more." But the demand for further food gradually ceasing from the domestic population, at a time, when the staple of the land still remaining uncultivated is such, as to prevent any possibility of exporting its produce with a view to profit, there could be no possible inducement to a further extension of agriculture.

Mr. Malthus very justly observes, in conclusion, that, " with regard to the principle of population, it is never the question whether a country will produce *any more*, but whether it may be made to produce a sufficiency to keep pace with an *unchecked* increase of people. This is doubtless the true state of the question ; and if there be any truth in the

principles maintained in this treatise, the produce of
a country, tolerably well governed, can easily be
made to keep peace with an *unchecked increase of
people*, that is, with an increase left to its own
natural progress.   But it is impossible to agree in
the corollary drawn by Mr. Malthus from this question as containing synonymous expressions ; "that in
England it is not the question whether, by cultivating all our commons, we could raise considerably more corn than at present; but whether we
could raise sufficient for a population of 20,000,000
in the next 25 years, of 40,000,000 in the next
50 years," and so on.   For we have seen, to a demonstration, that in the state of society now existing
in England, or, as it could by any possibility be
made to exist, these periods of doubling are altogether visionary and theoretic.

Such are the opinions of the principal political
economists with respect to the important question
treated in this chapter, with the observations
to which they have given rise.   Upon considering
them, it will occur to every reflecting mind, that
there is one circumstance strongly militating against
the opinion of those, who contend that agriculture is,
in all cases, the efficient cause of population.   It is,
that not one of those writers can point out, or has
made any satisfactory attempt to show, in what
manner a further extension of agriculture can be
made, after the commercial state of society is entered
into, by any other means than by a demand for produce from an increased number of mouths.   They
have contented themselves with saying that such
should be the policy, without ever adverting to the
practical impossibility of adopting it.   But surely a

more absurd and unpromising attempt can scarcely be imagined, than for a government to undertake to force the cultivation of inferior land, before an increased demand for its produce should render the employment profitable. It is quite ridiculous to talk of bounties upon the export of corn in such a case. They are altogether inadequate to the purpose in the advanced states of society. For since the foreign market is always supplied from countries in the purely agricultural state, where good land can be had cheap, a successful competition can never be carried on by another country where only inferior land is to be procured, and that at a high price. When to this is added the freight, which must also rise in proportion to the price of provisions in the home market, it seems absolutely impossible, consistently with common prudence, to grant a bounty upon the export of corn high enough to counterbalance such disadvantages.

That bounties upon export, and other encouragements to agriculture, may retard the diversion of capital to mercantile and manufacturing purposes to a later period, and encourage the cultivation of soils of a staple inferior to what would otherwise have been attempted, is probable : and it may be doubted whether every expense so incurred has not been a very useless and unnecessary waste of money ; for if capital can at such periods be more profitably employed in commerce and manufactures, we may rest assured, that the population thus produced will soon make it the interest of individuals to divert a portion of their capital to the land. But that bounties upon export can ever permanently encourage the cultivation of bad land, or any other agricultural speculation affording small returns, before there is an immediate and pressing domestic demand for the produce, is too untenable a proposition to deserve a serious answer.

———

I have now traced, (and, notwithstanding the extreme importance of the subject, I fear at almost too great a length), the various and conflicting opinions of political economists, with respect to the order of precedence between agriculture and population. I shall devote a few remaining paragraphs to an attempt to draw out a consistent system by reconciling, as far as possible, their contending arguments; and am disposed to think it will appear that, by overlooking the change which takes place in the interests and habits of the people as society advances, each writer has endeavoured to apply *universally* what, from the nature of the case, can only be of very *partial* application. There are, probably, periods in the progress of society, in which every proposition enunciated by each of the economists I have cited may be respectively true. But from the want of discriminating those periods, they have persevered in applying to one condition what is only true of another; and, by an attempt to establish a *general* principle, have exceedingly confused their argument, and fallen into many *particular* absurdities. There is a period in a man's life, when it is superlatively true that he ought to be sent to school, another when he should go to college, another when he should enter into a profession, and another when he should enjoy his ease with dignity; but it would be a very singular consequence to generalize any

one of these propositions, and to assert that he should
enter into a profession at twelve, go to college at thirty,
and be whipped at school in his grand climacterick.
But to resume the attempt to draw out a consistent
system from the contending arguments.

It appears, in the first place, that so long as a
country remains in the agricultural state of society,
that is, so long as agriculture continues to afford the
most profitable employment of capital, that department of industry will, with very few exceptions and
qualifications, be the efficient cause of all increase
in the domestic population;—and 2dly, as soon as
the best lands are appropriated, and commerce and
manufactures become the most profitable employment of capital, then *they* will be the efficient cause
of population;—and 3dly, from the demand created
by this population, must spring all further supply
of food from the soil.

To prove these propositions we must observe
generally, that the state of employment, or the demand for hands, is naturally the only criterion of
the numbers which, when called into existence, can
be reared to manhood and permanently supported.
Industry is consequently the main efficient cause of
population in all states of society. Nor does it by
any means appear so certain, as has been sometimes
declared, that the demand for hands will always be in
proportion to the actual supply of food. Where
great prospects are opening for an extensive increase
of commerce, of manufactures, of exportation; where
large capitals gained abroad are brought home to
set industry in motion in the parent country; or
great supplies of men for the army, navy, or foreign
colonies, are necessary to the welfare of the state;

it is evident that a great demand for additional hands will exist, whatever may be the actual supply of food. The demand for labour being derived indifferently from all the sources of industry, and population being regulated by that demand; it seems only necessary to inquire in what department of industry the principal demand for labour exists, in order to determine what species of it is the efficient cause of the increase of population. The answer to this in agricultural countries will evidently be agriculture; in commercial and manufacturing countries, commerce and manufactures: and we shall plainly perceive upon consideration that this is agreeable to the fact.

In those countries where the demand for labour is principally from the land, and its remuneration drawn from agricultural profits, the children, from generation to generation, are bred up in the occupation of farmers, and their sustenance is derived immediately from the objects of their labour. This simplifies the operation of society so much, that there is no room for doubt or mistake as to the efficient cause of population.

But as society advances, the question becomes more complicated. In a commercial and manufacturing country, however, it is still evident that almost all the increased remuneration of labour, or the fund from which the labourer is enabled to rear a family, is drawn from profits derived from commerce and manufactures. But the products of their industry do not immediately afford sustenance to the labourer as in the former case, but are necessarily exchanged for food. For some time after the agricultural state of society is passed, the quantity of surplus produce created by it is the fund upon which the

merchant and manufacturer draw for their subsistence; but it is their commerce and manufactures
which give them an effectual claim to it, and from
which therefore their support is actually derived; for
if they could not assert this valid claim to their share
of the surplus produce, it would certainly be exported
to a foreign market. Agriculture therefore, even
in this early period of the commercial system, has
no greater share in calling human beings into existence and enabling their parents to rear them, than
any other department of human industry. If this
admits of any exception, it is, that while the surplus
produce raised in the agricultural state continues
unexhausted, its existence, previous to the demand made upon it by the manufacturing population, may somewhat keep down its price, especially
if there be no active demand for it from abroad.
But when once population has overtaken this
quantity of surplus produce, then agriculture and
other employments stand precisely upon the same
footing, as to their effects upon population. The
former can no more be exclusively called the efficient
cause of it, than shoemaking, weaving, dyeing, or
any other exertion of industry that supplies a man
with objects to exchange against the necessaries of
life. Nor will any more corn be grown till an
effectual demand arises for it from some other department of industry, and some of these objects of exchange are presented to the notice of the cultivator.

The *proof*, then, of the three propositions, with
which I began my statement of this interesting
question, may be thus condensed.

1st, In the agricultural state of society, agriculture is the efficient cause of population, because the

demand for labour and its remuneration are derived
principally from that employment.

2dly, After a country has stepped out of the agricultural into the commercial system, but has not
yet increased its population sufficiently to consume
the surplus produce remaining from the agricultural
state, commerce and manufactures are the efficient
cause of population, because from them is now derived the demand and remuneration of labour. Population, however, is not yet the efficient cause of
any increase in agriculture, because a previous supply
of food already exists, and until that is exhausted
little more will be raised. Population therefore
cannot be the efficient cause of an effect which does
not take place.

But, 3dly, As soon as the commercial progress of a
country has increased its population, so far as to
consume all the surplus produce existing at the
period of its first emergence from the agricultural
state ; then commerce and manufactures do not
only constitute the efficient cause of population,
but this last is the sole efficient cause of all further
production of food, because the land remaining uncultivated is of such a quality, that an effectual demand upon it can only be made by the pressure of
domestic population against the actual supply.

These seem to be the grand outlines of the truth
upon this interesting question, though, from the
complicated nature of society in all its advanced
stages, and the irregularities introduced by the
mistaken principles of political economy upon which
most nations have occasionally been conducted, it
may be sometimes difficult to trace its progress, and
a few modifications may, in fact, be admitted.

Notwithstanding the general truth of the first proposition, for example, it may be observed that many simple manufacturing employments exist in the early stages of society, which have their proportionate share in the production of population : so that, in a modified sense, it may be asserted even here that population is the efficient cause of part of the existing agriculture ; because it is certain that, unless there were a demand for the produce somewhere beyond the bounds of the farm, little or no surplus would be raised. A demand is also frequently made from foreign countries. Their population therefore may likewise, *in some measure,* be called the efficient cause of agriculture in the country exporting the supply. These modifications, however, do not affect the general truth of the first proposition, and are not of much practical importance.

On the second proposition it may be briefly observed that, as artificial encouragements or discouragements to agriculture may advance or retard the period of a country's transition to the commercial state of society, so the removal of those artificial impediments, at any period after the step has been taken, may give a temporary start or depression to agriculture, and either retard or advance the arrival at that point when the commercial and manufacturing population shall have absorbed all the surplus produce previously existing. Thus, for example, should a country, from peculiar circumstances, such as seem to have influenced the United States of America, have commenced its commercial career before all its best lands are brought under cultivation, (which may be called the natural period of that change,) the removal of those circumstances, or small artificial encouragements to agriculture, will induce the capitalist again to prefer land to commerce for a time, and the country will revert for that period to the agricultural state of society, or rather will vacillate between the agricultural and commercial states: this will *retard* its arrival at that point where the augmented population shall have consumed the whole surplus produce. Again, artificial discouragements to agriculture will divert a portion of the capital to commerce for a period, and thus hasten the arrival of the people at the abovementioned point. But these vacillations will not affect the fundamental truths contained in the second proposition, nor the practical conclusions to be drawn from them. It may be observed too, that they are almost always injurious to the political interests of a country. I have little doubt that the late interruptions to the commerce of the United States of America have added to their solid strength, and given a fresh impulse to the progress of their population, by diverting more capital to their extensive soil ; and that they have thereby subtracted somewhat from the interval of time which must yet elapse, before they fill that commanding station in the western hemisphere, and in the naval and commercial enterprise of the world, to which they so ardently aspire.

On the third proposition we may observe, by way of qualification, that the importation of food, which is occasionally brought into commercial countries, will naturally impede the encouragement afforded by increasing population to domestic production. The population will then perform the same office towards the agriculture of a less advanced state, which the population of one more advanced formerly acted towards the country in question, when it was itself in the agricultural state. The imported food, being grown in plenty where good land is cheap, may appear capable, notwithstanding the freight, of underselling in the home market that of domestic growth on inferior land. But the skill, the capital, the superior industry, and the economical improvements in the mode of cultivation, which always attend the application of commercial capital to the soil, joined to the natural wish of all monied men to possess land, will usually be sufficient, for some time at least, to counteract the superior cheapness at which imported corn is raised in the country of its growth. And when the natural disadvantages can be no longer thus counterbalanced, but are in danger of too far reducing the profits, and consequently of checking the further progress of domestic agriculture; *then*, AND NOT BEFORE, government should interfere by protecting duties, and restore things to their proper level. For it should never be forgotten by the inhabitants of a country of extensive territory, that imported corn, however secure its arrival may usually be, should never be depended upon, but as a temporary instrument for supporting those, whose demand for food should ultimately elicit a further advance of domestic cultivation. It appears then that, notwithstanding these qualifications, the three propositions above stated are generally true, and may lead to practical conclusions of the greatest importance.

I trust also that the arguments, by which they have been supported, are sufficient to establish the truth of the fifth proposition to which I stand

pledged in this treatise :* viz. " That in the alternate progress of population and subsistence, in the
earliest as well as in the most advanced stages of
society, a *previous* increase of people is necessary to
stimulate the community to a farther production of
food, and consequently to the healthy advancement
of a country in the career of strength and prosperity:" together with the consequence derived from
it ; viz. " That the pressure of population against
the *actual* means of subsistence, or, more correctly
speaking, the excess of population *just beyond the
plentiful supply of the people's wants*, instead of
being the cause of most of the miseries of human
life, is in fact the cause of all public happiness, industry, and prosperity."

* See book i. c. iii.

CHAPTER IV.

Of the mischievous Pressure of Population caused by accelerating its Progress considerably beyond the natural Rate.

HAVING in the last chapter established the order of precedence between food and population in the several states of society, it is now time to revert to that part of the second fundamental principle of this treatise, which relates to the causes by which population is made to press mischievously against the actual supply of food: and first, of that which is derived from encouraging the progress of population considerably beyond its natural rate. I endeavoured to show, in the first chapter of this book, that *not every* encouragement by which population is increased beyond the natural rate will necessarily lead to a mischievous pressure, but that cases may occur in which it is attended with circumstances leading to great positive good. But a general rule may perhaps be laid down, by which to distinguish the probable effect that would follow in all cases, excluding for the present all moral considerations. It may I think be safely asserted, that, wherever a corresponding encouragement is afforded to industrious exertion, either by fortuitous circumstances or by the act of government, there the progress of population may safely be encouraged beyond its natural rate, and *vice versá.*

We have seen also, that in free and regular governments, in the advanced states of society, the in-

crease of population cannot be very rapidly accelerated, and is itself one of the most powerful encouragements to the further exertion of industry on the
soil; and that in the *less advanced* states of society
there is always a surplus produce of food; consequently the whole population cannot generally press
either mischievously or otherwise against the total
supply of food. These considerations should seem
to reduce the subject of the present chapter within
very narrow bounds, unless we encroach upon the
third and fourth fundamental principles of this treatise, which embrace the moral part of the subject.
Important objects, however, may still be comprised
under this head; for there are certainly methods in
the earlier stages of society, by which population is
encouraged without any reference to industrious exertion, and consequently where the pressure of a
part of the people against *their* means of procuring
subsistence produces much individual want and misery, although the whole population may not press
against the total supply of food.

The following case may be stated for an example:
Even in the advanced stages of the agricultural state
of society, great carelessness is apt to prevail respecting the appropriation of small portions of inferior
land. It appears at first sight indifferent to the possessor of an hundred acres of good land with hands
enough to cultivate it, what becomes of seven or
eight detached acres of inferior and neglected soil
lying round the corners of his hedges. But let us
suppose seven or eight miserable hovels erected upon
these acres, the land converted into potatoe gardens,
and each maintaining half a dozen human beings, for
whose labour the condition of society, (according to

the principles on which it should be conducted,) offers no demand ; and he will begin to lament too late that his indifference to the neglected portion of his property has permitted such a nuisance to grow up upon it. Let us suppose the prevalence of this system general in a country, and its government will presently discover that its duties towards the people have been grossly neglected. It by no means follows that the population thus reared would tend to encourage industry by lowering the price of labour, (as they certainly would do had they their labour only to depend upon for procuring the means of subsistence ;) because in the case supposed, the produce of the land attached to the cottage is sufficient to afford a subsistence compatible with idleness. This removes the necessity of that mutual dependance between the employer and the employed, so essential to good order in every community. The care and observation of the higher orders is entirely removed from the lower; and the natural consequence of *such* a state of disconnexion between them, (notwithstanding all the fine sentiment concerning the advantages of independence among the lower orders,) has always been found practically to lead to vice and insubordination. It would be strange indeed if uncontrolled and unmitigated ignorance could end in other results. The first generation of these interlopers therefore will scarcely be reared, when either property will become insecure, the laws set at nought, and violence become prevalent; or a system of severity must be adopted in the practice of the government abhorrent to all rational liberty, and finally aggravating rather than allaying the symptoms of the disease. For in these kinds of contests the government is always ultimately defeated; in the long run severity wears itself out against so dense a body of resistance. When the government is overcome, the proprietors, who come into immediate contact with the danger and the evil, have little chance of success. They can only palliate for a time by submission. Their sturdy neighbours may be induced to assume the character of tenants without the feelings of that condition; and all the disorder, idleness, and profligacy of the feudal system, (without even its limited subordination to the immediate superior,) will be introduced into a society having no fair claim to them. But this palliation is merely temporary, and must necessarily end in further aggravation; for the children of the immediate possessors will enforce their demand of a settlement by the same cogent reasons which their fathers found successful. If waste land of a good staple beyond the limits of cultivation had still existed to be occupied, as in North America, these applicants would be a blessing rather than a curse to their country. But if, as in Ireland, the mass of the land is appropriated, what resource is there but, either, that they be left to starve, or that further portions of the land already cultivated be allotted to the claimants, till employment can be found for them in regular departments of industry foreign to the soil. But in such a condition of society it is to be feared that the establishment of manufactures would offer no resource for the employment of the superfluous hands.

The want of subordination, and the insecurity of property incident to the system, will more than counterbalance the natural effect of the cheapness of labour, in tempting the capitalist to turn his

views to manufactures. The immense surplus of
hands in the uncivilized parts of Ireland has scarcely
tempted a single capitalist to transfer his industry to
those devoted regions. There appears therefore to
be no probable result, but a continued contest between the pressure of severity in the government
against the people, and that of misery in the people
against the government; between the outcry of a
depressed and starving population, and the fears of
a proprietory prevented in all its legitimate views towards the accumulation of capital. A more deplorable
picture of society, a condition more devoid of hope,
a state of political darkness more impervious to a
single ray of light, can scarcely be imagined. Yet
it is impossible to deny that a mischievous encouragement of population, beyond its natural rate of progress, is, at least, the immediate cause of the evil.
If either the proprietors had used more precaution
in preventing their waste lands from being settled by a
race whose labour was surperfluous in the place of
their settlement, or if the government could have
found the means of opening sources of industrious
employment for their children, in situations where
the abatement in the progress of population, natural
to the advancement of society, could have had its fair
operation; none of the evils just recited would probably have occurred: for the individuals, instead
of multiplying in miserable hovels, devoid of all
concern and taste for the comforts and decencies
of life, would have been drawn off from their
native villages, for the regular supply of the
mercantile and manufacturing towns, or for the
other departments of industry. I think it may be
safely affirmed that the general spread of such a

population, as is here reprobated, over the face of a country, can only be the result of a long course of misgovernment and of misdirection of public industry, and that it is a reproach to any nation. A few individuals might have so settled in particular districts, wholly through the apathy and neglect of the proprietors; but a general system of the kind argues something worse than neglect or apathy on the part of the government.

Upon investigating the foundation therefore of this unnatural encouragement to population, we find that it resolves itself into misconduct on the part of the government and the proprietors of land, and ignorance and evil customs on the part of the people.

The remedy, to be effectual, must be gentle and slow in its operation; for the task is nothing less than to correct the sturdy prejudices, and to alter the inveterate habits of a numerous population. A gradual elevation of the religious and moral character of the natives; the introduction of a taste for the comforts and decencies of life; laws enlisting the self-interest of the proprietors to second these philanthropic objects, and to prevent the further progress of the evil, by charging them with the support or employment of the superfluous population which they encourage to grow up under their eye; these, joined with enlightened measures for the promotion of domestic industry, and honourable distinctions conferred on those, who are zealous and active in devoting their time and talents to the amelioration of their country, would in the course of time operate a happy change, and in some degree atone for the long neglect which had diverted a portion of the people from their just and legitimate functions in the commonwealth, and encouraged them to produce a race of human beings which can only be contemplated as a dead weight in the scale of society.

Let it be observed, however, that this superfluous population does not press even against the actual supply of food, of which, by the supposition, there is still a surplus produce; for the country must be yet in the agricultural state of society to engender such a nuisance, or at least not far enough advanced from it to have consumed its surplus produce, and render inferior land valuable. But the idle and listless beings, who have been called into existence, can make no valid claim to any share of this produce, (which will still be exported) but are miserably subsisting on the produce of their own potatoe garden. Great quantities of corn were, till very lately, exported even from those very parts of Ireland where the wretched and starving cotters are most numerous and most miserable. A population of this description, therefore, is a mere excrescence on the body politic, which might be eradicated to its great relief, could the operation be performed without infringing upon the laws of humanity, or endangering the system. But since it would be too severe for the humanity of the faculty to advise, and too difficult for the skill of any operator to perform, the only remaining resource is to try the method of absorption, slow and tedious as the process may be, and largely as it may draw upon the patience of the subject.

It will be perceived that a picture, not very dissimilar to what has been here exhibited, would soon be produced by the general extension of a system of charity often recommended by benevolent individuals, who suppose that the condition of the people would be materially ameliorated by building cottages on all waste lands, and endowing them with portions of land, large enough to support the tenants. That such schemes of charity in a few instances, and carefully superintended by sagacious proprietors, have produced much individual happiness I rejoice in believing. But any general prevalence of the system would doubtless lead to all the inconveniences detailed in the preceding pages, because it would increase the population, without augmenting the demand for labour by depressing its price.

Throughout the whole of this chapter, I have constantly borne in mind, that in a free and Christian country every human being born within its limits will by some means or other be supported : and it is the method by which this support is bestowed that renders the competition between the necessities of the lower orders, and the superfluities of the higher, alluded to towards the close of the second chapter of this book, available in favour of the former. The ordinary fluctuations of employment in such a country will always keep up a sufficient number of distressed persons to establish that competition in full vigour. To destroy it, by turning the balance wholly on the side of the necessitous, would be ruinous to industry, and would prevent all accumulation of capital. The utmost vigilance should therefore be exercised by the proprietors of a country not to suffer the natural operations of society to be impeded, by permitting a population to settle itself upon their estates, for whose employment there will probably be no demand. The best mode of effecting this appears to be to keep the number of tenements, as nearly as possible, within those limits which will only accommodate the persons, whose labour is wanted in the district where they are born, together with their families. All the *parents* will then be industrious. The system of charity, alluded to in the first chapter, may then be applied to such of these families as are too numerous to be supported by the average rate of the parents' labour, that the children may be reared for the supply of those districts which do not keep up their effective population; but no useless hands will permanently remain a burthen upon the proprietors, absorbing their profits without any return to them or to the country : and the competition between the necessities of the poor and the superfluities of the rich will be maintained at the point most favourable to the exercise of enlightened charity, and to the accumulation of capital to be applied in opening further resources of industry. As these are developed, more tenements will be of course erected, because a larger supply of hands will be wanted. But the consequent increase of the people will be sound and healthy, because no *parents* will exist, whose labour is not generally wanted in the places of their residence ; nor any children be reared, who will not ultimately be turned to account, either in replacing their parents, in emigrating to places where their services are required, or in occupying new stations of industry in the places of their birth.

The reader's mind may perhaps be prepared, by the considerations offered in this chapter, to admit the validity of a principle, which I am strongly disposed to consider as of universal application, viz. that the only methods by which the progress of population can be *mischievously* advanced beyond *its natural rate,*

are by neglecting to promote, or by violently interfering with the morals and the industry of the people.
So long as these are duly fostered, and permitted to
have their free course, all the natural causes of abatement in the progress of population, and the natural
encouragements to the production of food, will be
successively introduced as society advances : but if
the influence of morality, or the current of industry
be checked, either by permitting the introduction of
idle and licentious settlers, or by any other means,
these salutary principles can of course be no longer
operative ; the stream will be choked up, and a
loathsome vermin will pullulate in the filth and mud
of the overloaded channel.

I do not mean to imply, that mankind will permanently proceed in multiplying its numbers where
there is a total stagnation of industry—quite the
contrary ; but their habits will then permit them to
approach much nearer to that point, where the food is
meted out to each in the smallest possible portions
that can support existence. To that extent therefore population will be encouraged, and in a mischievous and unnatural manner ; that is, in a manner
contrary to the ordinary course of society, and the
evident designs of Providence ; nor will any thing
check its progress but the violent pressure of human
misery against the means of subsistence.

In confirmation of this argument, I would, in addition to the facts referred to in this chapter, confidently
appeal to the details in the first book of this treatise
respecting Spain, China, and the South Sea Islands,
and to the observation of any one who will take the
trouble to investigate the condition of the people in any
declining country.

Should any one be disposed to object, that the arguments of this chapter are in opposition to those in the first chapter of this book, recommending under certain circumstances an artificial acceleration in the increase of the people; I would observe, in reply, that it is with a view to the different periods, in which the increase of people takes place, that I deprecate that contemplated in this chapter : and I do so upon these grounds—1st, that the quality of the population raised under the former system will be of a superior stamp, both in healthiness and industry; and 2dly, that the increase is uniform in its operation, and particularly applicable to those periods in the progress of society when its effects are most wanted; namely, the commercial and manufacturing periods, in which alone any large sums can ever be wanted for the charitable support of numerous families. Whereas the population, raised under the system deprecated in this chapter, will be most numerous when it is least wanted; namely, towards the end of the agricultural, and the early stages of the commercial states of society. It is also irregular and uncertain in its progress and numbers, and consequently in quality the most remote that can well be conceived from any fitness for the purposes of regular industry. I consider this difference as a signal instance of the distinction, which Providence has placed, between the production of similar effects by moral and immoral means. When an enlightened charity constitutes the motive and the object of the act, as in the poor laws of England, Providence overrules the effect so as to produce indeed an increase of people, but a still greater increase of industrious employment. Where an indolent apathy permits encroachments and irregularities, as in the cases stated in this chapter, the effect is indeed likewise an increase of population, but a much greater increase of idleness, vice, and misery. The causes of the disorders of states are manifold; but if they could all be traced to their origin, I believ that the seeds of a very large proportion of them would be found in the idle and licentious habits of such an extraneous and neglected population, as it is the object of this chapter to deprecate.

We are then again conducted to the important conclusions to which every preceding part of this inquiry tends—that industry is the legitimate parent, and the firm supporter, of population, as well as the natural regulator of its quantity and quality; and that when thus produced and regulated it can never *mischievously* press against the means of its subsistence. That the industry here spoken of (when taken in its enlarged sense) includes and supposes a due attention to the moral condition of the people is of course implied, and will be more fully shown when we come to consider the two last of the fundamental principles laid down at the outset of this treatise.

CHAPTER V.

Of the mischievous Pressure of Population, caused by depressing the productive Energies of the Soil considerably below its natural Powers.

IT is obviously true, that the natural powers of the soil to afford a further supply of produce vary with every advance of a country in the progress of society. In the agricultural state, that is, before all the rich lands are appropriated and brought into cultivation, the powers of the soil are great, and capable of affording a considerable supply of produce at a comparatively small expense in cultivation. In the commercial and manufacturing state, that is, when the lands remaining unappropriated and waste are of inferior staple, and commerce and manufactures are consequently the most profitable employment of capital, the natural powers of the soil are gradually contracted, and can only afford a further supply of produce at a continually increasing expense in cultivation.

That the expense of bringing waste land under cultivation continually increases with the advance of society and population, will be evident if we consider the gradation as to quality, in which lands, generally speaking, are reclaimed. Those of superior staple, which will pay best, are of course reclaimed the first, and so on, in succession of inferiority, till at last none but the most barren and ungrateful spots are left waste. Municipal laws, and the rights of property, will of course introduce trifling irregularities in the

march of this system, but as men may usually be depended upon for following their own temporal interests,
it may be argued upon in general as regular and un-
remitting. The necessary consequence then of this
progressive recurrence to inferior soil is that, at each
succeeding step, the cultivator has to grapple with a
more ungrateful subject, and must therefore incur an
increased expense in rendering it productive ; and
that nothing but the certain prospect of being remunerated for that expense in the price of the produce
will induce him to undertake the task.

It follows from these facts, that the very same circumstances, which in the first case may afford ample
encouragement to the productive energies of the soil,
may in the last depress them very considerably below their natural powers ; for as the only encouragement to produce any article is to be found in the
profit accruing from it, after all the expenses of production are paid, it is obvious that, when these expenses are high, they cannot be compensated by the
same encouragements which may have proved fully
sufficient while the expenses continued low.

It is obviously true also that, where the public institutions of a country are of a liberal and expensive
nature, and the land and its products are highly
taxed to support them, these expenses must also
be added to that more immediately incidental to cultivation, before we can determine what will actually
encourage or depress the productive energies of the
soil. A community, for example, which from the
profits expected from its agriculture engages to support establishments for the religious instruction, the
moral education, and when necessary for the charitable support of its people, or which has entered

into an agreement with monied capitalists to pay them a portion of produce by way of interest for capital advanced, will of course discover that all these expenses must be added to those arising from the natural condition of the soil before a fair balance can be struck. What may constitute a fair encouragement therefore to the agriculture of a country shrinking from any of these undoubted and imperative duties or necessary engagements, may yet considerably depress that of another which performs them, even although both countries may be found to have reached, in other respects, the same point in the progress of society.

Again, it is obviously true that where the condition of a country is found to be on the *expensive* side of all these alternatives; that is, where it has both advanced far into the commercial and manufacturing systems, has incurred a public debt, and has also established liberal and expensive institutions for the comfort, happiness, and morality of its people, to be defrayed from the produce of its soil, the foundations of its agricultural prosperity are completely different from those of other countries, where no such conditions of society exist. Still greater encouragement will be necessary, in such a country, to prevent the depression of the natural powers of the soil, than where only one or two of those extraordinary sources of expense exist: and this is perfectly fair. It is impossible for a nation, any more than for an individual, to enjoy the advantages of an expensive establishment without defraying the cost. It is dishonest to set up such an establishment without the means of paying for it; and it is equally unmanly and inconsistent, having once established it upon a fair estimate of means, and reaped the expected advantages, to shrink from the necessary payments, or to envy those nations who have been willing to forego the comforts, or to desert the duties, in consideration of escaping *the expense.* In short, it is as vain as it is childish, at once to grasp at the advantages of riches, and to long for the disincumbrance of poverty.

If these reflections are just, we shall at once perceive that, to avoid the evils arising from depressing the productive energies of the soil below its natural powers, the application of general principles will scarcely be sufficient. A particular inquiry into the state of society, in which the country in question may happen to exist, is as necessary here as in estimating the force of the principle of population : and in the adoption of any practical measures a knowledge of the state of surrounding countries is equally important. For, practically speaking, it cannot be doubted that in a large society of nations it is impossible to rely upon each individual nation, or even upon a majority of them, for a constant adherence to general principles ; especially on questions of vital interest to their neighbours, who are, I fear, almost necessarily their rivals. No man can be more ready than myself to admit, that general principles, when universally adhered to, are the best foundations of individual policy, because they constitute the best security of individual as well as of general prosperity : but, as I have elsewhere taken the liberty to remark, " the science of political economy, being a set of conclusions drawn from general principles, is of course intended for general application. It is presupposed that all the nations concerned in any question involving those principles will fully act up to them, because it is their interest to do so; or if any particular nation refuse so to act, that it will suffer for the deviation to the advantage of the rest. This supposition, in ordinary times and cases, or in times the same as when the principles of the science were laid down, is perhaps correct, and may often have been justified by the event; but the case is very much altered when the ordinary systems of policy are completely overthrown by extraordinary causes." Now I think it will be found in practice, that the prospect of ruining or materially injuring a rival nation has always been considered a cause sufficiently *extraordinary* to justify a departure from general principles, even under a full acknowledgment of their use and advantage in ordinary times: at least, I am sure that any nation which should venture to rest the fundamental principles of its political system upon a contrary expectation would wilfully place itself in great and imminent jeopardy.

Fully admitting therefore the theoretical expediency of general principles on the subject before us, and that, according to every fair conclusion to be drawn from them, population would not necessarily press to a mischievous degree against the means of subsistence, although the natural powers of the domestic soil were insufficient to afford those means, because food might be purchased by the products of the people's industry from other countries where the powers of the soil are sufficient; yet this admission is by no means conclusive of the question: for the reasons above mentioned, the temptations which such a state would afford to the hostility of rival nations is so great, the effects which would be actually produced by depriving any considerable portion of the people of their accustomed means of subsistence, are in truth so dreadful, that nothing short of absolute necessity can justify a great and extensive country in submitting to a permanent dependance upon imported food.   But if the natural tendency of population to increase be not abated as society advances in its progress, but retain (as it is asserted to do) all its original vigour, even in the highest stages of its progress, and when the productive powers of the soil are necessarily very limited, it is evident that this absolute necessity of a permanent dependance upon imported food must at length occur; the idea of ultimately placing the community in a state of comfort as to their means of subsistence from the domestic soil must be abandoned as hopeless; and there should seem to be a limit in the progress of wealth and civilization beyond which no prudence, no public spirit, no attention to public and private morals can carry any people; a point from which they must necessarily begin to decline, and a principle of decay which no obedience to the commands of God can obviate.   This is a very disheartening prospect, and one that I should be exceedingly reluctant to entertain; because it involves a principle of apathy in the cause of public virtue and happiness, by the necessary anticipation of their speedy decay.   For it is impossible to doubt of their transient existence, when once they come to be considered as necessarily dependant upon the prevalence of general principles; that is, upon the universal consent of nations in a course of conduct upon which no two have been ever found practically to agree.

But if the natural tendency of population be such as I have endeavoured to prove in this treatise; and if by a fair adherence to moral and political rectitude, that natural tendency may actually be made to operate, so as to introduce, without any countervailing increase of vice and misery, a gradual abatement in the progress of population as society advances and the inferior soils only remain uncultivated, we at once recognize a conservative principle, which may carry on the society in wealth and happiness to an indefinite period : at least in so far as the principles of population and production are concerned, there is no assignable limit to the existence of a state so conducting itself.   Under the blessing of Providence, and in conformity to its laws, such a community may remain for ages a standing monument that the permanence of prosperity may always be commensurate to the wisdom and virtue of the people.   For as the powers of the soil diminish, the demand for its produce decreases also ; and we have already seen that, before the powers of the soil are altogether exhausted, the demand for its produce will have been altogether stationary by the arrival of the population at its point of non-reproduction.

But although the powers of population and production will both gradually abate of the rapidity of their progress as society advances ; yet while they are still proceeding, however slowly, it is necessary that this abatement should take place, *pari passu ;* that is, that there shall be no abatement of production except as there is a corresponding one of population ; but that due encouragement should still be given to the production of food on inferior soils, in proportion as the continued progress of population creates a demand for it : otherwise the conservative principle will be destroyed, and either an increase of vice and misery, or an uncertain dependance upon foreign produce, will be necessarily introduced, and the permanence of the public wealth and happiness thereby endangered. But as the temptation is always great for a country in an advanced state of society and supporting expensive establishments by taxes upon agricultural produce, to avail itself of the importation of foreign corn from the agricultural countries, where it may be had cheap, rather than to cultivate its own inferior soil at a great expense; and as the difficulty is also considerable in finding the means of confining the people to the latter expedient, when the former appears to be their more immediate interest, it seems necessary in this part of our inquiry to enter into a consideration of those means: for this purpose, it is my intention, in the following chapter, to discuss the principles upon which corn laws ought to be constructed; that is to say, the principles upon which the powers which we know still to exist in the soil of a country to return a further produce may best be called into action.

CHAPTER VI.

An Inquiry into the Principle of Corn Laws.

IT appeared from the last chapter, that all corn
laws are a departure from the general principles of
political economy; and, in so far as they have a tendency
immediately to raise the price of corn, may generally
be considered in the light of a tax paid to the grower
by the community at large, to ensure either the
safety of the state by securing an independent
supply of subsistence for the people, or the ultimate
cheapness of corn by encouraging its plentiful
growth by a temporary rise in its price. Corn laws
then are only to be justified upon grounds of general
advantage to the whole community. Their expediency should never be argued upon other grounds.
But when this general expediency is once plainly
established, the specific object being to afford protection to one particular branch of national industry,
because it is thought of vital importance to the
welfare of the whole, the argument must then of
course turn upon the sacrifices by which the rest of
the society can give this special protection. Having
previously determined it to be for their own, because
for the general good, they should always bear these
premises in mind, be careful to investigate the subject dispassionately, and not to suffer their jealousy
to be excited by the necessary result, if it should
end in proving that some expense must be incurred
to purchase the expected advantage. A continual
vacillation between the pursuit of a desired good

and the abandonment of the sacrificies necessary to obtain it, is a system of policy equally pernicious and contemptible.

In the early stages of society, before the best lands are all appropriated and brought under cultivation, laws enacting a bounty upon the exportation of corn will give an extraordinary and immediate impulse to agriculture. But as much of the additional quantity of produce thus raised will eventually be brought into the home market, the ultimate result of this temporary rise will be a gradual but considerable and steady diminution in price. This was partially the case in England at the beginning of the last century, when, after a long system of discouragement and of impolitic enactments respecting agriculture, bounties were given upon exportation, and high duties laid upon the importation of corn. These wise alterations operated like magic, and placed England in some respects in the situation of a newly settled country. Good land, long in waste from former discouragements, could be procured at a cheap rate ; and the soil being fresh and producing abundantly could be cultivated with a large profit, and returned an abundant surplus produce. The effects were such as might have been expected : the people were plentifully supplied with food at a very reduced price, and so large an exportation of grain nevertheless took place, that the annual average was never less than 300,000 quarters; and in the 20 years of greatest prosperity, viz. from 1740, to 1760 it amounted to 700,000 quarters of all kinds of grain. The present condition of the soil of France, lately liberated from the feudal system and other oppressive impediments in the way of agricultural enterprise, may probably lead under proper encouragements to the same results; and corn in that country may for some years be both cheap and very plentiful.

Such is the natural result of corn laws enacting a bounty upon exportation and imposing duties upon importation, during the agricultural state of society, or rather until the best and richest lands of a country are all appropriated and cultivated. But as society advances, as none but inferior lands are left to be brought under cultivation, as capital is gradually diverted to the then more profitable employments of commerce and manufactures, and as a mercantile and manufacturing population absorb by degrees all the surplus produce of the best lands, and create a demand for further produce from soil of an inferior staple; we immediately perceive that the political question is completely altered. Bounties upon exportation are no longer necessary, because the demand which they are intended to produce is already made to a sufficient extent by the mercantile and manufacturing population at home. They would moreover, if enacted, be a mere dead letter, not only because the utmost exertions, which can be made upon the inferior land yet remaining uncultivated, cannot permanently do more than supply the increasing demands of its own inhabitants, but also because, if a surplus produce for exportation could be raised upon such land, no reasonable bounty could enable it successfully to compete in the foreign market with corn grown upon the superior soil of the agricultural countries, especially where any considerable expense, by way of freight or otherwise, is to be incurred in the transport. The bounty therefore can never operate till the domestic supply exceeds the internal demand by some impediments in commercial speculations, forcing an extraordinary portion of capital into those upon land. But this is merely a temporary alteration; and, upon the whole, we may safely assert that bounties upon export cease to operate when a country has decidedly advanced into the commercial and manufacturing state of society, and only inferior lands remain uncultivated. For, to sum up in a few words the preceding argument, the high price of corn induced by the increasing demand for food will always exceed that at which the agricultural nations can raise it, at which therefore other nations may easily purchase it; consequently, at which it can be sold when exported by the manufacturing nation. The law then encouraging exportation must be a mere dead letter, unless it contain the ruinous and unfair enactment of an excessively high bounty. Happily, however, it becomes useless too by the force of circumstances, because a superior impulse is given to agriculture by the demand from a commercial and manufacturing community.

But another system of policy then becomes imperative, namely, to protect the agriculture carried on upon the inferior lands now brought under cultivation from interference and eventual ruin, arising from a competition with corn grown upon the rich and unembarrassed soil of the agricultural countries. It is obvious that this can only be done by duties upon importation, tending to keep up the price in the domestic market sufficiently high to remunerate the cultivator of inferior land. From the nature of things these duties must vary, and they must vary

so as to increase as society advances. For of the
inferior lands, the best remaining will upon the
average be of course first brought under cultivation,
leaving at every step in the progress only others still
inferior to the last, to be cultivated at an expense
continually increasing. The protection therefore to
be effectual must vary with every step, so as to cover
that continually increasing expense. Thus, as I
observed before, a people must pay, and ought justly
to expect to pay, for every advantage they draw
from their advancing wealth and happiness by the
progress of society. They may choose whether they
will enjoy or forego those advantages; but having
made their election they must not shrink from the
necessary consequences of the alternative they have
chosen.

We see then that, to ascertain the nature and extent of the encouragement necessary to the prosperity of domestic agriculture upon inferior soils,
many facts must be previously inquired into. As
first, the average capability of the country to raise
actually, or within a reasonable period of encouragement, produce enough for its own consumption;
because upon this will not only depend the possibility
of placing it ultimately in a state of independence
upon foreign supply; but the circumstance will also
materially affect the prospect of immediate competition from the corn-growing countries. This will be
treated in the remainder of this chapter.

Next we must also take into our calculation the
several component parts of which the expense of
raising produce upon inferior land is made up; as 1st,
Rent, or landlord's interest and profit upon his capital
laid out in purchase or improvement: 2dly, The ex-

pence of cultivation, or tenant's interest and profit upon his capital and labour; and lastly, Taxes and all other outgoings imposed upon land. Considering also the variable and uncertain amount of agricultural produce, especially upon inferior soils, we must always recollect that no corn laws can fulfil their object of encouraging the cultivator of such land, unless they secure to him a high price in years of deficient produce, a moderate price, or what is called the growing price, in years of average produce, and a low price in years of extraordinary plenty. Lastly, care must be taken that all these component parts do not make up a total of expense to be paid by the consumers of domestic agricultural produce, that would cramp or discourage the growth of domestic commerce and manufactures, by increasing their necessary cost so as to encourage a competition from the commerce and manufactures of foreign countries. For, after all, the demand created by the increase of a commercial and manufacturing population can alone, for the reasons stated in a former chapter, open a market for the sale of raw produce grown upon soils of a staple continually diminishing in value. These points will be treated in following chapters.

We have now to consider, in the remainder of this chapter, the effect which the capacity of a country to raise within itself produce enough for its own consumption should have upon the nature of the encouragement necessary for the prosperity of domestic agriculture. When a territory is of small extent, and fully peopled with a commercial and manufacturing population collected into large towns, (such as the small European republics exhibited during their vigour and prosperity,) it is evident that it *cannot feed itself,* and that it must permanently depend upon imported corn. The whole system of its laws will be framed with this view; and as states of this description seldom excite a general jealousy, especially among the agricultural nations, and their demand for foreign corn does not extend to any great positive quantity, they may with prudent precautions go on prospering for ages under such a system. In truth, many advantages with respect to regularity of supply and uniformity of price will in such a case result from it. In the first place, whenever such a country depends mainly upon importation for its regular supply of food, a stated encouragement to the exporting countries will always produce a stated supply, which will be grown by them for the specific purpose of feeding the importing country. It will therefore be generally sure of a sufficient and regular supply, one main ingredient producing uniformity of price. In the next place it will be affected in a very slight degree by the variableness of seasons, and by any eventual deficiency of the crops in the corn-growing countries; for as their surplus produce considered in the bulk is at all times more than sufficient for the limited supply of the small commercial states, and the deficiencies of one country will probably be compensated by the redundancy of another, their prices are regulated more by the wants of the importing nation than by the average growth of their own. This has been fully established by incontestable evidence.* Here then is another ingredient, securing almost to a certainty a regular uniformity of supply and of price in

* See Evidence before the Lords' Committee, 1814.

the corn market of an importing country not capable of feeding its own population, but permanently depending upon a supply of foreign produce.

The practical conclusions however are exceedingly altered when we come to apply them to an extensive and highly manufacturing country, which in average years is nevertheless capable of supplying the whole of its inhabitants with food the growth of its own soil. For in this case any considerable demand for imported corn must of course depend upon the state of the preceding harvest at home. There will be no permanent demand for foreign corn as in the former case; and of course the exporting countries will not regularly grow corn for its supply. They must be tempted by a previous knowledge of an extraordinary demand, indicated by an extraordinary increase of price in consequence of a deficient harvest. But such a supply from the regularly exporting countries is in the nature of things distant and uncertain; and after all it may perhaps be brought into the country at a loss to the importer, in consequence of a plentiful year succeeding one of deficient crops, or of a *glut* caused by excessive importation into a market of the precise extent of whose wants no previous knowledge could be obtained. This last result will inevitably occur, if the neighbouring countries not usually exporting corn should have been blessed with a plentiful crop, and able to forestall those usually exporting in the deficient market; as was the case of France with respect to England, in the year 1814.

All these circumstances must render the supply from the corn-growing countries to one nearly feeding its own population in average years very uncertain

and precarious; and in such a country it seems next
to impossible to establish a regular and permanent
equality in the price of corn, which must fluctuate in
proportion as Providence has been more or less boun-
tiful in blessing the labours of the husbandman with
increase. Temporary exceptions to this result may
certainly be shown; as in the case of a deficient crop
at home, when the neighbouring countries have been
blessed with an abundant harvest. Under these
circumstances if the importation of their corn be
freely admitted into the country where the crops
have been deficient, the price of its scanty produce
may be reduced either to the average level, or to
that at which the grower could only have been remunerated for a plentiful crop; a condition under
which nothing but speedy relief can save *him* from
ruin, and the *country* from an ultimate fluctuation
of price much greater than that which would naturally have ensued.

We see then the difficulty of establishing an uniform price of corn in a manufacturing country principally depending upon its own resources for the food
of its people, together with the improbability of
always ensuring a certain supply from abroad to
meet the eventual deficiencies in the crops of such a
country. The unavoidable conclusion therefore, in
every view of policy, seems to be that domestic produce should be encouraged by any means consistent
with the general welfare of the community; that
from a supply *almost* sufficient for the people, it
should be made to afford one *altogether* so. We
know that the inherent powers of the soil are
always sufficient for the purpose. The difficulty,
however, of calling them into action may still

be considerable. Nor indeed does it appear possible, in a country where the inferior lands are extensively cultivated, to secure a fair prospect of remuneration to the corn grower, without measures involving what the general consumer will be apt to call a hardship upon him, and what really is an immediate sacrifice on his part. For it is evident that the same price, which in a plentiful year will more than remunerate the grower for an abundant produce, will expose him to ruinous loss in one of deficient crops, when the quantity he could carry to market may perhaps be reduced one half. But inferior lands are peculiarly subject to the hazard of a deficient crop, and in a given number of years they occur very frequently. If therefore by the admission of foreign grain at a price constituting a fair remuneration for an average crop, the price should be kept at the same level when the domestic produce is scanty ; although the circumstance would in the first instance be extremely favourable to the general consumer, it would be ruinous to the agriculturist, and therefore ultimately injurious to the permanent interests of the whole community.

To say that corn is the measure of value, and that the cultivator would be renumerated by a diminution in the money price of wages and other articles of consumption, is an argument contrary to fact. For it has always been found practically impossible to establish an average in the money prices of the necessaries of life, at all corresponding with the fluctuations in the price of corn. It certainly affects them in some degree, and in proportion as the purchase of bare food, or rather of mere bread-corn, constitutes the expenditure of the people. But

many necessaries in general consumption, even among
the labouring classes, in countries at all advanced
into the commercial and manufacturing state of society, are very remotely if at all affected by the price
of corn.   If these necessaries, therefore, by taxation
or other causes, continue dear, the labourer who requires them cannot, or least ought not, to work cheap.
But a high rate in the wages of labour, of whatever
component parts they may be made up, and a low
price of its products, can never be permanently maintained; they are conditions altogether incompatible
with the prosperity of industry, whether exerted on
the land or on other objects.

     To the limited extent, however, in which the
wages of labour are actually affected by the price of
corn, the general consumer, *i. e.* every order of the
state except the agriculturist, is immediately bene-
fited by a reduction of price; although if that reduction be produced by importation, and be also sufficient permanently to discourage agriculture, this
immediate benefit will soon resolve itself into an
ultimate evil, by diminishing the demands for all the
products of industry from the numerous class of cultivators, and by the insecurity of the substituted
mode of supply for the food of the people.   The whole
question, therefore, is reduced to this.   What immediate sacrifice will a manufacturing community,
supporting expensive establishments by taxes upon
the land and labour of the people, make to secure to
themselves the permanent advantage of an independent supply of food from their domestic soil, and
a permanent demand for domestic *manufactures* together with a large contribution to the taxes from
a prosperous and increasing class of cultivators?

Will they for this object incur the risk of losing a portion of the demand which they might otherwise expect from foreign nations for their manufactures? and to what degree will they consent to suffer this loss? Certainly not to the extent of risking any permanent decrease in the whole amount of the commercial and manufacturing population; because such a result would at once destroy the demand for agricultural produce, which it is the object of the whole argument to find the means of supplying. But in estimating its probable extent it may be useful to recollect, that although this risk is apparently increased by every step made in the progress of society; because as the land yet remaining uncultivated decreases in quality, the premium for cultivating it must be increased *pari passu;* yet we may also conclude that the improved machinery, the perfect state of public credit, the freedom and security of property, which are all necessary to the existence of a highly civilized and manufacturing state of society, usually confer advantages on the products of their industry even in foreign markets, which are frequently found in practice more than to counterbalance even a considerable difference in the price of labour. They also produce effects on the home market, tending to something like an uniform price in corn of domestic growth, by the accommodation afforded to the cultivators in times of difficulty. It should seem, therefore, that by making an immediate sacrifice for the encouragement of domestic agriculture, a clear advantage is gained over the opposite system. For a great and opulent class of domestic consumers are at all events preserved, affording a permanent and certain demand for manufactures; while the foreign demand, which at the best is comparatively precarious, appears not to be subjected to any very material additional risk.

If indeed, in a country which nearly or just feeds its population from the produce of it's own soil, it were possible to establish a monopoly of food, so as to prevent its sinking in price in proportion to its plenty ; and thus to deprive the consumer of his fair advantage in a plentiful crop, in return for his sacrifice in favour of the grower in the event of a deficient one ; much might be said against the necessity of such sacrifice being ever made : for the extraordinary profit of average or abundant years might, and probably would, more than compensate the deficiencies of scanty crops. But the very idea of a monopoly of agricultural produce appears to me to be a prejudice. It is perfectly fair and just, and the well understood interest of the public, that every proprietor should be permitted to make as much of his property, as a fair contemplation of the demand and supply will enable him to make. If he attempt to make more, not the public, but the speculator himself must suffer. This is peculiarly true of agricultural produce. That man must be very superficially acquainted with the first principles by which markets are regulated, if he does not know that a corn-grower, holding back his produce to enhance its price when no actual scarcity exists, must ultimately be obliged to bring it to market at a *reduced* price; and that holding it back when there is a real scarcity is the greatest possible public benefit; because it tends to enforce œconomy in the use of grain, and to make the general stock last the longer. The result is, that the public instead of paying first a *high* price, and afterwards a *famine* price, without the means of a constant supply, is furnished with a re-, gular though scanty provision at a scarcity price. So closely on this great question of practical policy are public and individual interests united.

I have heard it said, in answer to arguments in favour of affording protection to the cultivator of inferior lands against a ruinous competition from the agricultural countries in the home market, that cheapness of corn generating cheapness of labour, and thus encouraging the rapid increase of a manufacturing population, their demand affords a higher encouragement to cultivation than can be accomplished by any protecting duties. Now I should be the last man to deny that, after a country has acquired prosperity in commerce and manufactures, the demand from its manufacturing and trading population can alone produce a further supply of food; for some of the fundamental arguments of this treatise depend upon that obvious truth. But the question here to be determined is not whether such a demand is not so created *somewhere*, and generally speaking; but whether it shall be made to operate on the agriculture of foreign countries, or on that of the manufacturing country itself: and the object of the proposed protection is to place the inferior land of the latter on a level with the superior land of the former : to afford it, in short, *artificially* that preference which, *cæteris paribus*, will *naturally* be given to a resource that can be had at home, rather than to a more precarious supply from abroad at an equal expense. The truism therefore, that a manufacturing population affords the best encouragement to agriculture in certain states of society, has evidently nothing to do with the question before us, unless the means exist by which that encouragement may be made to operate upon the domestic soil. These means can only be afforded, in a state of society where poorer soils only remain to be cultivated, by protecting them against the competition of the richer soils of the purely agricultural countries.

Still, however, the manufacturing population must exist and increase, or the demand would not be created for any augmentation at all, either of domestic or of foreign produce. So that the encouragement to be given to agriculture is a question of degree, and it must obviously not be carried to an extent that would injure commerce or manufactures, either by materially affecting their export to foreign countries, by raising the price of labour to an exorbitant height, or by diminishing the sale of goods in the domestic market. To ascertain whether due encouragement can be afforded, without some of these pernicious consequences, in any given country, it is expedient in the first place to inquire into the necessary expenses that must be defrayed by the cultivator, before he begins to calculate upon those profits which are to determine the propriety of his continuing or relinquishing the objects of his pursuit; for these expenses must evidently be exceeded by the price paid for the produce by the general consumer, in order to give the cultivator the means of continuing his industry.

They are, as before remarked,—1st, Rent—2dly, Tenant's expenses—and 3dly, Taxes. Of each of these then in their order.

CHAPTER VII.

An Inquiry into the Nature of Rent.

THERE are few subjects on which more extraordinary notions seem to have prevailed among political economists than on the nature of rent, and
consequently there are few, on which a greater mass
of prejudice in general is found to exist. Dr. Adam
Smith says* that " the rent of land, considered as
the price paid for the use of land, is naturally a
monopoly price. It is not at all proportioned to
what the landlord may have laid out upon the improvement of the land, or to what he can afford to
take" (that is, I presume, without loss of capital
or fair interest upon it) " but to what the farmer
can afford to give." Now, with great submission,
I venture to deny the whole of this statement;—and,
first, that the rent of land is a *monopoly* price,
or, as Mr. Malthus explains it,† " the *excess* of price
above the cost of production." I suppose, of course,
that the price of the raw material is to be included
in the costs of production, and is to be expected to
return a fair profit, otherwise no man would enter
into the speculation. Now this price, in the case of
land, is the capital and labour employed to purchase
or reclaim it; and including a fair profit upon them,
there is certainly no monopoly price fixed upon the
rent of land, which is as fairly open as any other

* Book i. c. xi.
† Inquiry into the Nature and Progress of Rent, 1815, p. 2.

species of profits to the competition arising from the demand and supply of the article in the market. I venture
also to deny that there is, upon the average, *any excess*
whatsoever in the price of the products of lands above
" *the cost of production.*"   It is certainly true, that
the sum that can be paid in rent must be determined
by that which remains in the hands of the immediate
cultivator from the sale of his produce, after all his
expenses of production, and his fair profits, are paid.
So must the interest of a manufacturer's capital be
paid from the sum which remains to the retailer,
after deducting his necessary expenses and profit.
But surely this interest can never be called " the
excess of price ABOVE the cost of production;" because it is, in fact, the bare return of a part of that
cost.   *Profit* is indeed made up of such excess in
price; and when that profit can be increased at the
will of the manufacturer, a *monopoly* may be said
to take place, because a price is then superadded
beyond that which a fair balance of demand and
supply would otherwise indicate.   But from the
nature of agricultural products, no such increase can
take place on the profits accruing from them, and,
consequently, on rent which is taken out of them,
and the amount of which depends upon them.   This
will, I think, appear from the following considerations.

   It is obvious that, after the first appropriation
of land, that is, after the first emergence of society
from the savage state, a man cannot become the
proprietor of a tract of ground without paying a
capital sum for the property, either in clearing, draining, embanking, and other objects necessary to be
fulfilled previous to the actual labours of the culti-

vator of raw produce; or else to replace the capital, and reward the skill and industry, of the original proprietor who performed those operations, together with his fair profits. This constitutes what may be called the *price* of land as distinct from the mere cost of cultivation, or expenses of the actual occupier. It is the interest of the sum thus paid as the price of land, which constitutes the rent of land, and which must of course be added to the mere expense of cultivation, before a fair calculation of the *whole* cost of production, or of raising raw produce for the market, can be made. And I venture to assert that, so far from being a monopoly, competition and other causes have always kept rents so comparatively low, as to afford upon the average of landed property a diminished REAL remuneration to the landlord or receiver of the rent as society has advanced; I mean, that the interest of the sum originally expended in the purchase and clearing of the soil of any given country, will afford to its receivers a continually decreasing *proportion* of the comforts and enjoyments of life, as those comforts and enjoyments are augmented by the progress of society, and of commercial and manufacturing prosperity; and that the landlord will consequently sink in the scale of society. It is notorious that, in rich and commercial countries, a capitalist, who can make 10, 15, or 20 per cent. in commerce, and 5 per cent, without any cost or labour, in the public funds of his country, often procures little more than 3 per cent. interest upon capital invested in land with a view to rent. This is at least one very singular feature in the chain of proof, that the rent of land is fixed upon the same principles with a monopoly price of goods. In truth, it appears

that land, so far from paying from its produce, as society advances, a continually increasing substantial surplus above the whole cost of production, including
the capital originally laid out, (although it may not
perhaps pay a continually decreasing actual profit,)
does certainly return a profit, bearing a continually
decreasing proportion to the profits of other stock
and labour. For, in the first place, it may be observed,
that when the first proprietor originally cleared the
ground in the early stage of society, and during the
whole continuance of the agricultural state, the
produce of land being the only profitable employment of capital and of labour, the owner of any quantity of it, although his money income might be small,
could of course command a larger comparative portion of labour and capital, than when other profitable
employments compete with him for the possession of
them. And again, when the commercial and manufacturing career is entered upon, and the capital
created by them is sometimes vested in land, although
the sum in money paid for the price of an estate may
be much less in nominal amount than the land
would sell for in the following century, when the
society has made further progress, and other modes of
investing capital become more numerous; yet the
actual or *real* value of that smaller sum of money,
or the comparison it bears to the general value of
labour and commodities, may, and in truth certainly
will, be greater than that of the larger sum subsequently paid as the price of the estate, because the
competition for capital, from other sources of employment, would of course bring down the actual
value of income derived from land as compared with
other profits. It appears indeed that the pleasure

and consequence derived from the possession of land will make the capitalist content with a smaller return from it than from other sources of profit.

Again, although an estate, which originally cost 10,000*l.* in money, when the produce of the estate only sold in the market at such a price as afforded a rent of 350*l.*, money being scarce and taxes low, may now pay a nominal rent of 1000*l.* a year, yet the landlord, from the high price of labour and commodities, arising from the commercial competitors and the pressure of taxation, may now be a poorer man, notwithstanding the nominal increase of his income; and if the country, during the interval in which this increase of rent has been accumulating, has been making a rapid career in commercial wealth, he certainly will be at least comparatively a poorer man, because the competition against him will have been continually increasing. Nor are these conclusions shaken by the obvious consideration that rents must sustain a *real* rise upon the old lands which have been actually cultivated, before due encouragement can be given to the clearing and cultivation of unreclaimed soil of an inferior staple. For if the profits of other sources of industry have sustained, from the same causes, a still greater *real* elevation; that is, if they will exchange for a still larger proportion of labour and commodities than this partial increase in the rent of land will purchase, which in a rapidly improving country would probably be the case, it is obvious that the rise in this last, though *real* as far as it goes, does not give the landed proprietor any substantial elevation in the scale of society. On the contrary, his condition is comparatively depressed, because he becomes entitled to a smaller proportion of the general wealth of the country. With respect to the general mass of landholders, there cannot be a doubt that they possess greater advantages with low rents and few burthens, than with increased rents and high taxes. In England, for the last 20 years, rents in general have borne a far less proportion to the gross produce of the land, than they did before that period; a fact perfectly conclusive of the present argument.

Surely, when we take all these circumstances into consideration, it is impossible to conceive any epithet less justly applicable to the rent of land than a *monopoly price*, since it is open to fair competition, and is only a reasonable, and frequently a very low, remuneration for capital expended, and consequently is not caused by the excess of price above the whole cost of production, but is only a portion of that cost.

Neither does Mr. Malthus's exposition of the *nature* of the rent of land appear much more satisfactory. Admitting it to be caused by the excess of price above the cost of production, he ascribes this fact to the *fertility* of the earth, affording a surplus produce of the necessaries of life beyond the wants of the cultivator; * and as this surplus produce is of a nature (according to his theory) to create a certain demand for itself by raising up a population to feed upon it, the market consequently cannot be over stocked; † so that the very abundance of the produce, by raising up competitors for it, tends to keep up the price, and consequently to afford an excess of profit above the cost of production, which is said to constitute rent. With respect to the fact upon which this theory rests, viz. that a surplus produce of the neces-

* Inquiry, &c. p. 13.
† The present state of the English corn-market affords a practical answer to this supposition.

saries of life will always raise up consumers, and will
therefore pay a price beyond the cost of production
higher than the other products of industry, I shall
be satisfied with referring the reader to a former
chapter, on the order of precedence between population and production ; only observing, in addition, that
the fact, if it were consistent with experience, must
necessarily be too slow in operation to produce the
effect required ; since the population supposed to be
called into existence by the surplus produce cannot
make an effective demand in the market till some
years after they are supposed by the theory to have
kept up the price by such demand. And, in the
next place, it is only by a previous reduction in the
price of the necessaries of life, annihilating the excess of price, upon which the whole argument turns,
that the supposed population with their demand
could be called into existence. I cannot therefore
see the force of the distinction made by Mr. Malthus
between the surplus profits of land employed in
raising the necessaries of life, and those arising from any other species of productive industry.
Nor can I think that the amount or the nature of
rent is affected by any quality inherent in the raw
produce such as he has assumed ; but which to be
effectual in the manner supposed, even at a distant
period, must first have annihilated beyond recall the
effect which is supposed to be produced.

But, in truth, are any of these fine-drawn speculations at all necessary to give a rational, intelligible,
and consistent account of the nature and origin of
rent, as well as of every other revenue derived from
capital and industry ? It is clear that no product
will be originally brought to market unless the de-

mand for it is sufficient to remunerate, first, the capitalist who erects the machinery, the warehouses, and
provides other dead or inactive stock, and keeps them
in repair ; and next, the person who purchases the raw
material, and employs his own and his servants'
labour on the manufacture, and who conveys the
article to market.

The produce of land therefore will not be originally
carried to market, unless the demand for it shall
afford a price sufficient to remunerate the purchaser
or clearer of the land for his capital, as well as the
farmer for his capital and industry ; for land will be
suffered to lie waste if such encouragement be not
given, upon the same principle that will prevent a
manufactory from being erected at a considerable expense, unless the material intended to be manufac
tured will repay the interest of the capital employed
in the buildings, repairs, and machinery, as well as in
the raw material and labour more immediately connected with the product. It is true that, after the
first mentioned capital has been expended, the land
cleared or purchased, or the manufactory and machinery set up, and the product brought to market, the
price of that product may be so reduced as to annihilate the value of the capital originally expended, and merely to leave a profit upon the ordinary
or routine expenses of the manufacture or of cultivation. Cultivation or the manufacture however might
still be carried on for a time, and until they required
to be renewed by a fresh application of capital,
although the capitalists who first set them going
would be ruined. But it is evident that all further
investment of capital in the same pursuits would be at
an end; and if the reduction of price arose from

foreign competition, the capital annihilated would
have been gratuitously conferred upon foreign countries, to the great injury of the country of its growth.
If the reduction of price arose from domestic competition, the loss would be a salutary hint to other capitalists to change the direction of their capital from a
department wherein the supply is found to exceed the
demand.

But here a very broad distinction is found between capital employed in agriculture and in manufactures. With respect to the latter, it is problematical, and therefore a matter of inquiry, whether
the check may have arisen from overtrading, or from
foreign competition? But, with respect to agriculture, if we consider what has been stated in former
parts of this work upon the continually decreasing
value of the land that is forced into cultivation, by an
augmented demand for its produce, and from increasing population, we shall at once perceive that, so long
as the public prosperity is in a progressive state, that
demand *cannot be checked:* therefore if the price of
the produce in the market originally created by that
demand should during its continuance permanently
sink, so as to annihilate the rent, or the fair profit of
the capital laid out in bringing inferior land into a
a productive state, the effect must be wholly ascribed
to foreign competition; and the capital thus destroyed
by the ruin of the domestic capitalist would be gratuitously given to one employed in furthering the prosperity of foreign countries. Now it is a question in
which both justice and expediency are eminently involved, how far a government is at liberty to permit
the annihilation of large and profitable capitals at
home, creating a great demand for all the products

of domestic industry, by the transfer of their elements to foreign countries? And it is a still more
important question, and not less easy of solution,
whether any immediate or apparent advantage proposed by the advocates of such an expedient can be
otherwise than ultimately destructive to the country
which has recourse to it?

Nevertheless, it is still true that, rent, to whatever fluctuations it may be liable, from these or
other causes, seems clearly to be nothing more nor
any thing less than the remuneration of the capital
employed in purchasing and clearing land, the amount
of which remuneration, as well as that of every
other species of industry, must be regulated by the
demand for its products. Its payment is as necessary as the payment of any other fair return to the
permanence of the actual state of prosperity in which
the concern may happen to be, as well as to its
further progress in a successful career; for it is that
out of which all accumulation to be expended in
further improvement, or in the renewal which becomes necessary in all perishable materials, must proceed. It is no *monopoly*, but equally subject to be
regulated by *fair* competition with all other profits of
capital; and the principle upon which rests the expediency of affording it protection from *foreign* competition seems to be in no material degree different
from that, which should regulate the conduct of a
government towards other vital sources of domestic
industry.

The nature and the amount of the necessary protection will depend upon various circumstances, both
in the country in question and in the surrounding
countries; but the principle is universal and unavoid-

able, that provision must be made for the payment of rent from reclaimed land, even of the lowest staple, before a reasonable expectation can be entertained of any further progress in domestic cultivation. These are the general principles which appear to connect the rent of land with the common interests of the state. They may be followed out into a great variety of detail, but enough appears to have been already stated for the purposes of this treatise, and to afford data for ascertaining how far a provision can be made for the payment of rent in any given state of society, without injury to the general interests of the commonwealth.

CHAPTER VIII.

An Inquiry into the Expenses and Profits of the Tenant.

BEFORE we proceed to inquire into the particulars of the expenses and profits of the tenant, it is necessary to distinguish accurately between that proportion of the price of produce out of which they are to arise, and the portion reserved for the payment of rent. The comparative amount of each of these is materially different, in the different conditions of society. We have seen in the last chapter that land is originally brought under cultivation, at least after the earliest stages of the agricultural state of society are passed, under the expectation of procuring in the shape of rent, a profitable return for the capital expended. This truth is not affected by the circumstance, that the land is occupied by the proprietor himself who originally reclaimed it, or by his descendant; for they are equally entitled to expect a fair return for the capital originally laid out, whether or not they may choose to add thereto the profits arising from the immediate application of their own skill and labour, and of a further capital in the actual cultivation of the soil. When land, however, has been once reclaimed and brought under cultivation, much of it will probably continue in that state, even although the price of its produce should be just sufficient to replace the cost of cultivation only, with a profit upon the tenant's capital equal to the average rate of profit in other departments of industry; and this although the landlord's capital should be altogether annihilated. The landlord would, in fact, then become the occupier, and be degraded from his former rank in society to that of a farmer. This effect, if general throughout the independent proprietory even of the inferior lands only, would be attended with consequences sufficiently lamentable to the general interests of the community, by a diminution of demand from the great consumers of all the products of industry, and by interposing a positive bar to all further improvement. It would not be altogether and immediately fatal to the existing agriculture; but would only constitute the lowest point at which it could at all continue to proceed even for a limited period. It may be useful then to inquire, what portion of the price of raw produce is made up of the actual expenses and profits of the cultivator, by deducting therefrom that which is superadded upon account of rent? Now we have seen that the portion, which constitutes rent, undergoes a comparative diminution, with respect to the mere expense of cultivation, in proportion to the progress of society, and to the necessity of having recourse to inferior lands for cultivation, or to an increased outlay of capital in the management of lands already reclaimed. For as the immediate cultivator must be remunerated, in the first instance, for his capital, it is evident that in proportion as he is obliged to increase that capital, in order to raise an equal quantity of produce, he must deduct the interest and profit upon it from what he would otherwise be able to pay in the shape of rent; unless they are compensated by improvements in the modes of agriculture, by which the produce raised by the labour previously employed can be increased in an equal degree. This however is seldom found to be the case, especially on inferior soils : we may therefore estimate the portion of the price of produce from these soils resolvable into rent as very small. If we consider the burthen of taxes generally imposed in such an advanced stage of society, as leads to the cultivation of inferior soils, and add it to the other agricultural expenses, we may perhaps estimate the portion resolvable into rent, even where a brisk demand exists for the produce, at not more than one-fifth of the whole price in the market, leaving four-fifths for the ordinary expenses of production, and for the farmer's profit on his capital. We have abundant evidence that upon the poorer soils of England not more than a fifth of the gross produce is paid to the landlord in the shape of rent, and that this proportion gradually increases to a fourth as the staple of the soil improves in quality. Supposing therefore that so wild an idea should enter into the head of a statesman as to annihilate all rent from inferior lands, and proportionally to reduce it on those of a superior staple, in order to afford raw produce at a cheap rate to the general consumer, we perceive that his utmost efforts could do no more than reduce the price one-fifth without throwing land out of cultivation, and thereby ultimately raising the price of its produce much higher than his notable expedient would immediately have depressed it. Suppose the *growing price*, including rent, to be 80s. for a quarter of wheat, the total annihilation of the rent would reduce it to 64s. which would constitute the mere current expenses of cultivation, and the questions for the public to consider, are, 1st, whether this difference of price would compensate the state for the ruin of its most efficient class of domestic consumers;—and 2dly, whether in a course of years agriculture could be carried on without the assistance of capital for the various offices of renewal and improvement, which always fall upon the landlord, or, in other words, upon the rent, and are not included in what is called the growing price of corn, or capable of being defrayed from the profits of the tenant.

Now whatever may be thought of the first of these questions, it seems morally certain that unless that portion of the rent, which a prudent landlord accumulates to meet the necessary wear and tear, and the occasional deterioration going on upon his estate, be added to the growing price of raw produce in the market, over and above the remuneration for the labour and ordinary profits of the occupier, cultivation must very soon decline, and that in no slow degree; especially on lands of inferior staple. For it is only by dint of a liberal application of capital that they can at all be brought to a productive state. An application of capital equally liberal, in what is called *high farming*, is also necessary to keep them in a productive state; and a very trifling diminution of such capital will give rise to a process of deterioration, which will proceed in a rapidly descending ratio: for such lands, when once neglected and exhausted, are with great difficulty restored. It is not, however, easy to conceive that, even were the price of produce reduced by foreign competition so low as only to remunerate the grower for his current expenses, the payment of all rent would be immediately and *ipso facto* annihilated.

There would for some time be a constant struggle between distresses of the landlord and those of his tenant. The former would naturally press for his accustomed rent to defray his current expenses; and the latter who had expended some of his former profits on the land, in expectation of an increased return in the course of his lease, would, for a period, advance a portion at least of his rent from former savings rather than forego all chance of remuneration from the return of better times. He would, in plain terms, do what a great proportion of the British farmers have been lately constrained to submit to, viz. he would pay his rent for a time out of his capital. The end of this process would however be the absolute impoverishment of both, and the consequent inability of either to make the smallest effort for the necessary renewal of those improvements, by which the land first became capable of affording a surplus produce for the market. This argument applies also, though in a somewhat less degree, to lands of a superior staple. So that I do not hesitate partially to agree in the truth of Mr. Malthus's position* that " if under the impression that the high price of raw produce, which occasions rent, is as injurious to the consumer as it is advantageous to the landlord, a rich and improved nation were determined by law to lower the price of produce " (to the bare expenses of cultivation, or) " till no surplus in the shape of rent any where remained ; it would inevitably throw not only all the poor land, but all except the very best land, out of cultivation, and probably reduce its produce and population to

---

* See Inquiry into the Nature and Progress of Rent, p. 35.

less than one-tenth of their former amount." At least I am persuaded that this would be the natural tendency, and that the lamentable result could only be averted by the necessary recurrence of very high prices of produce, in consequence of the rapidly diminishing supply, which, in spite of any law, would virtually restore high rents, and induce the capitalist again to set out in the career of cultivation from the point whence he started, perhaps a century or two before. So that the ultimate result might possibly be nothing more than throwing back the country a century or two behind its natural station in the progress of society.

We see then that where the investment of capital in agriculture meets with due encouragement, the office of renewing the improvements, and replacing the eventual deteriorations and wear and tear of the land, falls upon the rent or capital of the landlord, and not upon the profits of the tenant. It forms no part of his expenses, which are confined principally to the wages of labour, and the wear and tear of stock and implements, and taxes. Of each of these in their order.

CHAPTER IX.

Of the Wages of Labour.

THE wages of labour are evidently another constituent part of the price of raw produce; but this proposition is liable to many modifications, arising out of the circumstance that wages are also themselves affected, as to the money amount of them, by the price of raw produce itself. This influence is partly nominal, and partly real. It is nominal in proportion to the degree in which the consumption of the labourer consists of raw produce, because his remuneration is of course the same, whether he receive 10*s.* in wages when that sum will purchase a bushel of wheat at 80*s.* the quarter, or 8*s.* when wheat is sold at 64*s.* the quarter. But it is *real* in proportion to the degree in which the consumption of the labourer consists of other articles besides raw produce. For any rise in wages consequent upon an increased price of corn will evidently confer upon the labourer an additional command over every article of his consumption except raw produce, in proportion as the rise in his wages exceeds his additional outgoing in the article of corn. It will enable him, for example, to purchase just so much more of grocery, tobacco, leather, clothing, &c. This principle has been rendered so perfectly clear by Mr. Malthus in his Inquiry into the Nature and Progress of Rent (p. 47, and seq.), that it is unnecessary to enter into any detail of the proof by which it is established. But a consequence necessarily follows which seems to have escaped observation, but which affords a signal instance of the principle of compensation to all ranks of the people, as society advances, contended for throughout this treatise. It is in the early stages of society, and in them only, when the artificial wants of individuals are few, and luxuries are scarcely known, that wages of labour are entirely expended in the purchase of raw produce. The peasant, who is then the only labourer, lives in rude and hardy plenty; himself and his children duly fed, he is happy and contented, nor feels a wish for articles which the simple structure of society has never brought within his notice. His immediate superior, the farmer, exhibits to him no provoking contrast of refined and luxurious enjoyment. Nor are the habits of the resident landlord's families, from whose servants and dependants the customs and wishes of the lower ranks are frequently derived, of a nature calculated to foster artificial wants. In such times the rough hospitality of the hall differs rather in quantity than in quality from the more sober plenty of the cottage; they are both derived almost exclusively from the immediate application of the raw produce of the neighbourhood. To constitute the happiness of the labourer, therefore, in that stage of society, nothing more is necessary than that a certain portion of raw produce should always be exchangable against the fair exertion of his industry. And a nominal money-rise of wages occasioned by a rise in the price of corn, as it leaves his real remuneration precisely where it was, neither improves nor deteriorates his condition, but leaves him as it found him, that is, happy and contented.

But as society advances, as manufactures bring into immediate contact in towns the labourer, the master manufacturer, and the independent proprietor living on the fruits of former industry ; and as commerce and riches introduce among the two last mentioned classes artificial comforts and enjoyments arising from the extraordinary profits of labour, it is both reasonable to conclude and fair to expect that a portion of this improvement in the condition of the other ranks will be claimed by the lowest. They will by degrees adopt as necessaries many articles which their forefathers either never heard of, or looked upon with contempt, as absurd and pernicious refinements. And it is ridiculous to suppose that, when once these principles have been engrafted into the general habits of the people, they can be torn away without endangering the vital principle of society. It is curious to observe the progress in which the general use of wheaten bread, and of the products of the East and West Indies, have been introduced into general consumption among the lower ranks in England. A Yorkshire peasant, whose father would have thought himself injured past redemption had wheaten bread been substituted for his oat-cake, by an apprenticeship to a clothier or cutler in one of the country towns not only becomes himself a consumer of wheaten bread, but the progenitor of a permanent set of such consumers. His sister, whose parents were satisfied with a competent portion of home brewed beer, by a few years service in a merchant's family not only becomes herself a consumer of tea and sugar, but the mother of a permanent posterity of such consumers. In process of time these new habits travel from the towns to the furthest recesses of the agricultural villages, and a lasting change is introduced into the mode of the people's subsistence. That the condition of the labourer should keep pace then with the progress of artificial enjoyment in the rest of the society, it is necessary that a real increase should take place in the wages of labour; that is, that the fair exertion of a man's industry should exchange against a larger portion of the comforts and conveniences of life than it did in the more simple stages of society; or else that the deficiency should be made up to him in some other way.

I cannot help considering this result to be as fair in theory, as it is inevitable in practical operation in a free country. And it appears to me to be no less tyrannical than impolitic in the proprietors or government of a country to attempt either to counteract its effects by depressing the real wages of labour by positive enactment, or to avail themselves of the increased wants of the labourer, by obliging him in unfavourable times to labour for their supply beyond the fair degree which his bodily strength will bear without ultimate injury, or for a smaller sum than will supply his reasonable wants and those of his family. A machine overworked will the sooner wear out. But a man worn out must, in a christian country at least, be supported by the rest of the community without any further profitable return from himself. It is therefore with some indignation at the want of feeling, and some contempt for the want of policy exhibited, that I have noticed the approbation bestowed upon the economical effects of low and fluctuating wages in Scotland, where rents, it is well known, are extraordinarily high. It appears to meet with the singular approbation of some political economists, that in dear years a workman, finding himself deprived of his usual enjoyments, is naturally excited to greater industry, and is desirous of working extra hours for the purpose of obtaining those comforts to which he has been accustomed; because " this disposition," it is said, " must naturally increase the supply of labour in " the market." But have these gentlemen considered the ultimate sacrifice by which this additional supply of labour is procured ? That it is by forcing exertion precisely at that period when the human frame is least capable of affording it; when the mind and body are both lowered by personal distress and the penury of a dependant family. A witness before the Committee of the House of Lords, respecting grain and the corn laws, being asked concerning the relative prices of work done by the piece in Scotland, when grain has been dear, and when it has been cheap, answers,—" In the year 1813, I contracted with a man to build some rods of masonry work, and the workman informed me that *in consequence of the hardness of the times* he executed that work at a *lower rate* than he would have executed it in years in which the prices of grain were lower." Another witness states; 1st, " I have always considered that when grain and other provisions *rose*, both manufacturing and agricultural labour fell. On the contrary, when provisions and grain fell, manufacturing and agricultural labour rose: the reason is obvious. Supposing there are in any one parish 100 labourers, who are able to do the work of that parish ; if provisions rise those labourers will do *double work ;* of course there being only a certain demand for labour, the labour falls." Being further questioned he says; 2dly, " very often he does *too much work* and works *beyond his strength* when grain is very high ; at other times he is idle when grain is low." The witness further stated ; 3dly, " that in a dear year his bailiff requested permission to have some particular work executed then rather than at any other time, because he could do it so much cheaper, *a great many labourers being idle* from having little work, in consequence of those who were employed doing *double work.* I desired him" says the witness " to go on with that labour likewise, and he actually contracted for very large ditches at sixpence an ell, which I do not think I could now do under from a shilling to eighteen pence, in consequence of the fall in provisions." Now in the first of these answers we have the fact, that when the labourer is least capable of extra work, he is ground down by a forced exertion of *double work.* In the 2d we have one extremely natural consequence, that he " does too much work, and works beyond his strength, when grain is very high ;" and 3dly, we have another consequence equally natural and almost equally humane and profitable to society, viz. That this double work and exhaustion of one portion of the labourers by excessive exertion tends to exhaust the other portion by actual starvation, in consequence of their having " *little work*" to do, at a time when a very great deal of work is absolutely necessary even to provide a scanty supply of food for themselves and their families. I am aware that if the mortality naturally to be expected among the last mentioned portion of the people should actually take place, the price of labour would again rise very high, and upon the return of plenty would encourage a rapid reproduction of people. But, considering the intervening misery and the great fluctuation in the rate of wages necessarily attending the process, and the dreadful disparity of condition introduced between the lowest and all other ranks of society, I think that a reasonable doubt may be entertained both with respect to the humanity and the sound policy of the whole system. And a mode of remunerating labour will surely appear preferable which secures regular comfort to the labourer in return for the fair and average exertion of his industry, and a regular rate of payment to the employer, whereby he can calculate beforehand, with some degree of accuracy, the proportion which his means bear to the work which he must hire labourers to perform. It is with most unfeigned pleasure that I quote the following passage from a note in Mr. Malthus's " Inquiry into Rent " (p. 48), where he incidentally alludes to the evidence upon which I have just commented. " With regard to the unusual exertions made by the labouring classes in periods of dearness, which produce the fall of wages noted in the evidence, they are most meritorious in the individuals, and certainly favour the growth of capital. But no man of humanity could wish to see them constant and unremitted. They are most admirable as a temporary relief; but if they were constantly in action, effects of a similar kind would result from them as from the population of a country being pushed to the very extreme limits of its food. There would be no resources in a scarcity. I own I do not see with pleasure the great extension of the practice of task work: to work really hard during twelve or fourteen hours in the day for any length of time is too much for a human being. Some intervals of ease are necessary to health and happiness, and the occasional abuse of such intervals is no valid argument against their use."

Upon the whole then I conclude that the comfortable subsistence of the labourer by a competent rate of wages, is an indispensable constituent part of the price of raw produce in a free country; that, as society advances, and the expenses of cultivation increase, and the consumption of the labourer is changed from an exclusive subsistence on raw produce to one compounded of corn and other articles not materially affected by the price of corn, wages must absolutely undergo a *real* rise. And that a country has no alternative between providing some method by which this *real* rise can be paid without injuring its general industry; or entering upon a retrograde course in society by giving up all those employments and the cultivation of all those lands which have rendered the rise in wages necessary.

In this view of the subject I apprehend the resource pointed at in the first chapter of this second book, which seems to be supplied by the spirit of the English poor-laws, may be found useful. Its consequences, as applicable to the case immediately before us, evidently are to prevent any great fluctuation in the rate of wages, to preserve a regular and constant rate of employment throughout the whole population, attended with a regular and fair remuneration, and this without precluding extra exertion for increased wages where an extraordinary effort is occasionally required by the manufacturer to complete a sudden order or answer a sudden demand. But there is no grinding down of the frame of the poor man, by extracting from him double work at the time when he is least capable of performing his average portion, but in return for his regular exertion of that portion a corresponding supply of his necessary wants is secured to him.

It will of course be asserted in reply to this reasoning, that both the price and the supply of labour will be regulated by the demand for it. Now that the *price* of labour will *for a time* be regulated by the demand I am ready to admit; but I must be permitted to deny that the *supply* of labour will in the natural course of things follow the demand as in the case of ordinary commodities, and, therefore, that its *price* will *ultimately* be regulated by it. The supply of labour is of too slow a growth to follow the demand for an increased quantity, before the want of such increase has annihilated the causes which created the demand itself. And labour is composed of sensitive materials too much dependant upon regular wants and habits, to accommodate itself rapidly to the decreasing wants of a retrograde society, without effects very dismal to the labouring classes, and very detrimental to all the other classes of society. So that in neither case will the state of the supply readily accommodate itself to the state of the demand.

For let us suppose that a high price of labour indicates an increasing demand for it, and encourages marriage and the production of children to supply that demand. It is evident that the new stock of

labour thus created will not come into the market
for 16 or 17 years at the soonest. And in the mean
time what will be the necessary consequence of the
high wages? That from the decreasing exertion of
some of the labourers, the capitalist will have a diminished command over the supply of labour at the
very moment that his interest and that of the State
require that it should be considerably augmented.
But the want of this supply, by enhancing the price
of wages still further, must of course check the progress of industry which originally created the demand, and this soon after the first start is given to
the population. By the time, therefore, that the
children begin to make an effective demand upon the
food of the country, the means of their parents for
affording them that food will be proportionally diminished, by the decreasing demand for their labour and
by diminished wages; and it will then remain to be
seen by what means the redundant supply of labour
actually in the market, or rising up for its supply,
will by its reduction accommodate itself to the reduced demand. It is clear that this can only be
done by the extinction of the superfluous population,
in consequence of the misery and distress introduced
among them by want of employment. I think myself, therefore, upon the whole justified in denying
that, in the natural course of things, the supply of
labour in the market will accommodate itself either
to an increasing or decreasing demand, with sufficient
rapidity and ease to secure the anticipated advantage
to the capitalist in the first case; or to prevent the
most extensive misery to the labouring classes in the
last case. The whole result of a reliance on such an
hypothesis would be nothing else than great fluctua-

tions of profit to the employer of labour; great fluctuations of price to the consumers of all the products of labour; and still greater fluctuations of condition to the labouring classes themselves, who are " unquestionably" (as Mr. Malthus observes with equal justice and liberality) " of the greatest weight in any estimate of national happiness."

I know, in short, but one method by which the supply of labour can be made immediately to accommodate itself to the demand in the market; and that is, by anticipating the production of the materials, which may be called into action when the demand is increasing; and providing for their due preservation against a more convenient season, when the demand is decreasing. I have shown that this anticipation and provision can be made without *any expense to the* WHOLE *society*, by the means pointed out in the first chapter of this second book.

But this is not the case with respect to all the particular portions of the community; for where the process is to be applied to a highly manufacturing state, the reasoning in the same chapter and in various other parts of this treatise, concerning the spontaneous distribution of the people, will show that the anticipation must be made chiefly at the expense of the agricultural part of the society; because the reproductive part of the people, from which the in creased supply of manufacturing as well as of all other labourers must come, exclusively resides in the agricultural districts. The provision also for their due preservation, when unemployed and in unfavourable seasons, necessarily, although not so exclusively, falls upon the produce of the land.

If the *whole society*, therefore, wish to preserve

the advantage, and to secure the *ultimate* saving accruing from it, in the constant supply and regular and uniform price of labour, under all the varying circumstances of demand, and in the well-being thus diffused throughout the great mass of the people, both employers and employed, it must be content to pay for them by an *immediate* enhancement of the price of the produce of land, upon which the principal expense of the process exclusively falls.

I have thought it right to place this subject in the chapter on the wages of labour, rather than in that on taxes or any other out-goings; because in fact it is much more nearly connected with wages than with any other subject. It is of little importance what denomination is given to the sum paid by the occupier of land for the support of his labourers and their families. It constitutes substantially, and as to all its political effects, the wages of their labour.

In estimating the extent of the sacrifice necessary to be made by the general consumer to enable the agriculturist to support this among his other burthens, it is customary to have recourse to the average prices of corn. But in a country which in ordinary years supports its own population, but is exposed to the risk of high prices in years of scarcity, averages are usually deceitful, and indicate a price higher than that which may be considered as sufficient for all the purposes of remunerating labour. But " as a people" (as Sir James Steuart observes) " does not live by averages, but every year's plenty or scarcity must affect them relatively to itself alone;" the corn grower in such a country will always require

protection in scarce seasons; because then with diminished means he continues to support more than
his fair proportion of the labouring part of the community. Although the price of his produce in plentiful years will always be below the average, its increased quantity will remunerate him for the diminished price; and a high protecting duty against the
import of foreign corn will probably be a dead letter.
But in scarce years the agriculturist, for the abovementioned reasons, will require the protection of a
high price against the competition of foreign corn in
the home market, if it were only upon the consideration of the enhanced sum he is obliged to disburse
in wages; and as it is then only that protecting duties will really operate, it is chiefly to ignorance of
the true principles of political economy, or to a selfish forgetfulness of them, that the violent prejudices against the establishment of such a protection in
a highly commercial and manufacturing country of
extensive territory are to be attributed. Upon the
whole, I think that the contents of this chapter have
fairly established that a free and commercial country
of extensive territory, wishing to preserve its prosperity in full vigour, and provide for the happiness of
all classes of its people, should endeavour to secure
such a remuneration to the agriculturist in the price
of his produce as will enable him, besides his other
expenses, to pay such wages to his labourers as shall
afford them and their families a reasonable participation in the general improvement of the commonwealth.

This may be the proper place for stating that, in
an advanced state of society where not more than
the fifth of the gross produce of a mixed arable and

pasture farm is paid in rent to the landlord, the expense in wages of labour, (as nearly as can be estimated from the average of returns made to the board of agriculture respecting the expense of cultivating 100 acres of arable land) will amount to a sum somewhat less than the rent.

CHAPTER X.

On the Remainder of a Tenant's Expenses, including Taxation, and on the Profits of his Farm.

THE cultivator's profits are evidently what remains to him after payment of his rent, of the wages of labour, of the wear and tear of stock and machinery, of other expenses of cultivation, of common interest on his capital, of taxes to the government, and of tithes where they are due. Of the two first items we have treated in the chapters immediately preceding. The wear and tear of stock and machinery, including the use of the team, on a mixed arable and pasture farm in England should amount to about two thirds of the rent; the seed and manure, which constitute the other expenses of cultivation, to about as much; tithe and rates to something more than half the rent; common interest upon capital to about one third of the rent; taxes to the government to about one tenth of the rent. From eight to ten per cent. should afterwards be left on the farmer's capital as his clear profit, to compensate the risk incurred and the labour bestowed, to accumulate for further investment, and to provide for his family.

On a farm worth 30*s.* an acre, we will suppose the necessary capital to be 12*l.* an acre, or 1200*l.* upon 100 acres. The gross produce of the 100 acres should then be worth about 750*l.*, and the sum would be thus apportioned according to the preceding estimate.

Although I am now arguing upon general principles, I have given the calculation according to the average out-goings of an English farm; because it is capable of being more easily referred to the test of fact and experience.

	£
1. Landlord's rent	150
2. Wages of labour	140
3. Wear and tear, including team	100
4. Seed and manure	100
5. Tithes and rates	80
6. Common interest on capital	60
7. Direct taxes paid by tenant, exclusive of property tax	15
8. Farmer's clear profits on 1200*l.* capital, not nine per cent	145
	£ 750

I do not conceive that the application of capital and industry to lands of moderate or inferior staple could be successfully made, or would in fact be persevered in in a commercial and manufacturing country even of extensive territory, at a permanent remuneration much lower than that which I have here stated. The competition for capital from other employments would prevent its diversion to the soil, until the price of produce should be sufficiently enhanced by the increased demand from the commercial and manufacturing population to afford that remuneration to the landlord for clearing, enclosing, draining, and improving, the land; and next, to the farmer, for capital, skill, and labour, employed in the regular cultivation. Should produce, therefore, be permitted to come from other countries at a cheaper rate, such land would never be cultivated or improved at all:—

at least it would be carried no further than to a state of coarse pasture.

Of the two first of these items I have already treated at large, and shall only add here that, including about 30*l.* from the item intitled rates, which according to the reasoning in the last chapter should be added to that entitled wages of labour, the two first items make up considerably more than two-fifths of the whole out-goings. If, however, there be any truth in the reasoning of the two last chapters, they are payments indispensably necessary to the welfare of the community. But in case of any defalcation in the due returns for the produce of the farm, they are the first that would cease to be paid; because an inferior state of cultivation could still be carried on upon the land by a considerable reduction in them.

Of the next item, viz. wear and tear of horses, stock, machinery, and implements, it may be observed that a portion of this expense involves indirect taxes to the government; and the remainder is devoted to setting industry in motion in other profitable departments. Any diminution therefore in the power of making this payment would be doubly injurious to the commonwealth; first by affecting the revenue, and next by depressing the general industry of the community. But such diminution would certainly ensue upon a depression in the price of produce, because like the two former items, this also could be trenched upon without absolute ruin to the farmer; he might still raise an inferior description of produce, and continue to live.

The next item, including seed and manure, is also indicative of a farm managed in a thriving manner; and, in case of an alteration of system by converting a large portion of arable into rough pasture, the expense would be saved. But it would be a most fatal saving in a commercial and manufacturing country; for, by checking the productive power of all the inferior lands, and by throwing them into such a state of waste as would require many years to reclaim, the community must be necessarily forced to have recourse to a permanent supply of foreign corn; and the capital and industry hitherto flourishing at home, would be transferred to foreign countries: to say nothing of the other inconveniences which have been stated as the consequence of such a calamity.

In the next item, tithes are the only article left for consideration; and in the view we are now taking they do not call for many remarks. Being a tenth of the produce, they will of course increase or decrease with the amount of that produce. But they constitute an out-going the relative amount of which cannot be diminished, as may be the case with all the other items. So long as the tithe owner is paid in that manner, the payment is very properly secured to him by law, in such a manner as to prevent the possibility of evasion or diminution. It has the preference over all other payments, and must therefore be deducted from the gross amount of the produce, before any calculation can be entered into of what the remainder may be capable of performing.

I cannot let this subject cross my path without one observation. However desirable it may be, both to the tithe owner in his professional capacity, and to the country with a view to the investment of capital in agricultural improvements, that a general commutation should, if possible, be made for this proproperty; yet, as far as it affects the farmer or mere occupier of the land, it is I think in ordinary times clearly advantageous to him. If no such out-going existed, a third would probably be added to his rent; that being, I should conceive, not an unfair valuation of the tenth of the gross produce of a farm, upon the average of farms. But from the difficulty in the mode of collection, from the liberal feeling of many of the clergy towards their parishioners, and from the general custom which the prevalence of this feeling has established, I will venture to affirm that the utmost value is not taken in one parish in a hundred in any country where tithes constitute the payment of the clergy. The *occupier* therefore, if a tenant, is the last man who ought to complain of that out-going.

The next item, viz. common interest on capital, is of course an absolutely necessary condition of its investment, and ruin must inevitably follow if it should continue permanently not to accrue; ruin to the individual by the loss of his fortune, ruin to the state by the destruction of its capital and industry.

Yet be it observed, this interest can only accrue upon the supposition that the price of the products of the farm is sufficient previously to discharge all its necessary out-goings, and to leave at least this surplus; which, it may be well to repeat, is not the *profit* that is to induce the capitalist to enter into further agricultural speculations, but merely the return which is to prevent his capital from being annihilated.

Of the direct taxes to government, which form the subject of the following item, it is scarcely possible for the tenant to pay less; and, property-tax excepted, the article is too trifling to deserve further consideration. There are other taxes, however, paid ultimately by the landlord, which constitute a more serious out-going, and, being levied in the first instance on the occupier, have of course the precedence of any payment of rent.

There is moreover one tax which, although not paid immediately by the landholder, falls so heavily upon agriculture, and operates so injuriously upon all classes of country residents, that I can let pass no fair opportunity of exposing its bad effects. I mean the tax upon malt, where malt-liquor has been the accustomed beverage of the people. When the duty is high, it operates nearly as a prohibition to the poor cottager, who was formerly accustomed to brew this liquor in small quantities for the consumption of his family; and the proportion of grain used in the great breweries, for the supply of country public houses, is by no means sufficient to compensate to the farmer the loss of demand from individuals of the lower classes. The effects, therefore, upon agriculture are obviously of a ruinous tendency; and those upon the morals of the people are still more serious. The *taste* for malt liquor is by no means eradicated from an English palate by the want of power to manufacture it at home. But, after tea or some other substitute has been provided for the family, the father is reduced to carry any surplus earnings to the public-house, where alone he can gratify the *reasonable* appetite which he inherited from his fathers. But the habit of frequenting the ale-house is no sooner acquired, than the appetite becomes *unreasonable*. Profligate and illicit means are resorted to for its gratification; wretchedness and beggary are introduced into the cottage; and, although the whole process has the appearance of adding to the revenue of the state, it does in fact greatly injure the industry and resources of the community, and saps the main pillars of public happiness and security.

We now come in conclusion to a most important article—the profits of the tenant; that which is to induce him to invest his capital in the cultivation of the soil, and which is to enable him to accumulate a further capital for similar investments. To deny that it is the interest of the community that these profits should be high, would be to deny an obvious truth; and it seems undoubtedly true also that their *general average* must rise with the necessity created by the progress of society for investing capital upon inferior land. For the increased price of produce necessary to make a return for that investment, and which is in fact the cause of it, and the continuance of which can alone keep inferior land in cultivation, must of course raise the profits of capital already invested in the cultivation of land of a superior quality, where produce can be raised at a cheaper rate. This will not admit of dispute if we consider that, produce of the same quality bearing but one price in the market, the cultivator, whose expenses compared with the amount of his produce were before so low as to enable him to make a profit by selling it cheap, must now make a superlucration, when the price rises high enough to remunerate the grower, whose expenses are high when compared with the amount of his produce. But this super-lucration must of course come out of the pockets of the consumer, and will therefore raise by its amount the general average of agricultural profits. It is true that a large portion of this superlucration will soon be added to the landlord's rent; but this will neither occur so rapidly nor so completely as to deprive the tenant of a considerable share in the advantage. The effect of this improvement will be to raise the relative condition of the farmer in society, and to induce persons possessing such capitals, as would authorise them to assume the rank of gentlemen, to invest them upon hired land; large portions of which will be accumulated into one farm; and a considerable increase in the quantity of surplus produce, the invariable consequence of large farms, will take place. This is also a necessary ingredient in a well constituted community, when society has advanced far in the commercial and manufacturing career; for the "free hands" as Sir James Steuart calls them, (that is, persons not employed in agriculture,) increasing with every step in that progress, a corresponding increase in the surplus produce which the agriculturist can spare to send to market of course becomes necessary for their food. But we have seen that the primary cause of this train of consequences is to be traced to the large profits of the tenant, inducing considerable capitalists to assume that character. The increase of those profits is therefore absolutely necessary to the public welfare as society advances, and constitutes the farmer's share of that general amelioration which should devolve upon every rank of the community from that advancement. The following passage from Mr. Malthus's "Inquiry into the Nature of Rent," p. 40, throws considerable light upon this subject. " I have no hesitation in stating that, independently of irregularities in the currency

of a country, and other temporary and accidental circumstances, the cause of the high comparative *money*
price of corn, is its high comparative *real* price, or
the greater quantity of capital and labour which must
be employed to produce it; and that the reason why
the real price of corn is higher, and continually
rising in countries which are already rich, and still
advancing in prosperity and population, is to be
found in the necessity of resorting constantly to
poorer lands—to machines, which require a greater
expenditure to work them, and which consequently
occasion each fresh addition to the raw produce of
the country to be purchased at a greater cost. In
short, it is to be found in the important truth that
corn, *in a progressive country*, is sold at the price
necessary to yield the actual supply; and that, as
this supply becomes more and more difficult, the
price rises in proportion."

If then it be desirable that a country should continue in a progressive state till it has reached its
point of non-reproduction, and if the power of extending cultivation and increasing produce " depend
entirely upon the existence of such prices, compared
with the expense of production, as would raise rents
in the actual state of cultivation;" in other words, if
the tenant's clear profits upon his *present* rent are
high enough to enable him to accumulate capital
and increase his *future* rent, so that cultivation may
proceed briskly, and agriculture extend itself in proportion to the wants of an increasing population;
then it follows as a necessary consequence, that it is
the interest of the state to take care that the tenant's
clear profits shall at least suffer no abatement. But

this involves greater sacrifices than every one who would agree in the abstract conclusion might perhaps be willing to make.

There may be many who will agree, that the average high price of corn in England, for example, " is the necessary result of the great superiority of her wealth and population, compared with the quality of her natural soil, and the extent of her territory;" and that, to preserve her in the same progress of prosperity and power, that average high price must be continued; who will yet hesitate to look the real difficulty of effecting this object in the face, or possess strength of mind enough to resist the temptation offered by the French or German agriculturists, who will be ready enough to offer corn at a low price, upon the simple condition of transferring British capital to their territory. The alternative is certainly tempting to the immediate feelings of selfishness, when we refer back to the schedule at the beginning of this chapter, and find the list of expenses, which must all be discharged by the general consumer to their full amount out of the price paid for raw produce, before the tenant's profits, the last item in the list, but so necessary to the prosperity of agriculture, begin to accrue. For it is evident, that these profits are nothing more or less than the net surplus after all other outgoings are discharged, and are, strictly speaking, " the excess of price above the cost of production," as hath been incorrectly asserted to be the case of rent. It is also clear, that if the state of cultivation be deteriorated by the diminution of any of those outgoings, the clear profits, (though perhaps not absolutely annihilated,) will be diminished in a still greater degree. The alternative therefore is fairly before the public, either to make the necessary sacrifice for the perseverance in a progressive state of prosperity, or to enjoy the present moment, at the risk of a progressive state of decay in future. They should recollect, however, that when the option is made, it will be too late to retrace their steps, and a little too absurd to complain of the consequences.

I should here have concluded this brief investigation of agricultural profits and expenses, were it not for the peculiar circumstances under which the agriculture of England now labours with respect to this item of tenant's profits.

After a protection, which has certainly been more than sufficient, as the event has shown, against the competition of foreign corn, an apparently permanent diminution in the price of raw produce has nevertheless ensued, which has not only annihilated the tenant's profit on inferior land, but has also materially trenched upon the item next liable to be affected, viz. the landlord's rent, and which must, if not remedied, as a natural consequence, soon affect the other outgoings, and the general state of cultivation, of revenue, and of every branch of national prosperity.

I think it will be peculiarly instructive to the advocates for making England again a country exporting corn to perceive that, although the surplus produce above the wants of the whole community, for which they so strenuously contend, now presents itself to their wishes, and that this surplus has lowered the price of corn so as to distress the agricultural interest to the greatest degree, and therefore so as to give more than a reasonable facility to exportation, yet, in point of fact, none has been exported, but the whole has been kept at home, and has glutted the domestic market. Now the cause of this seems very evident. Although the price of corn is low compared with the expense of raising it in England, it is still high compared with the expense of raising it in the agricultural countries; it therefore cannot compete with them in the foreign market; it has not therefore been exported; and it is not very unsafe to predict that, so long as the same relative circumstances continue, it never will be exported; at least, not permanently. The advocates for rendering England a permanently exporting country must first ruin our manufactures, throw all our inferior lands out of cultivation, and reduce our population *within* the limits of the supply from the lands of superior staple. They may then attain the object of their desires by exporting the surplus. This point may perhaps deserve a more minute investigation, as the advocates for the system of exportation from England have some plausible facts on their side connected with the progress of agriculture during the last century : into these I shall briefly enter.

Before the Revolution, the agriculture of England was comparatively in a very wretched state. The abuses of purveyance, the licenses for monopoly, and the unbounded permission given to the importation of corn, were impediments to cultivation so intolerable, that much of the best land of England lay waste, and had done so for centuries. It is indeed impossible that other consequences should have followed the confined or mistaken policy of our princes before that period, who rather had in view to draw a revenue immediately from the corn trade than, by regulations on more enlarged and liberal principles, to encourage the improvement of agriculture and the general prosperity of the country; and thus to secure to themselves the power of levying a revenue of twenty times the amount. So true it is, that selfish policy, grasping immediate advantages, without regard to future consequences, always defeats its own ends.

From the year 1570, many laws were made verbally encouraging agriculture, by allowing exportation; but they embarrassed it with duties of from 10 to 50 *per cent. ad valorem;* and, with very trifling exceptions, allowed an unlimited importation.

At the Revolution, a different policy was adopted; *bounties* were then given upon exportation; high duties were laid upon corn imported; and twelve years afterwards, (in 1700,) the duties payable on exportation were in all cases abolished. But the high duties upon importation being often evaded, from the difficulty and neglect in ascertaining the price of corn in the home market, the system was completed in 1732, by a law obliging the grand juries, at every quarter sessions of the maritime counties, to present the average price of corn, and the justices to transmit them to the officers of the customs at the ports, in order to enforce a fair and strict collection of the duties. These wise alterations operated like magic, and placed England in some measure in the situation of a newly-settled country. Good land, long in waste from former discouragements, could be had cheap; farms easily procured; and the soil being fresh, and producing abundantly, could therefore be cultivated at a large profit, as soon as it was eased of a part of the discouragements under which it laboured. The effects were such as might be expected; the people were, with very few exceptions, plentifully

supplied with food at a moderate price; and so large
an exportation of grain shortly took place, that the
annual average was never less than 300,000 quarters; and in the twenty years of greatest prosperity,
(from 1740 to 1760,) it amounted to upwards of
700,000 quarters of all kinds of grain.

Now this effect of the corn-laws, established after
the Revolution, is the ground upon which those who
think a recurrence to the same system would *now*
produce the same effect rest their arguments. But
do they consider the different condition of the internal
demand for corn, and the state of the soil yet uncultivated, between that period and the present? Do
they reflect upon the manufacturing population now
existing, which then was not even thought of? The
demand from whom must operate, at least as much
as any bounty could do, in securing a market for
such corn as the cultivator can bring to it under the
present state of the soil?

If any part of these considerations have escaped
their attention, I think that a recurrence to them,
and to the facts which were contemporary with the
laws which are accused of having checked exportation, will operate a conviction on their minds. From
the year 1732 to 1760, England continued to make
large exports of corn: from 1760 to 1767, the exporting balance gradually decreased, till, in the last
year, it wholly ceased, and has never since been resumed. During this period, the price of corn had
been gradually rising from 1*l.* 19*s.* to 3*l.* 4*s.* the
quarter. Yet, be it carefully observed, it was not
till the last of the abovementioned years, 1767, till
the export of corn had ceased, and till its price had
thus risen, that even a temporary law was made pro-

hibiting the export; and this was enacted in consequence of disturbances from the scarcity and dearness of corn, and petitions to parliament from London and other places; and no permanent law for the purpose was made till 1773, six years after all exportation of corn had finally ceased. Unless therefore it be considered logical in reasoning to ascribe an effect to causes which succeeded it in the order of time, I think it perfectly evident, that the balance turned from the exporting to the importing side, not in consequence of any statutes, but from other causes; and these causes are clearly to be traced in the rapid increase of manufacturing and commercial industry and population during the same period, which not only absorbed all the surplus produce derived from the land and formerly exported, but which also created a demand for a still further supply: and the reason why this supply was not produced from the domestic soil of inferior staple, as it naturally would have been according to the principles of this treatise, was because the laws prohibiting the export also, absurdly enough, encouraged the import of corn, thereby establishing a competition between the *best* lands of foreign countries and the *inferior* lands of our own for feeding our own people. It is natural enough that on this system we should have gone on importing corn, and encouraging the capital and industry of other countries at the expense of our own till the error was discovered. But the rapid increase of population and industry nevertheless continued to afford so strong a stimulus to cultivation, in spite of a low protecting duty, that it still proceeded in some degree upon the inferior lands, and kept our supply of food so nearly up to our demand that the permanent requisitions from abroad never exceeded from a week's to a month's consumption, according to the state of the harvest. But this has of course brought so much inferior land into cultivation, and has so much enhanced the general and average expense of raising produce, that, as I have before fully explained, it is utterly absurd to suppose that it can ever be made to compete in the foreign market with corn the growth of the purely agricultural states.

I trust that these arguments are sufficient to convince the advocates for making England a country permanently exporting corn, that the period for success in such a scheme has long elapsed, and that they are neither entitled from precedent or fair reasoning to entertain any such expectations, while she retains her commercial and manufacturing greatness.

But it may be asked, how comes it then that a a surplus produce, (Jan. 1816,) actually exists beyond the wants of the community, which it would be certainly advantageous to the grower to export if he could find the means? Whence, in short, is derived this extraordinary glut in the corn market to which we have so many years been strangers? The solution of this question may perhaps be thought to lead to considerations of too temporary a nature to be admitted into a work of this description. But I venture to hope that a perusal of the following arguments will correct this opinion. The circumstances under which we are now labouring must be of frequent recurrence in all free and extensive countries, far advanced in society, liable to be engaged in hostilities with their neighbours, and wisely exerting themselves to establish an independent supply of food for the people from their native soil. They will doubtless recur, perhaps with aggravated force, in future periods of our own history. An investigation of them is therefore surely not superfluous in a work professing to treat fundamentally of the principles connected with the comfortable subsistence of the people in the advanced stages of society.

CHAPTER XI.

On the Causes of the present Depression, and of the Fluctuations which have lately taken place, in the Price of Agricultural Produce.

I CONCEIVE that no man accustomed to consider the principles upon which the demand and the supply of the corn-market are regulated, and who recollects the history of the last two eventful years, can hesitate in pointing out, with a considerable degree of confidence, both the proximate causes of the present state of things, and the origin from which they sprung. It is demonstrable, as a general principle, that when markets are for any considerable period overstocked with an article, the importation of which is prohibited, the glut must necessarily be produced by the existence of a surplus produce of domestic growth. A temporary effect of this nature may certainly be produced by distress among the growers, from want of accommodation arising out of a suspension of credit, or from a panic concerning the progressive deterioration of prices. Either of these causes would induce them to pour their produce into the market in greater quantities than the demand would absorb, would reduce its price, promote a wasteful consumption ; and, when the temporary effects had ceased, the natural result of such a process would be a subsequent and rather sudden elevation of price : for the country would be gradually exhausted of its produce, while the increased demand remained in full vigour. The wasteful habits introduced by previous plenty would not be immediately corrected, and, when the stock to supply them began to fall short, a considerable rise of price would of course ensue. That these causes have in some degree operated to produce the present glut in the market, and that those effects are reasonably to be expected, especially if the ensuing harvest be not very plentiful, is, I think, undeniable. The general want of that accommodation which the farmers have for years past experienced from the country Bankers, whose resources of credit have now failed, have rendered it necessary for tenants to force their corn into the market with a simultaneous effort, in order to procure money for the payment of their rent, their taxes, and other out-goings : while the consequent reduction of price renders it necessary to sell so large a quantity of produce, in order to realize the sums actually due from the cultivator to his creditors, that infinitely more than the fair proportion of the growth of the country has been prematurely forced into the market. At the same time, the general stagnation of credit, and want of money for speculation, have prevented the purchase of any large quantities of corn for the purpose of storing, with a view to resale at a profit. The alarm of the farmers, lest a still further depression should ensue, operating upon their conviction that, at all events, their produce must ere long be carried to market, must have hastened their efforts to anticipate this further depression by a speedy sale, and, by adding to the mass in an already overstocked market, must have tended, like most other effects of panic, to aggravate the danger it was the object to avoid. Under these circumstances it is not true, as I have lately seen it asserted, that the consumption of corn does not increase in some proportion at least to the depression of its price. When cheap, it is converted to many purposes for which substitutes are used when it is dear. I have no doubt that grain has been used for many months past where potatoes are the usual food in ordinary times. The supply and the consumption having therefore both exceeded their usual proportion, it follows, as a strictly logical conclusion, that unless the future growth shall be equally in excess, the ultimate consequence must be a comparative scarcity and rise in price. And as there is no reason to conclude that the growth will be sufficiently in excess to counteract the effects of one unfavourable or even average harvest upon the diminished breadth of corn, to which the low price has induced the cultivator to contract his efforts for the ensuing crop, I have little doubt that a gradual rise in the corn-market will, ere long, be established, unless the next harvest should be uncommonly abundant.

In the mean time however it may be asked, how is the agricultural interest to be relieved from the distress consequent upon the depression in the price of produce, which has been proceeding in a constant state of aggravation for the last two seasons? To this it may be answered, that in so far as they were entitled to, or could receive relief from, the unfair competition of the foreign grower, it was granted, though somewhat late, during the last session of parliament. In so far as their distress, notwithstanding that relief, is now to be attributed to an excess of the supply actually grown above the diminished demand in the market, the relief can only proceed from the

300 CAUSES OF THE PRESENT DEPRESSION.

agriculturist himself. He must of course adapt his supply to the demand. This is obviously the only cure. The abolition of rent, of tithes, of taxes, of every other out-going foreign to the expenses of cultivation, can have no possible effect, till this necessary condition is fulfilled. For if the supply be greater than the demand of any article that must necessarily be brought to market within a given time, the price must of course sink below the cost of production, whatever that cost may be. The farmer would not gain one-half penny by getting rid of all those out-goings ; but the price of corn would *naturally* sink, in the first instance, till it reached that point in the *scale of loss,* at which the most distressed cultivator should find himself obliged to dispose of his produce. It would *in fact,* however, soon sink much lower ; for the ruin of the owners of the rent, of the tithes, of the taxes, who are the public creditors, would successively take so many consumers out of the market, that the forementioned *point in the scale of loss* would be continually lowering, until the gradually con-tracting supply should be no more than barely suffi-cient to answer the gradually decreasing demand in the market. But it is difficult to say, how many retrograde steps in the progress of society the country must in the mean time have made.

Now I think there are many circumstances which lead to the conclusion, that the growth of corn in the United Kingdom has been in excess above the demand for the last two years. In the first place, the quantity of foreign corn brought into it, in addition to an abundant domestic supply, before the Corn Bill of 1815 began to operate, must have decreased *quoad hoc* the demand for grain of English growth. In the next place, the demands of government for the army and navy, for the maintenance of prisoners of war, and the necessary waste of food in all the transfers of it incident to the operations of war, all of which have constituted very material items in the demand for many years past, and have therefore operated long enough to produce their effect on the agriculture of the kingdom, have on a sudden either partially or entirely ceased. And as the difficulties thrown in the way of the free circulation of corn by the continental system and our disputes with America obliged us to draw upon our domestic agriculture for the greater part of the abovementioned demands, the supply no longer wanted now preponderates as a dead weight on the unfavourable side of the balance in the market. Without entering into minute calculations of the quantities of corn thrown upon the market by the cessation of these demands, the fact that they *have produced a surplus* is capable of demonstration. For if the agriculture of the country was previously sufficient without material assistance to supply the wants of the domestic population as well as the foreign demands just alluded to, which is proved by the small amount of grain imported of late years, then it follows as an incontrovertible conclusion that, when the last quantity is added to the first in the home market, there must be upon the whole an excess of supply above the demand; and this excess being proved, I apprehend no man will hesitate in admitting that it can only be cured by reducing the supply to the demand. This necessary alteration of system is only one among many effects of the complete revolution in almost every course of transactions, public and private, which has been induced by the sudden transition from an habitual state of war with almost all the world to a general state of free and liberal intercourse. If England be true to her principles, if she show as much vigour, wisdom, and perseverance, in meeting the first difficulties of peace, without departing from the principles upon which her permanent prosperity must always rest, as she exhibited during the protracted difficulties of war without departing from her principles of moral and political integrity, the transition will be made without danger, and in a short period she may sit quietly down to enjoy her reward. The elements of mischief, in the mean time, however, must be expected to work busily : doubtless, in many cases without any bad intent among those who may call them into action. General principles will probably be applied to particular circumstances, with as much eagerness and confidence on the *corn question* as we recollect them to have been urged on the *bullion question*. But the natural good sense of the country will meet them in the same manner, and the result of experience will in this case, as it did in that, tend to the confusion of the interested and ill-intentioned, and the conviction of the candid and sober-minded disputant.

In the case immediately before us, of a market overstocked by excessive growth, it is easy to foresee how the cultivators themselves will apply the remedy. Finding grain a drug in the market, they will be induced to diminish the breadth of land sown, and to convert it to other purposes of cultivation, until the price of grain again rises in the market; and, as the present cheapness of food will probably give an impulse to the increase of population, a further demand will soon occur, which will restore the profitable cultivation of grain to the lands now diverted from it.   This alternating process will certainly produce a fluctuation in the price of corn ; and, generally speaking, it is certainly true that, after the agricultural state of society is passed, an independent supply of grain cannot be raised upon inferior soil, without some fluctuation of price in the market.   It is the rise of prices which produces further cultivation, and the consequent production which again depresses the price till increasing population calls for a further produce.   But these fluctuations will never be very great, in the natural course of things, in any free and industrious country possessing plenty of capital.   A trifling rise in price is a sufficient indication to the capitalist where he can lay out his money to advantage ; and in a rich and flourishing community the competition is usually rather among the possessors of capital for its profitable investment, than among the possessors of profitable employments for the use of capital.   A small rise in the price of grain would always carry a corresponding portion of capital to the soil, and the quick returns will prevent that trifling rise from being aggravated into a high price.   The fluctuations of price can never therefore be very great in the ordinary course of things, where the distribution of capital is left to its free course: and it would be plainly absurd to ascribe the great fluctuations of the present moment to any causes, which ought to influence the legislature in the adjustment of the permanent interests of agriculture as connected with those of the other classes of society.   So great a depreciation in the value of produce could never have occurred without the violent revulsion produced by the sudden stoppage of the demands created by a protracted war. To argue therefore upon the inconveniences arising from such an unnatural fluctuation as the ground for recurring to a system of supply permanently dependant upon other countries, a system, too, which would be occasionally subject to fluctuations still greater, and to consequences infinitely more fatal, is as I have ventured to assert, plainly absurd. It was just the sort of argument used upon the bullion question, and its application rests on grounds very analogous. A sudden effect wrought by violent and temporary causes was presumed to have arisen from the regular and natural operation of general principles; and a remedy was recommended arising out of those principles, which would evidently have been ruinous, if its advocates were (as they now confess themselves to have been) to a considerable extent mistaken in the cause of the evil.

Just in the same manner we now find a crowd of writers ascribing the present unnatural fluctuations of price to the system of forcing an independent supply of food from inferior soil, as if they were the natural and unavoidable consequences of that system, and contrasting with it what they are pleased to call the steady and uniform prices of a supply dependant upon importation from foreign countries. It is really edifying to behold the coolness and courage with which these œconomists come to the conclusion—that it would now be expedient to throw away all the capital which has been expended upon our domestic soil of inferior staple, to ruin past recal the large class of general consumers who subsist upon its cultivation, and to transfer their industry and resources to rival nations! Even if their premises were true, their conclusions would scarcely be admissible, since, for reasons given in a former part of this book, the fluctuations consequent upon *their system* would be greater and more frequent than those we have lately witnessed. But their premises being plainly false and exaggerated, inasmuch as the fluctuation is the consequence not of the present system, but of a violent interference with it, arising out of extraordinary causes;—it should seem that their argument fails in all its parts: and, if there be any truth in the propositions maintained in this and the preceding chapters, the application of their argument in practice would certainly lead to national ruin.

I shall perhaps be asked by the advocates for steady and regular prices of corn, Are we then to give up all hopes of this great desideratum, attended as it is by uniformity in the price of other articles, by a steady rate of wages, an even tenour in the value of capital, and the general comfort which flows from these effects among all classes of the community? I answer, that *perfect uniformity* in the price of raw produce appears to be a mere phantom of the imagination, after the agricultural state of society has been passed, and inferior soils begin to be cultivated. If the people depend upon a domestic growth, the variation of the seasons upon a supply sufficient on the average must sometimes produce cheapness as the consequence of an abundant harvest—at other times dearness as the consequence of a deficient crop. If they depend upon the growth of foreign countries, the variation of the seasons there, the uncertainties of commerce, the impediments of war, the prohibitions of hostile governments to export an article from its bulk not easily smuggled, will always introduce more or less of precariousness in the supply, and consequently of fluctuation in the price. And if the demand extend to a large portion of the people's food, the disorders introduced by these interruptions may be very fatal to the peace and good order of society. It should always be recollected in this argument, that a country possessing political power liable to excite general jealousy, ventures permanently to depend upon the foreign supply of so essential an article as food, with infinitely less security than small commercial republics; and that it will be exposed to much greater fluctuations from political causes.

Since then some fluctuations must be expected under either system, the question is—Under which system will they be the least, after a country begins to subsist upon the produce of its inferior soils? Now I apprehend that an independent supply from the native soil, and the encouragement of domestic cultivation, by fixing the price at which foreign corn may be imported at that point which is just necessary on the average to remunerate the grower of domestic produce for the clearing and cultivation of soils of the staple of those last broken up, will best effect the object in view. As society advances, this price must of course rise in proportion to the necessity for cultivating soils of still inferior quality to those last occupied. But we must recollect also that the advancement of society is necessarily accompanied by an abatement in the progress of population : so that before the period when none but the worst soils remain unoccupied, the demand for further production recurs at intervals successively more distant.

We may too, I think, always be reminded, in reference to the effects upon commerce and manufactures, of the high price at which these last supplies from the worst soils can be procured, that the principal object of commerce and manufactures for export being to realize capital for investment at home, and to assist in carrying on a people in a healthy career of industry and cultivation; it follows that, in proportion as a country advances to a fulness of population and production, external commerce and the export of manufactures become comparatively of less importance to them. In proportion as England shall be peopled and cultivated towards the utmost point, its commercial intercourse with other countries may perhaps be profitably confined to the mere exchange of commodities for mutual comfort and convenience, without any view to the realization of fresh capital. The main springs of her wealth would then be found to be almost exclusively in her internal trade.

But to return from this digression. I have stated that the protection of domestic agriculture, by an importation price just high enough to remunerate the cultivator of soils of the staple of those last broken up, seems to be the most effectual method of preventing great fluctuations in the price of produce under the ordinary course of things, in a commercial and manufacturing country; indeed of confining all fluctuation within the limits necessarily set by Providence in its regulation of the seasons.

I think that this will appear to be true, when we consider that the price can scarcely ever rise materially higher; because it will be so very far above that which corn bears in the exporting countries, or any of the other countries with which they have dealings, that the instant the ports of the highly commercial country are open, corn must almost necessarily flow into them, as to the most profitable market to which it can be carried : of course this is predicated of ordinary times, and the chances of war and other similar impediments are excepted in the argument. Neither will the price ever sink very far below the importation price, except in very plentiful harvests at home, when the excess in quantity will remunerate the grower at the reduced price. For under the ordinary circumstances of the country, inferior lands will not be broken up without a demand for the produce raised upon them. And upon the first indication given by sinking prices, that such demand is supplied, the progress of breaking up such soils will of course be checked. In plain terms, men will not cultivate without such a price for the produce as will pay the cost of production ;—at which price foreign corn comes into competition and checks a further rise. By these means, therefore, all material fluctuation is prevented, and it is reduced to an alternation between such low and moderate prices, on the one hand, as result from plentiful and average crops; and on the other such a moderately increased price as a scanty crop, notwithstanding the depression caused by imported corn, may be supposed to cause. In this last case, indeed, the grower will not be *entirely remunerated,* but must take his share with the rest of his countrymen in the infliction of Providence. But, upon the whole, the progress of agriculture will be maintained ; the system least liable to fatal interruptions will be pursued; and fluctuations in price as far prevented, as can be supposed possible during the advanced stages of society in a production of so precarious a nature as the growth of corn.

CHAPTER XII.

*Recapitulation of the last Five Chapters, and the
Conclusion deducible therefrom.*

AT the close of the sixth chapter, I observed that
the question concerning the encouragement to be
given to agriculture is a question of degree; that it
must obviously not be carried to an extent that
would either permanently injure commerce, and especially manufactures, by materially affecting the exportation of them to foreign countries, in consequence
of an exorbitant rise in the price of labour at home;
or that would check the sale of goods in the domestic
market.

I further observed that, to ascertain whether due
encouragement can be given to agriculture without any of these pernicious consequences, it is expedient in the first place to inquire into the necessary expenses that must be defrayed by the cultivator, before he begins to calculate upon those profits
which are to determine the propriety of his continuing or relinquishing the objects of his pursuit.
For these expenses must evidently be exceeded by
the price paid for the produce by the general consumer, in order to give the cultivator any profit at
all. This inquiry has been carried on in the four
chapters preceding the last; and the result seems
to be, that in a country far advanced into the commercial and manufacturing state of society, enjoying a free constitution, and that wishes to preserve
and improve those blessings;—1st, a rent sufficient

to return fair interest for the capital invested in the land;—2dly, wages high enough to afford to the labourers and their families a fair participation in the improving condition of the whole society;—3dly, money sufficient to keep the stock and implements upon the farms in a thriving and serviceable state;—4thly, the power of keeping the land in heart, and sowing the most profitable crops;—5thly, the support of the moral and religious institutions of the country;—6thly, the fair return of the farmer's capital;—7thly, the necessary taxes to government;—and lastly, increasing clear profits upon the farmer's capital—constitute the encouragement necessary to the successful progress of agriculture. Be it observed, that they are not stated as essentially necessary to the prosperity of agriculture *in all countries;* but to its co-existence with the peculiar condition and advantages of a free and commercial country. The question then arises, *can* it co-exist with those peculiar advantages? Can the general consumer in a commercial and manufacturing country afford to defray all these necessary expenses without destroying commerce and manufactures, the very sources of agricultural prosperity in such a country? In short, can the infant be supported without destroying its nurse while it still requires her milk? I am disposed to think it can.

In the first place let it be considered that there are no consumers of manufactures, and objects of commerce, so certain and so constant as the domestic cultivators. Let us refer again to the schedule at the beginning of the last chapter but one, and we shall find that at least two thirds of the sums there specified are expended by the farmer, or by those who receive the sums from him, in such objects. Rent, wages, wear and tear, tithe, taxes, and at least the interest of the farmer's capital, are in a considerable portion so expended. The sum, therefore, paid by the general consumer in the price of raw produce is circulated, till a large portion of it is conveyed to the merchant or manufacturer, in the price of his commodity: and the circulation of it, with its return to the farmer through the agency of the manufacturing labourers, promotes industry and comfort among all classes of society. But let us suppose the farm lying waste, and the outgoings from it consequently annihilated; the whole of this circulation is of course at an end. The *existing* labourers receive no wages, and can therefore spend none, but must be supported by a tax on the manufacturer so long as he is able to support them; the landlord receives no rent, consequently he can purchase no commodities. The clergyman receiving no tithe is in the same predicament. So are all those whose industry and employments were promoted by the expenses of the farmer. Now supposing the produce formerly raised on the farm to be imported at a cheaper rate, what compensation does the merchant or manufacturer obtain for the above-mentioned loss of his domestic market, and of property to the state? I will grant that he is enabled to export his manufacture at a somewhat cheaper rate; yet surely he can never expect permanently to do this to the extent of converting the labourers and farmers, previously employed as cultivators, into manufacturers; nor to that of compensating to himself the loss he has sustained by expelling them from the domestic market. To say nothing of the precarious nature

of foreign trade, especially of the market for exported manufactures, it cannot be too often repeated
that, in a highly commercial state of society, *a very
large portion* of the cultivators are employed on in.
ferior land, and must therefore be ruined by a free
competition with the cultivators of the purely agricultural countries. Their disappearance then from the
manufacturer's market is at once a certain and
enormous loss: and I am persuaded that nothing
but the difficulty of procuring an accurate estimate
of the comparative value of manufactures sold in
the foreign and domestic markets respectively could
ever lead the manufacturer to suppose, that this
certain loss could be permanently compensated by
his eventual success in the foreign market. If therefore the alternative were that he must lose one or
the other, it is presumed that he ought not to hesitate. But is this, in fact, the alternative? Certainly
the sacrifice of the cultivators of inferior lands is a
great and certain loss to the commercial and manufacturing market at home. But does the high price
of produce, necessary to the maintenance of that
cultivation, as certainly deprive the merchant and
manufacturer of their success in the foreign market?
I will cite an authority better than my own upon
this subject. (See Malthus' Grounds of an Opinion
on the Policy of restricting the Importation of Foreign
Corn, p. 31.) " It may be said, perhaps, that a
fall in the price of our corn and labour affords the only
chance to our manufacturers of retaining possession
of the foreign markets ; and that though the produce
of the country may not be increased by the fall in
the price of corn, such a fall is necessary to prevent
a positive diminution of it. There is some weight

undoubtedly in this argument. But if we look at the probable effects of returning peace to Europe, it is impossible to suppose that, even with a considerable diminution in the price of labour, we should not lose some markets on the continent, for those manufactures in which we have no peculiar advantage; while we have every reason to believe that in others, where our colonies, our navigation, our long credits, our coals, and our mines, come in question, as well as our skill and capital, we shall retain our trade in spite of high wages. Under these circumstances, it seems peculiarly adviseable to maintain unimpaired, if possible, the home market, and not to lose the demand occasioned by so much of the rents of land, and of the profits and capital of farmers, as must necessarily be destroyed by the check to our home produce.

" But in whatever way the country may be affected by the change, we must suppose that those who are immediately engaged in foreign trade will benefit by it. As they, however, form but a very small portion of the class of persons living on the profits of stock in point of number, and not probably above a seventh or eighth in point of property, their interests cannot be allowed to weigh against the interests of so very large a majority.

" With regard to this great majority, it is impossible that they should not feel very widely and severely the diminution of their nominal capital by the fall of prices. We know the magic effect upon industry of a rise of prices. It has been noticed by Hume, and witnessed by every person who has attended to subjects of this kind. And the effects of a fall are proportionately depressing. Even the foreign trade will not escape its influence, though here it may be counterbalanced by a real increase of demand. But, in the internal trade, not only will the full effect of this deadening weight be experienced, but there is reason to fear that it may be accompanied with an actual diminution of home demand. There may be the same or even a greater quantity of corn consumed in the country, but a smaller quantity of manufactures and colonial produce; and our foreign corn may be purchased in part by commodities which were before consumed at home. In this case, the whole of the internal trade must severely suffer, and the wealth and enjoyments of the country be decidedly diminished. The quantity of a country's exports is a very uncertain criterion of its wealth. The quantity of produce permanently consumed at home is, perhaps, the most certain criterion of wealth to which we can refer."

Many other writers have expressed their opinion that the effects of a high price of labour, on the export of manufactures, will be more than counteracted by the superior skill, capital, and industry, of which high wages are one necessary consequence. Those, who have done me the honour occasionally to look into the tracts which I have published, well know that I am no advocate for *gratuitously* establishing such an elevation in the price of labour as shall put the foreign commerce of a country unnecessarily even to the slightest risk. An important part of my argument on the Poor Laws (see Short Inquiry, &c.) rests upon the effects which they have in favouring foreign commerce, by preventing the inordinate rise of wages during a brisk demand for hands. But when the question is, not whether a gratuitous sacrifice shall be made, but whether, in an alternative presenting unequal risks, that side shall not be embraced where the chance of injury is undoubtedly the least, it is certainly gratifying to find political economists of high character agreeing in opinion, that where the injury to be apprehended is *undoubtedly* the least, there it will, *in all probability*, turn out to be none at all: and that if the domestic capital, skill, labour, and enterprise of a nation are kept flourishing and entire, its commerce and the export of its manufactures will rest upon a principle of vigour more than sufficient to overcome the competition of any rival country, possessing an advantage only in the single article of low wages.

I think, then, that I am authorized in concluding that it is both consistent with the interests, and within the power of a free country far advanced into the commercial and manufacturing state of society, to preserve its agriculture in a flourishing condition, by securing to the cultivators an increasing price for raw produce in proportion to the expenses they must incur in bringing inferior land into cultivation. Such a price is evidently the natural effect of the progress of society and of population, and can only be prevented by permitting the policy and resources of countries, in other states of society, to flourish at the expense of the country in question, and to amalgamate themselves too closely with its interests; a permission always problematical in politics, and, in nine cases out of ten, decidedly injurious. A fair commercial intercourse between rival nations is a bond of union; but with them, as with individuals, too close an intimacy is apt to lead to dangerous separations. We may return then to the principle which forms the title of the fifth chapter of this book, from which the whole of the subsequent argument has branched out, and assert that the encouragement to agriculture, here contended for, is necessary to prevent the mischievous pressure of population, caused by depressing the productive energies of the soil considerably below its natural powers.

CHAPTER XIII.

Recapitulation and Conclusion of the Second Book.

THIS book, which contains the political application of the argument held in the first book of this treatise, has been constructed with the single view of showing the *legitimate* consequences deducible from that argument on the important and fundamental questions that relate to the comfortable subsistence of the people, as society advances towards those stages where the means of providing that subsistence is often found to be a matter of intricacy and difficulty. It would be impertinent to enlarge in this place upon the close connexion between these consequences and all the higher departments of politics. "There are counsellors and statesmen," as Lord Bacon says, in his observations on the speech of Themistocles, "which can make a small state great, and yet cannot fiddle; as on the other side, there will be found a great many that can fiddle very cunningly, but yet are so far from being able to make a small state great, as their gift lieth the other way, to bring a great and flourishing estate to ruin and decay. But let counsellors and governors be held in any degree '*negotiis pares*,' able to manage affairs; be the workmen what they may, *the work* is the main object; that is, the true greatness of kingdoms and estates, and the means thereof." Now there can be no doubt that a compact, vigorous, and well-knit body is an indispensable quality of "*the work*" or instrument with which statesmen are to operate. They may be furnished with all knowledge, yet if they have not such an instrument to wield, their wisdom will be of no avail. Of what effect, for example, is the power of such a country as Spain in the hands of a statesman, except to encumber his march? and certainly her statesmen have for many generations been much addicted to *fiddling*, or, in Lord Bacon's words, " to those degenerate arts and shifts to gain favour with their masters and estimation with the vulgar, which deserve no better name than fiddling." So far therefore from making a small state great, they have brought their great and flourishing kingdom to ruin and decay, and have made it almost an useless incumbrance in the political system of Europe. Whereas the power of Great Britain, from the circumstance that it has regulated its internal polity upon the principle of Themistocles, has been found to preponderate in the scale of the world, when cast into the balance by her statesmen against the most powerful nations.

But this is by no means the whole case. Political greatness is of trifling value, nor can it be of long duration, unless it rest upon public happiness. France had political greatness enough, and to spare, but it rested upon public misery and the degradation of the people, and therefore could not stand the test of a well combined attack. The comfort and happiness of the people then lie at the bottom of the national strength, and consist in their industry and comfortable subsistence, or rather in the comfortable subsistence which is the natural result of their industry, under the regulation of wholesome laws.

If the first book of this treatise satisfactorily proved that there is no inherent principle in the constitution of society which necessarily prevents this condition from being fulfilled at any period of its progress, or from continuing in vigour for an indefinite period when once established, I trust that the contents of this book have been equally successful in showing the specific means by which the condition may be practically realized.

It has shown, first, (see c. i.) that population, having a natural tendency to keep within the powers of the soil to afford subsistence, a well regulated community may safely encourage its increase, either with a view to public strength or private happiness, because in such a community that increase will certainly be accompanied by a contemporaneous extension of agriculture.

It has shown (c. ii.) that the tendency inherent in the principle of population to keep it within the powers of the soil can never be destroyed, because, among other reasons, it appears that, as society advances, the number of the people never presses against the *mere necessaries* of life, but only against the luxuries of the higher orders. And further, (c. iii.), that population, being the cause of the production of food in the higher stages of society, it is only necessary to permit that cause, under due moral regulation, to operate its legitimate effect until the people naturally cease to reproduce their own numbers, in order to prevent any permanent pressure of their wants against the means of subsistence. But in order to enable the *natural* increase of population to operate its legitimate effect in increasing the production, of food, several precautions are necessary, all of which however are also essential to the people's happiness, independently of any view to their comfort.

able subsistence: as, first, (c. iv.) To prevent any *unnatural* acceleration in the progress of population whereby an *idle* and *unemployed* people might come to press perniciously against the food, which is only increasing at the natural rate indicated by the demand of the industrious consumers who have a fair equivalent to give for it. Secondly, (c. v.) That the productive energies of the soil shall not be depressed below their natural powers, so that the industrious consumers shall be disappointed of their fair expectation of subsistence, in return for the remuneration they are prepared to give for it. To prevent this depression it appears, (c. vi.) that as society advances, and food is raised, at an increased expense, upon land of inferior staple, the cultivator should be protected from the competition of corn raised by the capital and labour of foreign countries, who can still cultivate it on good land at a small expense. And to secure to the domestic cultivator of inferior land such a sufficient price for his produce, as shall induce him to persevere in his useful occupation, and tempt others to enter into it, it appears also necessary, that that price should cover the following outgoings; viz. (c. vii.) a fair rent to the landlord; (c. viii.) the tenant's fair expenses and profits, consisting of, 1st, (c. ix.) such wages to the farmer's labourers as shall maintain them and their families in comfort and decency; 2dly, (c. x.) such a sum of money as shall keep his stock and implements in good order; as shall keep his land in heart; as shall pay his moral and religious instructors; his taxes to the government; and, after all, shall not only afford him common interest for his capital which is necessary merely to save him from ruin, but shall also afford him a liberal clear profit upon that capital in reward for his industry and exertions.

It does, I trust, appear that, under the operation of the principles established in the first book of this treatise, the production of all these objects lies within the compass of such laws as a free people may not only cheerfully live under, but by which they will find their political condition and private happiness materially improved. The people must indeed contribute their share to the production and permanence of these blessings, by the adoption of a reasonable and moral system in their private and public conduct. The force of no political institutions that ever were promulgated is sufficient permanently to carry on the public prosperity, when opposed by a profligate and discontented, and consequently a factious people; a consideration which should convince mankind, if any thing is capable of working the conviction, of the paramount influence of morals over politics. But so long as the people will faithfully and steadily adhere to such a system, there seems to be no *political* necessity that their condition should ever alter for the worse. The conservative principle involved in the propositions maintained in the first book of this treatise seem to guarantee society from that principle of decay connected with the progress of population, to which it has been assumed to be *necessarily* liable from its very constitution and essence. There is evidently no *physical impossibility* of maintaining the people in comfort, from their internal resources, up to any given period of time.

It must, however, again be pressed upon the reader's attention that, in order to induce a people faithfully and steadily to adhere to their system, something more is necessary than a mere conviction of its political utility. This conviction has ever been too weak to overcome the indolent or selfish propensities of mankind. To become effectual, it must be aided by public principle, which can only be founded in moral knowledge and integrity, which, again, can find its source in no other spring but sound and pure religion. This, to use a simile of Sir James Steuart, is the top of the pyramid. If it be not contracted to this point, but its summit left bare and exposed by the omission of the apex, the storms will enter, and the edifice must gradually decay, and crumble into ruins.

It is partly for these reasons that I venture to add a third book to this treatise, containing the *moral* consequences deducible from its fundamental principles. I have also been induced to make this addition, because some departments of moral conduct, most nearly affecting the comfort and happiness of mankind, derive a peculiar character from the principles of this treatise, distinct from that which my opponents have endeavoured to impress upon them. This is particularly true of many objects relating to the exercise of charity, to the marriage of the lower orders of the people, and to a few other points which are detailed in the following book. I trust that they will be found not altogether wanting in interest or novelty—nor, above all, in TRUTH.

BOOK III.

CHAPTER I.

*Application of the third Principle—That the Ten-
dency of Population will neither be materially
altered nor diverted from its natural Course, (as
exhibited in the foregoing Chapters,) in a Country whose Government, Laws, and Customs, are
founded, in the main, upon Principles of Religion,
Morality, rational Liberty, and Security of
Person and Property, although these Principles
may obtain only an imperfect Influence.*

THE preceding books of this treatise have probably
been successful in establishing the connexion between the principles of sound politics and of pure
morals, as well as in exhibiting the dependance of
the most important conclusions in political economy
upon the preservation of rational liberty, security of
property, and the consequent promotion of industry.
The whole foundation of the argument in the preceding books resting upon the *spontaneous* operations of men as society advances, the enjoyment of
rational liberty in their actions, and of security in
their persons and properties, is of course implied. It
is unnecessary therefore to dwell upon the applica-

tion of that part of the principle at the head of this chapter, which refers to liberty and security, any further than to claim admission for the obvious fact that their theoretic perfection is not necessary to ensure the free and unimpeded progress of society. The history of our own country is more than sufficient to show, that where the government and laws are founded, *in the main*, upon the principles of liberty, partial deviations and individual exceptions will not impede the general march of the commonwealth in its career of happiness and prosperity.

The religious and moral part of the principle, which forms the title of this chapter, not having incidentally fallen under discussion to the same extent, we shall now proceed to investigate and apply it.

It has been already shown that the progress of society depends upon the *spontaneous* operations of mankind, in the pursuit of that course, which Providence has chalked out as leading to general happiness and prosperity, and that any deviation from it is always accompanied with proportionate difficulties and disorders in the machinery of the commonwealth.

But men's *spontaneous* operations are of course dependant upon their wills; and as the will of man is naturally liable to be perverted by selfishness, by short-sighted views of immediate interest, and by the external temptations which surround him, all of which are continually soliciting him, with a view to his individual interest, to depart from the course which leads to the general wealth of the community, it is obvious that some higher principle is required than those usually presented to our notice by writers on political economy. Now it is not easy to discover where a principle is to be found sufficiently powerful to counteract this natural bent towards evil in human society, except in the department of morals.

Again, as the healthy progress of society depends upon the pursuit of that course which Providence has chalked out as leading to general happiness and prosperity, the question of expediency is of course involved in it. But if there is one fact more fully established than another, to the satisfaction of every candid investigator of human actions and opinions, it is the uncertainty of the conclusions drawn from mere *political* expediency, which, as an excellent writer has observed, are the result merely of man's "judgment of probabilities." But as no two men ever formed the *same judgment of probabilities*, some further rule of reference is of course required for the regulation of men's actions and opinions. And it may be asked, with some confidence, where is a rule of reference to be found sufficiently capacious to include all the debateable points respecting the will of Providence in the government of human society, and sufficiently incontrovertible or authoritative to bring the debates to a conclusion, except the rule given by the great Architect of society for the preservation of his own work? This rule, it will not I apprehend be denied, is that of *moral* expediency, not always as it may be deduced from the law and the light of nature, (which only removes the difficulty one step, and still leaves the conclusion as open to debate as before,) but as it is plainly expressed in the precepts of Revelation, which, as Dr. Paley observes, are as much intended to regulate the conduct of men as members of the community, and as citizens of the world, as in their capacity of private individuals. Indeed, although this truth has been too frequently overlooked, I can never bring myself to believe that it was ever really doubted by any one who seriously reflected upon the subject. There is scarcely a Christian precept which does not refer to man as a member of society. To suppose then that the constitution and progress of society was no part of the design of him who gave the precepts, is about as reasonable as to deny that the British parliament in passing the Mutiny Act has any view to the stability and discipline of the army. The truth seems to be, that men, even very honest and well-intentioned men, have found the principle rather more difficult in its application to public than to private affairs. Moral integrity is sometimes accompanied with present sacrifice, and frequently with apparent risk; and conscientious persons, not fully impressed with the practical conviction of God's *particular* superintendance, may doubt how far they are justified in incurring that risk, and making that sacrifice on the part of the public, at which they would not hesitate in their own individual case. It requires, in short, a stronger conviction of the *ultimate expediency* of moral conduct, than many public men have the good fortune to acquire, to induce them, as trustees for the public, to forego the temptation of an apparent political advantage, although of doubtful aspect as to moral expediency. They too often acquiesce therefore in the radical separation attempted to be set up between morals and politics in affairs of legislation.

The object then of this third book is to show that, in so far as the questions discussed in this treatise are concerned, a reference to moral expediency, where the express commands of God cannot be discovered, and to Revelation, where its commands are ex-

pressly intimated, is a perfectly safe principle upon which
to determine the choice of any particular alternative in
political conduct; and that moral calculations are in
no respect to be postponed in favour of those which
have a more immediate reference to the science of
government. I trust that the result of this inquiry will
prove, that there is no moral *incapacity* inherent in
the constitution of society which impedes its regular
and successful progress in improvement up to the
remotest period in which the community will
abide by the rules projected and divulged by Providence for the regulation of their conduct. For
if the progress of society depend upon a regular and legitimate increase of population, industry,
and civilization, and these again are derived from a
reasonable adherence among the mass of the people
to the laws of religion and morality, then it seems
undeniable that religion and morals are more sufficient to secure the progress of society, than the
dry results of political economy; that these without
the other are like false reckonings at sea, by which
the ship is liable to be wrecked on the first rock
which lies in its track. In truth, what dependance
can be placed upon a political calculation with respect to the general conduct of individuals, when
there is no security that those individuals will guide
their conduct by any general rules? And what security is it possible to obtain that individuals will so
guide their conduct but that which is derived from
moral and religious sanctions—that is, from sound
principles leading them to a knowledge of their
duty to their fellow creatures and to society, and
infusing a hearty desire to fulfil it? These, therefore,
and these only, are the key stones in the arch of
civil society; till they are inserted the fabric is in

danger, and the work of the architect is incomplete. If they are removed, no symmetry of proportion nor the nicest calculations of science can preserve the fabric from destruction.

Upon the whole then I think myself justified in arguing as a general truth that, as the *natural* course of human society depends upon an adherence to such principles as have been deduced from an observation of the best constituted commonwealths, so these principles are themselves discovered, established, and confirmed, not so much by a scientific investigation into the grounds of political expediency, as by a due inquiry into, and regard to, the demands of religion and morals upon the conduct of the people and the government. Thus guided the people will spontaneously arrange themselves as the true principles of political economy would suggest, and indeed must so have arranged themselves before any principles at all could have been deduced from an observation of their political condition. Without a due regard to morals and religion, I am perfectly ready to admit that the *selfishness of mankind* will be so far from leading to such an arrangement as I have contemplated, that it is the main cause of all the deviations from what I presume to call the *Providential course of society ;* that it lies at the bottom of all that vice and misery which, in the system I am desirous to oppose, has been ascribed to the progress of society as its necessary consequence. It is here, indeed, that the foundation of my argument may be said to rest. I assert that Providence has placed a fallen but rational creature in a world where a constant resistance to his evil propensities, and to the temptations which foster them,

is necessary to his happiness both in his individual
and social capacity ; that he has pointed out to him
the means by which that resistance may be effectually
carried on ; and that as he has made the happiness
of the individual dependant upon the degree in
which he perseveres in that resistance, so has he
made the happiness and well-being of society no less
dependant upon the degree in which the mass of
individuals pursue the same course.   If society,
therefore, make any progress at all, it must be in
consequence of the obedience of the individuals com-
posing it to the commands of God, that is, of their
resistance to the evil and selfish and savage passions
which obstruct that progress.   So that the Providential course of society runs directly counter to
human perversity, and depends entirely. upon the
degree in which it is subdued, and man in some
degree restored to his original constitution and
dignity.

I am aware that it may here be objected, that
since Society is composed of individuals whose
proneness to evil is admitted, and there is reason to
suppose that few of them fully and effectually resist
it, it seems rather inconsistent to argue that the
Providential course of a society thus constituted
should run in a contrary direction.   I admit that
this objection would be conclusive, were the universal
obedience and sinless perfection of individuals necessary to such a gradual improvement in their condition as the healthy progress of society requires.
But a reference to fact and experience proves that
this is by no means the case.   We see many societies
advanced to a high degree of happiness and civilization, not indeed where morals are generally relaxed

and religion neglected, not indeed where the laws themselves are founded in injustice and immorality, but certainly where the opposite virtues are merely sufficiently prevalent to render them upon the whole the ruling principles upon which public and private conduct is regulated. The *degree* of happiness and civilization will of course depend upon the extent to which the habits and dispositions of the people prompt them to a ready obedience or to a profligate resistance to such laws; but as long as the principle of virtue is strong enough to maintain them in the respect of the people, and to ensure a general obedience to their enactments, so long will the society continue to advance, and the spontaneous arrangements of the people to produce those political effects which have been detailed in the preceding chapters of this treatise.

If this hypothesis be just, it must follow of course that any principle of conduct, which is allowable on grounds of morality and religion, cannot be politically mischievous, since those grounds are asserted to form the criterion to which, and to which *only*, political expediency can *with certainty* be referred. In other words nothing can be politically expedient that is inconsistent with morals and religion; and every thing plainly consistent with them is politically expedient as a fundamental principle of action. Here then another very wide field of difference is opened between the principles of this treatise and those which it is my object to oppose. By these many actions, perfectly allowable upon moral and religious grounds, some indeed which appear to be specifically commanded as branches of our duty, are concluded to be contrary to the well-being of society, and alto-

gether inconsistent with the views of Providence
for the government of the world. The course of
nature is set up against the divine laws, and the
principle of political expediency against the revealed
will of God.

Now there are two ways of attacking positions
of this nature, either by asserting at once that Providence is a better judge of its own work, and consequently of what is *expedient* to keep it in due
course, than any human philosopher can pretend to
be; which at once precludes all argument except as
to what really is the revealed will of God. The
other method, and upon the whole perhaps the most
satisfactory, in so far as the proof can be clearly made
out, is to show that, upon fair principles of philosophy
unaided by higher authority, the duties which are
commanded, and the actions which are permitted,
are in themselves *expedient* and in their consequences beneficial to society: and while we carefully abstain from any idea that the *authority* of
the divine laws is at all affected by our necessarily
confined notions concerning their expediency, we
may be thankful that on many important points of
practical conduct the proof of that expediency lies so
much within the scope of our intellectual faculties. The
last is the method which I mean to pursue on the
present occasion, and shall in the following chapters
select the most prominent of the actions and duties
connected with this inquiry; first endeavouring to show
the extent to which we are commanded or permitted
to practise them, and then to exhibit the degree in
which the expediency and advantages of practising
them can be proved from the arguments of the two
preceding books.

CHAPTER II.

Of the Nature and Extent of the Duty of Charity.

IT is surely superfluous in these days, and most emphatically so *in this country*, to enlarge upon the absolute and unconditional nature of the duty of charity; or to assert that it is strictly speaking a moral duty, and that we are commanded to practise it for our own improvement and the profit of others, without any nice reference to our notions or presumptions concerning its political expediency. " Let every one of you assist his neighbour in whatsoever business he hath need of you:" (Rom. xvi. 2.) " Give to him that asketh thee, and from him that would borrow of thee turn thou not away:" (Matt. v. 42.) " Give, and it shall be given unto you," &c. (Luke vi. 38.) " The liberal soul shall be made fat, and he that watereth shall be watered also himself: (Prov. ii. 25.) " Be not forgetful to entertain strangers:" (Heb. xiii. 2.) with many other texts of Scripture, are positive injunctions enforced by sanctions having no reference whatsoever to political expediency. Yet if it be true, as asserted, that population has in all cases a tendency of itself to exceed the supply of food for its support; since we can scarcely, by the nature of things, assist the poor in any way without encouraging them to produce, and enabling them to rear, a greater number of children, or at least without prolonging the existence of the objects of our charity; it is evident that by every exertion of it we

are only increasing the quantum of human misery.
While we assist some we are proportionably depressing others, and adding to that number which is
already exuberant to a fault. It is impossible to
parry this conclusion; and although the humanity
of many who profess to admit its truth, especially
of the author of the Essay on Population, very naturally recoils from the proposition, nothing can more
strongly mark its practical deficiency when applied
to the exigences of human life than the manner in
which he endeavours to escape from it. They say
that general principles should not be pushed too far;
and that cases may occur where the good resulting
may more than overbalance the evil to be apprehended. But if the *principle* be true, how is it possible to know that the beings we thus *exalt* may be
more worthy than those so *unjustifiably depressed?*
If the world be already miserable because it has
a continual tendency to repletion, all charity which
encourages marriage among the lower orders in order
to promote happiness and morality, which assists
women in child-birth, which promotes vaccination
and the cure of painful and distressing diseases,
which helps in short any of the poor to rear their
children in soundness of body, which bestows relief
upon the old who have not saved a provision from
their youthful earnings, which saves in any manner the
life of one whose death would set his fellow-creatures
more at ease, is a criminal indulgence of individual
feeling at the expense of the general welfare of mankind: since by the exercise of any one of these
charities towards one individual, we reduce another,
who may deserve it less, to the same distress from
which the object of our benevolence is relieved.

This is the plain, manly, and consistent conclusion to be drawn from the premises. He who is
thoroughly convinced of the truth of the latter must
of course think it his duty, however painful it may
be, to act up to the former. Nor can this opinion
or conduct be at all altered by a mere recommendation from the person who, as he thinks, has established the principles, not to push them too far, because the benefit he may bestow upon one individual
may perchance be greater than the injury he will
certainly do to another. He may reasonably doubt
this ; and the doubt may serve very strongly to fortify
the natural inclination, of which we are most of us
too sensible, to keep our money in our pockets.

Again, the goodness and justice of the Divine
Providence, in the precepts it has laid down for the
exercise of our charity, are no less implicated in the
conclusions referred to.   In addition to the texts
just quoted, we are commanded *absolutely*, and
without any reference to its effects upon society, " to
give unto the poor sufficient for his need," " to deal
bread to the hungry," " to cover the naked," and so
forth.   The law is represented as of the highest
obligation, and not only strict, but generous obedience to it as the most decisive test of faith. This
is too broad a principle of duty to be palliated or
denied : and being so, we are surely justified in pre-
suming *à priori*, that a compliance with it can never
endanger the welfare of those towards whom it is
exercised, by enlarging the boundaries of vice and
misery amongst them. Nor is it easy to reconcile
our minds to the solution of this difficulty, which
has been attempted, by saying, " that the Scriptures
command us to give to the poor, but are quite silent

as to the *utility* of such a virtue." Undoubtedly, if in any case the commands of God appear to our finite understandings to be inexpedient in their particuliar application to human affairs, we bow with humility, and conclude that their *general* expediency has reference to the universal scheme of things, which the wisdom of the Creator has removed far beyond the blinking imbecility of mortal ken. But on a subject of such daily importance to us as the practice of charity, it would not be without an obstinate struggle, nor without exquisite pain, that a philanthropist could be brought to rest its expediency solely on an argument so abstracted. He would rather argue, that if we conclude charity to be a virtue, we can hardly admit its consequences to be vicious; and whether or not his abilities would enable him to refute arguments that may be brought forward to prove them so, he would no more admit the truth of those arguments, than he would the falsehood of the Newtonian system, because its founder could not explain the cause of gravitation; or the non-existence of the electrical energies of various bodies in nature, because the primary cause of electricity is beyond the scope of our knowledge. To be *told*, therefore, that the delightful sentiments arising from the practice of this virtue are " baseless illusions," should not disturb his repose in the least; and so far from seeking for consolation in a forgetfulness of the truth, he should immediately have recourse to the expedient of reminding himself of it. For the truth must evidently be, that since God is an all-wise and all-good being, who made the world, and is intimately acquainted with the principles upon which it is conducted, whatever he commands *must*

OF THE DUTY OF CHARITY.

337

be expedient for the benefit of man, whether we
can prove it so or not. Actually to bring forward
that proof must nevertheless give a sensible pleasure,
though it can impart no additional conviction, to a
truly rational mind.

It is therefore gratifying to reflect, that the conclusions to be drawn from the first part of this
treatise, with respect to the exercise of charity to
the poor, leave the expediency of the practice of
that virtue not only open to the utmost extent, under
the control of discretion, to which a benevolent
heart may find pleasure in its exertion; but by
rendering every rational mode of relief innocent and
praise-worthy, they afford to all, according to their
means, the opportunity of obeying the commands of
God by the exercise of this sublime duty to their fellow creatures.

For if population, in well-governed states, hath a
natural tendency to keep within the powers of the
soil to afford it subsistence as society advances in
its progress, the trifling impulse given to it by the
most unbounded exercise of charity of which any
record exists, or which any reasonable man would
anticipate, can scarcely give an important counteraction to that natural tendency. The supposition that
it would do so is merely theoretical, like most of the
other arguments which pretend to prove the tendency of population to exuberance. They assume a
probability contrary to all experience of the past,
and to all future expectation; namely, that because
charity is enjoined upon man without limit, therefore, unlimited alms-giving will be the result.—
Whereas whoever reflects for an instant upon the
various impediments which continually operate upon

the human heart, in opposition to the universal pre-valence of that practice, need be under no extreme apprehension that it will ever tend to general extravagance.

Moreover, we shall find in a subsequent chapter, (see chap. iv.) that as the exercise of charity is necessarily limited by the number of the legitimate objects of it, so these objects are continually changing their numbers during the progress of society, and will always bear a proportion to the means of relief in the power of the community. Indiscriminate alms-giving is not charity, but profusion ; the objects of judicious alms-giving increase in proportion to the whole number of the people, the farther society advances from the agricultural stage. But the natural rate of the increase of population also undergoes a proportionate abatement, as was fully proved in the course of the first book, and affords room for an enlarged exercise of charity without the danger of producing a vicious excess of population. It can scarcely therefore be necessary, with a view to the general welfare of society, to repress the influence of the virtue upon the charitable exertions of individuals.

This will be still more apparent if we recollect that all money permanently bestowed in charity to those who are *really* unable to work, may in one sense as certainly encourage industry, as if it were paid in the first instance to the industrious labourer. For while it does not necessarily hold out encouragement to the able and the slothful, it is immediately paid away by the person first receiving it for objects, the products of industry. It operates as an increased demand for those products ; and where freedom and security of property give scope to industrious exertion, those products, whether they consist of food, of manufactures, or of objects of foreign commerce, will certainly be supplied. If it keep in action a mouth which would otherwise be closed for ever, the demand for food thereby created will cause its production as certainly as if the rich man had spent his money so bestowed in building a summer-house, or digging a fish-pond.

To prosecute these observations to their full extent, as exemplified in our own country, is an important object which I have elsewhere endeavoured to fulfil. But I think it expedient in this place to enter my solemn protest against a very witty retort to which I perceive that the argument lies open. It may perhaps be said, that according to this reasoning, there would be no public injury in supporting the whole labouring population by donations in money, since they would immediately go to the purchase of necessaries, and thus to the encouragement of industry :—while it is evident that if all could be so supported, none would work to produce those necessaries. In answer to this piece of pleasantry it may be sufficient to observe, that the office of charity consists entirely, either in supporting those who *cannot* support themselves, whose number is necessarily limited ; or in making up to others the deficiency which their own fair exertions leave in their power of supporting their families, whose number is also limited, and by the principles of this treatise is continually decreasing as society advances in its progress, and fewer individuals exist in a situation and capacity to rear large families. When giving away money extends beyond these limits, it becomes (not charity, but) thoughtless profusion. Within these limits, and well administered, it can scarcely have much effect in diminishing industrious exertion, since it is only bestowed in proportion as such exertion is *impossible* or *insufficient*.

It has been asserted that charity exercised in the mitigation or extirpation of mortal diseases, is in its effects entirely nugatory, because it does nothing more than merely dam up one of the necessary drains by which the overflowing current of human life is discharged, and that the accumulating stream will soon open for itself another outlet. Now I have admitted in a former part of this treatise, that a certain proportion of premature deaths seems to be a Providential condition of society in each of the stages through which it passes, though the proportion is certainly affected by moral causes. But if there be any truth in the general principles of the first book, it is certain that as society advances, and the procreative power of mankind abates of its force, if the proportion of premature deaths be not diminished, there would be danger of a too rapid decrease in the progress of population. Should, however, the current of mortality not be checked, as society advances, by the mitigation or extirpation of diseases, it is evident that the proportion of deaths to the population, instead of being diminished, will, upon the whole, be materially increased; because the assembling of large numbers into towns, and the other artificial habits incident to a commercial and manufacturing society, have all of them a natural tendency to increase the number and aggravate the intensity of existing diseases. In the natural course of things, therefore, the current of death will be enlarged at the very time when the interests of society command that it should be contracted. But let the species of charity here adverted to interpose with its assistance, and affairs will resume their healthy progress: lives will be saved where living men are wanted, and the stream of existence preserved at an uniform level.

Surely this is no unpleasing instance of the manner in which Providence adapts the laws which regulate the progress of society to the moral expediency of those commands which he has imposed upon mankind.

I trust that the different practical conclusions deducible from the arguments of this treatise and those to which they are opposed, with respect to the general exercise of charity, are sufficiently obvious without further illustration :—that those here maintained have at least the advantage of being consistent with themselves, with the commands of God, with the known precepts of morality, and with true benevolence. I am pretty confident also, that there will be no necessity to advise a departure from the *principles* of conduct laid down, in order to make the *practice* square with precepts which every enlightened Christian must allow to be reasonable.

From the whole of the argument, then, we seem justified in concluding that, in so far as the exercise of real charity is concerned, there is nothing which can materially interfere with the natural tendency of population to keep within the limits of the productive powers of the soil. I cannot but think, however, that we are entitled to go farther, and to assert that the rational exercise of this virtue is calculated to give additional force to that natural tendency: 1st, by the impulse which it affords to industry, in the manner just explained, and thereby to the progress of society towards its higher stages;—and 2dly, by the moral sensibility and mutual intercourse which it establishes among all ranks of the community, whereby the habits, which repress any tendency to a mischievous increase of population, are made to operate preventively with a force more than sufficient to counteract the positive encouragement which is supposed to be afforded by charitable donations. That these habits are the offspring of the charitable intercourse of the rich and enlightened with the poor and ignorant, is well known to all those who are practically conversant with the subject. It is the neglected and degraded poor man, abandoned to the solitary reflections of an uninformed mind upon his cheerless prospects and situation, who ceases to respect himself, or to feel any of that enlivening principle within him, which diverts his attention from the mere sensual and physical wants of his nature, to the comparative decencies and comforts of life. It is this man, who, feeling himself an object of indifference to others, is actuated by the same feeling towards the rest of the world. He becomes morose, brutal, and *selfish*, in the lowest sense of the term. His natural feelings in these respects not being corrected by intercourse with more enlightened men, nor softened by a sense of obligation to his superiors, and of the interest he has in their approbation, he becomes careless of his future conduct, and is driven at the impulse of the first temptation that is offered to his passions. Restrained by no check, moral or natural, by no sense

of respect towards others or himself, he is impelled
to the multiplication of his species like the brutes
that perish.   And I am ready to acknowledge that
the population thus raised is checked only by the
rule which regulates the number of the brutes; viz.
by the perpetual contest between the powers of procreation and the principle of destruction—a rule
which, when applied to the human species, involves
almost every modification of vice and misery.

But let the fair form of charity be introduced, and
society assumes an aspect altogether different.   The
sullen and hardened heart of the previously neglected
individual is awakened to the sympathies of our
common nature.   Finding that he is respected by
others he begins to feel some respect for himself, and
to acquire an indistinct notion of the moral equality
of mankind.   He learns by degrees that the poorest
tenant of the meanest cottage possesses a soul of
equal value, in the eye of its Maker, with the
lord of the surrounding districts; and if he be the
inhabitant of a free country, that he possesses also a
body of equal value in the eye of the legislature.
Having a powerful friend that feels an interest in
his proceedings, his reflections on his temporal condition are also cheered and enlivened.   Gratitude
will sometimes find a place in his heart; and from
this seed alone, with judicious culture, may spring
up a plant in the shelter of whose branches all the
gentle and moral qualities incident to his situation may repose.   But should that sentiment be too
refined for his perceptions, the bare conviction that
a man more powerful than himself has taken charge
of his welfare, and has assumed some responsibility
that his exertions to better his own condition shall

not be altogether fruitless, elevates the tone of his feelings, invigorates his efforts, and imparts a glow of hope to his heart, and of satisfaction to his countenance. The whole man, in short, is changed, and his habits are renewed with him. The principle of respect to his superior, and the wish for his approbation, will aid the principle of respect for himself, in restraining him within the bounds of decency and morality; and the population which he is the instrument of raising, being produced in conformity to the laws of God and the moral institutions of his country, will, as we shall perceive in a following chapter, be a sound and substantial addition to the powers of the commonwealth. Thus it is that the moral virtues act and re-act upon each other; and if the general exercise of charity has, on the one hand, a tendency to extend the limits of population beyond the natural boundary, it has also, on the other, qualities inherent in its very nature sufficient either to counteract that tendency or to convert it into a blessing.

I have seen a poor deformed cripple in a workhouse attain his 20th year with not a spark of moral culture, with ears through which the accents of kindness and encouragement were never directed to his heart; the object of complete neglect, if not of scorn and contempt, to all by whom he was surrounded. His mind not highly endowed by nature, completely blunted by hard usage, approached to idiotcy, and his countenance exhibited a mixture of sullenness, envy, and despair. I have seen this miserable object taken by the hand of a benevolent individual, his rags exchanged for decent clothing, *strange* words of kindness and encouragement ad-

dressed to his astonished ear, a spelling-book placed
in his hand, his steps directed to a sunday-school,
and flattering approbation bestowed upon his earnest
but quite abortive effects to learn to read.   Although
little actual knowledge was imparted, a more complete moral revolution was never observable in man.
The eye before dejected was lighted up with joy and
hope; the countenance, distorted with envy and
furrowed with the deep lines of despair, relaxed into
a cheerful smile; an interest for his own improvement was excited in his mind, and kept alive by the
consciousness that his benefactor *cared for him.* The
smile of pleasure, with which that benefactor was
constantly greeted, imparted a joy only to be equalled
by his humble thankfulness for having been the instrument of such a change in the heart of a fellow-
creature.   But if these were his feelings as a philanthropist and a Christian, I think that he might also
fairly indulge some sense of gratification as a *politician.* The dirty and vicious habits, to which this
poor creature was formerly a prey, were far from in-
capacitating him from becoming the father of a
family as wretched and denuded as himself.   He
would have been satisfied to lie down with his
partner in the hovel of the workhouse, and to pullulate without control.   But feelings of decency and
self-respect have now induced better habits.   His
mind is diverted towards objects more remote from
the brutal part of his nature, and it is probable that
he will, at least, become a harmless if not an useful
member of society.

I trust that one serious reflection will not be considered by fastidious readers to be here misplaced.
It is intimately connected with the direction of our

charity. If the mere sense of the love bestowed by an earthly superior, and of the interest taken in his welfare, is capable of working such a moral change in the heart of an inferior, how strongly are we encouraged to direct our charitable exertions towards awakening the same feelings in a much more exalted degree, by a display of love and of benevolence, the knowledge of which (although the highest intelligence cannot fully comprehend, nor the most sensitive heart appreciate it) will yet be imparted to the dullest and most ignorant in proportion to their need? The poor and the ignorant man, who is improved in his moral habits by intercourse with a benevolent superior, will have those habits immoveably fixed, and exalted into spiritual affections, by opening to him the means of intercourse with a Saviour, whose charity as far exceeds all human efforts of benevolence, as the influence of his example and assistance upon moral conduct is superior to the force of human influence or example. The test, therefore, by which the sincerity of individual charity should be tried, must have reference to this most exalted species of the virtue. The main ingredient in true charity consists in the personal sacrifice which it involves. He therefore can scarcely be called truly charitable, who does not confer all the benefits in his power upon the objects of his charity, especially if those which he withholds would be attended with a greater sacrifice to himself than those which he imparts. How then can he be said truly to practise the virtue, who gives that which has reference chiefly to the temporal condition of the object, and which it is creditable in the world to bestow, while he withholds something else, which has reference to the eternal welfare of the objects, but the means of imparting which may eventually involve the sacrifice of popularity or of some other worldly interest?

I would recommend these observations, in an especial manner, to the higher ranks of Irish proprietors, especially of those who usually reside at a distance from the properties and the people whence their revenues are derived. It will be recollected that in the sixth chapter of the first book it was shown, upon indisputable Irish authorities, that moral and religious instruction afforded the only ray of light to cheer the almost hopeless gloom which overspreads that country, where atrocities, that almost exceed what feudal tyranny contrived to produce, are frequently perpetrated by the ignorant and barbarous population. The resident philanthropists of Ireland are so convinced of the reality of the evil, and of the only practicable remedy, that they have lately made a most forcible and judicious appeal* to their countrymen of the United Kingdom, and especially to the absentee proprietors of Ireland. I am sorry to observe that it has been every where answered with greater alacrity than among the last-mentioned class of persons. The pledge which I gave in the sixth chapter of Book i. (p.103), to say something of the means by which the objects of moral instruction in Ireland

---

* See Three Reports of the " SOCIETY FOR PROMOTING THE EDUCATION OF THE POOR IN IRELAND ;" of which the Rt. Hon. David Latouche and Co. are treasurers. The comprehensive plan of this society is admirably adapted to the peculiar circumstances of the Irish population: and the parliament of the United Kingdom is so convinced of its utility, that it granted 7000l. to the trustees, for the purpose of erecting a central school in Dublin, from which masters might be sent to other parts of Ireland.

may be carried into effect, induces me to lay the following observations before her proprietors.

Considering, then, the great variety of religious sects in Ireland, and that the majority of the people dissent from the established church, and are in the thraldom of a religion, the fundamental principles and chief protection of which are ignorance and bigotry; it seems to follow that individual exertions can alone be efficacious in instructing their minds, and raising their moral condition. The government has no machinery in such a country by which it can operate upon the universal population, or even upon the majority of them; for the sort of instruction which the establishment, as a professional body, would wish to impart, must necessarily be received with jealousy and distrust by those who are opposed to it. Individual influence in its particular sphere can alone be sufficient to counteract such disadvantages. The society which is referred to in the note above offers the means to every individual who feels disposed to establish schools in his immediate neighbourhood, and calls upon those who, in conscience and honour, are bound to take an interest in the welfare of the Irish poor, to enlarge these means, and to apply them to their legitimate ends. That this appeal has not been sufficiently answered is a lamentable fact; but well knowing the candour and generosity of the Irish character, I shall indulge in no unnecessary severity, but simply state for the consideration of those whom it may concern a few plain facts.

I have now before me a list of 121 Irish absentee proprietors, respectively enjoying revenues drawn from the land and labour of Ireland, of the annual amount of 2000*l.* up to 50,000*l.*; more than 80 of whom derive from the country an income exceeding 5000*l.* a year a-piece. I do not perceive the names of five of these gentlemen as patrons or subscribers to the " SOCIETY FOR PROMOTING THE EDUCATION OF THE POOR IN IRELAND." But I think they will feel some compunctious visitings when I state that, in the Appendix to the Third Report of that Society, is to be found a paper containing the " Prospectus of the EDINBURGH SOCIETY for Promoting the Education of the Poor " (not of Scotland, but) " of IRELAND." Let the Irish proprietors resident in England peruse the following admirable statement of the views of these benevolent Scotsmen, extracted from that Prospectus, and then refuse, *if they can*, to join in instituting a similar society in London.

" If there be any one circumstance which has more than another contributed to exalt this country to the high rank which she holds among the surrounding nations, it is the acknowledged superiority which she enjoys in respect of the means of education. This is an advantage which invariably leads to the most beneficial results. A good education directly tends to raise the standard of morals, and to improve the character of those who enjoy it—to excite and diffuse a spirit of useful exertion—to increase the energies of the mind, and to bring them to bear with more effect on all the objects of human pursuit—to meliorate the condition of individuals and of society, and to promote the general happiness of life. Hence every friend of humanity will desire to see the benefits of education widely diffused, and will co-operate with any rational plan by which that end is likely to be accomplished.

" In Scotland, though much may still be done to extend and improve the education of the lower classes, there is *comparatively* little to be done. Through the universal establishment of parochial schools, that valuable legacy of the Scottish parliament to their country, education is obtained at such a moderate expense that almost all classes of the community have excess to it. And the lower classes have in consequence attained a measure of knowledge, of moral cultivation, and intelligent industry, which is not found in the same rank of society in any other country.

" In England, the education of the lower orders was for a long time less attended to than the generous character of the country, and the progress of civilization in other instances, might have led us to expect; of late, however, the attention of men of the first eminence in station, influence, and character, has been directed to this important object; and plans have in consequence been formed, and measures adopted, which promise the happiest and most extensive success.

" Ireland, unfortunately, does not in this respect exhibit the same favourable appearances with the other divisions of the British empire. Though it possesses many advantages friendly to the improvement and comfort of the inhabitants, it is notorious that no adequate result has hitherto been derived from them.

" Nature has been liberal to that country; the soil is fertile, and the climate is mild; the spirit of the people is high; their minds are inquisitive and reflecting; their disposition generous and ardent; they are lively and active, equal to any exertion, and capable of any attainment: yet, with all this, it appears from the united testimony of all who have written on the state of Ireland, that the character of the native inhabitants is low, and their circumstances wretched in the extreme.

" To this unhappy state of things, different causes, moral and political, which it is here unnecessary to specify, have probably contributed ; but there can be no question, that one cause which has had a predominant influence on the circumstances and character of the Irish is the want of education. Through the injurious influence of that powerful cause, which still exists to a degree that is hardly credible, the natural advantages which they enjoy are in a great measure lost : intellect, capacity, warm affections, generally unimproved, and often ill directed, bring no suitable benefit to the possessor of them; it is well if they be not made the means of precipitating him deeper into vice, and increasing his power of doing mischief.

" At a time when the tone of philanthropic feeling is more than ordinarily high—when the benevolent of every denomination are zealously exerting themselves to minister relief to their fellow-men, in different countries, and under different descriptions of suffering or of want ; so large and so interesting a portion of our fellow-subjects cannot surely be suffered to continue in their present unpropitious circumstances ; circumstances in which it is manifest that their intellectual energies are cramped, their moral character depressed, their personal happiness obstructed, and the welfare of the state materially injured. In this case the most forcible considerations that can be addressed to the mind—humanity, justice, sound policy, patriotism, true Christianity—all concur in calling loudly on Britons to consider the state of the lower classes in Ireland, and to assist in the design of ameliorating their state, by furnishing them with the necessary means of moral and religious instruction.

" This generous design, to which we wish to call the attention of our countrymen, is not entirely new. The education of the poor in Ireland has, at different periods, attracted the attention of the public mind, and different measures have been employed to promote it. Free schools were at an early period established in several of the large towns, and have since been extended to some parts of the country. Provision is also made, at a great expense, for maintaining what are called the Protestant Charter Schools. These establishments have, however, been productive of very limited effects. The utility of the Charter Schools has been much impeded by the narrow and exclusive principle on which they are instituted, none being received into them but the children of Protestants, or of Catholics who allow their children to be educated in the Protestant religion ; and though the free schools are conducted on more liberal principles, being open to the children of parents of every religious persuasion, yet their number is so small as to be altogether inadequate to the wants of the community."

The Earl of Selkirk is President of this society.

But although the communication of religious knowledge is merely a department of *charity* as far as the exertions of individuals are concerned, it is also a matter of *positive political duty* on the part of the legislature and government of a country. The neglect of it interferes more with the progress of society and the good of the commonwealth, and is more likely to introduce the peculiar evils arising from an abuse of the principle of population, than the relaxation of all other laws; because these have ever been found insufficient to restrain men from crimes, and from imbibing habits unfavourable to the decencies and proprieties of life, while their hearts continue depraved, and their wills unsubdued : whereas religious instruction, by converting the heart, and subduing the will, affords, in proportion to its prevalence, an effectual control over men's outward actions. There is in particular a department of this duty peculiarly connected with the subject of population, which, on that account, and also because it has been hitherto grossly neglected by most governments, cannot be omitted in this treatise—I mean a legislative provision for the more enlarged performance of religious rites, and for imparting public instruction, in proportion to the gradual increase in the number of the people. It is taken for granted, that no Christian, or even rational government, can neglect the primary duty of establishing, as an essential part of the constitution, what it conceives to be a pure religion, calculated to afford sound and uniform principles of moral practice to its people. Still less can it be thought probable that, having provided such an establishment, any government in its senses will undermine its foundations by entrusting its management to weak, corrupt, or ignorant superintendants. For such conduct would at once annihilate all the political advantages of the institution, by rendering it contemptible in the estimation of the very people, whose minds it had elevated in its purer days into a condition to appreciate the value of what they had lost. But yet, it is not altogether sufficient to establish a pure religion, and to

place it under the superindence of able, learned, zealous, and spiritual pastors, unless provision be also
made for enlarging the frame of the establishment,
and for conveying public instruction to the people in
proportion to the wants of an augmented population.
The people will be driven without the pale of the
church as much by the want of physical power in
their pastors for the performance of their duties, as
by the corruption of their doctrine, or the abatement
of their spiritual zeal.   And it is no less cruel than
absurd in any government to permit the exigences of
a pure and spiritual church insensibly to extend
themselves beyond the physical powers of its appointed pastors.   Despair of performing their whole
duty will often lead to a total dereliction of any
performance at all ; and even where it has not this
lamentable effect, where the zeal of a minister is not
relaxed by the obvious disproportion of his means to
his ends, still a large portion of the people must
either be abandoned to ignorance and depravity, or
consigned to the spiritual direction of persons, of the
moral consequences of whose instructions the state at
least has no sufficient assurance, and therefore cannot
be absolved from the charge of a gross dereliction of
its duties towards the people.

It seems impossible to deny that these conclusions
are justly applicable to every state, where the population has greatly extended itself, or been accumulated
in large masses in new situations, without a proportionate increase of public schools and of established
churches and ministers.   If the evil has continued
long enough to render the disproportion considerable,
it will be extremely difficult of remedy ; for the new
population will necessarily be fixed in the sectarian

habits in which it has been educated; and wherever its numbers approach to an equality with the adherents to the established church, these last will be considered merely as *another sect;* they will be disliked as a *privileged sect;* and a great and dangerous jealousy will exist with regard to any measures that may be thought necessary for checking the progress of the evil in the only legitimate way; viz. by spreading the knowledge of the established doctrines through the medium of public instruction, and by increasing the number and enlivening the zeal of the established clergy.

It is in this state of things however, that the purity and spirituality of an established church is brought to a severe but wholesome test: if its doctrines be corrupt or its practice impure, it must presently sink under the accumulated load of neglect within, and of opposition from without. It is certainly not too much to assert that no Roman Catholic Church, nor any heathen system of religion, could endure this *rude trial.* But if the doctrines of the establishment in question be scriptural, and its practice pure and liberal; if in short, upon a candid comparison of its doctrines with the Bible, and of its precepts and practice with their moral effects upon the heart and life, it has a clear advantage over the opposing sects in the estimation of an enlightened people; a well-grounded hope may be indulged. For truth, especially religious truth, will ultimately triumph; and the means in the case before us are as obvious as, under Providence, they are certain of success. Legislative enactments for the supply of existing deficiencies in schools, churches, and ministers; the appointment of zealous, able, and spiritual superintendants; a reference by them on all occasions to the original doctrines on which the church in question may have been founded, or seated in the hearts of the people; and the encouragement of evangelical learning and practice among the inferior clergy, will restore the stray sheep to the fold, and with them will also return the moral, decent, and regular habits, by which the natural tendency of population to keep within the bounds of subsistence is sustained in vigour.

In the department of charity connected with moral and religious instruction, the general establishment of schools in proportion to the increase of population seems to require a few more remarks, especially with a view to their moral uses. As society advances, as commerce and manufactures increase, and a country makes rapid progress in the accumulation of public and private wealth through the knowledge, ingenuity, skill, and dexterity of its people, it is undeniable that they are thereby exposed to greater temptations to immoral conduct. The propensities of man being adverse to his moral welfare, it follows that, in proportion as his other faculties thrive while his moral sense continues torpid, he will become the more mischievous instrument in society, and the more exposed to Divine anger. Now in the first place it is evident that no state has a *right* to build up any portion of its prosperity at the expense of the eternal welfare of its agents, and what is still more conclusive it has not the *power* to do so. It may make the attempt, but in a short time it will miserably fail; for adversity, not prosperity, will be the result. With a view either to conscience or policy, therefore, it cannot neglect to make religious and moral instruction co-existent with every step in the progress of other knowledge. To impart such instruction may be strictly and correctly defined to be the sole end and object of the education of the people, as far as the state is concerned with it. Individual interest and exertion will apportion the supply of all other knowledge to the demand, much more correctly and beneficially than can be effected by any public institutions; and it is certain that, when the supply exceeds the demand, the peace and good order of society are in danger.

It is the perception of this last-mentioned truth which for so long a time left doubts upon the minds of well-meaning persons in England as to the propriety of a general system of education. The truth is, that the object for some time was not well defined; there was much said at the outset of the new opinions upon this subject which are happily now become so prevalent, about exalting the condition of the lower orders, enlightening their understandings, enlarging their minds, infusing into them a greater spirit of independence, and various other objects peculiarly liable to be misunderstood by minds rendered jealous by the abuse of similar language during the progress of the French revolution. It was observed that, as every step in the scale of society was fully occupied, the temporal condition of the lower orders could not in one sense be raised but at the expense of the higher; and that the spirit of independence in its most obvious sense was already sufficiently prevalent. It would certainly have been a much shorter and more effectual method at once to have stated moral and religious instruction as the object; and all sober and enlightened men would then have perceived that the consequences could not have been otherwise than good, both to the state and the individual, the condition of both having materially increased the number of their temptations without a corresponding augmentation in the means of resisting them. This perception would have been aided by a reflection which I ventured to make seven years ago, (and subsequent events have been far from contradicting the hypothesis, or weakening the force of the argument,) that the first ingredient and elementary principle of all temporal prosperity, the confidence and respect of mankind, is always absent from the unjust man and the unjust nation. Each may prosper for a time; but on the first change of circumstances every one will desert them, and their fall will be more rapid than their exaltation. Whereas we have the highest authority for asserting, that an apparent dereliction of temporal advantage for the sake of virtue will be often repaid with interest in this world. Though dangers press around us, yet if we turn our eyes to the continent of Europe, and back upon ourselves, we must be ungratefully blind not to acknowledge the situation of our own country to be a signal instance of the truth of that assurance; and no less mad not to preserve the same claim to the same distinction by diffusing as widely as possible the only knowledge which entitles us to it; and by imparting none which may interfere with this most important branch of improvement."

It must be observed, however, that the fulfilment of this duty, and the general diffusion of moral instruction among the people, does certainly in one respect " exalt their minds;" it clears and regulates their moral sense, and affords them an undeviating rule by which they may judge concerning the general interests of morality, as well as their own individual duties; and also concerning the equity and propriety of the laws under which they live. It is very true, therefore, that in countries where the laws are of an immoral and tyrannical nature, or where the higher ranks are sunk in indolent and selfish habits, or immersed in vicious gratifications, public opinion, enlightened by moral instruction, will interpose a very *inconvenient* impediment to perseverance in such a system. It is not perhaps too much to say that a moral and intelligent people cannot continue to be governed upon such principles, or permanently kept in subordination under such a degenerate race of superiors. Nay further; although the general system of government may be fair and good, yet the general spread of moral instruction will render the people very quicksighted into the particular instances of inconvenience and oppression, which may still remain to be remedied. They will by degrees be anathematized in the public opinion, which in a free country is no uncertain symptom of their speedy reformation. In England the general abhorrence in which the slave trade is held arises perhaps more from the generous feelings than from the strictly moral sense of the people; but it is so strongly fixed in the public opinion that no efforts could ever restore that abominable traffic. Upon the same principle it is easy to foresee that, if the people generally imbibe correct notions on morality, it will be absolutely impossible long to retain any laws or customs, whose moral tendency can be clearly shown to be pernicious, however precious they may be in the eyes of those who fancy that they have an interest in the preservation of them. This, as I have just observed, is a very *inconvenient* bar to those who are interested in the duration of abuses.

Now whether the erection of the tribunal of a morally instructed public opinion be upon the whole advantageous or useless to a state, is a question upon which an English and a Spanish statesman would probably hold different sentiments: sentiments will also vary concerning it in proportion to the conviction entertained of the paramount influence of morals over political prosperity. My own opinion of course is not doubtful: as I firmly believe that the progress of a country in population, in strength, and in happiness, depends upon the private morality of its citizens and the public morality of its laws and institutions, I hail with the greatest satisfaction any arrangement powerful enough to overcome the temptations which are continually opposed to the influence of those blessings. I am therefore, a decided advocate for the establishment of a tribunal, before which the contending interests of the several classes of the community can be ultimately carried, to be determined upon a free discussion of their moral or immoral tendency. However troublesome such a court of reference may be considered by professional politicians, it cannot well be abused, or perverted to the detriment of the state. I have always thought it to be one of the brightest ornaments and most glorious attributes of a free constitution, and far superior to its other attribute of political liberty, which, great and admirable as it unquestionably is, is sometimes liable to abuses destructive of the very objects it was intended to preserve. These observations will not I trust be thought irrelevant to the

questions under discussion, although they are not
perhaps the most obvious inferences which they present. Few charities can be of a more complete and
exalted nature than those, which by one and the
same process ameliorate the individual, improve the
spirit of the government, and promote the permanent and healthy progress of the commonwealth
in the career of society.

I should be sorry, however, that the foregoing statement should be so far misunderstood, as to give rise to
the idea that the slightest intention exists of mark-
ing with approbation the captious spirit, which may
sometimes induce men to convert their moral knowledge rather into an instrument of offence against
the character of their neighbours, than of correction
for their own dispositions, or for public immoralities.
The best reformer is he who will take *one individual*
in hand, viz : *himself*. But in a free country every
citizen has also a duty to perform towards the public.
If he be well instructed, the performance of this
duty will be duly regulated, and will not degenerate
into offensive interference with his neighbour, as it
certainly would, were his sense of freedom to operate
upon an ignorant and profligate mind. He will,
however, gradually acquire something like a correct
sense of the moral tendency of the laws and customs
which influence his condition, and if he find himself
or his neighbours inconvenienced by any of them,
he will be furnished with some ground of fair judgment concerning their expediency or necessity.

It is not every state certainly which could afford
to endure such a scrutiny. But I will venture to
assert, from long reflection upon the theory and
practice of the British Constitution, that our own

country may cheerfully submit to it, and will derive essential benefit from the result. Our general system of manners and legislation rests on moral and liberal principles. The few exceptions which may be taken, are of a temporary and adventitious nature, and may be easily and safely remedied, when once the public opinion is agreed as to the principle upon which amendment shall be conducted. Let a general system of instruction, then, establish this principle in sound morals and religion ; and a standard of reference is provided by which the people may in the first place learn the value of the blessings they actually possess, and, be guarded against the efforts of profligate politicians to excite discontent in their minds. In the next place they will be able in some degree to judge concerning the necessity of such reparations as all human institutions do constantly require, and concerning the bounds within which they should be confined. A principle, therefore, both conservative and invigorating is introduced into the system, which, where the constitution is originally sound, may protract existence to a very remote period.

CHAPTER III.

On Economical Systems of Charity, by which the Poor assist in Providing for themselves.

I ENDEAVOURED in the former part of the last chapter to prove that the most enlarged exercise of charity, in the judicious relief of real distress, is not only consistent with, but actually conducive to public wealth and happiness, when they are founded on the principles maintained in this treatise. It will lead to no inconvenience from the encouragement which it may be thought to afford to population, because, as society is advancing, the fluctuations of employment increasing, and cases of individual distress consequently becoming more frequent in proportion to the number of the people, the progress of population is also continually decreasing in rapidity. The lives, therefore, saved by the relief of distress are more than counterbalanced by the natural abatement in the procreative power of the human species, and no redundancy ensues. In proportion as the virtue is called into exercise, means are provided for its innocent operation. But although this is a wise and a beautiful feature in the dispensations of Providence, it does by no means exclude the expediency of all such precautionary measures as shall render the people as independent as possible of subsistence by mere alms-giving. Such measures are no less advantageous to the moral than to the political condition of the people.

With this view many plans have been suggested, to enable a labouring man, by his own prudence and exertion, to assist in obviating the effects of those fluctuations in his temporal circumstances, to which the inhabitants of a populous and commercial country must necessarily be exposed. These plans are exclusively a feature of the advanced stages of society, because it is in such only that the fluctuations in the condition of the lower orders renders them necessary, and because they can only be successfully promoted in a country where property is secure, and public credit high. For these reasons I believe they have been scarcely known, except in our own country, and perhaps in a very limited degree in Holland. An attempt or two has been made in France, particularly at Chaillot near Paris, where a society was established, holding out to persons of both sexes after they have reached 70 years of age, or sooner if infirm, a comfortable subsistence for the remainder of their lives, upon consideration of a monthly payment, progressively advancing from the age of 10 to that of 70. Not long ago it is asserted that there were nearly 100 aged persons, whose appearance evidently bespoke their having occupied stations above the lowest ranks of society, living under the protection of this institution in happiness and contentment.

But it is in Great Britain only that institutions of this nature have either prevailed in sufficient numbers, or have been brought into so complete a system, as to offer fair grounds for investigating their moral and political effects, or for comparing the respective advantages of the several plans which have been acted upon. Considering the general

ignorance of the parties principally interested, viz.
the lower orders, it may be affirmed that none of
them have either fully answered the proposed end,
or are likely to be effectual, without the assistance
and superintendance of the higher orders, or at least
of the legislature : and this consideration fairly brings
them within the scope of an argument on the different modes of exercising charity.

Without entering into a minute distinction between plans having the same or nearly similar objects
in view, it will be enough to divide the economical
institutions of this nature into two classes, consisting—1st, of Friendly Societies or Benefit Clubs;
2dly, of Banks for the savings of the poor. The
objects of both are highly laudable; holding out
future recompense in return for present prudence
and self-denial. But the comparative merits of each
are by no means equal, as I shall presently have occasion to show.

The friendly societies are by far the most ancient
of the two institutions. Sir Frederic Eden, in his
laborious and useful work upon *the Poor*, endeavours
to trace them back to the remote periods of our
history, and believes that he has discovered analogous objects in the ancient Gilds of the Saxon times.
It is sufficient for our present purpose to state that
the modern societies took their rise about 40 years
ago, and gradually increased in numbers to between
5 and 6,000 societies, containing an amount of members equal to 8 in 100 of the whole resident population. The professed object, for the attainment
of which the rules are constructed, is to afford to
every member, in consideration of his small monthly
payment while in health, reasonable relief in case

of sickness or infirmity ; and usually a sum of money to his widow in case of death, and another sum to defray the expenses of his funeral. Doubtless they have partially fulfilled their objects ; but various circumstances have attended their operation in practice, materially detracting from the speculative advantages which were anticipated from the institution of them.

The vital principle of success is, of course, the economy and profitable use of small sums, and the nice calculation of chances, providing that the engagements entered into for pecuniary payments shall not exceed the probable accumulations. The constitution of the friendly societies has been defective in both these particulars. The demands upon the funds have exceeded the accumulations from various causes : —as 1st, The admission of members comparatively advanced in years upon the same terms of payment with the young and vigorous, whereby more than a profitable proportion of disabled members have been thrown upon the funds for support. 2dly, The out-goings for burials, for sums to widows, and other payments distinct from the main object of supporting helpless age upon the savings of youth, have not generally been calculated, in projecting the rules and rates of payment, and tend injudiciously to exhaust the funds. 3dly, The frequent meetings at the public-house for the monthly payments, the annual feast, and the funerals of members, if they do not tend to exhaust the funds, undoubtedly introduce habits that accelerate the period at which the members will become a charge upon them.

It is certainly true that the landlord of the public-house is the person who thinks himself principally

interested in the maintenance of the club. So much
so, that in most country villages it is called Mr. A.'s
club at the White Hart, or Mr. B.'s club at the
Green Man, &c. But the interest of the landlord
can of course tend only to one point. It is not,
therefore, with so little reason as Sir Frederic Eden
seemed to suppose, that it has been asserted " that
the members of friendly societies, from being accustomed to assemble at ale-houses, are not only sti-
mulated by interested landlords, but encouraged by
the contagion of ill example in habits of drunkenness :—that the money which is spent on a club-
night is entirely lost to a labourer's family ;—and
that there are various ways in which the earnings of
industry might be applied more advantageously to
the morals of the labourer and the comfort of his
family ;"—it may be added also, with more certain
prospects of ultimately attaining the professed end
of securing a provision for old age and infirmity.
For when to these causes of excessive demand upon
the funds, it is added that these funds themselves
are not managed with such minute attention to
economy, as is necessary to secure the best interest,
and the most rapid accumulation of the small sums
continually coming in, the frequent bankruptcies of
the clubs need excite no surprise. I fear it is too
often the case that, by the time any large portion of
the original members become aged and infirm, the funds
fail, and those members are thrown upon the parish.
Although they have paid their quota during the
vigour of their age, and are now looking for the promised reward, they are excluded from the new institution which immediately rises from the ruins of the old
one, under the patronage of the landlord of the public-

house ; but into which, of course, are only admitted
members who have the apparent means of earning a
livelihood without immediate assistance. This process,
be it observed, does not diminish the number of clubs,
but only neutralizes the benefits they are calculated
to confer.   There is the same appearance of prosperity on the face of any official returns made to
Parliament or to the constituted authorities.   Yet, if
consequences be closely investigated, the result seems
to be that a set of vigorous consumers is provided
in succession to the landlord of the public-house,
who do in fact assist one another during the flower
of their age in certain agreeable and some useful
objects of minor importance, but are so far from
providing effectually for their professed undertaking
to secure the independence of their members as they
advance in years, that they defraud them at that
critical period of their just claims, and do absolutely
rather subtract from, than add to, the comforts of
their families. Sir F. Eden somewhere observes, when
discussing the merits of a society which did not require of its members regular meetings at the public-
house :—" This is an omission which would discourage associations in a country village, where labourers form friendly societies, not only in order to
secure themselves a competent support in old age or
sickness, but *likewise* in order to spend a convivial
hour with their neighbours, and to hear what is
often (as Goldsmith says) ' much older than their
ale,' and generally as harmless—the news which
has been collected by rustic politicians."

The conclusion which the same writer draws from
the whole of his investigation into the effects of
friendly societies is to be found in the following

extraordinary passage. " These institutions do not aim at *perfection,* but *improvement:* They are not intended to be that " faultless monster which the world ne'er saw ; " but it is a *sufficient* proof of their *excellence,* that they are congenial to the social habitudes and prejudices of the labourer ; and that if they cannot *correct* the inclination (which is too often caused by hard labour) for conviviality and dis-sipation, they at least *convert* a *vicious* propensity into an *useful instrument* of economy and industry ; and secure to their members (what can seldom be purchased at *too dear* a rate) subsistence during sick-ness, and independence in old age."—(See conclusion of chapter on Friendly Societies, in Sir F. Eden on Poor Laws, vol. i.)

I do not think that Mandeville himself could have laid down more singular principles of *excellence* and *improvement,* especially when the objection evidently is not the want of " *correction,*" but the absolute encouragement " of *vicious* propensities." But it seems that even this is not " too dear a rate" at which to purchase " subsistence in sickness, and in-dependence in old age : " and that *vice* is thereby " *converted* into an *useful instrument.*" Happily, the moral knowledge of the people of England ren-ders it scarcely necessary to visit the profligacy of this sort of reasoning with any serious severity of remark. It may be useful, however, to show its utter absurdity in a practical point of view, by re-ferring to the inefficacy under which this very *useful instrument* has always laboured for producing the advantages which were anticipated from its assist-ance.

It appears then that, so far from securing to the

members " subsistence in sickness, and independence
in old age," it usually fails in permanently producing
either of those results; it frequently ends in defrauding the most praise-worthy members and the oldest
subscribers in the clubs of the fruits of their perseverance ; and the encouragement which they afford
to conviviality and dissipation is an *useful instrument* for few other purposes, except to fill the coffers
of the brewer and ale-house keeper, and through
them of the excise, at the expense of the morals of
the cottager, and the comfort and happiness of his
family.

Such I fear are too frequently the results of benefit clubs ;—and such *I am sure* will invariably be
the consequences, wherever they are conducted upon
Sir F. Eden's principle of " converting a *vicious* propensity into an *useful* instrument of economy and
industry."

Now surely the strongest advocate for the *jollity*
of the lower orders, (he who aspires with most eagerness at that cheap popularity which is acquired by
flattering the vice which is the peculiar disgrace of
our people in every eye but their own,) will scarcely
hesitate to admit that it ought not to be professedly
introduced for the furtherance of an object which it
can scarcely fail to defeat. It is bringing too great
a disgrace even upon their own system, and not
giving drunkenness fair play, to palm upon it more
than its legitimate evil consequences; to make it the
instrument of defrauding as well as demoralizing its
subjects. Upon their own principles, therefore, they
should keep it clear from all pretensions to produce
economical results, lest the obvious disappointment
that must ensue should operate in producing dis-

gust in the people's minds against this very laudable and useful feature of our national character.

Be it admitted by all means, notwithstanding the experience of the Scots, that a British soldier, sailor, or husbandman, is never worth a farthing for service, till he has spent his last farthing of money in rioting and drunkenness.   Let no rational man presume to entertain any doubt whatsoever that he would become indolent, or a coward, or a milksop, or a puritan, or a methodist, if he could be prevailed upon to carry his savings to a place of secure deposit at a distance from the ale-house, and expend the interest with his family in rational and *really* social indulgencies.   Let no one undertake to dispute the position that it is mere gratuitous theory to suppose that a poor English labourer, or soldier, or sailor, can make any savings from his hard-earned pittance, although in every parish, regiment, or ship, where the opportunity has been afforded, great numbers have eagerly availed themselves of it.   Let all these wise axioms be received as oracles ; but let the authors of them be consistent, and fairly encourage drunkenness and extravagance, according to the laudable precedent established in some parts of the army on the 25th and 26th of every month; and of the navy whenever *some* ship's crews receive their wages.   Let them not act so unfairly by their own system, as to attempt to establish upon it the opposite virtues of prudence and economy.   Human institutions, as Sir F. Eden well observes, do not aim at *perfection ;* and it is too ambitious for any moral philosophers, whose system has fairly secured all the advantages of drunkenness and dissipation, to grasp at the further rewards of sobriety and morality.

For this last-mentioned purpose, however, we will
now proceed to inquire into the merits of the second
species of institution mentioned at the outset of this
chapter, viz. :—Provident banks for the savings of
the poor, allowing interest for small deposits, with
liberty of withdrawing either the whole or any part of
them, as the future necessities of the person deposit-
ing may require. So many intelligent writers have
entered into details concerning the nature of these
institutions, that I shall be satisfied with referring to
those tracts which appear to me to give the most
satisfactory accounts of them.

The description of the establishment at Ruthwell,
near Edinburgh, by Mr. Duncan, the minister of
that parish, is interesting and instructive, because it
contains a clear account of the first successful attempt in this career of usefulness.

The observations on banks for savings, by the
Rt. Hon. G. Rose, contain, like all that gentleman's publications upon similar subjects, much sobriety and good sense, and many useful practical
directions. He gives at length the rules of a bank,
lately established at Southampton, by which deposits
not less than a shilling are received, which begin to
bear interest at 4 per cent. when they amount to
12s. 6d.; and when the sums lodged by any depositor
shall amount to 25l. the same are to be withdrawn,
or at his option may be invested in the public funds,
for which, as well as for the receipt of the interest,
the institution will afford him every facility. Mr.
Rose then proceeds as follows.

" Under these articles it will be seen that the depositors will be under no obligation to continue their
payments into the bank a week longer than they shall

choose: they may stop when they shall find it inconvenient to go on to make the savings, without incurring any forfeiture; and they may begin them
again when they can afford to do so; with perfect
freedom to withdraw their money, without inquiry,
whenever they shall have occasion for it for any purpose. And to prevent a possible mistake as to the
property of any one in the bank for savings, each
depositor will have in his own possession a paper, in
the nature of a receipt, in which will be entered
every sum he shall deposit."

" But as it may frequently happen to persons in
the lower classes of life not to know how to go about
purchasing stock or to receive the interest, (whereby
those few who now make savings frequently lose
them, by entrusting them in improper hands, to the
great discouragement of economy in others,) the institution undertakes to do both : so that the depositors
can be put to no inconvenience by being obliged to
withdraw their money."

" The advantages of these Institutions are too
obvious to make it necessary to say much upon them,
I will therefore allude only very generally to them.

" *Apprentices* on first coming out of their time,
who now too frequently spend all their earnings,
may be induced to lay by 5*s*. to 10*s*. a week, and
sometimes more, as in many trades they earn from
24*s*. to 50*s*. and 60*s*. a week.

" The same observation applies somewhat less forcibly to *journeymen* in most trades whose earnings
are very considerable, from not beginning so early,
and to workmen in many branches. With respect
to these it has been made evident to me and to many
members who attended the mendicity committee

in the last session of parliament, that in many instances when the gains have been as large as above
stated, the parties have been so improvident as to
have nothing in hand for the support of themselves
and families when visited with sickness, and have
consequently fallen immediately upon the parish.
In some instances the tools and implements of their
trade have been carried to the pawnbroker, whereby
difficulties are thrown in the way of their labour
being resumed on the restoration of health. I will
not however admit that habits of improvidence and
thoughtlessness are always the offsprings of vice, as
I am persuaded they are often the consequence of
ignorance or accident.

" *Domestic Servants*, whose wages are frequently
more than sufficient for their necessary expenses.

" *Carmen, Porters, Servants in lower conditions*,
and others, may very generally be able to make
small deposits.

" It is a trite observation that drunken men are generally the best workmen : no one however will believe
that drunkenness can advance skill ; the plain fact
is, that such workmen earn a great deal more than
is necessary for their ordinary maintenance, and not
knowing how to dispose of the remainder, they
spend it in drunkenness and dissipation of the worst
kind.

" With respect to *day Labourers*, the full advantage
cannot be expected to be derived at first, as far as
relates to married men with families ; it too frequently happens that where there are two or three
children, it is all that the father can do to support
himself and those dependant upon him with his
utmost earnings ; but the single man, whose wages

are the same as those of his married fellow labourers, may certainly spare a small weekly sum; by doing which he would in a reasonable time have saved enough to enable him to marry with a hope of never allowing any one belonging to him to become a burthen to the parish.

" Nothing is so likely as the encouragement of a plan of this sort, to prevent early and improvident marriages, which are the cause, more than any others, of the heavy burthen of the poor's rate. When a young single man shall acquire the habit of saving he will be likely to go on, till he shall get to gether as much as will enable him to make some provision for furnishing a few necessaries to assist in the support of a family, before he thinks of marrying.

" This is an attainment that every man who has the good of his country at heart must certainly wish for, without going the length of Mr. Malthus (whose patriotism will not be doubted) in desiring to prevent marriages taking place till the parties can state a probability of their being able to maintain the family which they are likely to have.

" If the full effect of this shall not be experienced instantly with respect to the class I am now speaking of, it can hardly fail of being produced as the rising generation of labourers shall get up; when a large proportion of the whole class will probably become depositors.

" At Edinburgh it is in proof that there is frequently an emulation among persons working in the same shop or manufactory, who shall save most during the week to deposit on the following Monday.

" I may here ask if the mind of man can invent any thing more likely than this to revive and to bring into action the old spirit of abhorrence to receiving parish relief.

" The success at Edinburgh and at Bath has been very considerable ; more so at the former than the latter, from the establishment having been earlier there, as well as from the greater extent of the city, and the greater variety of occupations of the lower class of its inhabitants.

" It is on that experience I rely more confidently than I should have done on the theory of the plan, excellent and unexceptionable as it is; it is going on in Scotland, according to the latest accounts, with increasing prosperity."

Such is the result of Mr. Rose's judgment, and I feel the greater pleasure in cordially assenting to it, having the misfortune widely to differ from some subsequent observations upon friendly societies, which are to be found in the same pamphlet.

By far the clearest and most useful statement however, which I have seen on this subject, is comprised in the third edition of a small anonymous tract, printed at Edinburgh and sold in London by Messrs Longman and Co. entitled, " A SHORT AC- COUNT OF THE EDINBURGH SAVINGS' BANK, con- taining Directions for establishing similar Banks, with the Mode of keeping the Accounts, and con- ducting the Details of Business." * The author begins by observing, that " the only effectual me- thod of assisting the poor is to encourage industry, sobriety, and economy among them, to excite and animate their own exertions, and aid them in securing

* Since this was written, a very clear and able pamphlet upon the subject has been published by Mr. Barber Beaumont, which is to be bought of Messrs. Cadell and Davies, in the Strand.

the full advantages of their success." After indulging, as is usual and natural with writers on the other side of the Tweed, in some remarks of considerable severity against the English Poor Laws, he proceeds as follows: " That much of the evil may be traced to the want of economical and provident habits among the poor themselves is unquestionable. The earnings of health and the wages of labour are made to meet only the daily expenditure, and the poor man is not careful to lay up any small sum which might be easily saved after the supply of his daily wants. The economy of nature points out the salutary maxim— that the season of plenty should provide for the season of want, and the gains of summer be laid up for the rigours of winter; for the abundant harvest of one year is intended to supply the deficient crop of another, and to be husbanded for the approaching season of scarcity. But this lesson of experience, though inculcated often with the most painful efficacy, is seldom duly appreciated till the calamity comes, and the season of preparation is past; so that the accidental occurrence of a rigorous season, or de-fective crop, with its constant attendant an increase in the price of the necessaries of life, is met without preparation, and must be endured without the mitiga-tion which a little prudence might have effected. Even for the approaches of infirmity and old age, though long contemplated, provision is not always made; and against the cheerless helplessness of the union of these with poverty there is no remedy but in the casual relief of the public or the parish.

" These habits of thoughtlessness and improvi-dence are not always the offspring of idleness or vice; they are as often the effects of ignorance or of acci-dent. The want of *a place of deposit* for the small sums which a poor man has it in his power to lay up, prevents him from thinking of doing so, and from acquiring a habit which is the foundation of so many virtues. Many would gladly adopt the plan if the facilities were brought within their reach : but while there is no means of placing these small savings beyond the reach of temptation, by withdrawing them from their immediate controul, the slightest invitation to squander them is too seldom resisted; or if not spent, they are lent to those who never repay them."

After these observations, the author proceeds to enter into a detail of the establishment of the savings' bank at Edinburgh, of its rules and regulations, the mode of keeping the accounts, and of the ample success with which it has been favoured. Although these are points of considerable practical interest, and many of them, especially the mode of keeping accounts, bear the stamp of originality and ingenuity, it would be obviously improper to enter into them in this place. I shall therefore take leave of this interesting pamphlet, after extracting the following conclusive arguments.

" The same wages are given to a man before he is married, and to one who has a large family. A larger sum even than two shillings weekly might be advantageously saved by the first class, which is too often spent in dissipation ; and if the advantage of saving a little stock be once felt, early and improvident marriages are likely to be less frequent than they are at present. During the ten or twelve first years of marriage the labourer's difficulties are greatest : his children are then young ; they stand in need of education ; and the mother's exertions are much occupied in attending to them. During this

period of life, the saving may be less; but after that
period, the children begin to support themselves, and
the parent may increase his rate of saving, so as with
former savings to lay up a provision for old age.

" In this country (Scotland) nothing more is wanting than to show the labourer the best means of securing part of his wages, and it will be done. The
advantage of doing so is abundantly felt, and a little
encouragement will make the extension of savings'
banks universal.

" It is certainly the interest of the higher ranks to
encourage this most promising experiment which has
yet been made for checking the extension of poor's
rates, which comes also recommended by its beneficial
influence upon the poor themselves, by removing one
great temptation to dissipation and idleness, encouraging at the same time honest, sober, and religious
principles."

———

After this comparison of the respective systems of
friendly societies and savings' banks, drawn both from
experience and the opinions of the several advocates
for each, I think it beyond dispute, that many
grounds of preference, both moral and political, exist
in favour of the latter. Every farthing saved is not
only preserved to the individual who saves it, but is
made the most of by accumulation. Both the principal and the accumulated interest are at any time
within reach of the depositor, upon *a formal demand*,
in case his necessities should at any time require him
to break in upon them ; and this power is evidently
superior to the privilege held out by the Friendly
Society, inasmuch as its beneficial influence extends to

the whole family, whereas the assistance offered by the Friendly Society extends only to the individual member, whose wife or children reap little collateral assistance. The *formal demand* is also a very useful condition; it implies *deliberation* before the savings are withdrawn; and few men will deliberately perform an imprudent or extravagant act. The money therefore will probably not be withdrawn without absolute and pressing necessity, and by no means upon so slight a temptation as would induce its disappearance from a deposit in the cottager's table-drawer. The spirit of accumulation is also a growing principle, and the poor man who has saved five pounds will much more probably exercise industry, sobriety, and self-denial to add to it other five pounds, than he who has yet received no practical proof of his power of saving, or of the advantages attending it.

The moral consequences are equally important : but it is perhaps enough to say of them in general, that every association connected with the savings in the bank is directed towards the social enjoyments of the domestic circle, which I will venture to assert are at least *a necessary condition* of all the poor man's virtue and respectability. Whereas the associations connected with the Friendly Society all tend towards the ale-house. I will therefore take the liberty of applying the language used by the advocates of the latter, with some trifling alterations to the former. These institutions do not aim at *perfection*, but *improvement*. They are not intended to be " that faultless monster which the world ne'er saw ;" but it is a sufficient proof of their excellence, that they are congenial with the social virtues and domestic enjoyments of the labourer; and although they do not prevent the inclination (often caused by hard labour) for occasional indulgencies in his family circle, they at least convert an innocent if not a virtuous propensity into an useful instrument of economy and industry, and secure to their members, (what can seldom be purchased at too dear a rate,) relief to their families under the pressure of difficulty, subsistence during sickness, and independence in old age.

The more I reflect upon the causes which tend both to demoralize and to deteriorate the temporal condition of the lower ranks in England, the more I am disposed to think, that the general prevalence of savings' banks, together with a diminution of the malt-tax, and the shutting up of two thirds of the ale-houses and liquor-shops, would operate, under the influence of moral and religious instruction, and of our other public institutions, in securing to the country a permanent supply of honest, healthy, and contented peasantry.

In conclusion, I must notice one objection which I have heard against the banks for savings. It has been insinuated, that so strict an exercise of economy must necessarily introduce a stingy, sordid, and calculating spirit among the lower orders. That their thoughts will all be so completely absorbed in the means of *saving*, that they will be apt to forget the more generous and public spirited art of *spending*. Now this apprehension is akin to those which some persons profess to entertain lest a tradesman should be too scrupulously honest, a clergyman too pious, a woman too modest, or a magistrate too firm ; lest society, in short, should be cursed with too much of a good thing. And truly honesty, piety, modesty, and a strict execution of the laws, are not less adverse than

a sober, moral, and independent race of people to the
wishes of those whose principal object in life is centred in irregular indulgence. Doubtless the prevalence of that *generous* spirit among the lower
orders which has been immortalized by the saying of
Mr. Hobson, who, when accused of stinginess, defied
any body to prove that he had "*ever denied himself any thing*," is much more favourable to the views
of such persons. But with respect to any other
species of generosity, no reasonable philanthropist can
well doubt that a poor man *must* practise economy
before he has the power of being generous to *others:*
and even a superficial observer of the operations of
the human mind, in any rank of life, will soon be
aware, that the prudent, the patient, and the self-
denying, are not only more accessible than the
thoughtless and extravagant to the claims of misery,
but that it is almost exclusively from them that acts
of real and unmixed charity do at any time proceed. In a word, if, according to the old proverb,
generosity be a vice unless it be preceded by justice,
the poor man has too many claims arising out of the
one to be enabled to practise the other, without a
strict adherence to sobriety and economy. With respect to a *calculating* spirit among the lower orders,
it can never be otherwise than convenient, both to individuals and the state, except where the object is to
make them perform acts, or acquiesce in proceedings
from which, upon fair calculation, they ought to abstain. But this is a principle of deceit; it is not that
upon which it is the interest of a free and moral
government to conduct its operations, nor, in truth,
is it that upon which the prosperity of *any* government can permanently endure.

CHAPTER IV.

General Conclusions with respect to the Exercise of Charity.

WRITERS, who have been in the habit of comparing the sums expended in charity in different countries, have too frequently forgotten to compare also the state of society prevalent in each, and the comparative means which they in consequence possess of meeting the demands made upon their charity. There are some conclusions upon this subject that appear to be just, but which I do not recollect to have hitherto seen submitted to the public.

Charity, in the sense in which it is now under discussion, may be said to consist of such pecuniary relief as individuals, notwithstanding the fair exertion of their industry, may stand in need of to relieve their necessities, and of such pecuniary expenditure as may be found useful in promoting moral instruction, and habits of industry among those who want either the will or the power to obtain them by their own exertions. It follows then, that the objects of charity vary in number and differ in degree in different countries, as the several states of society are respectively prevalent in their different gradations. In the agricultural state of society, the necessity for donations in money to support existence must be very small indeed; for food is plentiful; and the exertion of any kind or quantity of labour meets with a high reward. Moral education, however, is here peculiarly necessary, in consequence of the insulated manner in which a race of cultivators must necessarily live, whereby that restraint which the opinion of the vicinage imposes upon moral conduct, is scarcely at all prevalent.

In the mixed agricultural and commercial state of society, individual distress will be more prevalent, from the partial fluctuations of employment, among the commercial part of the community; objects of charity, positively in want of food, will therefore occasionally present themselves. But as the price of provisions must still be low, as the commercial employments will be principally of a durable nature for the supply of the domestic population, and the *real* wages of labour will still be high, the necessary expenditure in charity to persons in want of food will not yet be great. Hospitals for the relief of casualties, and public institutions affording employment to those who suffer a temporary interruption in their own pursuits, will, in ordinary times, be probably sufficient to maintain the comfort and happiness of the people. But as augmented commerce attracts the people into towns, and increases their temptations to licentious indulgence, while the high remuneration of labour affords them opportunities of gratifying it, both moral education and moral precautions of a charitable nature should scrupulously attend every step in their progress. Public schools, a rational provision for a church establishment, gaols so constituted as to promote the reformation of offenders and be really a terror to the evil-minded, (which may strictly be called *national charities,*) now become indispensable to the public welfare.

As a country proceeds from the mixed agricul-

tural and commercial state towards the highly
manufacturing and commercial, every department of
charity must necessarily be enlarged. We have seen
that the produce of the soil can only be increased at
an augmented expense from inferior land, as a previous demand elicits it; that fluctuations in the
price of food are the necessary consequence ; that a
continually increasing proportion of the people comes
to reside in towns, to be employed in manufactures
for exportation, and in pursuits which prosper or
decline according to fortuitous circumstances, and
most of which are not very favourable to the general
health of the persons engaged in them. It is evident
therefore that a much larger number of individuals
must occasionally be exposed to the pressure of want,
under circumstances which render it much less easy
to relieve them.

Occupations are comparatively full; food is comparatively scarce ; the operations of society become
more complicated; and it requires the charitable exertions, both of the state and of the superior orders
of society, to prevent the comfort and happiness of
the people from declining. Liberal provision for
temporary distress, the support of the children of industrious parents, private societies combining industrious employment with pecuniary aid, and assisting the poor in laying up a provision for future difficulties, are absolutely necessary for the purpose. It
is obvious also that dangers of a moral nature increase
in the same proportion. Almost every circumstance
I have mentioned as attending this condition of
society adds to the temptations of the people, without
diminishing their power of resisting them. In addition, therefore, to the moral precautions of a charitable

nature, applicable to the former conditions of society, an increase of the established clergy in proportion to that of the population, especially in large towns, a provision of the same nature for national schools, the means of putting a speedy end to the trifling disputes and bitter contentions of a people in the constant collision of interests, by the cheap or gratuitous administration of justice in cases of minor importance, fall within the public department of moral charity at this period. Private societies for the distribution of the Scriptures, for the circulation of sound and orthodox tracts, calculated to keep the spirit of pure religion and morals alive among the lower orders, and personal attention to the moral wants and habits of their respective neighbourhoods, are requisite from such of the superior orders as wish to make the due return to society for the augmented comforts and enjoyments which its progress has afforded them. I think, too, that I may add, that a view to the diffusion of these blessings among the foreign dependencies of a state, is both a positive duty, and a becoming tribute to Providence, where it has favoured their successful establishment at home.

It appears, then, that every step in the progress of society imposes a corresponding necessity for the enlargement of every description of charity which is promoted by pecuniary expenditure. But it may also be observed, that means of meeting the demand are increased at least in an equal proportion.

The accumulation of capital, and the elevation of a larger portion of the people into the superior walks of life, are indispensable concomitants of all progress in commercial and manufacturing industry. The number of persons upon whom the duty of charity is imposed, and their power of amply fulfilling that duty, are therefore augmented in full proportion to the increase of the legitimate objects of charity; and the onus upon the country, though increased in absolute amount, is perhaps lightened with respect to its comparative power of bearing it. This may be illustrated by a dry arithmetical calculation.

Let us suppose the nominal capital of an agricultural country to be 5,000,000*l.*, and the sums expended in charity to be 50,000*l.*, or 1 per cent.; that in its progress to the mixed agricultural and commercial state its nominal capital is increased to 20,000,000*l.*, and its charitable expenses to 150,000*l.*, or three fourths per cent; it is evident that the sum expended, though thrice in amount, is a fourth less burthensome to the country, provided the expense is fairly apportioned.

Again, at its arrival in the highly manufacturing and commercial state, its nominal capital may be increased to 200,000,000*l.*, and its expenditure in charity to 1,350,000*l.*, and yet the country, and each individual in it, may expend a smaller portion of its means in the exercise of that virtue than when only 150,000*l.* was laid out. Nor would it be fair to estimate the comparative distress at the two periods, or the number of persons receiving relief, according to the difference in the two sums; for it is well known that, as wealth accumulates, the real value of money decreases as compared with its nominal amount, and a larger sum is necessary to purchase an equal quantity of the necessaries of life. If we suppose this difference between the last two of the above mentioned periods to amount to one fourth, we must of course deduct that proportion from the increase of distressed persons, which the difference between the two sums would otherwise indicate. The same allowances must of course be made in comparing the charitable expenditure of two separate countries in different conditions of society. In England the nominal increase of the poor's rate, from 1783 to 1803, was from 2,130,000*l.* to 4,200,000*l.*, or 2,070,000*l.*, which is apparently near double. But the price in the necessaries of life during the same period had increased one third. That proportion therefore, or 1,400,000*l.*, must be deducted from 4,200,000*l.*, in order to ascertain the real increase of persons supported by charity during the period; which, instead of being nearly double, as appears upon the face of the account, will then turn out to be something less than one third; for the increase of expense, if money had continued of the same nominal value, would only have been from 2,130,000*l.* to 2,800,000*l.*, as will be evident to any one who will take the trouble to arrange the figures on the back of a letter. The increase in the number of persons to be supported, must of course have been in the same proportion, viz. less than one third: but the revenue of England, or the power of supporting them if the expense were fairly apportioned, had considerably more than doubled in the same period.

If the reasoning contained in this chapter be at all just, there surely cannot well be more idle declamation, than what we frequently hear concerning the extravagance of the expenditure in charity in some countries, grounded upon a comparison with the trifling sums paid in others, where the bulk of the people apparently enjoys equal comfort and happiness. It is obvious that the reasonable expenditure for the purpose of keeping the people in a comfortable state, and the means of meeting it in an agricultural country like America, must be greatly less than in mixed agricultural and commercial countries, like France and Scotland; and these again must bear a small proportion to the necessary expenses and the means of a highly manufacturing and commercial nation, such as England. To make a comparison, therefore, between these countries or between others in a similar condition respectively, with a view to charge that which makes the greatest expenditure with extravagance, appears to be not more reasonable, than it would be to murmur that the head of a large family, enjoying an ample fortune, should dedicate a greater sum to the support and assistance of his poor relations, than the head of a small family in circumstances comparatively narrow.

But perhaps it may be objected, that if the necessity for the exercise of charity increases with every step in the progress of society, individual distress must of course increase also, and the general condition of the people be deteriorated. To this it may be answered that, where the demands of charity are duly answered, the general happiness of the people is rather advanced than trenched upon by the increased extent of charitable exertion. I should upon the whole conceive that a peasant would be more happy in the power of sending his children to a village school within half a mile of his cottage, or a town-resident to one within half a furlong, than the cultivator in an agricultural country could be in the scanty and occcasional intercouse which he could have with any instructors at all in the insulated situation of his residence ; and that the children in the former case would be more likely to turn out blessings to their parents. In Canada, I am credibly informed, that the means of procuring instruction are so scanty, that even many members of the legislature cannot sign their names. Though government, through the exertion of some benevolent men in authority there, are about to use means for affording greater facilities of instruction.

Again I should conceive, that a poor man who fractures one of his limbs in a highly civilized country that fulfils its moral duties as to charity, and is instantly carried to an hospital, where all the comforts and skill attendant upon such a state of society are employed towards his cure, enjoys some trifling advantages over the peasant of the agricultural country, who may meet with the same accident in the middle of a large wood, 100 miles distant, even from the scanty comforts and deficient skill which are usually found in such countries.

Once more—although the ordinary fluctuations in the condition of the labouring part of the community are necessarily greater in the most advanced than in the previous stages of society, yet I should certainly be disposed, from personal observation, to assert that, where the measures for meeting the consequences of these fluctuations, which have been detailed in former chapters of this treatise, are duly called into action, as in every moral country they will be, there the poor man's condition is upon the whole more desirable than in the earlier stages of society. For not only are the ordinary fluctuations met and remedied, but the extraordinary fluctuations

also. He feels secure that, if he is himself industrious, his family will meet with due support, both
when their ordinary expenses are greater than he
can afford, and also when accident imposes upon
them any extraordinary difficulties. And when the
support, although given as a modification of charity,
is confined to these two cases, it is both desirable in
theory, and true in fact, that the sense of degradation attached to personal relief under any form
should gradually wear away, and attach itself only
to cases of distress induced by idleness and profligacy. In all others it comes by degrees to be considered as a provision due by law or custom from the
society at large, in return for the general advantages
received by its progress in wealth and prosperity.
This observation especially applies to the case of
the poor-laws in England, where we frequently hear
it stated, in terms of lamentation and reproach, that
12 in 100, or nearly an eighth of the resident population are *reduced to the state of paupers*, subsisting upon *charity ;* whereas it is well known to
all persons conversant with the execution of the poor-
laws, that at least one third of those persons are
the offspring of industrious parents of large families,
who receive their subsistence from the state by a
legal provision, involving no disgrace or imputation
upon the receivers, and conferring great and important
benefits upon the state in its present condition of society. Strictly speaking, therefore, it cannot be considered so much in the light of *charity* under *any* of its
modifications, as in that of a tax upon property,
which when duly apportioned, is calculated, as I
have shown in a former chapter, to produce economi-

cal results highly beneficial both to the agricultural
and commercial interests of the community.

It appears then that just comparisons concerning
the charitable expenditure of different countries
must include a review of the different states of
society in which they may be; and that when the
argument is stated merely by comparing the nominal
amount of the sums expended in each, to be just,
it must be applied only to two places where the
people are in similar circumstances. These comparisons, however, when fairly drawn, are not without
their use for many purposes.

In an interesting volume entitled " *Collections
relative to the systematic Relief of the Poor, at different Periods and in different Countries,*" published for Crutwell, Bath; and Murray, London;
many such comparisons are instituted with great
candour and sagacity, both with respect to ancient
and modern states. They are well worthy of the
notice of philanthropists, and seem to bear out the
compiler in several conclusions highly important to his
own country. One of them is stated by him in the
following words :—" Whatever may be the state of religion, government, morals, and police, the sums annually devoted to the relief of the infirm and poor are
not so small as to warrant the vain suggestion which
many delight to propagate, that the sacrifice of property to the support of the poor in England, by the
operation of the poor's law, is greatly disproportionate
to that which common humanity devotes to the
object in other countries. That the legal allotment
of a portion of the public wealth, to the support of
those whose labour has been or may be beneficial to

the public, is in any view of national policy more disadvantageous to the community than the leaving all who are in want to seek at large for the charity of individuals—is a conclusion to which I conceive an observer would never be led by an examination of the state of the poor and the effects of charity in catholic countries." In Naples and Milan the sums expended in charity are larger in proportion to the population than in Liverpool and London, yet no one who has seen the four cities will dispute the superiority of the condition of the people in the two latter. Edinburgh, which has no extensive poor's rate, applies nearly as large a sum to the support of its poor in proportion to the population, as Liverpool contributes, including its very high poor's rate. But the situation of the poor in Liverpool and Edinburgh is probably upon a par with respect to comfort. We see then that, where the moral duties of charity are duly performed, there its professed objects will be attained; and this by a pecuniary expenditure not greater than will be extracted by the pressure of misery against the fears or feelings of individuals where the moral duties are neglected. The difference in the two cases will not be so much in the expense as in the effect. In one the people will be happy, decent, moral, and industrious; in the other they will be wretched and brutal, and profligate and slothful. The same author, after a review and comparison of the condition of the poor in England, Scotland, and Holland, where legal relief to the poor is part of the law of the land; and in Ireland and other countries of Europe where no such laws exist, concludes with stating his conviction that " it will certainly be found that the charities of other coun-

tries have never, at any period, been so conducted as
to relieve the poor of an equal population so adequately as the poor's law, with less encouragement
of idleness or with better stimulus to industry." Of
course both the adequacy of the relief, and its effect
upon the moral and political condition of the poor,
must depend upon the sagacity, attention, and perseverance with which it is administered; and in
these respects Holland perhaps stands first in economical prudence; Scotland first in moral precaution,
and second in economical prudence; and England
second in moral precaution, but clearly and decidedly
the last in economical prudence.

The difference perhaps is upon the whole made up
in England by the strong bond of union and reciprocal
attention which exists between the higher and lower
orders, much of which may possibly be traced to
the long period during which the poor laws have
been in operation amongst them; whereby a conviction has been worked among the higher ranks
that, if the condition of the poor be neglected, the
ultimate consequences must be an increase in the
compulsory expenditure for their support. I trust
that I shall stand excused for quoting, as the conclusion of this chapter, a passage formerly written
by me upon the good effects which flow from such
an intimate connexion of interests between the
higher and the lower orders as is produced by our
system of poor laws. " It may be admitted as a
general axiom in the politics of a free and extensive
country, that when once a strong bond of reciprocal
interest is established between the higher and lower
orders of the community, the statesman's task is
half performed to his hand; and that such a people,

by their native energy and internal resources, will
not only preserve the integrity of their own empire,
but must by the force of their institutions gradually
triumph over their enemies. In Scotland, the feudal
system prevented the introduction of a state of degeneracy similar to that of Ireland ; and as poor
laws have for a very long time subsisted in Scotland,
poor's *rates* have been regularly called into operation
in proportion as the feudal system has worn away,
and commerce, manufactures, and tillage, have usurped
the seats of baronial splendour, and encroached
upon the idle hospitality of the lords of the waste.
An institution which produces such phenomena in
society must necessarily rest on grounds of deep
moral and political expediency. It has been asserted
by some, particularly by foreign writers, to be the
millstone around the neck of England, which must
at length engulf her in a sea of ruin ; and we are
willing to admit that it is, in the spirit of our other
institutions, calculated for a state of progressive
prosperity ; but that it may accelerate our downfall,
should the circumstances of the country begin to
decline. But to compensate this evil we think it
will appear that, under Providence, so long as the
several ranks of the people are true to themselves
and to each other, such a state of declension is not
within the scope of probability : and we have yet
to learn that a law or institution is objectionable,
because it is inconsistent with a selfish neglect of
duty in those for whose government it is intended."

CHAPTER V.

Brief Recapitulation of the preceding Chapters upon Charity.

CHARITY is confessedly a moral duty enjoined in the Holy Scriptures, and is therefore to be practised in conformity to the commands of God when they can be clearly discerned; and where they are silent, it is to be regulated by the best lights which can be acquired from considerations of moral expediency. *Within* those limits, I think it has appeared from the preceding chapters of this book, that no political mischief can arise from the most unbounded exercise of the virtue. *Beyond* those limits, donations in money, under the guise of charity, partake not of the nature of virtue but of thoughtless profusion, and tend more to encourage profligacy than to relieve distress.

That the due exercise of charity can produce no political evils connected with the principle of population has, I think, appeared from the consideration, that the virtue is never called into action so as materially to affect the numbers of mankind, until the natural rate of their increase becomes so slow by the progress of society, that the impulse given to it by charitable exertions is rather an advantage than otherwise to the state. That the sums bestowed in charity will be sufficient to supply all her legitimate demands, *and also* to satisfy the demands of the idle and profligate who would willingly subsist upon them without any exertion of industry, is more

than we are justified in inferring either from history
or experience; although there are many countries
where the last mentioned abuse of charity absorbs
more money than its legitimate use, and there are
few where the practice of the virtue is conducted
in the most judicious and economical manner. The
question is resolved therefore more into one of judgment in the mode of distribution, than of comparative expenditure. And the most liberal and enlightened exercise of charity, so far from forbidding,
absolutely requires the adoption of every expedient
for inculcating religious, moral, sober, and frugal
habits among the lower orders; for encouraging them
as far as possible to provide for themselves, and to
rise independent of the aid either of the public or
of individuals, to the utmost extent to which the
state of society under which they are living will
allow. But as their natural power of effecting these
objects is altered by almost every step in the progress
of society, it follows that assistance from the state
and from philanthropic individuals must come in
aid with increased activity as society advances, and
the natural means of the poor themselves are diminished. Happily also it has appeared that both the
means and the will for granting this aid increase in
at least as great a proportion as they are wanted, in
every moral and well regulated community. In one
parish of London there are more charitable institutions both public and private than in the whole
Empire of China; and the effects upon the people
respectively may be contemplated in the first book
of this treatise. Nothing then can well be more
absurd than to sit down and murmur at the superior
expenditure of charity in any particular country

over another, without taking into consideration the moral and political condition of each. Nor can it well be disputed that, where the moral and political condition of the people is in the most enviable state, as compared with others in the same stage of society, there the charitable institutions must be constructed upon the truest theory, and most effectually carried into practice. For these institutions have so direct a bearing upon the condition of the people, at least in the advanced stages of society, that it can scarcely be said by those who disapprove of their extent, that the people are happy and comfortable, not through the influence of those institutions, but *in spite of them*, and by the counteracting force of the other laws and customs by which the people are affected.

Upon the whole then, perhaps, we may conclude that politicians may safely discard their apprehensions that the practice of charity, as commanded by Scripture, or as it results from moral expediency, will ever be found in excess among any people; or that preserved within those limits it can ever be misapplied. And thus upon this great practical question, as well as upon all the rest which we have contemplated, the conviction accompanies us through all its bearings and ramifications, that Christian morality is the only solid foundation for the political welfare of the people.

CHAPTER VI.

On the Propriety of affording a free and equal Option of Marriage to all Classes of the Community.

THE following passage occurs in the eleventh chapter of the fourth book of Mr. Malthus's Essay. " Nothing can be more clear than that it is within the power of money and of the exertions of the rich adequately to relieve a particular family, a particular parish, or even a particular district. But it will be equally clear, *if we reflect a moment on the subject,* that it is totally out of their power to relieve the whole country in the same way, at least, without providing a regular vent for the overflowing numbers in emigration, or without the prevalence of a particular virtue among the poor, which the distribution of this assistance tends obviously to discourage." The preceding chapters may, perhaps, have satisfied the reader that a power does exist of relieving a whole country without providing for overflowing numbers by emigration ; because numbers will not, in fact, overflow. It is the object of the present chapter to show to what extent the prevalence of the particular virtue among the poor, which the exercise of charity is said to discourage, affects the principle of population, and consequently whether the option of marriage may not be afforded to the lower ranks of society upon moral considerations only, and be left perfectly free upon grounds of expediency, and even upon those of political arithmetic."

On this subject, conclusions the most important to the moral good and general happiness of the people depend upon the truth or falsehood of the principles maintained in this treatise. The following proposition has been repeatedly drawn from the principle of population, as it is laid down by those writers whom it is my object to oppose; viz. moral restraint, that is, involuntary abstinence from marriage by those who cannot support a family of the average number, (accompanied by abstinence from irregular intercourse,) until the pecuniary affairs of the parties are absolutely in a condition to support a family of the size that may eventually be born to them, is the only method of escaping the vice and misery incident to a redundant population. Now as the lower orders are evidently the only part of a people who cannot support a family, if they choose to give up other enjoyments in exchange for the domestic, it follows that the rule of involuntary abstinence from marriage applies exclusively to them, and that it is necessary to the public welfare that *they* should continue single, and of course unpolluted, to a comparatively advanced period of life. At the same time the advocates of this opinion are compelled to admit that such a *general system* of restraint among the lower orders is, from the nature and constitution of mankind, extremely difficult and improbable; and that supposing the abstinence from marriage *only* to be attained, there would be great danger of encouraging the worst vices among them. The attempts to weaken this objection to the system consist principally of a comparison of its result with other crimes and vices to which it is asserted that the opposite course of conduct, or the encouragement of marriage, would lead;

which are said to be great, but which I must beg
leave to think (from an extensive observation of the
lower orders) by no means the greater of the two.
Again, they are compelled to admit, that, " considering the passion between the sexes in all its bearings
and relations, including the endearing engagement of
parent and child resulting from it, it is one of the principal ingredients of human happiness;" and we may
surely add, that its lawful gratification is the great constituent of the happiness of the lower orders, who
do not profit in proportion with the rest of the community by the progress of civilization : at least it
does not afford to them, as it does to the higher ranks
of society, any mental substitute for these interdicted
gratifications. Even an attentive perusal of Mr.
Malthus's confessedly Utopian state of society, described in his chapter on " the effects which would
result to society from *the general practice*" of such
double abstinence as is above described, will undoubtedly show that almost all the moral advantages
and happiness resulting from it attach exclusively to
the feelings and condition of the higher orders. The
people should therefore be entitled to retain that
which they possessed in the earlier stages of society,
and for which its further advancement has afforded
them no substitute.

But, say the supporters of the new opinions, if the
lower orders do not alter their conduct in this respect
with the progress of society, an increase of misery,
and a multiplication of deaths by famine and various
other diseases, must be the inevitable consequence.
To prevent this lingering misery, therefore, if we
attempt to facilitate marriage as a point of the first
consequence to the morality and happiness of the

people, to act consistently, we should facilitate and not impede the production of mortality. Instead of recommending cleanliness to the poor, we should encourage the contrary habits; we should make our streets narrower, and implore the return of the plague; we should build our villages near stagnant pools, and encourage settlements in bogs and morasses. We should above all reprobate those benevolent, but much mistaken men, who have foolishly thought they were doing a service to mankind, by projecting schemes for the total extirpation of particular disorders. Truly, according to the dilemma here stated, it appears that great and irremediable vice and misery, in some shape or other, is what a reasonable man must expect to find the lot of the larger portion of his fellow-creatures, even supposing them to practise the degree of virtue and morality which has been found to exist in the best regulated and most civilized societies; and that one great and inevitable source of vice and misery is gradually increased among the lower orders, without any counterpoise, in proportion as the situation of the other ranks is ameliorated.

But can this be the ordination of Providence? Has he made the attainment of moral virtues so unequally possible among men? It is impossible to believe it upon any authority less than his own positive declaration. Nor is it any defence of the justice of such an arrangement to say, " that at some particular periods in the progress of society men are more strongly tempted in a particular manner than at others;" for it is evident that, according to the preceding exposition of the plan of Providence, it is not a substitution of one species of temptation for

another, but an exoneration of a degree of temptation from the higher orders, to place the burthen
upon the shoulders of the lower. It seems that the
last are the only persons to whom the option of early
marriage is to be denied, though they have at the
same time fewer enjoyments to substitute for it, and
infinitely fewer means of avoiding the temptations
to vice, which an involuntary abstinence from marriage necessarily multiplies. Their mental resources
being most deficient, they are more in want of other
gratifications, and of the means of humanizing their
minds by the enjoyments of the social affections.
Whereas the higher and middle orders, who want it
least, have a perfectly free option of marriage.

The denial of this fact, which is sometimes attempted, cannot, I think, be maintained. That their
pride, their desire to retain the enjoyments attached
to a life of celibacy, the profits arising from pursuits
with which the care of a wife and family is incompatible, the various pleasures and advantages, in
short, which in a civilized state men in the higher
and middle classes must sometimes resign upon
marriage, prevent them from entering into that contract for fear of losing those advantages, is very certain ; and the result forms one of the leading arguments in the first book of this treatise. But they
have evidently the power of choice. If they choose
to sacrifice one enjoyment for the sake of the other,
by descending a degree in the scale of society, they
may gratify their wishes with innocence, and exchange a part of their pecuniary or other advantages
for the comforts of a family. If they prefer the
ease and disincumbrance of a single life to the social
comforts of the marriage state, they can never have

a right to complain of the sacrifices by which alone those enjoyments can be innocently obtained, since they are of their own imposing. Before they can prove that vice or misery arising from an involuntary abstinence from marriage are any part of the lot bestowed upon them by Providence, they must prove that the same Providence hath made the enjoyment of luxury, and the acquisition of riches, a necessary condition of their existence.

Providence, for example, cannot be arraigned for reducing a man to the necessity of abstaining either from marriage, or his wine; nor would it be any mitigation of the crime of irregular intercourse, if a man should say that, by the constitution of human affairs, he could not enjoy the comfort of a wife without parting with his bottle. He has it clearly in his power to support the former in health and temperance, if he choose to abstain from the latter;—the choice is his. But when he has made it, he is certainly bound to abstain from illegal gratification, having the power of enjoying that which is legal. As this, however, is not the case with the poor, if it could be proved that they, among whom perhaps the natural passion is at least equally strong, with less power of escaping its effects, be absolutely precluded from the option of an early marriage; if the weight of the greatest of all temptations be laid exclusively where the smallest means of resisting it are bestowed; if there be no possibility of bestowing upon the lower orders the gratifications which their religion holds out as innocent, and the domestic enjoyments of a family, (those cordial drops in the cup of a poor man, which by lulling his most restless passions to a repose that his intellectual faculties could never

produce, lift him to a level with his superiors in the
scale of happiness and contentment, and in the power
of practising the moral duties);—then may we be
tempted to think that the impartiality of Providence
may be plausibly impeached, and that the sins and
vicious indulgences of the lower orders must be held
harmless in its sight. To say in defence of so partial
a dispensation, "that the Scriptures most clearly and
precisely point out to us, as our duty, to restrain
our passions within the bounds of reason ; and that
it is a palpable disobedience of this law to indulge
our desires in such a manner as reason tells us will
unavoidably end in misery ;" would scarcely be admitted as conclusive in any place where the hearers
were not restricted from answering, so long as the
argument is exclusively used in reference to the
lower orders; which in this question of the free
option of marriage or celibacy it certainly is, according to the reasoning just referred to.

But let Providence speak for itself on this occasion,
and in language of its own inspiration. St. Paul
who, in addition to his inspired wisdom, was a man
of the world, and a politician liberally educated,
takes occasion to address the Corinthians upon the
subject of matrimony. They were natives of a rich
luxurious city, employed in many occupations sufficient to engross a man's whole and undivided attention, (as is the case in every advanced stage of society;)
and where of course it would have interfered with
the general and individual prosperity that all should
have been distracted from their attention to pursuits
advantageous to the public by the care of families;
he therefore writes thus to them. " It is good for a
man not to touch a woman ; nevertheless, to avoid

fornication, let every man have his own wife, and let every woman have her own husband :" (1 Cor. vii. 1, 2. 9.): and to the Hebrews, a nation in a somewhat less advanced state of society, he says, " Marriage is honourable *in all;* but whoremongers and adulterers God will judge :" (Heb. xiii. 4.) The meaning of the former passage plainly is, that it is proper enough, there is no harm, that a man should abstain from marriage provided he can abstain from women ; but let him, who finds he cannot otherwise abstain, have recourse to matrimony. That this is the true meaning appears from what follows : " I speak this by permission, not of commandment ; but every man has his proper gift of God ; one after this manner, another after that : I say therefore to the unmarried and widows, it is good for them if they abide even as I" (in a life of celibacy) ; " but if they cannot, let them marry." The meaning of the whole is so direct that it is impossible to mistake it. It is plainly this : in a complex society some may serve their country by devoting their whole time and talents to the advantage of the public in naval, military, commercial, or political pursuits ; others to the exclusive service of God and the souls of their fellow-creatures ; to severe study or to literary labours. Others again by marriage may serve both God and their country in bringing up families, and leading them in the paths of religion and virtue. Let those, then, who can contentedly devote their whole time to the former pursuits, and by distracting their minds continue pure from carnal indulgences, remain single even as St. Paul. But if ever they find their purity in so much danger that they cannot otherwise preserve it, let them marry ; " for whoremongers and adulterers God will judge ;" and so long as men have it in their power to marry, if they cannot otherwise remain pure, there is no just ground of complaint against this condition of celibacy. Such then is the judgment which the omniscient God has promulgated concerning the force of the strongest and most necessary of the natural passions, and to such an extent has he allowed indulgence to be innocent. Marriage is held forth as the universal method of such indulgence, and it is clear that the recommendation has to do with feelings and situations that will occur in every state of society, whether the population be full or scanty ; that it applies to the inhabitants of crowded cities as well as to the village peasant : therefore it is to be presumed (as the principles of this work maintain) that God hath provided the means of a sufficient supply of food for any increase of people which the compliance with such permission will ever be found to produce. The precise and positive rule is one of the most universal application, and therefore, in the case supposed, may universally be complied with without reference to any other circumstance. Moreover, marriage being permitted in the cases just stated, it follows most clearly that it is permitted to the young among the lower orders, as soon as they are emancipated from the paternal superintendance, and find their temporal circumstances in such a state as to induce them to suppose that their comforts would be increased by matrimony. " Let the *younger women marry*, bear children, guide the house, give none occasion to the adversary to speak reproachfully :" (1 Tim. v. 14.) And here we have one among a thousand instances, that the method appointed by Providence for preserving and improving one virtue is made the indispensable condition, and the means of practising, many others; for without early marriage, how can a parent hope properly to fulfil the various duties of education, maintenance, and provision for his children. " Ye fathers, provoke not your children to wrath, but bring them up in the nurture and admonition of the Lord; having them in subjection with all gravity : " (Ephes. vi. 4.) " If any provide not for those of his own house, he hath denied the faith, and is worse than an infidel : " (1 Tim. v. 8.) There are many other commands to the same purpose given to parents, a compliance with which requires much of the undivided attention of a great portion of life, and can hardly be performed by those who marry when they have yet but few active years remaining. Enough, however, has been said to prove the positive nature of the scripture doctrine upon this subject, and to show that there is no room to misapply the opinion* quoted from Dr. Paley, (Mor. Phil. b. ii. c. 4.) by stating that, according to the genuine principles of moral science, "the method of coming at the will of God by the light of nature is, to inquire into the tendency of an action to promote or diminish the general happiness." Indeed this passage should never have been quoted, without the qualification given to it in an early part of the same chapter of the " *Moral Philosophy*," that such a method is merely recommended as the *best remaining* to discover the will of God, when we cannot come at his *express declarations*, which must always guide us when they are to be had, and which must be sought for in Scrip-

* Malthus's Essay, b. iv. c. 2.

ture. (Paley, Mor. Phil. b. ii. c. 4.) When these are express, as we find in the case before us, there is no further room for controversy. Nor can a more dangerous road to scepticism be marked out, than to set up against them, or in explanation of them, any thing so very variable and doubtful as the opinion of philosophers concerning " *the tendency of an action to promote or diminish the general happiness.*" The arguments of this treatise, for example, and those to which they are opposed, arrive at precisely contrary conclusions as to this *tendency* in the case before us. How far the latter can stand the test of that criterion by which, according to Dr. Paley they should be tried, it is for the candid reader to determine. I will only remark in confirmation of my own reasoning that, during a long and attentive observation of the habits and manners of the poor in England; I have never observed a moral and prudent young man, of whatever number of children he may have been the father, in a state of misery. On the contrary, I have generally found the numerous families of moral, healthy, and youthful parents in a satisfactory state as to external circumstances, and greatly superior in these respects to the peasantry of any of the foreign countries in which it has been my lot to travel, or of whom I can obtain any authentic account. So strictly true in politics is the saying of the Psalmist: " I have been young, and now am old; and yet saw I never the righteous forsaken, nor his seed begging their bread."

In the mean time, I think myself justified in remarking that, such being the difficulties and inconsistencies of the opinions respecting population which I am now opposing, when connected with the subject of marriage, it may be worth while to inquire how far the system adopted in this treatise will alter the conclusions to be drawn, and bring them more into unison with the apparent equity of the Divine dispensations, with our sense of natural justice, and with the express commands and unqualified permissions of Scripture on the subject :—and whether this combined inquiry will not prove that every man, in every station of life, has equally the option of contracting matrimony, if upon a due consideration of his temporal circumstances and moral feelings he may think proper to do so, without any necessary injury, from the principle of population, to the society in which he lives.

We have seen that, as civilization advances, the number of those who spontaneously prefer the advantages of celibacy to those of the married state continually increases ; and that the power of propagating their species in many of those who choose the other alternative is at the same time continually diminishing. We have seen that, in proportion as these effects arise, the necessity increases that the re-productive part of the people should remain at least as fruitful as before. The re-productive part of the people are principally the lower orders, who, while the agricultural state of society existed, married early, and reared as large families as they could procreate, because progeny in that state of society is equivalent to wealth : they must, therefore, do the same now in order to make up for the deficiencies left by the non-reproductive part of the people. But the lower orders are precisely the persons who, in a well-regulated government, would most wish to enter early into the contract of marriage, because

the blessings arising from it are almost the only innocent enjoyments within their reach. According
to the system of this treatise, therefore, it is not
only possible for the lower orders generally to marry
early, without any evil consequence from the principle of population; but it is absolutely necessary
that many of them should follow their natural inclinations in this respect, in order to produce that salutary increase of people which is connected with the
prosperity and industry of a nation. Therefore to
leave without inquietude " every man to his own
free choice," though evidently insufficient to guard
against evil, according to the opposite *principles*, is
fully so according to those maintained in these pages.
I venture to assert as a general position that, in a
well constituted and industrious community, every
man who chooses it may marry without prejudice to
the state, as soon as he can procure a decent habitation, and perceives a fair probability that the regular fruits of his exertions will enable him to maintain a wife and two children at the least; and I will
further express my belief that, in no stage of society through which *such a* community passes, will
the reasonable exertions of an industrious youth fail
of affording him such an average return. Occasional
fluctuations in the demand for labour must of course
be allowed for, and temporary relief provided by
laws enacted for that purpose.

To give any positive encouragement to marriage
further than to point it out to the people as their legitimate resource against irregular indulgence, must
depend upon the particular situation of polity in
which a country may happen to be placed; but never
to *discourage* it directly or indirectly appears as

consistent with sound policy as it is with the dispensations of Providence, and the commands of religion.
Providence does not seem to have intended any restraint upon the higher and middle classes in the exercise of their option as to marriage or celibacy, but
leaves to every one his power of selecting his own
method of passing through his state of probation in
this respect. HE doubtless foresaw the election that
a large portion of them would make, and has converted it into the means of balancing more equally
the temporal advantages and happiness of each rank,
and the several temptations to which each should be
exposed. The reasoning, therefore, is by no means
impaired by the consideration (to the limited extent
in which it is true) that, if those who now voluntarily abstain from marriage from the above-mentioned causes should choose the other alternative,
population might have a tendency to advance too
rapidly for the diminished power of the earth to supply it with food. Such a supposition is nothing more
than an assertion that, if the world and the dispositions of mankind were differently constituted, affairs
would not go on so well; a proposition which I
should of course be among the last to deny. But as
the truth now stands, we observe that, by a beautiful arrangement, so common in the dispensations of
Providence, a provision is made to arise from the
silent and unobserved operation of man's propensity
to better his condition, which at once ensures the
political welfare of the community by keeping up
the population, and enabling it to make a further
progress, while it facilitates alike to the poor and
the rich the practice of virtue, by exposing neither to
a degree of temptation from which the other is exempt.

It appears then, upon the whole, that no moral impediment to the progress of society, or to the natural tendency of population to keep within due bounds, is to be apprehended from as general a prevalence of matrimonial connexions as the existing state of society will admit; nay that a perfect liberty in this respect is essential to a healthy progress. We perceive that the principle of population introduces no new duty, nor any necessary increase of vice and misery as society advances, and the land arrives nearer to its point of complete cultivation.

I must here be permitted to remark, that a general attention to the moral duties is as necessary to connect the happiness of the people and the public prosperity with the propositions established in this chapter, as with any of those which have preceded them. If husbands or wives be drunken, idle, and profligate, whether they be young or old, their families will be in some way or other a burthen to the state.

But I think upon the whole that an early marriage, and a young family, is a strong incentive to sobriety, industry, and decency, in a poor man, wherever his moral and religious instructors come in aid of his natural feelings of affection towards his wife and children. I have seldom seen the workings of good advice upon natural affections fail in their effect, except in old and very hardened profligates; and I have very frequently beheld the combination of the two effectual in reclaiming a loose and thoughtless character.

I should be sorry however to be so far misunderstood, as to be thought to assert that it would be consistent with the good of the state, to afford to every idle and abandoned stripling the means of entering into the marriage contract, although he possess neither the will nor the intention of labouring for the support of his family, nor be in a capacity to have set before him in a forcible manner his duties in these respects. For truly I have never yet been able to discover, nor should I be very industrious in searching for, any scheme of polity which can enable the machinery of society to work freely and profitably, notwithstanding the general neglect of moral habits and precautions.

But my meaning and intention in this chapter have been to prove that, where fair and reasonable attention has been paid to the moral education of the lower orders, and a fair and reasonable provision made for renewing in their minds, by the aid of an able and faithful ministry, the fading impressions of their early instruction ; there it is not only consistent with the welfare of the state, and the comfortable subsistence of the people, but absolutely essential to a due progress in wealth, population, and prosperity, that individuals should be left at perfect liberty to form their resolutions as to the contract of marriage upon grounds entirely distinct from political considerations, and that it is perfectly feasible to relieve every distress which may eventually arise from the effects of the principle of population upon such a system of liberty, *in the whole country* as well as in particular families, parishes, and districts.

I must be excused, therefore, for again reminding the reader that Christian morality is, after all, the hinge upon which the argument must turn in this as in every other part of our inquiry ; that without this support it is a matter of perfect indifference to the comfort and happiness of a people upon what political principles the laws and customs of society with respect to the matrimonial contract are established. The vices of either system will outweigh its advantages, without the general prevalence of this ruling principle.

Before the close of this chapter, I must beg leave to contrast its conclusions with those of Mr. Malthus upon the same subject. He states (book iv. chap. 10) that population is plainly redundant, unless the poor are in a condition to maintain *all their children.* Marriages therefore should be delayed till the parents are in such condition, that is, till the price of labour, joined to their savings, will enable them to support a wife *and five or six children,* without assistance: and if we cannot attain these objects, all our former efforts will be thrown away. (book iv. chap. 11.) Now surely no one who has traced the effects of the progress of society in the preceding pages will hesitate to admit the utter impossibility, *in the more advanced stages,* of paying wages to *all* labourers high enough to enable the *married* to support so large a family without assistance. According to Mr. Malthus's hypothesis, therefore, either the labouring poor must generally be condemned to celibacy, or the society be thrown back towards the agricultural state.

CHAPTER VII.

*On the Influence of the Principle of Population,
and of the Progress of Society, upon the individual Virtue and Happiness of the People.*

HAVING shown that in *some important and controverted points* the principle of population leaves
the political expediency of moral conduct, and the
conditions of public virtue and happiness, precisely
where it found them, it now only remains to establish the truth of the same propositions as general
axioms. For this purpose we must inquire whether
any of those natural arrangements of society, which
have been pointed out as contributing to the simultaneous progress of food and population, do, generally speaking, increase the intensity of vice and
misery; or whether the result of those arrangements
be not rather a general compensation of enjoyments,
leaving the increase or decrease of *vice and misery*
entirely dependent upon the general conduct and
habits of people, with reference to morals and religion; and lastly, whether we cannot thus establish
the glorious conclusion—that an eminently vicious
people will at all times destroy itself, and a moderately
virtuous one support itself, and flourish. There will
then remain, to complete the object of this treatise,
only the fourth fundamental principle—that the tendency of population will operate in advancing the
happiness and prosperity of a people *in proportion to*
the prevalence of liberty, to the purity of the popular

religion, and the soundness of the public morals, habits, and tastes of the people.

It has I think been somewhere observed, that every attempt to explain the cause or ultimate object of moral evil in the world will fail; and if a new revelation were given to turn this dark inquiry into noon-day, it would make no difference in the actual state of things. An extension of knowledge would not reverse the fact that human nature has through every age displayed the clearest proofs of innate depravity, nor could it weaken the probability that it will still continue to do so, whatever were the reasons for giving a moral agent a constitution, which it was foreseen would soon be found in this condition. I am thankful, therefore, that it is not necessary to entangle ourselves in these depths, but only to be convinced that, *cæteris paribus*, the average quantity of evil that affects mankind is not necessarily increased as society advances.

It is evident from the preceding chapters, that the classes whose situation in life is changed by the progress of society are the non-reproductive classes, that is, the higher ranks generally, and the lower and middle ranks resident in towns. Among the higher ranks, I think, after what has been stated, that the principle of compensation is so self-evident as not to require any additional illustration in this place. But I am aware that some difficulty may arise from the situation of the people in large towns, which form so considerable and so necessary an ingredient in the composition of an advanced state of society. In order to investigate it fairly, with reference to our present inquiry, it is evidently necessary to distinguish between that quantity of vice and misery which actually exists in many towns, where no adequate pains have been taken to improve the morals and the police, and that quantity which has been assumed to be *necessary* to produce the requisite abatement in the progress of population. The last is clearly all that can be justly ascribed to the dispensations of Providence in this argument; and when it has been reduced to its proper quantity, we must proceed (if any remain) to ascertain how far it may be sufficient to counterbalance the superior exertions of virtue, which the state of society producing many towns enables us to make.

Occasion has already been taken to show the high proportion which the average number of deaths to the population in towns bears to that in the country, and that a great portion of this extraordinary mortality takes place among infants and young children. But a certain number of premature deaths occurs in the country as well as in towns, and it is probable that the most favourable condition can hardly reduce it among the lower orders to less than one-third of the number born. As far as my personal experience goes, I should be disposed to think that the average was rather more. Now, as to these individuals themselves, who shall say that their condition (thus early taken from the world) is not to be envied by those left behind? The principal question, therefore, as to the sum of misery produced by this increase of premature deaths, seems to be the degree in which the parents are affected by it; and the immediate point to be determined in the case before us is, how much more heavily this species of grief presses upon parents residing in towns, than upon those in the country. As this is one of the chief drawbacks which we shall have to make from the numerous advantages of civilization and commerce, I shall endeavour to investigate its extent with some precision. The number of births produced by each marriage must of course be various in different situations; but there is good reason to believe, that the average of four to a marriage in towns, and six in the country, may not be far from the truth. Now, as half the number born in towns dies in childhood, each married couple must of course lose two children on an average. In the country, where it has been fully proved that the majority of the numbers born live to be married, we will calculate the number of those who die in childhood at one third; for the waste of life among persons who are just adult is very small in the country. But as each married couple here produces six births upon an average, if one-third die in childhood, the loss they sustain is of two children each, as we have seen to be the case in towns; so that the average pressure of grief upon each married couple is *in quantity* precisely the same, and the difference between them appears to be in the *proportion* which the loss of each bears to their whole stock, which in the townsman's case is one half, in the countryman's one third. The loss is in the same proportion as if two men, one possessing an income of 4000*l.* and the other of 6000*l.* a year, should each be deprived of 2000*l.* a year. On the face of this account there certainly is a comparative disadvantage on the side of the townsman; but if we consider that both the contract of marriage and the residence in the town are voluntary on the part of the parents suffering the loss, as well as the numerous advantages and enjoyments by which they are tempted to place themselves in that situation, their whole lot may well bear a comparison with that of the country residents. That such is the opinion of the people themselves is evident from the eagerness with which every situation in great towns is sought after by the residents in the country, and from the infrequency of the opposite course of conduct. We may, therefore, fairly conclude that the general increase of misery is not very great, if any at all. Nay, we think, that we may fairly assume that there is upon the whole an increase of happiness, particularly when we consider the superior capacity for enjoyment which the townsman's mental improvement gives him, and the superior means of attaining it afforded by the higher remuneration of his labour.

It remains to inquire how far the abatement in the progress of population which is incident to the existence of towns is caused by an increase of the vice of which they are said to be the hot-beds. Upon this subject there are some curious facts to be found among the writers who have turned their attention to it. I have selected the two following; the first of which is highly honourable to the sect upon whose society the experiment was founded. It struck Dr. Perceval, (see Perceval's Essays on Population, p. 41. Ed. 1776.) that the principles and manners of the Society of Friends, though often made the subjects of illiberal censure and ridicule, might afford them advantages over other bodies of men, with respect to the duration of life. The diligence, cleanliness, temperance, and composure of mind by which the members of this society are distinguished, in towns as well as in the country, might reasonably be supposed to contribute to health and longevity; and as there are no persons among them in abject poverty, and few immoderately rich, this more equal distribution must lessen the sources of disease, and furnish every individual under it with the necessary means of relief. These considerations excited his curiosity to know the proportion of deaths among the Quakers of Manchester; and he was gratified by Mr. Routh, one of the Friends, in the most obliging manner, with the following information. The society consisted of 81 males and 84 females, 54 married persons, nine widowers, seven widows, and 48 persons under 15 years of age.

The births during the preceding seven years had amounted to 34, and the burials to 47; about 1 therefore in 24 of the Quakers in Manchester died annually; whereas the proportion of deaths among the inhabitants of the town at large was as 1 to 28. This difference, which is directly the reverse of what would occur were vice and intemperance the only causes of mortality in towns, Dr. Perceval afterwards reduces to a level, by supposing, that the Quakers had few or no accessions to their number by new settlers or converts during the seven years. This must have considerably increased their proportional mortality; because, as new settlers generally arrive in towns in an adult state, and the chief mortality takes place in childhood, they must of course raise the proportion of *inhabitants* to the *deaths*, and also of *births* and *weddings* to the *burials*, higher than they would otherwise be. If this cause did not exist, he conceives, that the general proportion of deaths to the population in Manchester would be at least as high as among the Quakers, perhaps something higher; but it cannot be denied, that the proportional mortality among these last is *naturally* very near as high as among the other residents of the town, notwithstanding the difference in the temperance, regularity, and cleanliness of the parties. That " the want of vivacity in the people of this sect," and " the sedentary lives of their females," tend materially to shorten the period of their existence, will not probably be admitted by any philosopher or physician. What then remains but that we come to the conclusion, that the causes which shorten the period of human life in towns, however they may be sometimes aggravated by vice, are fully sufficient, without any such aggravation, to produce all the effect contended for in this treatise, and to render the inhabitants of towns, supposing that they conducted themselves as temperately and as virtuously as the Quakers, a non-reproductive part of the population of the state. Dr. Perceval (see Perceval's Essays on Population, p. 56) has afforded another fact to prove that the quantity of vice usually existing in towns does not materially alter the otherwise natural rate of the progress of population. By a careful comparison of the difference in the proportion of deaths between the town of Manchester and the villages immediately surrounding, he found that the yearly mortality in the former bore a proportion to the whole population, very nearly, if not quite, double to that in the latter;—yet " both live in the same climate, carry on the same manufactures, are chiefly supplied from the same market," and their habits of life, their morals, and their manners, cannot therefore be very different. Supposing the fact as established by the Quakers to be out of the question, there can probably be no difference of vice in these two situations sufficient to account for their different rates of mortality; and the two facts taken together render it absolutely certain that such is not the cause. We must evidently, therefore, have recourse to the other circumstances in which towns differ from the country; and these are chiefly, confinement from such exercises as render the body vigorous and robust; an atmosphere unfavourable to the duration of life; and the weaker spark which originally animates the frame of the townsman, and which refuses to carry his existence to the same extended period as the more vivid fire which glows in the frame of the countryman.

Some of these circumstances are caused, and all of them are compensated, by the superior degree of mental exertion necessary to the townsman, that cannot fail to impart to him a portion of refined enjoyment to which the peasant must be a total stranger. Nor has he ever felt the want of the more efficient properties of the body. Although he is born an animal less vigorous than the peasant, his native air affords him a state of personal feeling as comfortable, fits him as much for the less hardy and laborious occupations in which he is employed, renders him as free from pain and as capable of the quiet enjoyments suited to his station, as the air of the country affords to the rough peasant flushed with the boisterous amusement of athletic exercises.

I am aware that it has been the custom among a set of philosophers, who are too little scrupulous con-concerning the effects of their sophistry upon the public good, to decry the effects of civilization, and to enlarge upon the degradation induced on the human mind by commerce and extended manufactures. They assume, that the moral degradation of the inhabitants is commensurate with the degree in which the division of labour exists in a country; and suppose, that when the public prosperity has been raised to a great height by the minute subdivision of labour, the *ideas* of the people will in each class be limited to the performance of one single manipulation. The only mistake in this proposition seems to be, that the word *ideas* has been used instead of *hands;* unless, indeed, it is intended to assert, that men receive their ideas through their fingers' ends, or the palms of their hands! A man's *hands* may be limited to one single manipulation; and, in proportion to the adroitness with which he performs it, his ideas may wander at large. A weaver, for example, long before his apprenticeship is expired, may throw the shuttle to and fro by mere habit, with little mental exertion, or even attention; and he is in constant intercourse with a large society of men, whose minds require only the proper pains, which it is the duty of every government to take in providing for their cultivation, to turn the activity, naturally resulting from the collision of ideas, to the moral advantage of the individual and of the community. Let any man set a ploughboy and a mechanic to an employment which requires ingenuity and thought, and with which both are unacquainted, and it will presently be seen which has had most opportunity of cultivating his mind and improving his faculties. Let any man revert to the origin of those who in revolutionary times have risen from the lowest orders into consequence; or of those who, in countries where liberty and equal laws give every man a property in the works of his head as well as of his hands and confer distinction upon those who are successful, have risen from obscurity by works of inventions or genius; and then let him ascertain how many have sprung from the rude peasantry, how many from the inhabitants of towns? If the inquiry should turn out in favour of the townsman, surely the variety of ideas, and the solid advantages, which lead to or follow these results, may be fairly set down to his account as so much happiness; at least, as so much additional capacity for enjoyment, and, as I think, for moral improvement also. I cannot think, therefore, that the collection of people into towns *necessarily* induces any moral degradation among them; on the contrary, I am tempted to believe that letters and arts introduce into the morals greater advantages, if properly seized, than wealth does disadvantages, notwithstanding the absurd paradoxes of Rousseau and his imitators upon this subject; and I heartily subscribe to the striking illustration of the antient philosopher, " Quid enumerem artium multitudinem sine quibus vita omninò *nulla* esse potuisset. Quis enim ægris subvenisset ? Quæ esset oblectatio valentium? Qui victus aut cultus, nisi tam multæ nobis artes ministrarentur, quibus rebus exculta hominum vita, tantum destitit à cultu et victu bestiarum." (Cicero de Officiis, lib. 2.) Although, therefore, the townsman's life may be somewhat shorter in duration than that of the countryman, it may certainly be said to be longer in giving more enjoyment to the individual. As to the effect on the community, the spread of knowledge and talents will always secure freedom, at least in the practice, if not in the form, of governments; and the latter will usually by degrees adapt itself to the former. Unless the wisdom and magnanimity of the present Emperor of Russia shall anticipate the course of events by benign concessions, the natural progress of industry and improvement in that country will provide that its government shall not be despotic half a century hence.

In quitting this part of the subject, I cannot help remarking that if towns have been called the hot-beds of vice, they have deserved that appellation more from indolent despair than from necessity. The towns have hitherto by no means had fair play. Notwithstanding the extreme difference between the dispositions, manners, opportunities, and temptations of the inhabitants of towns and the country, not only have the same laws been thought adequate to the government of both, but too often those laws have even been relaxed in towns. Where regulation has been most wanted, it has been most neglected; and what is worse, religious instruction, the only sure foundation of all morality, has usually been more scantily provided in the same proportion. It is pleasing, nevertheless, to reflect, that if towns have been *actually* the hot-beds of vice, they have been no less the seats of exalted virtues. The most enlightened exertions for bettering the condition of mankind have been struck out by the intellectual collision of many enlarged minds collected into the focus of a great metropolis: and although we cannot quite vindicate from partiality the predilection for a city life, entertained by our great philosopher and moralist Dr. Johnson, I cannot either avoid thinking that he who would, if possible, reduce cities and towns to annihilation, rather than use due exertions for their improvement, and to render them more conducive to the views of Providence in making them a necessary condition of one state of our political existence, would, by the same rule, hang a boy for his first fault, rather than endeavour to root out the innate seeds of evil implanted in his mind.

But perhaps it may be said that the number of the childless and unmarried among the higher orders is a clear addition to the mass of public misery as society advances. To this it may be sufficient briefly to reply, that those qualities of the mind and body, which are least favourable to the production and care of large families are often the most so to other pursuits not less useful or advantageous, nor less capable of conferring happiness. It is upon these ranks that the task of mental thought for the whole society often devolves, and it is another instance of the gracious dispensation of Providence fitting every creature for its appointed end, that the mind is often most vigorous and capable of high cultivation in the most delicate frames of body. If a lad be prevented by a puny frame from joining in the boisterous sports of his schoolfellows, does he not find comfort and pleasure in books and contemplation ? And if, upon growing up into a man, he be not able to distinguish himself in the sports of the field, or in the robust pursuits of life, is it not often the foundation of a more substantial, noble, and lasting celebrity in knowledge, in eloquence, in arts—nay, since the modern improvements in warfare, frequently in arms ? Yet these are precisely the men who are the least likely to become the fathers of large families—a condition, if they fulfil the duties of it, that must evidently tend to subtract from their public utility. Strange as it

may appear, unless we revert to this solution of the
fact, the greatest heroes and most celebrated men
have in very many instances been childless, if not unmarried. But have they been therefore the more
miserable? By no means. That affection which
would perhaps have been engrossed by their families
has all been lavished on their country and on mankind. And, however great may be the satisfaction
arising from domestic endearments, the high-wrought
pleasure flowing from a consciousness of having conferred a benefit upon one's country and upon the
world—of having been the humble instrument in the
hand of Providence of furthering the moral and religious welfare—of increasing the general happiness of
mankind—or of deserving public applause and gratitude, will scarcely yield to it in intensity of delight.

If it be said that this applies exclusively to men,
it may be answered—that the names of many emi-
nent single women may be cited, both in this and
other countries, which show that the other sex have
their full share in the observation.

It would not, however, be reasonable or decorous
to close this discussion without some more particular
reference to the effect which the increasing celibacy
of civilized society has upon the comfort and happiness of the female sex. This, at first view, would
appear to be an unhappy one, for supposing the proportion of women to men to remain the same, the
former would of course seem to have a diminished
probability of enjoying the comforts of matrimony;
and it is not evident in what manner civilization
affords them a full compensation for this loss. The
will of Providence, with respect to the proportions of
men and women who are respectively born or existing

in the world, affords matter of very curious contemplation, and an interesting collection of facts has been made by various authors upon the subject. The learned Dr. Derham, (Physico-Theology, p. 175,) thought that he had grounds for computing the proportion of male to female births generally to be as 14 to 13, or that a 14th more of males were born than of females; and actual observation gives reason to believe, notwithstanding a doubt cast upon the fact by Dean Tucker, that the excess is generally about a 14th. (Dr. Perceval's Essay on Population, p. 74.) Dr. Price, however, says a 19th or 20th. This arrangement obviously appears calculated with a view to provide for the superior waste of male life in hazardous exertion, &c. which exists in every stage of society; and there would be nothing surprising in the discovery, that the proportion of females advanced in life actually existing in any state of society should, notwithstanding this excess of births, be equal, or even larger than that of males, in consequence of the increased mortality of the latter from those causes. But it does certainly appear at first a little singular that it should have been found (Dr. Price, edit. 1803, vol. ii. p. 106 and p. 132.) by a great variety of returns, that the mortality of males in the *earliest stages of life*, and even the proportion of *still-born* males, bears a very high proportion to that of females. (Price, p. 230.) It should seem therefore that the Author of nature established this proportion between the births, rather with a view to a particular weakness or delicacy in the constitution of males in very early life which makes them more subject to mortality at that particular period, and renders it necessary that more should be produced in order to preserve the due proportion between the adults of the two sexes. It appears that, taking an average from all the accounts which have been given of the existing number of males and females at a marriageable age, the superior mortality among the former has about reduced the sexes to an equality ; though it must be admitted that the proportion of this superior mortality of males seems to increase with the progress of civilization and wealth; to be doubtful in the purely agricultural state of society, where children are riches, and the prolific powers are exerted to the utmost by second and third marriages ; to be but small in country parishes and villages, larger in small towns, and greatest of all in cities. (Price, vol. ii. p. 133, ed. 1803.) But it is in none of those situations high enough to prevent the generality of women from marrying once, unless she should prefer the advantages of her state of celibacy to the prospects which the offer of marriage may eventually hold out.

The motives of her determination are probably merely personal. If she choose a single life, she has no more view of adding to the happiness of the rest of society " *by making room for other marriages without additional distress,*" (see Malthus's Essay, book iv. chap. 8. p. 550, 4to edit.) " than she has, in her preference of connubial happiness, of strengthening the power and population of her country, by producing sons to fight its battles," &c. As far as the motives of an action constitute a ground of respect, they stand precisely on equal terms : if they are appreciated according to their absolute utility in their generation, the difference will not be greater, supposing both to fulfil the duties of their station with equal integrity and zeal : and if superior respect be due to her who has exercised most self-

denial, and whose lot has been least enlivened by
social comforts, it might be equally difficult to say,
whether the cares of the married state, and the
labour, self-denial, and attention necessary in rearing
a family, do not counterbalance all that part of its
advantages which is denied to the single woman
in civilized society. The difference therefore between the agricultural state of society and those
more advanced in civilization, with respect to the
female sex, as far as it is connected with marriage,
will be two-fold: 1st—The superior delicacy and refinement of the latter state of society will induce
many more to decline marriage, because by accepting
it they would lose some of the artificial comforts they
enjoy in their state of celibacy, which women in a
less advanced state of society neither know nor feel
the want of: 2dly, The widow's chance of a second
and third marriage is smaller, because where the
number of men just of a marriageable age exceeds
that of the women, and children are riches, as in the
agricultural state, when by any accident a woman
becomes a widow before her time for child-bearing is
past, there will of course be a competition for her
among men younger than herself; whereas, where the
number of men of a marriageable age is only equal to,
or smaller than that of the women, as in the more advanced stages of society, it is probable that the elderly
ladies and widows will be neglected in favour of the
younger: at least we have the opinion of a great philosopher and moralist, that a man who acts on the contrary principle " does a foolish thing." (Dr. Johnson—
Boswell's Life.) For the reasons given in a former
chapter upon the option of marriage, it is clear that
the first of these conditions does not necessarily add

to the misery of the single woman, because she has her comforts, (and comforts which her conduct shows she esteems the most valuable,) in exchange for those which she refuses. With respect to the diminished chance of second or third marriages, the question is a very delicate one, and such as a *male* author cannot presume to determine.

He may, however, venture to suppose that it really is a small subtraction from female happiness incident to the progress of civilization; for, as it has been said that a woman who takes a second husband, pays the highest compliment to her first, by showing that he made her so happy as a wife that she is willing to partake of the same happiness a second time; it cannot but add something to the distress of the widowed state that an alteration in the condition of society should preclude her from an equal chance of paying this mark of regard to the memory of her deceased lord. But there is yet another condition of civilized society, which renders this case still harder, and seems to prove that, with the diminished chance of supplying the loss, the chance of enduring it is increased: for it appears (Price p. 132) not only that married women live longer than single women, but that, independently of the waste of adult males naturally to be expected in war, and other occupations of risk, the proportion of male to female deaths is evidently greater in the *more* advanced than in the middle periods of human existence, (Price, p. 230,) and that this proportion corresponds, in some degree to the progress of civilization. (Price, p. 134.) In New Jersey, a country at the time the account was taken in a purely agricultural state, the number of adult males was said to exceed that of the females; (Price, p. 133) but in the villages of Brandenburgh, in a great variety of English towns and villages, as well as in Sweden, the result was precisely the reverse. According to calculations accurately made from the data, it appears that, in the state of society of the greater part of Europe, though the proportion of male to female deaths approach more nearly to an equality at the ages of 30 to 35, (at which the number of married and child-bearing women (Price, p. 408) is greatest,) and between 40 and 45 when the female constitution is well known to be subject to particular risk ; yet there are no ages at which a *smaller proportion* of females does not die than of males, except the ages in which the number of deliveries of children is greatest : and *even then* the probabilities of living among the females are nearly equal to those of the males. The decrements of life however among males increase in proportion to those of the females, after 45 or 50 ; and of a married couple after that period an annuity upon the life of the wife would be worth on an average three or four years' purchase more than on that of the husband, in a state of society such as exists in the greater part of Europe. Now if the preceding facts be correct, the progress of civilization, and the congregating of people into towns, not only diminish the widow's chance of a second marriage, but increase her chance of becoming a widow ; not considerably however at any time, nor at all (as it should seem) before she arrives at that period of life at which her being a wife or a widow can no longer affect the population of her country. Nor does she incur this risk before the children have completed their education, and are able to do without a father's care, supposing the

marriage to have been contracted at that early period
which is most favourable to the interests of virtue
and morality, and, as we have seen, not inconsistent
with the public welfare considered in connexion
with the principle of population.

Now supposing (what appears to be the fact) that the
different chances in the agricultural and commercial
states are that, in the former, a man may only die a year
or 6 months before his wife ; in the latter three or four
years sooner, I should be the last man to assert that
this is no addition of misery to the lot of the woman.
Considering the great majority of suitable matches
which take place in civilized countries, and the height
of affection which an intercourse of many years
produces between two enlightened and tender minds,
it is by no means extraordinary that the grief upon
the interruption of this connexion is so great and so
incurable as it is frequently observed to be. Taking
then this observation as the measure of our judgment as to its quantity, it must certainly be set
down as an object to be placed in the balance against
the general advantages of the progress of civilization
on the condition of mankind. But, however this
superior mortality of males may affect the happiness
of the female sex generally, it does not necessarily
diminish their option of marrying once. For although
the total number of females, existing at one time
will always exceed that of the males, yet as the prolific power of the former ceases earlier in life, there
nevertheless may, and probably will, exist in every
society more men of an age to marry with prudence
than women capable of child-bearing. The numerical difference in favour of the women therefore will
chiefly be found in the comparative numbers of

aged men and women. For what purpose Providence
has ordained that the latter should exceed the former
is left with great deference to the speculations of
others : but I trust that no one will attempt to ex-
tract from the circumstance any argument in favour
of polygamy. Should any be so inclined, or tempted
either to believe with Mr. Hume that *all* regulations upon this head are *equally lawful,* or to think
with Mr. Bruce, that the number of wives should
be regulated by the law of nature ; he cannot too
soon be informed that by this same law of nature,
and consequently by Mr. Hume's principles of natural
justice, a man (in Europe at least) is only entitled
to one young wife, together with as many *old ones*
as he chooses to marry.

I think it will now appear that, all things considered,
the actual decrease in the number of marriages, which
attends the progress of society towards its advanced
stages, affords no proof of any *necessary* or material
increase of vice or misery among the female sex, and
it is curious to contemplate the gradual improvement
in their situation, during the advance of society from
the savage state treated in the fourth chapter of the
first book.

To conclude then. If, upon a deliberate review
of the *causes* which produce the abatement in
the progress of population as society advances,
any one should still incline to doubt how far they
have been calculated to operate upon the numbers
of mankind, without any *necessary* degradation
of their moral and political state; or should hesitate in assenting to the position that a fair and
practicable conformity on the part of a people to
the dictates of morals and religion is sufficient to

secure the salutary operation of those *causes;* let him reflect upon the following addition to the virtue and happiness of mankind conferred by the increase of commerce and civilization, taken absolutely and without reference to the moral and religious cultivation of the people by other means. The freedom introduced by the mutual dependence of all ranks of the people upon each other, and the more regular distribution of produce in commercial and civilized countries in consequence of every man's having a valuable consideration, either of labour or manufacture; to give in exchange for it,—the superior comforts which in some degree pervade even the lowest ranks in consequence of the further application of science to the common purposes of life,—and the intellectual enjoyments imparted to a large portion of the people, are among the least observed, but not the least important, of these benefits. The virtues peculiar to these states of society in Christian countries, though seldom traced to their scource, are equally true and indisputable. The intercourse promoted between different individuals and societies, and between one country and another, must tend to humanize the mind and to promote the spirit of philanthropy; and as the continuance of this intercourse must depend upon a general adherence to justice, integrity, and industry, it can hardly avoid introducing among the parties concerned a conformity with those virtues in principle and practice. The brutality and cruelty to inferiors, the arrogant contempt and surly pride, so conspicuous in the distant and scattered residents of agricultural districts, (which Mr. Barrow has so well illustrated in his account of the Boors of the Cape of Good-Hope, and for a smaller degree of which other nations might be quoted,) where the violent and tyrannical passions are not allayed by any respect for, or intercourse with, equals, disappear immediately amidst the personal collision and frequent reciprocity of kindness in a commercial community.   Commerce, too, when its liberal principles once come to be rightly understood, and it is conducted upon those of an enlightened system of Christianity, not only promotes peace over the several nations of the world, but may, and in fact often has, become the means of propagating that holy religion, for the reception of which it seems absolutely necessary that men should be, in some degree, civilized and acquainted with the artificial comforts of life. The extension of commerce, too, affords an opportunity of uniting many heads, many hands, and many purses for these glorious and benevolent objects, and give an increased chance of success in their pursuit. The superior impulse given to charity by this change of society has before been treated at some length: the magnificent instances exhibited, in our own metropolis are the admiration of Europe.   The improvement likewise of the intellectual faculties of man, under the influence of morals and religion, should certainly enable him the better to resist the temptations which may assail his virtue.

These are, perhaps, the chief benefits to the virtue and happiness of man bestowed by commerce.   That every commercial nation, or even any one of them, practises all these virtues to the full extent of their power is not asserted.   Bu that they are all within its power, and therefore that an all-wise and all-good Providence intended that they should practise them, is as certain as that many members of society do actually so regulate their conduct as far as their limited means allow. The *general* effects of commerce and civilization, however, are in a great measure such as are here stated; and these effects will become more universal with every spread of morality, and of that religion which has made commerce and wealth the instruments of improving and converting, instead of degrading and corrupting, mankind.

The whole amount then of the arguments of both sides, with respect to the relative virtue and happiness of the commercial and less advanced states of society, may perhaps be reduced to this—that each has its respective temptations, differing from those of the others in quality though not in quantity or degree, considering the means bestowed for resisting them. The practice of virtue, therefore, all things considered, is equally easy or difficult in all, according to the attention which is paid to the morals of the people; and happiness being dependant upon the degree in which virtue is practised, their several chances of attaining it are equal likewise. But (as Dr. Paley, Mor. Phil. b. vi. c. ii. p. 345., finely observes) " The final view of all rational politics is to produce *the greatest quantity of happiness in a given tract of country;*" and we may fairly conclude that the intention of Providence is the same with respect to the world in general. It follows therefore that, with an equal proportion of happiness in the possession of individuals, the more of them there are, the nearer will that intention be to complete its fulfilment. I trust therefore that, if it has been proved that the means ordained for replenishing the world with people are not generally attended with an increase of vice and misery, but that a moderate attention to the laws of religion and morality will prevent such an effect, it will go far towards rescuing the Divine Justice from imputations to which a contrary conclusion could scarcely fail to give rise.

Before we quit the third fundamental proposition, which has hitherto been the subject of discussion in this book, it may perhaps be necessary to make a short reference to the topics of liberty and security of property, which are included as conditions of that proposition. It is not my intention in any part of this treatise to enter into a minute investigation of those political blessings: they have frequently been discussed in separate treatises, and are sufficiently understood and appreciated wherever a capacity for enjoying them is found to exist; and as that capacity is of a moral nature, the enjoyment of the blessings depends more upon moral than political causes. It is evident however that, as the force of my whole argument depends upon the spontaneous operations of the people, arranging themselves, selecting their occupations, and forming their habits with a view to their real interests, a reasonable degree of freedom from those restraints which are not commanded by the moral law, is absolutely necessary to the successful pursuit of their objects. Their exertions would be cramped, and their spirit broken, by any interference with individual liberty and property which is not compensated by some superior advantage to the whole community. If I were asked what is the lowest degree of these political blessings which would prevent a community from actually receding in the career of public prosperity, I should perhaps cite the condition of the protestant monarchies on the Continent; and I should certainly place the point far below that at which we are arrived in our own country.

CHAPTER VIII.

Application of the Fourth Principle, viz. that the salutary Tendency of Population will have its complete Operation, in proportion as Religion, Morality, rational Liberty, and Security of Property approach to the Attainment of a perfect Influence.

AN ingenious and popular French writer, who had many and peculiarly favourable opportunities of observing human nature in various ranks among the nations of Europe, has a passage to the following effect. " In argument upon political if not upon moral questions, the difficulty with men is not to combat their sincere and unbiassed opinions, which would soon be settled by reason on one side or the other. But the real difficulty is to combat with success the opinions which men *pretend* to hold, which they have adopted from vanity, or self-interest, or ambition ; and which they have so amalgamated with their minds, as at length to be led by self-deceit into the belief that they are the sincere and honest results of their judgment.

" There is, therefore, no greater enemy to sincere and honest reasoning than self-love, and its several modifications ; no greater friend to it than a generous enthusiasm of sentiment which is prepared to sacrifice time, talent, personal gratification, or even life itself for the good of others. But self-love is greatly interested to laugh all such self-devotion, and therefore all true and honest reasoning, out of doors. When a gentleman says he is of such an *opinion,* one takes it for a delicate way of expressing that such is his *interest.*"

Now it is much to be feared that this is but too faithful a picture of the minds of the largest portion of practical debaters on questions of politics; and the reason appears very obvious. Political questions have from the beginning of civilized society been argued exclusively upon the principle of self-interest, somewhat enlarged perhaps from its bearing upon the mere individual, but still very much disjoined from moral considerations, and from those sanctions which refer the tendency of our thoughts and actions to their effects on the whole scheme of our social and individual existence. In education especially the science of politics is carefully insulated and kept apart from that of morals. We are taught to weigh all its propositions in the mere scale of worldly interest, and a powerful association is thus formed in our minds, which it is to be feared so far from realizing the beautiful hypothesis of the poet concerning the expansive power of self-love, is but too apt to reverse it. Self-love, instead of *rising from individual to the whole,* is too apt to sink from the whole to the individual.

Political economy is in an especial manner liable to this observation; for as it consists of a set of general principles, in conformity to which it is presumed to be the temporal interest of all parties to conduct themselves; it applies itself of course principally to the selfish feelings of mankind. But as no two philosophers ever agreed as to what really constitutes the temporal interest of men in the ge-

neral and enlarged sense contemplated by political
economists; and as every general principle of a
merely political nature is contingent in its application, and is obviously inapplicable where any of the
parties to a transaction refuse to be regulated by the
general rule; the science of political economy, as
now conducted, is of very confined use in practice.
The prospect of immediate and personal advantage
must ever be too powerful to be counteracted by
prospective views, resting upon *data* so uncertain
and precarious; and men do not fail to perceive that
they may justifiably decline a present sacrifice, when
the utmost penalty held out, is a contingency which
one half of the reasoners upon the subject assert to
be rather likely to produce good than evil. It is not,
therefore, surprising that the practical result of all
argumentation upon political economy comes to this;
that men investigate the conflicting opinions, till
they meet with one consonant with their immediate
feelings of interest; and in that they abide till circumstances appear to offer individual advantage from
a change of sentiment.

Now if there be any truth in these observations,
and if I have also been successful in the preceding
chapters of this treatise in proving that moral principle affords a certain standard of reference for the
political questions now under discussion, and that
nothing determined in conformity with it was ever
found otherwise than advantageous to the commonwealth; I think it follows as a natural conclusion
that the more complete is the sway which religion
and morals are permitted to have in determining
those questions, the more advantageous will the determination be in itself, and the more probable will

444 PUBLIC HAPPINESS PROPORTIONATE

it be that the parties concerned will adhere to it in opposition to present temptation.

But let us come a little closer to the point, which is to show that the particular tendency of population to keep within the powers of the soil will have its *complete operation,* so as to prevent any mischievous pressure even against the actual supply of food, in proportion as religion, morality, rational liberty, and security of property approach to the attainment of a perfect influence.

And first of religion. It will scarcely be denied that if every man conscientiously consulted its dictates as to the connexions which he formed, as to the diligence and sobriety with which he conducted himself individually, and as to the mode in which he regulated his social or charitable relations towards his fellow creatures; there would, by the principles established in the first book of this treatise, be actually no distress arising from the want of a plentiful supply of the people's wants. For on the one hand, no greater proportion of the people would elect to marry than the interests of the state required, nor any more children be brought into the world than the demand for industrious labourers would be able to employ as they grew up. And on the other hand as every man would be sober and industrious, he would contribute his full share towards the production of the comforts and necessaries of life, or towards the fulfilment of other useful duties. But it would of course be absurd to expect so general a conformity with the commands of religion, and I have only exhibited the picture with a view to show the consequences that would ensue from the reality, if it existed, in order to make it more apparent that the nearer we approach towards it the less difficulty will be experienced from any mischievous tendency in the population to press against the existing supply of food. For if complete conformity would insure complete success, and every step in advance be (as in the case before us it evidently is,) of itself a positive good and a solid acquisition, it follows as an undeniable conclusion that the degree of success will be in proportion to the degree of conformity.

Let us suppose, for example, a village or a family in which the doctrines and discipline of real christianity were cultivated and observed, and where its genuine effects of decency, sobriety, honesty, industry, and charity, with the repression of the opposite vices, were generally apparent; doubtless this family or village would be much more happy and prosperous, and especially with respect to its comfortable subsistence, than those which were regulated upon opposite principles. It follows then as a matter of course (if the principle of population be in fact adjusted as I have contended in the first book of this treatise,) that the more families and villages can be brought under the same regimen the greater will be the general happiness, comfort, and prosperity of the community at large. I have been induced to repeat this observation, because according to the principle of population as laid down by my opponents, the conclusion is in some respects different; and the consequences, although admitted with respect to a private family or a village, are denied to hold good with respect to the whole community.

If the reader, however, be disposed to agree in the view I have taken, he must not shrink from the necessary consequences, but apply the argument to his own conduct; and, (in so far as he possesses legitimate influence,) to the principles upon which the government of the state is conducted. The immediate effect of religion upon the individual mind of a statesman belongs to a department of inquiry less elementary than that pursued in this treatise. But if he believe that the machinery of society works freely for the benefit of the people in proportion to the prevalence of religion; and if he also acknowledge the duty, asserted by Dr. Paley, of endeavouring to produce the greatest portion of public happiness and prosperity in a given space of country; then he must of course, *as a mere politician,* be occupied in a continual struggle to increase the influence of sound, pure, and orthodox principles of Christainity. He will not be satisfied with that moderate portion of morality which may be thought barely sufficient to prevent the actual degradation of society, but he will aspire after that further and higher portion which shall urge it on to a continual state of advancement. He will never suppose that his task in this respect is concluded; for it would be to forget the principles of the system he has adopted, were he to rest upon any other supposition than that human affairs have a natural tendency towards the principle of evil, which requires incessant counteraction. It would be his policy then to countenance every institution, public or private, fulfilling the great objects of circulating the Holy Scriptures, of spreading the knowledge of their contents, and of extending the influence of their precepts among the people. Nor would he be prevailed upon to withdraw that countenance, although trifling inconveniences, from which no human institutions are exempt, may be thought to qualify their general usefulness. That the good outweighs the evil in the balance will be sufficient to influence his determination.

Above all, should a church establishment fulfilling these conditions be one of the public institutions of his country, he will consider it as so much the more entitled to his special care and protection as well as to his love and veneration, as it affords, from its fixed and permanent principles, the greater security against perversion and abuse, and an acknowledged standard of reference by which any deviation into the paths of heresy and immorality may be immediately discovered. Moreover, if the connexion of religion with policy be as close as I have ventured to assert in this treatise, I think it cannot be disputed that such a church establishment is emphatically a part of the political constitution of the state; and that it is strictly the duty of the government to provide means both for the efficiency of its ministers in learning and piety, and for an adequate increase of their numbers in proportion to the augmented wants of an increasing population. When these conditions are fulfilled, it obviously follows that official encouragement should be exclusively confined to the clergy of the establishment, since through its agency alone can the state have due security for the permanent instruction of the people in those tenets upon which its political prosperity mainly depends. And as in a free country men are only amenable for their public conduct to the laws, and this by a slow and tedious process, it seems absolutely necessary to the security of the state that no persons among the laity professedly hostile to the religious establishment, or even indifferent to its welfare, should be admitted to offices of dignity and influence. In a despotic country, where the will of the sovereign can instantly and effectually interpose, and where all dignity and influence centre in his person, greater latitude may perhaps be admitted without detriment.

These several conclusions can only be impugned by arguments which suppose either that the interests of policy are altogether independent of religion, or that the religious establishment of a country is not founded upon the orthodox principles of Scripture. But as the state in providing an establishment substantially denies the first of these propositions, and in fixing its particular doctrines virtually contradicts the other, it is undoubtedly bound to use every legitimate effort to secure the religious instruction of the people in the established tenets. If it be evident that a political establishment cannot endure in a free country unless the habitual opinions of the people are directed in a current favourable to its objects and principles, it is doubly so that, in a case so exclusively within the province of mind as religious instruction, an establishment formed for that purpose must fall to the ground, unless it possess the means of obtaining a permanent influence over public opinion. The duty of the statesman therefore, (and under that denomination I include every individual of influence in the state,) does not admit either of doubt or dispute. But his success will, after all, be contingent. If the establishment he supports be really founded in the pure doctrines of the Gospel, and has been duly and zealously set forth to the people in all its purity, it will doubtless secure their hearts against the inroads of all opponents. But if both, or either of these conditions be wanting, the spiritual arms, which can alone be fairly used in its defence will not be found of temper to withstand a vigorous attack, and the illegitimate weapons of persecution will be too often called in aid. It is superfluous to refer to the respective practice of the Roman Catholic and Protestant establishments in illustration of this remark. A few observations however may be profitably made upon the means of restoring the influence of a pure and orthodox established religion, from which the minds of the people have been partially alienated.

It is evident that this result can only have arisen, in the first instance, from the gradual debasement of religious sentiment in the educated part of the community, the influence of whose opinions and example will always extend sooner or later throughout the whole community. The religious establishment, consisting as it does of human agents, can scarcely altogether avoid the contagion. The spirit of the times, whatever it may be, will more or less affect it, and the tone of its doctrine and the strictness of its practice will be insensibly lowered, without shock- the feelings of the people, or being very clearly per- ceived by the establishment itself. The instructors of free agents are almost imperceptibly guided by the turn of mind which they perceive to be prevalent among their pupils. They have a natural, and in some respects a laudable apprehension of closing the minds of their hearers, against all improvement by shocking their prejudices and running counter to their preconceived opinions.

It is probable that causes of this description ope- rated in lowering the scriptural and orthodox spirit of most of the Protestant churches of Europe during the last century. The rise and progress of modern philosophy and liberality, which were only cant

terms for atheism and deism, insensibly corrupted
the sound and vigorous principles in which the Protestant laity of Europe were educated for more than
a century subsequent to the reformation. The taint
of the poison was transmitted to their posterity, and
seemed habitually fixed in the constitution of many
of the higher ranks of society. They could not bear
with patience the humbling truths of the Gospel, and
it is natural to conclude, from the causes just stated,
that those truths were in consequence less frequently
promulgated; and most certain it is, that scarcely
any desire was exhibited, either by the state or by
individuals, for affording the people augmented means
of instruction in the tenets of the establishment in
proportion to the evident necessity created by their
increasing number. But as every departure from
established principle necessarily leads in time to a
reaction, especially where freedom of discussion is
permitted, active and inquiring minds were led by
the obvious symptoms of degeneracy to compare the
doctrines, the sentiments, and the characters of
modern times with those which are associated with
our dearest recollections in the history of the Protestant Church. It was then that the benefit of
Establishments shone forth in all its lustre. The re-
action, it must be confessed, far exceeded the original
impulse of the force impressed, and was not a little
tinctured with enthusiasm and extravagance. But
it served to rouse the energies and restore the elas-
ticity of the body of the orthodox church; and her
fixed and permanent principles afforded an unerring
rule by which to judge of the extent to which a
salutary re-action might fairly be carried. But as the
uneducated part of mankind are prone to extremes,

it is not surprising that many would not consent to stop at this point, but have left far behind them the good old principles of their forefathers, who bled for that liberty of conscience which their posterity appear somewhat prone to convert into licentiousness.

Now if this be any thing like a just account of the origin of many of the modern sects, it will be more easy to discover the proper remedy than effectually to apply it. It may, however, be generally comprised in one short sentence: viz. a return to the good old principles, a deviation from which was the original cause of the evil, and a fervent but charitable zeal both in providing and profiting by the necessary means of imparting the knowledge of those principles in their true and genuine spirit to the great body of the people.

This remedy, I am happy to believe, is in rapid progress, and that its effects will daily become more visible in the augmented virtue and happiness of mankind. I shall not again repeat the arguments of this treatise, which prove that the elements of human society can securely rest upon no other basis; but it is impossible not to feel a sentiment of gratitude at the share which our own country has been permitted to bear in enlarging and strengthening it. Nor do I believe that any of my rational countrymen are so *exclusively English* as to suffer the alloy of a baser sentiment to mix with their genuine feelings of congratulation, that foreign governments are also raising a superstructure of public happiness and prosperity upon similar principles. The following treaty is a most noble and singular testimony to this fact. I have heard that some politicians, unable to appre-

ciate the genuine feeling and singleness of mind
which dictated its contents,

> " Advancing gravely to apply
> To th' optic glass their judging eye,
> Have bent their penetrating brow
> As if they meant to gaze it through,"

and have discovered a meditated attack upon the
grand Turk or an holy crusade against the Wahabis.
But a candid consideration will convince us, that
a document scarcely ever appeared containing stronger
internal evidence of unity in object and artless-
ness in design ; or, (if the circumstances under which
it was drawn up be considered,) reflecting greater
honour on the heads and hearts of the potentates
personally concerned in its composition.

The sighs and groans of their own subjects, and
the retributive sufferings of the French, had been
heard and contemplated by them as the ultimate
results of a long course of political transactions disjoined " from those true principles on which the
wisdom of God in his Revelation has founded the
tranquillity and prosperity of nations." The effects
were before their eyes, the causes were not doubtful,
and but one effectual remedy presented itself.

The sovereigns had the *moral magnanimity* boldly
to avow their determination to apply it. This term
is peculiarly apposite on the present occasion ; for
it was plain to foresee that the document would be
branded as little better than cant and hypocrisy, and
the framers of it as little better than madmen, by those
philosophers who, in their admiration of religion
without cant, are themselves a little apt to adopt
what I have seen well described by the term of *cant*

without religion. But truly if the document which follows be any proof of the insanity of those who signed it, one may be disposed to answer the persons who make the insinuation in the words of an English king, who, when informed by his courtiers, for obvious purposes, that one of his most distinguished naval officers was gone mad upon religion, replied, " I heartily wish, gentlemen, that he would *bite* you all."

The following manifesto was issued at St. Petersburgh on Christmas day, and precedes the treaty about which there has been some discussion in the British House of Commons.

" We, ALEXANDER I. by God's Grace, Emperor and Autocrat of all the Russias, &c.—

" Make known : As we have learned from experience, and its direful consequences to all the world, that the course of former political connexions between the powers of Europe had not those true principles for its basis on which the wisdom of God, in his revelation, has founded the tranquillity and prosperity of nations, therefore We, in concert with their Majesties the Emperor of Austria and the King of Prussia, have proceeded to establish an alliance, (to which the other Christian powers have been invited to accede,) in which we mutually bind ourselves, both for us and for our subjects, to adopt, as the only means of attaining that end, the principle derived from the words and religion of our Saviour Jesus Christ, who teaches mankind to live as brethren, not in hatred and strife, but in peace and love. We pray the Almighty that he may send down his blessing thereon ; yea, may this holy alliance be confirmed between all powers for their general welfare ; and may no one, unrestrained by the unanimity of all the rest, dare to depart therefrom. We therefore order a copy of this alliance hereto annexed to be made generally known, and "read in all the churches."

" In the name of the Most Holy and Indivisible Trinity.

" Their Majesties the Emperor of Austria, the King of Prussia, and the Emperor of Russia, having, in consequence of the great events which have marked the course of the three last years in Europe, and especially of the blessings which it has pleased Divine Providence to shower down upon those states which place their confidence and their hope on IT alone, acquired the intimate conviction of the necessity of founding the conduct to be observed by the powers in their reciprocal relations upon the sublime truths which the holy religion of our Saviour teaches—

" They solemnly declare that the present act has no other object than to publish, in the face of the whole world, their fixed resolution, both in the administration of their respective states, and in their political relations with every other government, to take for their sole guide the precepts of that holy religion, namely, the precepts of justice, Christian charity, and peace, which, far from being applicable only to private concerns, must have an immediate influence on the councils of princes, and guide all their steps, as being the only means of consolidating human institutions, and remedying their imperfections. In consequence their Majesties have agreed on the following articles:

" Art. I. Conformably to the words of the Holy Scriptures, which command all men to consider each other as brethren, the three contracting Monarchs will remain united by the bonds of a true and indissoluble fraternity; and considering each other as fellow-countrymen, they will on all occasions, and in all places, lend each other aid and assistance ; and regarding themselves towards their subjects and armies as fathers of families, they will lead them, in the same spirit of fraternity with which they are animated to protect religion, peace, and justice.*

" Art. II. In consequence, the sole principle in force, whether between the said governments or between their subjects, shall be that of doing each other reciprocal service, and of testifying, by unalterable good will, the mutual affection with which they ought to be animated, to consider themselves all as members of one and the same Christian nation, the three allied princes looking on themselves as merely delegated by Providence to govern three branches of the one family, namely, Austria, Prussia, and Russia ; thus confessing that the Christian world, of which they and their people form a part, has, in reality, no other sovereign than him to whom alone power really belongs, because in him alone are found all the treasures of love, science, and infinite wisdom, that is to say, God, our Divine Saviour, the Word of the Most High, the Word of Life. Their Majesties consequently recommend to their people, with the most tender solicitude, as the sole means of enjoying that peace which arises from a good conscience, and which alone is durable, to strengthen themselves every day more and more in the principles and exercise of the duties which the Divine Saviour has taught to mankind.

" Art. III. All the powers who shall choose solemnly to avow the sacred principles which have dictated the present act, and shall acknowledge how im-

* The Polish nobles formerly drew their swords when they turned to the altar to repeat the Creed, in testimony that they were ready to DEFEND *their faith* at the risk of their lives.

portant it is for the happiness of nations, too long agitated, that these truths should henceforth exercise over the destinies of mankind all the influence which belongs to them, will be received with equal ardour and affection into this holy alliance.

" Done in triplicate, and signed at Paris, the year of grace, 1815, 14th (26th) September,

  " (L. S.) FRANCIS.
  " (L. S.) FREDERICK WILLIAM.
  " (L. S.) ALEXANDER.
   " Conformable to the original,
    " (Signed) ALEXANDER.

Done at St. Petersburg, the day of the birth of our Saviour, the 25th of December, 1815."

Having now traced, perhaps at too great length, the conclusions to be derived from the application of the fourth fundamental proposition of this treatise as far as religion is concerned, we will proceed to a few brief remarks upon the department of morals. The general argument is here of course very similar to that which has just been submitted to the reader. If the happiness to be derived from the influence of morality be in proportion to the *extent* of that influence, the statesman cannot rest satisfied barely with that degree of it which may be just sufficient to preserve the state from convulsions : but he will aspire after that which shall at least exonerate every public law of the state from the reproach of tempting the people to immoral conduct. In England for example, although our laws are certainly constructed upon the general basis of moral principle, and are sufficiently so to secure a fair competence of public happiness and prosperity, yet I think that no candid philanthropist or statesman will hesitate in admitting, that both the people's comfort and the state's security would be advanced by still referring some of our laws to the test of moral expediency derived from its true source.

If that law, which precludes three fourths of the consumers of game from acquiring it in any other manner except by the corruption of all morals, and the destruction of all regular habits, in a great portion of our most valuable population, were altered so as to preclude these consequences, doubtless both the peace, comfort, and prosperity of the country would receive a material accession.

Again, if that desirable mixture of all the educated ranks and professions, which fills the benches of the House of Commons, could be there collected without something like a necessary corruption of a large class of the people, without temptations to falsehood, perjury, and a long train of subordinate crimes; there is no question but that it would be a considerable improvement in policy : there would be many more honest and industrious subjects; and enlightened gentlemen would themselves feel their own consciences upon certain subjects a little more at ease.

That both these political and moral objects might be attained with considerable facility and without serious danger I verily believe, as well as that a contemplation of the evils in their present state, and in a moral point of view, must infuse an ardent desire to attempt the remedy into the mind of every truly British statesman.

These few remarks are sufficient, in addition to what is scattered throughout the whole of this treatise, to illustrate the moral application of the proposition at the head of this chapter. I trust that they are sufficient to convince the reader that any political hypothesis which can be shown to lead to immoral consequences must be either false or inexpedient. If it be conversant with the essential nature of the principles, it must be false; for nothing can be essentially true which is essentially immoral, that is, contrary to the express will of God. If the hypothesis be exterior to the essential nature of the principles, and conversant only with their special application, it must be inexpedient, that is, unsafe to act upon; because the disorder introduced by its immoral consequences will *ultimately* much more affect the liberty and security which are necessary to the free operation of the principles, than can be compensated by any *immediate* or apparent advantage held out by the hypothesis.

Being then, as I trust, agreed upon these great and leading principles, we will now proceed to the remaining topics of this chapter, viz. rational liberty and security of property.

It is superfluous to remind the reader, that the liberty here contended for is simply a perfect freedom from the interference either of an oppressive government or of a licentious people, in the pursuit of just, good, and legitimate objects by individuals; and that the security of property intended throughout this treatise involves not only an abstinence from illegal exactions in the government, but also full security from the laws and the habits of the people, that neither they nor the government shall interfere with the free and equitable disposition of private property. The salutary tendency of population at once to keep within the remaining powers of the soil to afford subsistence, and also to give a continual impulse to the further progress of society, has been made to depend throughout my whole argument upon the spontaneous distribution of the people, and the free choice of their pursuits. It is necessary for these purposes that no material interference shall have prevented such changes as the altered circumstances of the society shall have made it the interest of the people to effect. Liberty and security therefore, as just defined, are essentially conditions of the argument; and it is evident also, that the salutary consequences to be expected will bear a tolerably exact proportion to the perfection and universal prevalence of those blessings.

I shall not in this chapter, any more than in the last, enter into a minute application of the deductions to be drawn from the establishment of this truth. The statesman who is convinced of it will not be satisfied in this case, any more than in those of religion and morals, to rest in bare mediocrity. He will consider every interference with the liberty of the subject, that is not absolutely requisite for the public safety, or counterbalanced by a very superior advantage to the whole community, as so much gratuitous subtraction from the power and happiness of the state: he will consider every tax, not imperatively requisite to support the dignity or the public credit of the nation, as a species of robbery; and every increase of establishments, unaccompanied by the discharge of corresponding duties, as little better than the propagation of authorized mendicity. He will especially deprecate these encroachments, from their tendency to annihilate the very elements of prosperity by interfering with the spontaneous arrangements of the people and their pursuits, and by introducing a mischievous disproportion between the rate of their numerical increase and the industry which is necessary to support it. He will, moreover, bend all his efforts to ascertain what specific means can best secure to the people the general prevalence of rational liberty and substantial security of property; and he will find no difficulty in admitting that these ends are not so much to be attained by particular enactments, prohibiting certain actions or pursuits which may be thought to interfere with general liberty and security, while the disposition of the people remains prone to evil through the predominance of ignorance or vice, as by the general establishment of moral and religious sanctions.

The constant pressure of prohibition against the general prevalence of vice and ignorance is so far from ever giving liberty and security for its results, that it can only end in anarchy or tyranny. But measures directed to the fountain-head, towards diminishing the evil propensities of the people by moral and religious instruction, are really effectual means of securing personal liberty and security of property, because they are the only effectual means of anticipating those evils that must eventually end in tyranny and anarchy; viz. severe laws, or popular licence. We cannot escape from this alternative. Nor is it possible to exhibit the political expediency of moral and religious culture in a stronger or more conclusive point of view, nor to show more clearly how essentially the permanent progress of public prosperity, the immediate political interests of the community, nay, the value of each individual's title to liberty and property, depend upon a due attention to that important object.

Upon referring to the contents of this chapter, I must be permitted to remark in conclusion that, although, considering the natural and inveterate propensities of human nature in all ages and nations, it would be altogether Utopian to expect to supersede the necessity of human laws or of political institutions by the general prevalence of virtuous tastes and conduct ; yet I do not see that this is any valid argument against admitting that the effect, although even without any hope of rendering it complete, will always bear a proportion to the means used for producing it; which is all that I am here contending for. We may be well assured that the means will never be copious enough to produce an universal effect; but they are abundantly sufficient to establish the expediency of instituting a further inquiry, whether the connexion of religion and morals with politics has not frequently been too much overlooked : whether the former have not been argued upon *too exclusively* with reference to the individual as to his own personal condition with a view to eternity, while his temporal interests, and the general condition of society have been supposed to be the exclusive province of the latter. How else can we account for the ardour with which men enter into controversies purely political as the sole foundation of their worldly prosperity, while they studiously avert their minds from all reference to moral and religious considerations as foreign to the subject, if not absolutely impertinent. Yet how is it possible for a statesman or economist to be more practically concerned in any subject than in one which, though it do not set up self-interest as the expansive principle of all public virtue, does nevertheless so far connect that powerful feeling with morals and religion, as to show that an adherence to them can alone afford sufficient security for the regular perseverance of nations or individuals in the principles of sound policy.

But perhaps the truth of these propositions will be more readily admitted than the possibility of drawing from them any practical conclusions. It may be said, and with great truth, that the great impediment to the general reception of principles of public and private conduct founded on pure morality evidently arises from the depraved tastes and habits of men ; from some objects of self-indulgence, or some fancied interests, which they consider at once as paramount in their estimation, and incompatible with a strict adherence to pure morality. The objections which I have frequently heard stated to the general introduction of religious and moral customs, and to the abandonment of habits and pursuits incompatible with them, when the duty is pressed home, are—that it may be all very true, but that, if reduced to practice, the result would in the first place impede the operations of society, or, if it failed of that effect, that society would scarcely be worth enjoying upon the terms.

Now this sort of feeling can only arise from grievous faults of education, whereby pernicious habits, pursuits, and amusements, have been intimately associated with, or at least too little dissociated from, the ideas of individual enjoyment and of political expediency. But surely this is no proof that the combination may not, by due precaution, be prevented? Once enlist these very feelings, tastes, and habits on the side of pure morals and religion, by impressing upon the mind of youth their close connexion with political expediency, public prosperity,

and the highest individual enjoyment, and the association is directly reversed.   I do not mean to assert
that the effects would also be *fully* reversed ; for the
new tendencies of the conduct will now be opposed
by the natural dispositions of the heart, instead of
running parallel with them as in the former case.
But it is impossible not to suppose that very considerable effects would be produced both upon individuals
and society.   One of the best of our old writers
observes that " the predominance of custom is every
where visible, insomuch that a man would wonder to
hear men profess, protest, engage, give great words,
and then *do just as they have done before;* as if they
were dead images and engines, moved only by the
wheels of custom.   Therefore, since custom is the
principal magistrate of man's life, let men by all
means endeavour to obtain good customs !   Certainly
custom is most perfect when it beginneth in young
years: this we call education, which is in effect but
an early custom.   But if the force of custom *simple*
and *separate* " (that is, operating individually,) " be
great, the force of custom copulate, conjoined, and
collegiate " (that is, operating upon society) " is far
greater ; for there example teacheth, company com-
forteth, emulation quickeneth, glory raiseth ; so as
in such places the force of custom is in its exaltation.
Certainly the great multiplication of virtues upon
human nature resteth upon *societies* well ordained
and disciplined;" (that is, pure churches, well regulated universities, &c. ;) " for commonwealths and
good governments do nourish virtue grown, but do
not much mend the seeds.   *But the misery is, that
the most effectual means are now applied to the*

ends least to be desired."   (Bacon's Essay on Custom and Education.)

But it is time to bring this chapter to a close, lest, under colour of a treatise on the elements of political economy, I be accused of coming down upon my readers with a general treatise of ethics. If the preceding observations apply to politics in general, they are especially true of political economy—the most important, because the fundamental, branch of all politics. The writers on this science, particularly of that part of it specifically treated in this work, have eminently discussed the objects of their attention as if they were distinct from moral considerations. Mr. Malthus, indeed, forms an honourable exception to this observation, by his care in tracing all his political conclusions on to their moral consequences, and has thereby submitted to his readers' consideration the whole question as to the expediency of adopting or rejecting his hypothesis. But by far the greater number of economists seem to have supposed that a bare proof of the general political expediency of their conclusions would lead to their universal admission and successful operation—a supposition contrary to the experience of all ages and nations, when applied to any thing so variable and uncertain as the judgment of men upon the application or effects of the best reasoned principles of political economy. The books, therefore, though by no means useless for the practical purposes for which they were intended, have had this mischievous tendency—that, being elementary parts of the education of youth of the higher orders, the fountains of political knowledge and legislative practice have been poisoned at their source:

and the great and leading principles, which should regulate both have been overlooked. Philosophers and legislators are brought up to consider the bare, and at the best uncertain, principles of political economy as sufficient to guide their conduct in promoting the welfare of mankind. The subject in this contracted and insulated view being in itself abstruse, and not capable of reference to any fixed or undeniable principles, is peculiarly the department of controversy. The science is divided, if we may thus express it, into so many different schools, each dogmatically adhering to opposite opinions, all equally convinced of the justness of their own conclusions, but no one in any great degree successful in improving the condition of society. The practical statesman having observed successive trials of each system, and finding none capable of attaining its professed object, becomes gradually indifferent to all, and disposed merely to have recourse to temporary expedients as difficulties arise, instead of anticipating them by a comprehensive view of remote causes and their consequences.

It is unnecessary to enlarge upon the debilitating effects of such a system of government on the commonwealth of a country, or upon its degrading effects on the habits and dispositions of the people. It is sure to engender general discontent, a dissatisfaction with the laws and the government, and a dereliction of all manly and self-denying principles. Surely then if we consider how perfectly innocent and safe is all reform that proceeds only upon the system of strengthening the spirit of the laws, by adapting them to a sound system of morals, it may be worth while to see what can be done for society upon that principle. Seeing

466 PUBLIC HAPPINESS PROPORTIONATE

that the effects of disjoining morals from politics have
hitherto been very unpropitious, let us at length begin
to try the effect of their combined force.

For this purpose I submit it again, with great humility, to the consideration of those whom it may
concern, whether an improvement in the system of
education may not be here suggested. If a scheme of
political economy were taught, in which the principles of the science should never be contemplated as
distinct from sound morals and religion, which constitute the real criterion of their truth and practical
utility, a new set of views and sentiments would in
time become habitual, and new elements of vigour
would be diffused throughout the decaying fabric of
society. That they would amount to a beneficial
improvement in the condition of mankind will
perhaps be the less disputed, if we consider that the
result promises to be rather the attainment of that
which all good men and enlightened statesmen have
in vain endeavoured to accomplish, than the introduction of any unknown or doubtful ingredient into
the political system. And the attempt may with
more readiness be made, because, supposing it to fail
of its whole object, it can only, as far as it does
succeed, lead to a practical enlargement of public
happiness, and of the moral and political force of the
people which makes the experiment.

If such a school were established, I would write
over the professor's chair—" Goodness, of all virtues
and dignities of the mind, is the greatest, being the
character of the Deity; without it man is a busy,
mischievous, wretched thing, no better than a
kind of vermin. Goodness answers to the theo-
logical virtue charity, and admits of no *excess* but

error; neither can angel or man come in danger by it."

I think the argumentative nature of the science would guard the practice of the virtue from running into error or enthusiasm, while a constant contemplation of the virtue would guard the practice of the science from degenerating into worldlimindedness; and both together would tend to form the useful and accomplished citizen of a free country—the real but practical Christian.

CHAPTER IX.

Brief Recapitulation of the Third Book.

IN the first chapter of this book I have endeavoured to show, as a general axiom, that there is no certain standard for political conduct except moral truth, nor any certain rule for the discovery of moral truth but a reference to the revealed will of God. Hence it followed as a natural conclusion that whatever is consistent with this last must be politically expedient, and that whatever is prohibited by it must be politically mischievous. I also attempted to prove that not only the discovery of what is expedient in political practice, but also the power and the means of adhering to it in political agents, are to be drawn from the same source ; for that all other sanctions, whether of argument, of interest, or of any other description, are too precarious and too little imperative upon the minds and wills of men to secure their perseverance in a straight course.

Having advanced these propositions as general truths in the first chapter, I endeavoured in those which immediately follow to show the specific application of them to some particular and controverted points of practice connected with this treatise. And first, in chapters two, three, and four, I prosecuted an inquiry into the nature and extent of the duty of charity. In the first of those chapters an attempt was made to prove that the first and most unbounded exercise of that part of true and rational charity which resolves itself into alms-giving, is perfectly compatible with the healthy progress of society and of population; because, as the objects of this charity increase in proportion to the whole number of the people, population also undergoes a proportionate abatement in the rate of its increase. Space, therefore, is afforded for the due exercise of almsgiving, without any undue encouragement to a vicious increase in the numbers of mankind.

It was however fully admitted and enforced, in the same chapter, that the moral and religious instruction of the poor is not only the most enlightened exercise of charity in individuals, but an imperative political duty on the part of the state; because it directly prevents or counteracts any eventual mischief which the injudicious exercise of mistaken charity in indiscriminate alms-giving may produce.

Since however the best of all charities are those which teach the poor to assist in providing for themselves, the object of the third chapter was to enter into a comparative estimate of the various plans for that laudable purpose. I trust that sufficient reasons have been given to justify the decided preference which I have ventured to entertain in favour of the recent institutions of Banks for the Savings of the Poor, equally on moral, political, and economical, views of the subject.

In the fourth and fifth chapters I endeavoured to detail the effects produced by the advancement of society into its higher stages upon the demand for the exercise of charity, and upon the means of meeting it; and to show that any comparative estimate of the sums expended in charity in different countries, which omits a full consideration of the state of society existing in each, proceeds upon principles fundamentally erroneous, and can only lead to practical mischief. It further appears from this chapter that the demand for charitable exertion, and the means of meeting it, equally increase as society advances, and that the effects thereby produced on the comfort and happiness of different communities respectively depend not so much upon the amount of the sums given, as upon the mode in which they are expended. Where the expenditure is guided by the rules of morality, public happiness and private comfort are the results; while the contrary system leads of course to opposite consequences. No apprehension therefore need be entertained in permitting the most unbounded exercise of charity, provided it be directed towards the proper and legitimate objects. Such are the results which I have endeavoured to deduce from an inquiry into the nature and extent of the duty of charity.

In the sixth chapter I have endeavoured to convince the reader that the people, and especially the lower orders, may be permitted, without detriment to the healthy progress of population, to enjoy an option of entering into the marriage contract or abstaining from it, determinable upon moral considerations only, and entirely free from the speculations of statesmen upon political expediency;—that this liberty is expressly allowed by the words of Scripture, and when enjoyed in conformity with its instructions will be not only free from any evil consequences of a political nature, but is absolutely necessary to a due progress in public wealth, civilization and happiness. These conclusions are strictly derivable from the fundamental principles of the first book of this treatise, and are drawn from the application of them to the question under discussion. I trust they have been sufficient to prove that, in a tolerably moral and well regulated community, it is perfectly feasible to relieve every distress which may eventually arise to individuals, from the enjoyment of such a system of liberty with respect to the marriage contract.

The object of the seventh chapter is to prove that the effects of the principle of population and of the progress of society have no *necessary* tendency to diminish the general sum of happiness enjoyed either by the whole community, or by the individuals of which it is composed, but that they only change the nature of the people's enjoyments; providing by a beautiful system of compensation, to all ranks of society, some countervailing advantage of a moral and political nature, for every necessary privation which the new arrangements of the community bring in their train; so that a good citizen will have an equal probability of happiness in every stage of society, in proportion as he discharges the duties which its particular condition imposes upon him.

In the eighth chapter I have endeavoured more fully to illustrate, and to apply to the practical purposes of statesmen, the fundamental truth that the salutary tendency of population, as well as every other condition of the healthy progress of society, will operate in proportion to the general prevalence of religion, morality, liberty, and security of property; that these four blessings, however, are in fact ultimately referable to the two first among them, the influence of which should be forwarded by every method within the power of the state; especially by early education and legal means for continued and permanent instruction. It follows too from this principle that a patriotic statesman ought not to sit down contented merely with that moderate degree of attainment with respect to these blessings, which is barely sufficient to carry on the progress of society, and is at liberty to relax his attention and exertion when he may think that point has been attained; because such relaxation would immediately afford scope to the natural tendency of human affairs to degenerate, and the healthy progress of society would be checked: but I have ventured to contend that, animated by the conviction that every improvement and increase of those blessings is in itself a source of happiness and prosperity, which can never be carried too far, he should make every attainment the step to a further progress : and though he may never positively reach the exalted point to which he may aspire, he will not only be enabled to counteract the natural tendency of human institutions to decay, but will also be rewarded by a conviction of having bestowed solid accessions of power and happiness on the commonwealth.

CHAPTER X.

On the rational Hopes that may be entertained of a progressive Improvement in the Condition of Mankind.

THERE is no point of view under which the subject discussed in this treatise assumes a higher interest, than in the conclusions which may be drawn from the different hypotheses respecting our rational hopes of future improvement in the condition of mankind. If the conclusions respecting the principle of population which it has been my object to controvert be just, it is evident that very slender hopes indeed can be entertained of any material amelioration. The progress of society according to those conclusions brings with it so many insuperable difficulties, insuperable even by any adherence on the part of the people to the laws of religion and morality, that we are compelled to submit to the disheartening conviction, that the best governed and most moral nation has no sooner reaped the rewards of its conformity with the commands of Providence, in the attainment of a high degree of general happiness and prosperity, than it must, by the inevitable laws of that same Providence, begin to descend in the scale of society, and to endure all those sufferings, which have been observed by political economists to be the constant attendants of such descent, so well described by Dr. Adam Smith as " *miserable*" and " *melancholy*." So that the statesman who advances his country the most rapidly in its career is only approximating it so much the nearer to its fall, and would have served his generation (or at least subsequent generations) better, had he bent his efforts towards repressing all those moral and political energies, by the developement of which a nation emerges from the stationary condition, which has been equally well described as " *hard* " and " *dull.*" The only prospect of obviating these consequences, even upon the hypothesis of those who differ from the conclusions of this treatise, is to be found in views of society confessed by themselves to be Utopian; or in applying to the great mass of the lower orders of mankind principles and arguments of too refined a nature to possess any general influence, except among the few who constitute the higher classes of society. *Involuntary* abstinence from marriage attended with moral restraint is to be increased, *among the lower orders exclusively*, as society advances, and as temptations to a breach of moral restraint consequently increase; and the propriety of this abstinence is enforced by arguments, and justified upon a principle of compensation, which can have no general reference whatsoever, except to the higher classes; such as the refinements of sentimental intercourse, the "distinction of a genuine from a transient passion," and the repression of love for a time " that it may afterwards burn with a brighter, purer, and steadier flame." Nor are the political expectations held out to us less brilliant and beautiful : " war," it is said, that great pest of the human race, would under such circumstances soon cease to extend its ravages so widely and so frequently as it does at present;" for " the ambition of princes would want instruments of destruction, if the distresses

of the lower classes did not drive them under their
standards." " Indisposed to a war of offence, in a
war of defence such a society would be strong as a
rock of adamant." (Malthus, book iv. chap. ii.)

Now, without laying any stress on the utter impossibility of maintaining the lower classes in such
a state as is supposed in these quotations, during
the necessary fluctuations of the advanced stages of
society, I do not think that it is quite consistent with
the experience of history to affirm, that nations, existing in the simple states of society which render
them incapable of offensive war, have usually been
able to oppose " a rock of adamant" to the attacks
of more powerful and ambitious rivals; but on the
contrary they have usually ended in becoming the
victims of their exclusive policy. Such a picture is
indeed nothing more than the delineation of the
peculiar comforts attending the weaker and less advanced conditions of society : its application, even
theoretically, to the more advanced stages, where the
loss of these peculiar comforts is, as I have shown,
more than compensated by other countervailing advantages, can only lead to error by setting up a false
standard of what is desirable. A commercial and
manufacturing nation, conducting itself upon such
principles, would tend towards its own destruction
by every step it should take in a career so obviously
incompatible with the rights and the intercourse it
is under the necessity of maintaining with respect to
other nations. The community, therefore, which
should first act upon this system would soon afford
an unanswerable practical evidence of the unsound-
ness of its general principle.

Again, we are informed that the only hopes of

ameliorating the condition of society is in the first place to cause a diminution of population. But then we are desired to consider " that this diminution is merely relative; and when once this relative diminution has been effected; by keeping the population stationary, while the supply of food had increased, it might then start afresh, and continue increasing for ages, with the increase of food, maintaining always the same relative proportion to it." (Malthus book iv. chap. iv.) Now to those who agree in the arguments of a preceding chapter, in the second book, on the order of precedence between food and population, this hypothesis of checking the increase of population till food is *previously* raised for its support will not require any further answer. The supposition of the practical possibility of such a system is altogether gratuitous, and is founded upon the mistaken presumption, that the springs of industry directed to agricultural improvement can continue in vigour in the advanced states of society, without a continually increasing demand for agricultural products. If, therefore, the only hopes of ameliorating the condition of society rest on the practical success of such an hypothesis, those hopes must be very slender and disheartening indeed.

We are further informed (Malthus, book iv. chap. v.) that the only condition under which early unions can take place among the lower orders in the advanced states of society is a *great mortality* among the adults. " To act consistently therefore, we should facilitate instead of foolishly and vainly endeavouring to impede the operations of nature in producing this mortality, and if we dread the too frequent visitation of the horrid form of famine, we should sedulously encourage the *other forms of destruction*, which we *compel nature to use*. Instead of recommending cleanliness to the poor we should encourage contrary habits. In our towns we should make the streets narrower, crowd more people into the houses, and court the return of the plague. In the country we should build our villages near stagnant pools, and particularly encourage settlements in all marshy and unwholesome situations," &c. Now if it be really true that, according to any hypothesis, early marriages cannot be permitted among the lower orders of a country without these absurd and miserable consequences, certainly that hypothesis offers no very encouraging prospect of the future improvement of mankind. But those who recollect the reasoning upon this subject in the sixth chapter of this book, will not probably entertain anticipations of quite so desponding a nature.

Again, we are told, with perfect truth, that if a man marry without being able to support a family, he must expect severe want ; a general truth which no one ever thought of denying. But the question is, what is that prospect of being able to support a family which authorizes a man of the lower orders to marry in a well regulated community? Is the possession of a decent habitation and the capacity to labour sufficient, or must he wait for something further in order to avoid bringing political mischief on his country and misery on a helpless family?

In answer to these questions, we are desired to suppose the general prevalence of such prudential habits among the poor, as would prevent them from marrying when the actual price of labour, joined to what they might have saved in their single state, would not give them the prospect of being able to support a wife and five or six children without assistance. " Undoubtedly" it is added, " such a degree of prudential restraint would produce a very striking melioration in the condition of the lower classes of the people." (Malthus, book iv. chap. xi.)

Now, with respect to the condition of the people themselves, if in any of the advanced stages of society they were to follow this plan, it is evident that they must remain unmarried all their lives, for in no case can such societies *generally* afford so large a remuneration to all its labourers married and unmarried; and every approach towards such a state of things would subtract just so much from the general industry of the country, would throw it into the declining condition, and gradually restore it through a long series of misery, depression, and consequent vice, to the purely agricultural state, when the six children might certainly be supported by their father's labour. But that this process would " strikingly meliorate the condition of the people" existing at its commencement will not I presume be contended; or that it would ultimately ameliorate their condition, will not probably be asserted by those who have done me the honour to attend to the reasoning contained in a former chapter, (see chap. vii.) upon the compensations afforded to every class of the community for the alterations made in their condition by the progress of society.

Neither would the effects of such a process upon the political condition of the country adopting it be more favourable than upon the private condition of its inhabitants. For in proportion as its advancement in prosperity has been a blessing, of course its retrocession must be the reverse, and the governing principle of the community would directly oppose the acknowledged desideratum of producing the greatest quantity of happiness in a given space of territory. It appears, therefore, that there must be something radically wrong in any hypothesis which pretends to make the happiness of the people dependant upon conditions so obviously calculated to introduce public degradation and private misery. Lastly, we are desired to recollect that the " laws of nature" say, with St. Paul; " If a man will not work, neither shall he eat." From which position we are desired to deduce this consequence as a law of Providence ;—that, let a man work with ever so great a degree of diligence and alacrity, he shall not the more be enabled to eat, (if he be a member of a civilized and commercial country) unless he also fulfil another condition with which it is impossible in such a country that he can comply :—viz. unless he abstain from marriage till he can certainly maintain a family consisting of a wife and six children.

The propositions which I have now detailed in this chapter, extravagant as they probably appear to those who have attentively perused the preceding treatise, are all strictly legitimate conclusions from the principles respecting population which it is the object of the present work to endeavour to refute. It must be confessed that they present a most desponding view of our prospects with respect to the future condition of mankind, a view the dreariness of which is only relieved, even in the estimation of those who present it, by the probable effects which education may have among the lower orders, in inducing them generally to assume habits which it is admitted to be next to impossible that they should assume, and which (to say the least of them) appear to be very far from consistent with the designs of Providence, and the express permissions of Scripture.

Without this condition, society as it advances, brings nothing but increase of misery to the most numerous and valuable class of the community; misery which can never be compensated in the eye of a just Providence, or of an enlightened philanthropist, by the eventual addition that may be made to the enjoyments of the other classes.

Such being the prospect opened to our view by the system just alluded to, let us inquire to what extent it may be improved, upon the principles maintained in this treatise.

For this purpose, and to avoid unnecessary repetition, I have only to recal to the reader's recollection the proofs of the fundamental propositions of the first book, and the application of them in the chapters on the direction and exercise of our charity, and on the free option of marriage. From these it will appear that the progressive abatement in the tendency of population to increase, as society advances, leaves ample space for consulting the happiness of the lower orders, both in the relief of their necessities, and in the permission of early marriages amongst them, without political injury to the state, or private injury to the individual. Nay further, I think it appears that this relief and permission, under the control of a moral and free government, are absolutely essential to the healthy progress of society;

that it is the interest of such a country in the advanced stages, that its lower orders should marry when they can procure a decent habitation, and the father has a fair average prospect of supporting two children by his labour; and that such being its interest, it is bound to provide, and will always have the power of providing, for the eventual maintenance of families consisting of a greater number of children, and for the eventual relief of such of the parents as may fall into temporary distress, from the fluctuations of employment necessarily incident to all complicated states of society.

The universal tendency of population to keep within the powers of the soil to bestow subsistence affords irrefragable proof that there is no *physical* impossibility that society should go on for an indefinite period advancing, and the community increasing in happiness and prosperity, under the laws and regulations of a benignant Providence. Still less can there be asserted to be any moral impossibility that they should so proceed. *Vice* and *misery* do not necessarily increase as society advances, unless counteracted by the general fulfilment of certain impossible conditions, which economists may choose to designate by the term *moral restraint*. But a people will gradually advance in moral improvement, as well as in temporal happiness and political prosperity, in proportion as they adhere to the general will of Providence, as announced in the precepts of the Holy Scriptures. Political speculations for the good of mankind, independent of these sanctions, will certainly fail of their effect; and if we examine to the bottom the instances in which they have failed, the want of success will plainly appear to have arisen from moral deficiencies. To take an instance from the English Poor Laws:—In parishes where they have been honestly administered, and where the people have had the advantage of zealous and spiritual instructors, the general condition of the society is superior to any thing the world can show. But where legislative enactments have been thought sufficient to supply the place of moral instruction, (instead of coming in aid of it,) half the advantages of the system have been lost by the counteracting effects of moral debasement. The chief advantages then consist in the security afforded by the system that attention to moral considerations will be revived by the pressure produced on the higher orders in consequence of the prevalence of moral debasement among the lower.

Various other instances might be cited in illustration: but they are I trust scarcely necessary to convince the reader who has advanced thus far in this treatise, that Politics, Morals, and Christianity, are dependant upon each other in the order in which they have been cited:—that the welfare of society, in its totality or in its separate parts, can no more be established by the principles of the first without a reference to the second, or of these without a reference to the third, than a finite straight line can be divided into two equal parts, without first knowing how to describe upon it an equilateral triangle.

According to the principles then of this treatise, our rational prospects of a progressive improvement in the condition of mankind stand thus: physically and politically speaking, there appears to be no natural or necessary impediment. But the extent to which the physical and political ability will be ren-

dered available to the purposes for which they were
bestowed, must entirely depend upon the degree in
which they are fortified and regulated by the prevalence of sound morals and pure religion. Whatsoever
therefore gives force to these, improves the scene
and vivifies the prospect. If this grand truth hath
been hitherto contemplated as little more than speculative in political systems, if the acknowledge-
ment of it hath been merely verbal and of course,
while its real influence has evaporated amidst the
contentious elements of worldly argument; doubtless
a practical conviction of its essential necessity and
active operation in all affairs of policy does of itself
open views of improvement of a cheering nature;
and considering the free course which, by the arguments of this treatise, the principle of population
appears to afford to the temporal happiness and moral
improvement of the people, the whole view is abundantly sufficient to confirm the conduct of the Statesman, and to animate the hopes of the Christian.

CHAPTER XI.

General Recapitulation and Conclusion.

THE judicious Hooker has the following passage: " God first assigned Adam maintenance of life, and then appointed him a law to observe. True it is, that the kingdom of God must be the first thing in our purpose and desires; but inasmuch as a righteous life presupposeth life, inasmuch as to live virtuously it is impossible, except we live; therefore the first impediment which naturally we endeavour to remove is penury and want of things, without which we cannot live."

In the foregoing treatise I have proceeded in some measure upon this hypothesis, having endeavoured to show in the first two books by what means a community is exempted from " that want of things without which they cannot live;" and in the third to exhibit the laws appointed for their observance when " maintenance of life " is assigned to them. But I have also attempted to do more than this. I have endeavoured to show further that the " observance of the law" secures " the maintenance of life;" that " a righteous life," or the influence of religion and morals in a community, not only " presupposeth," but is actually the condition of obtaining a competent portion of subsistence; and although " to live virtuously it is impossible, except we live," yet in proportion as we do in fact live virtuously, the difficulty of living at all, or of finding the means to support life, will disappear. It has been my object to prove the truth of this gracious dispensation of Providence, by showing, in the first book, the admirable proportions maintained between population and subsistence in every gradation through which society passes, and the dependance which the maintenance of this proportion has upon the general conformity of the people with the express commands of God for their government. It was proved that, preserving this conformity even to a very moderate extent, their comfortable subsistence is always secured by the conservative principle upon which the progress of population is regulated, notwithstanding the continual decrease in the productive powers of the soil; so that at no period, from the very infancy of society to the highest state of civilization at which any people can be conceived to arrive, and from the very commencement of cultivation to its fullest state of production and improvement, will a tolerably virtuous and well-governed population press perniciously against the means of subsistence derived from its native soil.

In the application of these truths, in the second book, the object has been to exhibit the means by which a moral people will employ their industry, in extracting a continual increase of subsistence from the soil of their own country to meet the demands of their augmenting numbers for food; and the precautions by which they will endeavour to secure this increase from waste and dilapidation. It is presumed to have been proved that, even in this department of the subject, which appears of a nature so strictly economical, success is very much dependant upon moral causes, through the influence of which economical measures will be efficient in raising produce for any increase of numbers to which a population so regulated will extend. There is therefore no *physical* impossibility of maintaining the people in comfort from their internal resources up to any given period of time.

In the application of the fundamental truths of the treatise in the third book, the object has been to exhibit the means by which the conservative principle, inherent in the progress of the population, is kept alive and regulated by the influence of religion, morals, rational liberty, and security of property over the customs, habits, pursuits, and spontaneous distribution of the people. And it is presumed to have been proved that the free exercise of all the virtues commanded in Scripture, and of all the moral obligations which can be deduced from an enlightened conscience, are not only compatible with, but to a considerable extent absolutely essential to, the salutary progress of population. Nay, more, that the progress will be salutary *in proportion* to the prevalence of moral and religious principles. There is therefore no *moral* impossibility of maintaining the people in comfort and happiness from their internal resources up to any given period of time.

The three books together may perhaps be allowed to exhibit something not far removed from a complete system of the elements of civil society, uniform in its tendency, agreeing with itself in all its parts, and strictly consonant with the revealed will of God, and with the moral laws thence derived. It shows that population may continue regularly increasing in numbers, wealth, and happiness from the first step in the career of society up to the highest point of civilization, under the operation of the laws which God himself hath appointed for their instruction, checked by no impediments but those which arise out of a wilful deviation from those laws ; and above all unembarrassed by any principle of evil necessarily arising, not from their own propensity to vice, but from their obedience to the laws which God has given them to counteract it.

Any approach towards the proof that such is the condition of human society in its fundamental elements must, I should think, afford sincere pleasure to every one who honours God and loves mankind. It must also animate his courage in the cause of both,—in the joint pursuit of piety and political knowledge. Few things are more discouraging to great moral exertions than the morbid doubts thrown around the question of their ultimate efficacy. A man requires to see clearly before he undertakes to act resolutely. There is not therefore a more certain method of paralyzing his efforts than by unfixing his principles, nor more efficacious means of invigorating his good resolutions than by showing the *positive certainty* of their advantageous results. It is surely, therefore, no small accession to the practical value of any system, that it exhibits one uniform and undeviating principle of action, applicable to every conceivable state of things, infallible in the production of profitable consequences, and usefully operative in proportion as it is called into exercise.

If the contemplation of such a system be useful towards the production, and animating to the progress, of the nobler sentiments among mankind in general, it should produce these effects in a peculiar manner among the ingenuous youth of the United Kingdom. They can scarcely take a step in their inquiries into the history and polity of their own country without tracing the consequences of such a system. Howsoever its vigour may, by lapse of time and partial neglect, have been permitted to droop in some of its departments, they will find in the construction of the system itself, that its founders looked to pure morals and sound religion as the fundamental principles of public prosperity. Our youth will therefore discover in the constitution of their own country, in church and state, at once the true foundations of national strength, and examples for the regulation of their own conduct and character as active citizens of a free country. If, during their perusal of the preceding view of the progress of society, they will bring the History of England to bear upon any one of the stages which have passed under investigation, they will probably find that the state has been carried through it with success, and made the transition to that which next succeeds, principally because it has in the main been governed upon the system recommended in this treatise; that is, that its laws and institutions have been founded in moral and religious principles, and that its leading statesmen, at the critical periods of its history, have usually referred their political measures to that unerring test. It will scarcely be denied, for example, that during the last century we have been profiting, almost exclusively, by the religious and political institutions left behind them by the great and good men who flourished at the REFORMATION and the REVOLUTION; that sound religion was the cardinal point to which all those institutions were directed, and, together with morals, afforded the principles upon which they were constructed. As little can it be denied that, during

the last century, if the institutions have not been permitted actually to decay, at least the spirit of some
of them has declined, and sufficient care has not been
taken to extend and apply them to the altered circumstances of the country. If it be asked wherefore is this? I should be tempted to reply, because
the cardinal principle was overlooked; because political sagacity was estranged from its legitimate com-
panion sound piety; and the effect of moral and political institutions upon the people was referred not to
the eternal principles asserted by God for the government of man, but to the degenerate passions of the
parties concerned, and to the temporary and particular interests of the passing moment.

Let the British youth compare the benefits conferred upon his country by Sir Robert Walpole, one
of the most celebrated statesmen of the last century,
with those which we inherit from the statesmen who
flourished 150 years before him; let the principles
and the character of each be investigated; and the
decided opposition will scarcely be entirely ascribed
to the different circumstances of the world at the
two periods. For the variance is certainly to the
full as great in principle as in practice.

If these were some of the causes of partial and
incipient decay, it is a much more agreeable, and not
a less profitable task to trace the causes of the partial and incipient improvement which has marked
the auspicious period of the present century. It
would, I humbly conceive, be a symptom of blind
prejudice to deny either that the moral and political
character of the *universal* English people (if I may
be allowed the term) has made a vigorous shoot in
advance, or that the cause is to be found in the

nourishment which has been betowed upon the root of the plant from the revived application of religious principle. These considerations are awfully instructive to such of my countrymen as are now in a course of training to fill the important and responsible offices of the state.

It would be an undertaking equally pleasant and profitable to follow the progress of the British commonwealth through the several stages of society, and to mark the instances of its partial deviation from, or courageous adherence to, sound principles, with the consequences arising from each. But the execution of such a task would evidently require a volume, to which indeed this which I have now brought to a close would be no unsuitable introduction. Whether I may myself presume to enter upon it must depend upon circumstances which it is impossible at the present moment to anticipate; for I possess no means of foreseeing to what extent the public may be pleased to sanction or condemn the present undertaking. If they determine to reject my principles, it would be useless to offer deductions from them until I have endeavoured to refute the arguments upon which the principles themselves may be rejected; failing in which, silence would be the part of wisdom.

But I hope, in all humility, for a more favourable result. Conscious as I unfeignedly am of the many defects in its execution; sensible as I must be that in so extensive and complicated an argument many insulated positions may be found, upon which misapprehension may lead to error, or wilful cavil to conclusions never intended to be drawn; still I cannot help entertaining a lurking expectation, that a connected and candid perusal of the treatise will recom

mend it to the unsophisticated minds of my countrymen. With this view I have endeavoured to infuse
into its pages the spirit in which they were written—
that of honesty, sincerity, and unaffected philanthropy.
To whatever other imputations the argument may be
liable, I trust that it will not be thought open to the
reproach of wilful perversion, cowardly concealment,
a morbid affectation of humanity, or a studied display
of moral and religious sentiment. I know that a fair
and manly argument will find favour and free admission with fair and manly minds, and such are eminently those minds to which this treatise is principally addressed. With respect to my own, I have
endeavoured to discipline it (though I trust from
more exalted motives) upon the principle of Epictetus
(in his Moral Essay upon the Book of Chrysippus,)
who thought that the more capable he presumed
himself to be of explaining his subject, the more
he ought to be ashamed if what he ventured to teach
others he did not take due care to practise as exactly
himself. This is, after all, the only solid proof of
a man's seriousness and sincerity: and I have ventured to cite it in this place, with a view to encourage those who may admit the truth of the reasoning
to give the same evidence of the sincerity of their
conviction. The principal satisfaction which the
eventual success of my labours can afford will be
found in that result.

I must be permitted to remark, in conclusion, that
there is something peculiarly animating in the prospect presented to our view. Although public and
individual happiness are made to rest upon the
basis of one uniform principle, certain in its effects,
and liable to no mistake in the application; success
is not dependant upon an unattainable degree

of perfection, which lies beyond the bounds of
hope or probability when applied to mankind in
general, but will be sufficient to reward exertion
far short of that extreme point, provided the course
of the pursuit tend directly towards it, and wander
into no devious tracks. Success, however, will be
ample in proportion to the degree of approximation
in which our exertions bring us to that point of
complete attainment, which every rational man sets
before him as the guide and end of his pursuit,
whether his object be of a temporal or of a more
exalted nature. Now it may be fairly asked, could
the goodness of Providence offer more persuasive arguments, or more encouraging conditions than certain recompense for moderate exertions, and a further
reward commensurate with any increase of them?
That compendious argument for sloth and indifference,
that the things of this world do not admit of perfection, and therefore that zeal in its improvement is
only an exhibition of folly or a waste of labour, is here
deprived of all its force ; at least, it is stripped of its
disguise, and its disgraceful motives are left naked
and exposed. We perceive that it is only necessary
to press forward firmly and courageously towards
the mark, however distant ; and to him that runneth
will be awarded a proportionate prize, in whatever
part of the course he may ultimately be found. None
will be entirely precluded, but those who are found
out of the course. These truths may be gathered
from the suggestions of natural conscience as well as
from the words of Scripture, of which the following
proof, extracted from the writings of a heathen moralist, may well excite a Christian community to
emulation :—

" We know that in this world perfection is not to

be attained; but it ought, notwithstanding, to be aimed at; because without keeping this unattainable perfection steadily in view, we cannot proceed far in what *is* to be attained; and for this purpose, perhaps, Providence indulged to us such an idea."

THE END.

ERRATA.

Page 30, line 2, *dele* comma after the word "pressure."
79, line 16, *for* similiar *read* similar.
81, line 12, *for* divest *read* divert.
98, last line, *for* prevert *read* pervert.
155, last line, *for* (Chap. vi.) *read* (Chap. iv.)
182, 7 lines from bottom, *for* propositions *read* proposition.
243, penult line, *for* are *read* is.
250, line 2, between the "any" and "excess" insert the word "extraordinary."
256, line 8, *dele* originally.
264, line 2, between the words "between" and "distresses" insert the word "the."
283, penult line, *dele* syllable "pro-".
320, line 3 from bottom, *dele* comma after "production."
334, line 11, *for* he endeavours *read* they endeavour.
336, line 4, *for* particuliar *read* particular.
350, line 6, *for* excess *read* access.
390, line 19, *dele* comma after "distant."

C. Baldwin, Printer,
New Bridge Street, London.

THE

FOLLOWING WORKS,

BY THE SAME AUTHOR,

Are to be had of the Booksellers for whom this Work is Printed.

1. A SHORT INQUIRY INTO THE POLICY, HUMANITY, AND PAST EFFECTS OF THE POOR LAWS. With an Appendix. 8vo. 8s. Hatchard, Picadilly.

2. A LETTER ON THE EDUCATION OF THE POOR. 8vo. 5s. Hatchard.

3. BOYLE'S REFLECTIONS, with a Preface. 12mo.

4. THE PRINCIPLE OF THE ENGLISH POOR LAWS, illustrated from the Evidence of Scottish Proprietors. 8vo. 3s. 6d.

5. A LETTER ON THE GAME LAWS, by a Country Gentleman a Proprietor of Game. 8vo.

6. A LETTER TO SIR HUGH INGLIS, Bart., late Chairman of the East India Company, on the State of Religion in India.